P9-AFO-010

MAKERS OF AMERICAN DIPLOMACY

From THEODORE ROOSEVELT to HENRY KISSINGER

MAKERS OF AMERICAN DIPLOMACY

From THEODORE ROOSEVELT to HENRY KISSINGER

Edited by
FRANK J. MERLI
and
THEODORE A. WILSON

CHARLES SCRIBNER'S SONS, NEW YORK

Copyright © 1974 Frank J. Merli and Theodore A. Wilson

Library of Congress Cataloging in Publication Data
Merli, Frank J.   1929–
    Makers of American diplomacy.
    Includes bibliographies.
    CONTENTS: v. 1. From Benjamin Franklin to
Alfred Thayer Mahan.—v. 2. From Theodore
Roosevelt to Henry Kissinger.
    1. Diplomats—United States. 2. United
States—Foreign relations. I. Wilson, Theodore
A., 1940–   joint author. II. Title.
[E183.7.M47]   327.73[B]   73-19866
ISBN 0-684-13786-0
ISBN 0-684-13797-6 Vol I (pbk.)
ISBN 0-684-13798-4 Vol II (pbk.)

This book published simultaneously in the
United States of America and in Canada—
Copyright under the Berne Convention

All rights reserved. No part of this book
may be reproduced in any form without the
permission of Charles Scribner's Sons.

5 7 9 11 13 15 17 19 c/p 20 18 16 14 12 10 8 6 4

Printed in the United States of America

To All Our Children

CONTENTS

PREFACE

These biographical essays—all especially commissioned for this collection—encompass a wide range of interpretive viewpoints and represent a significant dimension of the nation's international experience, stretching from the peacemaking efforts of Theodore Roosevelt's presidency to the cold war detente of Henry Kissinger. The figures we have chosen include the obvious presidents and secretaries of state, but to give the reader an idea of the variety and depth of American involvement in foreign affairs, we have also included a representative sample of second-echelon makers of diplomacy. In the selection of contributors we have attempted a balance, geographical as well as generational; but our emphasis has been on the new generation of diplomatic historians trained in the late 1950s and the 1960s. By allowing the contributors the widest possible range of interpretive freedom, encouraging them to find their own ways to illuminate the nature and significance of their subjects, and refraining from any attempt to reconcile opposing interpretations, we intended to avoid the dangers of a facile "consensus" approach and the pitfalls of a "problems" reader. We hope that the collection represents a fair cross section of the debate on the meaning of American diplomacy and the contributions of the men who have molded it.

Because the thrust of this collection is interpretive rather than monographic—and because we hoped to keep the book within manageable bounds—the citations and the scholarly apparatus that a more technical compilation might be expected to contain have been reduced. Omissions should not be difficult to rectify, however; in nearly every case the contributors have derived their essays from works in progress or recently completed in which full documentation can be found.

In the preparation of this volume we received the cooperation of many experts who read the essays for accuracy of information and validity of viewpoint and made helpful, perceptive comments on early drafts. To identify them might imply support for views they do not hold; so we have elected to thank them anonymously but publicly. In addition, Alexander DeConde of the University of California at Santa Barbara, Walter LaFeber of Cornell University, and Richard Leopold of Northwestern University offered helpful suggestions about contributors and the format of the book. Robert Beisner of American University played a key role in the planning stages of the project and has supported it throughout. Without in any way implicating these men in the imperfections this work may contain, we thank them sincerely for the generosity that prompted their responses to our requests for help.

The staff at Scribners, especially Elsie Kearns and Barbara Wood, have been cooperative throughout; their careful attention to detail has saved us from many errors. Mrs. Joan Jander of Dyer, Indiana, compiled the index.

Above all others, one person requires public thanks for his part in bringing this work to fruition. In addition to training both editors and a number of contributors (and coauthoring an essay), Robert H. Ferrell of Indiana University has read all the selections, offering incisive criticism. When the mechanics of the project and the difficulty of keeping so many historians in harness threatened to overwhelm us, his calm and judicious advice brought order and a measure of sanity to the operation. At every stage of the project he has been a wise and sympathetic counselor, and for his contributions we are deeply grateful.

The real heroes of the project are the authors, who struggled against an almost impossible deadline, who cooperated so fully in the task of putting the pieces together—and who so cheerfully suffered our sometimes heavy-handed commentary. For the merits of the work they deserve full credit. They have demonstrated that diplomatic history can deal imaginatively with ideas, that it can incorporate and refine new methodological insights from other branches of history and from other disciplines. Their efforts reveal that historians of divergent backgrounds, ideological commitments, and convictions can move beyond the partisanship and acrimony that have so crippled our field in recent years, that they can meet on common ground and cooperate in the search for a meaningful, verifiable past.

Thanksgiving Day, 1973   Frank J. Merli
                                                Theodore A. Wilson

INTRODUCTION

To choose the few men who form the subjects of these essays as pivotal figures—as the "makers of American diplomacy"—from the throng who have influenced the nation's foreign relations is certain to provoke displeasure at the selection of some or the omission of others. To attempt to assign responsibility for any idea or decision in foreign policy to a single individual is an equally thankless task. Diplomacy has always been a product of the actions of numerous persons and groups; as the international responsibilities of the United States have expanded in the twentieth century, so have the constituencies affecting the conduct of diplomacy. The creation of policy in a democracy derives from a complicated interaction of domestic concerns, political calculations, popular attitudes, seemingly irrational assumptions and beliefs—in short, from assorted, ill-defined, and often contradictory purposes. In such circumstances, designating certain men as personifications of the national will or agents of history may indeed appear a naïve approach to a complex problem.

History, in a sense, remains a composite of innumerable biographies, however, so such a task seemed worth undertaking; but it poses once again the eternal conundrum of free will versus determinism. To what extent, if any, does the act of an individual affect the course of events? Even if responsibility for a decision or a general policy could be clearly attributed to a single person, would not the problem of relating it to subsequent decisions and policies be almost insurmountable? Cause and effect relationships do exist, of course; but normally they are so amorphous and intertwined that attempts to unravel them lead more often to ambiguity than to certitude.

It often seems, to paraphrase one of our contributors, that the evil diplomats do lives after them, but that the good is often interred in the archives. Any attempt to find underlying congruities in the work of American diplomats confronts the problem of contemporary animosity and the biases of historians toward past efforts to manage the nation's affairs. The record suggests, superficially at least, that much of the work of American diplomats has been devoted to tearing down, in word if not in fact, the policies of predecessors. It would appear, therefore, that continuity has not been a dominant feature of United States diplomacy. Further, the special concerns of particular diplomats do not always seem directly related to the larger issues of national policy that transcend presidential administrations, the tenure of a particular secretary of state, or the effective influence of powerful pressure groups.

Such warnings merely restate the obvious: that the contributions of individuals, no matter how many, do not and cannot comprise the total of the American diplomatic experience. The essays in this collection suggest another observation, perhaps also self-evident: that those who have created and conducted America's foreign affairs have often responded to forces outside their control; their decisions have furthered aims and aspirations that they understood little and that interested them less. Statesmen must confront the crises of the moment without leisure to analyze the consequences of their acts. The limits these underlying factors place on the conduct of diplomacy have sometimes been more important than personal initiatives. Whether they know it or not, men are prisoners of the milieu in which they live and function and, with some rare exceptions, are constrained by the dictates of their own experience and the conventional wisdom of their age. Few transcend such limits; fewer still build lastingly or institutionalize their insights.

The following essays suggest at the same time that the participation in diplomacy of human beings, each bringing unique beliefs, patterns of behavior, principles, and ambitions to the common task of directing the country's international business, remains an absolutely essential factor in the diplomatic equation. Men, not abstractions such as Wall Street, the Eastern Establishment, or the United States, "make" diplomacy. These essays treat individuals who are in some ways representative, in some ways atypical, of the men who have conducted foreign relations in the twentieth century. They suggest the extent to which elements of personality (even idosyncratic behavior and personal foibles) have affected events. Issues of foreign policy and the forces that produce them transcend the purposes and preoccupations of individual statesmen; nevertheless, they can only find expression through the marvelously unpredictable, chaotic realm of human motivation and the decisions of fallible men. "No matter how 'ripe' the time," as David Brion Davis has said so well in another context, "there would be no coalescing of . . . opinion until specific decisions and commitments were taken by individual men. . . . Yet when all allowances are made for . . . trends and climates of opinion, one must ultimately come down to the men who precipitated change."[1] Understanding this fact, so obvious yet so often ignored, is a necessary beginning to any re-creation of the context of American diplomacy.

These essays on men who in some way have contributed to the making or implementation of American diplomacy were originally envisioned as informative but disparate pieces that would form a gallery of diplomatic portraits, reflecting internal meaning but perhaps offering little to assist the reader's grasp of the relationships that cut across eras and styles of diplomacy. Surprisingly, a process of selection that because of circumstance contained an element of randomness and guidelines that offered the contributors considerable flexibility produced something more than a mere "collection." The result demonstrates far greater continuity in the outlooks and actions of these diplomats than anyone had anticipated.

The past seventy-odd years have wrought amazingly few

---

1. David Brion Davis, *The Problem of Slavery in Western Culture* (Ithaca, 1966), p. 489. Professor Davis is discussing the rise of antislavery sentiment and John Woolman's part in precipitating it; but his point about individual responsibility applies as well to the diplomatic realm.

changes in the essentials of foreign affairs—a surprising statement unless one reflects on the basic components of the world views of Theodore Roosevelt or Henry Kissinger. Survival in a hostile international environment has remained the touchstone, and the options by which survival is to be ensured appear to be as restricted and fraught with peril today as in 1900. Power—its definition, articulation, and believability—stands at the center of the agonizing choices with which all American diplomats have struggled.

In the twentieth century convulsive and repeated changes in both the structure and underlying assumptions of American society and the environment of global politics have occurred. The resulting impact on American diplomacy seems to mark a basic shift in the purposes and methods of United States foreign policy, thus mocking any argument for continuity. Nonetheless, the objectives of American diplomats, as the essays on such apparently diverse personalities as Theodore Roosevelt, Willard Straight, Harry S. Truman, John Foster Dulles, and Henry Kissinger indicate, reflect a deep and abiding commonalty of interest among those who have shaped foreign affairs in this century. One common theme is, again, concern with power and awareness of America's significant role, because of its vast and expanding economic strength, in any tabulation of the global power balance. Allied with this concern has been persistent uncertainty about the nature and extent of America's responsibility, because of its great and growing power, for the melioration of conditions inhibiting lasting peace and universal prosperity. Except for a special few, the judgment of American leaders in the twentieth century has been to proceed with great caution in this strange new situation, to apply the nationalistic precepts of an earlier age, and to conclude that unilateralism, with all its limitations, is preferable to efforts to create some global community requiring the sacrifice of national sovereignty and freedom of action. In fact, it is possible to argue that the imprint of earlier views, especially the moral superiority of American aims, has combined with consciousness of America's staggering power to generate faith in America's ability to establish and maintain world order by unilateral action. Still, American diplomacy in the 1970s in many ways goes back to a less ambitious time and seems to differ little from the foreign policy goals of TR or Willard Straight. The following essays suggest that the ambivalence and widespread ignorance about the world that character-

ized popular attitudes and the views of most American statesmen
in 1900 still prevail.

In other ways, of course, the twentieth century has witnessed
an incredible transformation of America's role in the world. This
shift in status and involvement has brought along with it equally
striking changes in the process by which decisions regarding
foreign policy are made. As the twentieth century has unfolded,
the number of persons and organizations participating directly in
the making of foreign policy has increased enormously, and the
activities with which they have dealt have become more complex
and specialized. That circumstance has spawned a huge foreign
affairs bureaucracy and has resulted in its emergence as an
independent, seemingly uncontrollable force in the decision-
making process. In recent decades, presidents have chosen (or
have been impelled) to conduct diplomacy themselves, pur-
posefully bypassing a swollen, inert State Department. Ironically,
one effect has been to reemphasize the central role of the
personal dimension in diplomacy, the absolute necessity for
diplomatic initiatives to be backed by the credibility and authority
of the individual negotiator. *Plus ça change, plus c'est la même
chose.*

Reproduced from the collections of the Library of Congress

CAUTIOUS WARRIOR:

THEODORE ROOSEVELT

and the Diplomacy of Activism

Eugene P. Trani

As president and as extraordinary citizen, Theodore Roosevelt created a unique niche for himself in the American political pantheon. Much about TR is familiar, as John Blum reminds us in *The Republican Roosevelt*: "The teeth, the famous intensity, the nervous grimace, impelling leadership, physical courage, moral fervor—sometimes frenzy. . . . There are the busted trusts, the outdoor life, the nature fakirs, simplified spelling, rivers discovered, lions felled." These externals, the personal quirks and enthusiasms of Roosevelt's life, are well remembered; however, understanding of his purposes and policies during the seven years he occupied the White House lags far behind. This imbalance is especially noticeable in studies of TR and foreign affairs, in which

Professor Trani acknowledges the assistance of the Woodrow Wilson International Center for Scholars in the preparation of this essay.

1

carrying a big stick while speaking softly remains the accepted, if too easy, characterization of his diplomacy.

Of all the functions of the presidency, none fascinated Roosevelt more than foreign affairs. The stimulus of world responsibilities enraptured him, and he went out of his way to undertake tasks for himself and for the United States. TR always acted to promote the national interest, of course, but he relied always on his own perception of America's aims. He seldom consulted Congress on foreign policy, except when a clear legal obligation existed, and he was willing to stretch executive power to the limit and sometimes beyond.

More than any other American of his time, TR assisted in the emergence of the United States as a world power. He also forced the nation to assume some of the responsibilities that derived from its new role, though in this he was only partially successful. He viewed the cautious reaction of his fellow citizens to world affairs, especially the hectic struggle for power and prestige before the First World War, with impatience and often exasperation. As president, Theodore Roosevelt won much recognition for his country and diplomatic achievements crowded his tenure in office. The United States exerted dominant influence in Latin America, pushed into European politics, protected and expanded its interests in the Far East, modernized the army and expanded the battle fleet, and pursued an active and generally enlightened policy toward its new colonial dependencies.

That the United States would assume a larger role in world politics was predictable when Roosevelt succeeded the assassinated President William McKinley on 12 March 1901. TR's views of foreign policy derived partly from his background and partly from the intellectual currents dominant in America in the latter years of the nineteenth century. He was born in 1858 in New York City to a socially established and moderately wealthy family. He received a typical upper-class education—tutors, Groton, and Harvard—and profited from exposure to the cosmopolitan social milieu to which he belonged by right of birth. As a youth TR traveled through Europe and the Near East and, indeed, except for Thomas Jefferson, the Adams family, and James Monroe, was more traveled than any preceding president. He possessed an inquiring mind and read voluminously on a multitude of subjects from natural history to modern warfare, a catholicism of interests that continued into manhood.

A childhood fraught with illnesses, particularly a serious asthmatic condition, greatly influenced TR's personal development. He determined to overcome his body's weakness and launched in his early teens a strenuous program of walking, riding, and boxing. This struggle for physical vigor, which eventually was totally successful, greatly influenced his outlook on life. It was to be dominant in his style of conducting the duties of the presidency, especially foreign policy. Roosevelt's views also owed much to the influence of his father, whom TR later termed the "best man" he ever knew. The elder Roosevelt, a dedicated philanthropist, possessed a strong sense of *noblesse oblige* that the son inherited.

The young Roosevelt found a philosophical rationale for his inchoate enthusiasm for individual and national self-improvement in doctrines that came into favor after the Civil War, at the time he was reaching adolescence. By the end of the century, these ideas, based in large part on Charles Darwin's epochal treatise, *On the Origin of Species*, had metamorphosed into a new fervor for national expansion. Enthusiasm for America's "Manifest Destiny" swept the country, and Roosevelt found himself at the forefront of its advocates. This renewed expansive frenzy gloried in such phrases, advanced by Darwin and his popularizers, as "natural selection," "survival of the fittest," and the "law of the jungle." Proponents of the new Manifest Destiny believed the United States, as a result of its emergence as a world power, was a fit nation, a chosen nation, qualified to instruct backward countries, and, indeed, required to do so. The "white man's burden" was a reality, and it imposed tasks that could not be shirked.

Those who called for realization of the national destiny asserted that America must have possessions in the Caribbean, Pacific, and Far East. Their ideology was a carbon copy of the European imperialism then burning its way across Asia and Africa. During the administrations of Grover Cleveland, Benjamin Harrison, and William McKinley, the United States became involved in diplomatic crises throughout the world: it challenged Great Britain and Germany in Samoa and obtained the harbor of Pago Pago; it extracted from Chile a $75,000 indemnity and an apology for the killing in Valparaiso of two crewmen and the injuring of sixteen others from the cruiser U.S.S. *Baltimore*; it annexed Hawaii in 1898; and in 1895–96 it forced Lord Salisbury's government to arbitrate the boundary between British Guiana and Venezuela. The century closed with the Spanish-American War and acquisition of an overseas empire. Advocates of a strong foreign policy were well satisfied with the start that had been made; America had come of age and had moved into the mainstream of history.

Further progress could be expected as these men attained positions of authority in Washington and elsewhere. Theodore Roosevelt's advance to prominence was especially swift. While still a young man, he served as commissioner of the civil service, New York police commissioner, assistant secretary of the navy, and as a volunteer lieutenant colonel in the war with Spain. Though playing only a secondary role in the great decisions of the 1890s, TR was influential, serving as an effective publicist for the causes then in favor. He attracted popular attention by vigorously expressing theories of international relations in books, articles, and reviews. In America, such ideas became most closely identified with Roosevelt, because he was able to lend them a special glamor. As David Healy has noted, Roosevelt's views were neither strikingly original nor distinct from contemporary opinion, but they were "frequently and forcefully expressed, formed a coherent whole, and suited the temper of the times." Many resulted from discussions with a circle of friends, gathered over the years, some of whom owed allegiance to other governments, who were to help TR with foreign policy during his presidential tenure. This group included Henry Cabot Lodge; the Adams brothers, Henry and Brooks; William W. Rockhill, an acknowledged expert on Far Eastern affairs; and Captain Alfred Thayer Mahan.

As the century drew to a close, Roosevelt's views about the wisest course for America became more concrete and demonstrated a confident grasp of the complexities of international politics. He urged commercial and territorial expansion, favored the annexation of Hawaii, supported the construction of an isthmian canal, and, of course, championed the creation of a first-class navy. Above all, he advocated policies that would uphold the honor and interests of the United States. "I am not hostile to any European power in the abstract," he once said. "I am simply an American first and last, and therefore hostile to any power which wrongs us." Friendly competition with the nations of

Europe, in particular Great Britain, was acceptable, for TR held as a first principle faith in Anglo-Saxon superiority.

The challenge lay elsewhere. Reviewing Charles H. Pearson's *National Life and Character: A Forecast* in 1894, TR observed that the great task facing mankind was to bring peace to the world's wasted spaces. Lasting peace was not possible, he believed, until the civilized nations achieved some sort of domination over the "barbarous" countries. This was racism raised to the level of principle. He justified the exclusion of Chinese immigrants, for example, by asserting that "the American democracy," demonstrating impressive clearness of vision, had realized that the presence of Chinese would be ruinous to the white race. To be sure, backward races could attain superior qualities, thus deserving and commanding respect. TR admired the Japanese because they had kept only the strongest of their traditions, scrapped the rest, and emulated the civilized nations of the West.

Although he professed to believe only in just wars, any war in which Americans fought was by definition just, and so TR could describe the Spanish-American War as the most righteous conflict of the century. "All the great masterful races have been fighting races," he claimed, "and the minute that a race loses the hard fighting virtues, then . . . no matter how skilled in commerce and finance, in science and art, it has lost its proud right to stand as the equal of the best." In this respect, the author of *The Influence of Sea Power upon History* and well-known promoter of the U.S. Navy, A. T. Mahan, greatly influenced Roosevelt's thinking. His ideas were, in fact, a starting point for almost every conversation Roosevelt had about foreign policy. Mahan forced TR to consider problems in military-strategic terms and to worry a good deal about national security. He soon came to believe the nation's safety required expansion, including construction of a powerful navy as well as territorial acquisitions. Strategic concerns alone do not explain Roosevelt's ardent advocacy of expansion, however. The national character would benefit, for the American people would have to overcome the physical softness and moral slackness that inevitably accompanied the transition from a pioneering country to a wealthy, developed nation. Maintenance of national strength thus became for him one of the central problems of American society.

After the Spanish-American War, Roosevelt's view of the

world became more complex, for he recognized that the great
powers could clash with each other as well as with barbarians,
realized that power struggles in such places as East Asia affected
the balance of power in Europe, and learned that a nation that
threatened American interests in one region might share its
interests in another. He concluded that America should use its
status as a world power to increase its strength and prevent any
nation from injuring the United States or its friends, and he
warned that America could not renounce its international obligations and avow itself "merely an assemblage of well-to-do
hucksters who care nothing for what happens beyond [their
borders]." No longer did he gauge events solely in terms of
American interests, though these of course were paramount. He
still divided the world into a few great civilized powers, purveyors
of enlightenment and culture and protectors of law and order; but
he admitted that these nations were themselves engaged in a
constant conflict for supremacy, though he averred that the
conflict would remain peaceful.

In sum, TR's pronouncements on foreign affairs reflected an
increasingly shrewd and subtle assessment of world problems,
though this is often ignored because of the moral exhortations, the
evangelical commentaries that made Roosevelt seem almost an
anachronism after he left the presidency. Stripped of their
rhetorical embellishment, his thoughts do not now, in the 1970s,
appear outdated. If his presidential statements customarily contained moral and ethical appeals, he understood that in the
absence of any accepted body of international law and of an
agency to enforce its rulings the determinant in world affairs was
power, and he believed that as long as nations existed the loftiest
ideals were worthless unless backed by force. Thus, a weak
America invited attack and ultimately destruction. TR especially
feared those he described as "peace demagogues," men who
preached disarmament. While nations should be equitable in their
dealings, they must possess the capability and determination to
defend their own interests. For the United States, this meant
ability to ensure its new empire, including supremacy in the
Caribbean, extension of power in the Pacific, and construction of
a transisthmian canal for rapid movement of the navy from ocean
to ocean.

As TR was keenly aware, the changing structure of power
elsewhere in the world jeopardized these purposes. Looking

abroad, he beheld a British imperium in gradual decline and the rising strength of Germany and Japan. Such shifts of power were unacceptable to TR, a devout Anglophile. It had been with an approving nod that he had observed the rapprochement between the United States and Britain in the last years of the McKinley era, largely because of the work of John Hay, ambassador to the Court of St. James's and later secretary of state. TR believed the two English-speaking countries had to think and act as one. When as president he occasionally scolded the British, he did so not because of any serious disagreement but because contention of any kind had been permitted to arise. TR was dedicated to shoring up British power and was convinced that if England weakened fatally the United States would have to step in to maintain the world balance of power—against any and all contenders.

These sentiments were far in advance of the opinions of the American people. Indeed, TR's active part in world politics while president did not derive, as Raymond Esthus has noted in his study of TR's response to international rivalries, from any belief of the American public that the United States had an important stake in world affairs. Curiously, however, the public's indifference proved advantageous. President Roosevelt became a key figure in the two great power confrontations of his day—the Russo-Japanese War of 1904–5 and the first Moroccan crisis of 1905–6—mainly because the major powers looked to the United States as the one nation with sufficient disinterestedness to mediate these crises fairly. To be sure, the size and potential power of the United States and a growing fear of the likelihood of a general war made America's goodwill and diplomatic support a prize worth cultivating. Although foreign diplomats might believe that the president was able to use the power of the United States as he wished, Roosevelt recognized the limits on his freedom in foreign affairs. He understood the isolationist views of his countrymen and, though never fully reconciled to the cautious policies those attitudes demanded, accepted them as facts of life.

Perhaps the best example of TR's careful balancing of the American public's feelings and his own concern about the changing balance of power was his mediation of the Russo-Japanese War. This episode was both typical and atypical of his diplomacy: it brought together all of the Rooseveltian beliefs regarding foreign policy, from informal diplomatic contacts to a search for an orderly world ruled by the great powers; but at the same time TR realized that he could not easily intervene in an international conflict of such dimensions and complexity. More often than not, he permitted subordinates to conduct diplomatic negotiations, recognizing that a president has other responsibilities than foreign affairs which, if neglected, will produce domestic pressures inimical to everything he may hope to accomplish.

The period of the Russo-Japanese War, the era of TR's deepest involvement with personal diplomacy, was coincidentally a time when he served in all but title as his own secretary of state. John Hay, who had been in poor health for much of his tenure, died in the summer of 1905. In the spring of that year the president was already writing diplomatic notes that went to the Department of State, next door to the White House, for transmission to envoys abroad. His diplomacy was so personal that at times Mrs. Roosevelt was his principal adviser. In this respect TR emulated the diplomatic style of other leaders of his day: Théophile Delcassé, Bernhard von Bülow, Sir Edward Grey, Wilhelm II, and Edward VII.

One should note parenthetically that the president never had large differences of opinion with Hay, whom he had respected; the contrasts in their diplomacy largely were ones of technique. Roosevelt differed in his manner of obtaining information, for unlike Hay he had little faith in America's regular envoys. He was wont to talk with bureau chiefs, head clerks, anyone he trusted, in or out of the government. TR also disliked diplomatic formalities and especially despised the appellation "excellency" referring to the president, as he saw no need of a title. Procedural details irked him. He told American diplomats abroad to use common sense in dress and to wear whatever would please the sovereigns of the countries in which they served. He enjoyed breaking diplomatic traditions, such as the custom that supposedly prevented him from entertaining people of equal rank. He took a truant boy's delight in forcing dignitaries into horseback rides in Rock Creek Park or walks up and down the wooded hills along the Potomac—Roosevelt's head thrown up to catch sight of birds, looking like a grotesque, burly Peter Pan while his guests huffed and puffed behind. Underlying the levity and seeming lack of decorum, however, were sound purposes and a professional's shrewd assessment of personalities and policies.

When Roosevelt assumed direct control of the State Department in 1904–5, relations with Russia presented difficult problems. One centered on communications between the two countries; the Russian ambassador in Washington, Count Arturo Cassini, had few qualifications for the post and did not fit into the scheme of Rooseveltian diplomacy. Difficult to get along with and, what was worse in TR's view, untruthful, Cassini impeded harmony between the United States and Russia. His own government did not keep him fully informed, and the president sometimes knew St. Petersburg's plans before Ambassador Cassini himself. The channel of communication was no better at the other end. TR considered the American ambassador in St. Petersburg, Robert S. McCormick, politically important but diplomatically useless. In December 1904 he shifted McCormick to Paris and replaced him with George von Lengerke Meyer, then U.S. ambassador in Rome and an old Harvard friend.

With Japan the communication problem was not as severe. The American minister in Tokyo, Lloyd C. Griscom, though experienced, was not an important cog in Roosevelt's diplomatic machine. TR preferred to deal with the Japanese minister in Washington, Kogoro Takahira, who had the double advantage of being fully trusted by his own government and the president. Then, in 1904, the Tokyo regime thoughtfully sent over Baron Kentaro Kaneko, one of TR's schoolmates at Harvard, as director of Japan's publicity effort in America. Kaneko and Takahira monopolized the president's correspondence with the Japanese government, putting Griscom almost out of the picture. The stage was set for a study in contrasts during negotiation of the Peace of Portsmouth in 1905, with Cassini shouting at one and all, and Japanese diplomats supplying TR with reading lists about their country and, upon request, a jujitsu teacher.

The president's arrangement of relations with the Japanese and Russians displayed his liking for congenial envoys, reliance on personal channels of communication, and preference for what a later generation would call "summitry." He also consulted many persons outside government about foreign affairs. Prominent in this group, who collectively were sometimes known as the Tennis Cabinet, were the French and German ambassadors in Washington, Jean Jules Jusserand and Hermann Speck von Sternburg, and Cecil Spring Rice, a British diplomat who in 1905 was an adviser *in absentia*, for he was first secretary of the British embassy in St.

Petersburg. All helped negotiate an end to the Russo-Japanese War, as did William Howard Taft who after 1904 was TR's secretary of war. If between 1901 and 1909 the participants changed, the president's style of conducting foreign affairs varied little. When Roosevelt wanted a message conveyed to another government he would call upon someone he trusted to deliver it, a technique that at times was extremely important in TR's diplomacy. His use of personal envoys and total control of foreign policy—excluding not only Congress but many times the State Department—certainly served as significant precedents for presidents Woodrow Wilson, Franklin D. Roosevelt, and Richard Nixon, among others, and appears to have marked the beginning of an ever-greater concentration of authority over foreign affairs in the White House. Such techniques appear outdated to some in the 1970s when problems of international relations have grown so complex that it is almost impossible for a few individuals to conduct personal diplomacy; eventually they produced irritation in the Congress and discouragement in the State Department. They were necessary, however, at a time when Americans cared little about foreign affairs.

At the *fin de siècle* Roosevelt worried greatly about the Far East. The decline of Great Britain was most apparent in that region where Russians, Japanese, Germans, and French were hastily and, as it turned out, thoughtlessly carving out spheres of commercial and territorial influence. Western interest in China had increased throughout the nineteenth century: Christianizing, civilizing, commercializing. Divided and weak, China remained a nation despite invaders, jackals, and false friends. Roosevelt's view of China included approximately equal parts of religion and economics. He certainly supported the concept of the Open Door—that all nations deserved rough equality of commercial opportunity in the Orient—but his interest principally derived from strategic concerns, from recognition that the struggle over China made up only one part, though a most important one, of a world struggle among the great powers. Roosevelt had come to the conclusion that China could not control its own territory, and thus the China problem would be long-standing.

China's defeat by the Japanese in 1895 had inaugurated a new era, a time of wild scrambling for spheres of interest. The Russians extorted from the feeble government in Peking the right to build a spur of the Trans-Siberian Railway through Manchuria and to construct naval facilities at Port Arthur. The Germans got Kiaochow, the French Kwangchowan, and the British Weihaiwei. These concessions alarmed the then citizen Roosevelt because they seemed to endanger American interests, and because U.S. economic involvement in China, which had become important in the latter part of the nineteenth century, was rapidly increasing when TR assumed the presidency. The work of American missionaries, U.S. economic interests, and, most importantly, strategic considerations such as the need to protect the Philippines and Hawaii appeared threatened by possible turmoil in the Far East.

In the regions surrounding China two nations in addition to the United States—Russia and Japan—had become powerful, and TR's views toward this three-power imbroglio revealed a sophisticated understanding of the nature of international rivalries. Initially, he had not been hostile toward the Russians. Relations had been cordial, and as a student of history TR knew that Russia had shown its friendship during the Civil War. Later, the czar had sold Alaska to the United States. This procession of events led Roosevelt to write in 1898 that "Russia, and Russia alone, of European powers, has been uniformly friendly to us in the past." Shortly before becoming president his view changed. Russia's encroachments in the Far East at the time of the Boxer Rebellion challenged Anglo-American interests. The treaty powers had moved troops into China, and Russia, with its long Chinese border, virtually occupied Manchuria. By 1903 the Russians' failure to withdraw from Manchuria much disturbed Roosevelt, as did another event at this time, an outbreak of violence against Jews in Russia in April 1903. He publicly criticized Czar Nicholas II and the Russian autocracy; some months later he wrote of a strong respect for the Russians but warned: "Unless they change in some marked way they contain the chance of menace to the higher life of the world. . . . Our people have become suspicious of Russia; and I personally share this view."

Toward the Japanese the president's feelings likewise shifted during his tenure. Throughout his public life he was torn between admiration for the efficiency and fighting qualities of the Japanese and fear of their strength and military zeal. When Japan protested the possible annexation of Hawaii by the United States in 1897, then Assistant Secretary of the Navy Roosevelt had declared, "The United States is not in a position which requires her to ask Japan or any other foreign power what territory it shall or shall not acquire." After the Spanish-American War, he worried about

Japanese interest in the Philippine Islands. Then, in the years 1900–1904, admiration overcame fear and he became convinced that the Island Empire did not threaten American interests. Unable to use America's power to stop the Russian advance, the president saw the Japanese as a possible barrier to Russian expansion. He thoroughly approved the alliance between Japan and Britain concluded in 1902; he realized that the American people would not permit any U.S. role in the alliance (which would have been a massive break with the past), but, even without U.S. participation, the alliance offered protection to American interests. When the Japanese protested Russian policy in Manchuria, the president expressed sympathy, looking upon Japan not only as a protector of the Open Door but, even more importantly, of the balance of power in Asia.

From the beginning of the Russo-Japanese War in February 1904, TR's sympathies were with Japan. Two days after the Japanese suddenly attacked the Russian naval base at Port Arthur, the president noted in a letter to his son Kermit that for several years Russia had behaved very badly in the Far East, especially by being grossly overbearing toward Japan. "I was apprehensive lest if she at the outset whipped Japan on the sea she might assume a position well-nigh intolerable toward us." Roosevelt was nonetheless wary of too sweeping a Japanese victory in the conflict, for Japan might become "puffed with pride." He did not want Japan to become a threat to American commercial and territorial interests. The Japanese must not establish themselves in China, though they could have Korea; above all, they must guarantee protection for U.S. interests in East Asia. Such was the reasoning behind TR's desire for peace in 1904–5. He sought a balance of power that guaranteed the interests of the United States as well as those of the other nations concerned.

TR was also anxious to stop war between civilized powers, a conflict he believed bad for the world, and by mediating he assumed he could guarantee Japan the fruits of its victory, preventing another triple intervention. Whether or not Roosevelt wished to mediate the war in order to advance his own reputation as a great statesman, he certainly was eager to play a part in world events. He prided himself on his independence from British activities and may have wished to show the world he could act alone; but there is no evidence to suggest that TR sought personal

"GOOD OFFICES"

Harper's Weekly, *24 June 1905*

advantage from a conflict in which thousands of lives had been expended.

Throughout 1904, if without success, the president used every opportunity to press his good offices on the belligerents. He met with the Japanese minister several times and urged Japan to take advantage of its surprising military successes while he tried to ascertain the Japanese peace terms. He badgered the Russian ambassador so much that, to quote Secretary Hay, "Cassini throws a pink fit at any reference to peace." By late 1904, as Japan's military successes continued, the president decided the best course was not to take a public stand on the issue of mediation until assured that both powers would respond favorably.

The Japanese victory at Mukden in March 1905 further moved world opinion toward expectation of peace. The president warned the Russian ambassador that if peace were not arranged soon, Japanese terms would be much more severe. The Russians had one last chance: the Baltic fleet under Admiral Zinovi Rozhdestvenski, then steaming eastward around the Cape of Good Hope and rapidly nearing the Far East. That hope disappeared when, on 27 and 28 May 1905, Admiral Heihachiro Togo annihilated the Russians in the Tsushima Strait.

Three days after this battle, on 31 May, Foreign Minister Jutaro Komura instructed his representative in Washington to suggest to the president that entirely on "his own motion and initiative" he invite the belligerents to direct negotiations. Details were left to his discretion, but the Japanese government wished to avoid the impression of a direct approach to Russia on the subject of peace. Roosevelt swung into action. To make sure that his views were conveyed directly to the czar, the president instructed his representative in St. Petersburg to inform Nicholas that the contest was "absolutely hopeless" and that if the Russians would consent to negotiations Roosevelt would, on his own initiative and as secretly as possible, seek Japan's consent for preliminary talks. Roosevelt also got the German kaiser to support this effort by appealing to his cousin Nicholas. Roosevelt had reached a commanding position. No objection would come from Britain, Japan's ally; France, the ally of Russia, had internal problems; both Japan and Germany favored the intervention of the president. Only Russia remained to be brought into agreement.

The offensive succeeded. Ambassador Meyer requested an audience and pointed out to the czar the futility of the war, its unpopularity, the threat of revolution, and noted the president's concern, for Meyer had kept TR informed of Russia's internal difficulties. Nicholas agreed to negotiations, provided that Japan consent before the czar's acceptance was made public and that the conference be without intermediaries.

After long discussions and much difficulty, the belligerents chose their delegations, agreed on Washington as the meeting place (later changed because of the summer heat to the naval yard near Portsmouth, New Hampshire), and Roosevelt called the conference.[1] The president felt compelled to ensure that the negotiations did not fail. After the arrival of the plenipotentiaries he entertained them at Oyster Bay, his home on Long Island, the Japanese on one day, the Russians on another. He told both groups that this opportunity for peace must not be missed.

The peace conference began with a formal luncheon for the envoys at Oyster Bay on 5 August 1905. From there the delegates traveled to Portsmouth. By 18 August, after twelve formal sessions as well as several private meetings, it seemed that an impasse over two issues, collection of an indemnity and cession of territories, would deadlock negotiations and perhaps even wreck the conference. Japan demanded the island of Sakhalin, already under military occupation by its forces, as well as an indemnity; the chief Russian delegate, Sergei Witte, refused both demands.

Roosevelt again intervened to urge both sides to compromise, pointing out the advantages to each, and political pressure, more or less subtle, accompanied these exhortations. From the czar he gained for Japan the southern half of Sakhalin. His influence was decisive with the Japanese, to whom he stressed that they had gained what they had fought for: Korea and southern Manchuria. These arguments, plus the financial strains of the war, brought the Japanese to terms, removed the final obstacle to settlement, and led to signature of a peace agreement on 5 September 1905.

The Peace of Portsmouth was a personal triumph for Roosevelt. The conference had assembled on his initiative; he had convinced the Japanese and the Russians of the need for a settlement; his preaching made the powers think of moderate

---

1. At the opening of the conference, there was no armistice between the belligerents. At Japanese insistence an armistice would not be effective until the peace treaty was drafted and only shortly before its final approval.

terms; his influence convinced the Japanese representative, Komura, to modify Japan's demands even before the conference
began; and he kept the conference going by constant discussions
with the plenipotentiaries and their governments. Although the
war would have ended sometime, it seems that peace would have
been precious long in coming if TR had not intervened. To be
sure, Witte, by disobeying his czar's instruction to break off the
conference, aided Roosevelt, but the president's influence
brought the final compromise. It was for its day an impressive
performance, even if the results were more transitory and less
satisfactory than expected.

The Treaty of Portsmouth was the best possible solution for
the time, serving the interests of Russia and Japan as well as the
United States. Beyond immediate details of the negotiations, the
peace greatly enhanced the prestige both of the United States and
its chief executive. Portsmouth stands as the last of the personally
managed peace conferences and, in effect, it closed the diplomacy
of the nineteenth century. TR's success is all the more surprising
when one considers that the Russo-Japanese War was one of the
first chapters of the major power rivalries that have littered the
landscape of international relations in the twentieth century and
have proved almost impervious to mediation. TR succeeded where
later mediators, such as Woodrow Wilson and Franklin D. Roosevelt, would fail.

The treaty's importance to the United States lessened in the
years that followed, as the Rooseveltian power balance in the Far
East collapsed, but this was the result of alignments looking
toward the world war, Far Eastern instability, and the nature of
competing interests in that region. In the Russo-Japanese treaties
of 1907 and 1910, the two powers agreed to divide Manchuria
through control of the two major Manchurian railways. Immigration policy at this time became an issue of domestic American
politics as well, and it, of course, exerted tremendous influence on
United States–Japanese relations. Any residual pro-Japanese sentiments had almost disappeared by the time TR left the White
House and certainly played no part in the Taft administration's
Asian policy. Most important, perhaps, was a change in China, a
new nationalistic and antiforeign attitude, which had developed
as the nineteenth century closed and became even more powerful
in the early twentieth century. Roosevelt had discounted this last
factor, since he considered the Chinese a backward people and

did not believe that China could soon become a major power; here TR proved dead wrong. Still, much was to happen between 1905 and 1949 and China's performance in world politics between 1894 and 1905 gave Roosevelt little reason to doubt his judgment. Nevertheless, his policy of a balanced antagonism between Russia and Japan, an antagonism that would protect America's interests, eventually failed.

Seeing that it was no longer possible for the United States to avoid involvement in world affairs and that, contrary to the belief of many Americans, peace might not be a normal condition, Roosevelt spent a good deal of time between 1901 and 1909 insisting that his country recognize its international obligations and have sufficient resources in readiness to honor them. He was aware that revolutions in communication, production, and transportation had created a situation in which available power, not just potential, was necessary, especially because of the heightened nationalism of the early twentieth century. He urged preparedness, but, as John Blum has noted, "this was not simple militarism." Preparedness to TR meant development of natural resources, an increase in industrial productivity, and maintenance of the American people's moral character. It meant changes in the military forces, and during Roosevelt's tenure the army and especially the navy underwent large and, as the world war was to show, vital changes.

Roosevelt understood that the United States did not require a large standing army, but the poor performance of the army during the Spanish-American War had shown vividly the need for drastic reforms. Elihu Root, who had been appointed secretary of war by McKinley, understood the necessity for reform, but it was not until 1902, and then only with TR's support, that Root was able to concentrate on army reorganization.[2] He increased the size of the army, abolished the permanent assignment of officers to staff duties in Washington, and overhauled the educational structure, creating the Army War College. He reformed the antiquated

2. Between 1899 and 1901, Secretary Root had to deal with problems in Cuba, Puerto Rico, and a difficult and embarrassing insurrection in the Philippines.

militia system and, most importantly, introduced the principle of the general staff. The organization of the army became more effective, and its capabilities were demonstrated in 1917 when the United States next entered a major war.

As might be expected, Roosevelt devoted most of his attention to the navy. Applying Mahan's theories, he concluded that because of its two ocean borders the United States had to develop a strong navy, second only to that of Great Britain. He conducted a persistent campaign for more and bigger ships, the global voyage of the "Great White Fleet" perhaps being the high point of this effort. Congress responded by greatly increasing the navy between 1901 and 1909. Roosevelt did not always get his way, and his request for four battleships of the dreadnought class in 1908 was cut in half. Still, the navy grew and its facilities improved. It acquired a potential base at Subig Bay in the Philippines, leased a site (Guantánamo Bay) in Cuba, and obtained funds for a base at Pearl Harbor.

Sea power lay behind much of Roosevelt's attitude toward Latin America. Here he sought preservation of the Monroe Doctrine and protection of American rights. When European powers, especially Britain and Germany who possessed powerful navies, seemed to challenge American supremacy in the Caribbean, demanding settlement of debts by the Venezuelan dictator, Cipriano Castro, Roosevelt readied the U.S. fleet and brought the issue to the Hague Court. He acted not because he supported Venezuelan interests, but because he believed that preservation of order in Latin America, an essential element in United States strategy, required American initiative. This belief led to the famous—or infamous—Roosevelt Corollary to the Monroe Doctrine, which claimed an exclusive American right of intervention in the Western Hemisphere. Of course, TR added that such intervention would come only as a last resort, but the mere idea, proof of a double standard of morality, was repugnant to Latin Americans and many of the president's fellow citizens. In retrospect, it was perhaps not so radical an idea, since a large nation probably does have certain perquisites in its sphere of influence. Roosevelt's corollary and the right of intervention were later abandoned, the latter during the first term of his cousin, FDR; but events in subsequent years in Guatemala, Cuba, and the Dominican Republic suggest that such simple repudiations of basic interests are perhaps not really possible.

No single incident tarnished Roosevelt's reputation more than the Panama Canal affair. According to his critics, at the time and since, he was guilty of blatant imperialism, cynically fostering a revolution in order to obtain the rights to a canal. An isthmian canal had been one of his fondest dreams and was necessary in his view because the United States Navy needed to protect the country's increased interests throughout the world. Roosevelt stretched his powers in this affair by showing sympathy to those conspiring to revolt against Colombia, but he did not foment the revolution. The United States quickly recognized the new regime and concluded a treaty obtaining for itself exclusive rights to build a canal. A story (perhaps apocryphal) about his defense of these actions to the cabinet best illustrates the president's trouble. After speaking vigorously about all the criticisms leveled against him, he asked if he had answered the charges. Secretary of War Root, the only person present whose relationship with TR permitted a frank answer, replied: "You certainly have, Mr. President. You have shown that you were accused of seduction and you have conclusively proved that you were guilty of rape." Roosevelt perhaps did proclaim his innocence too loudly.

Once the canal rights were established, the president pushed ahead with construction and after administrative difficulties arose gave the whole job to the army under George W. Goethals, who carried the task to conclusion in 1914. While TR's methods in this episode can be and are properly criticized, they ensured the completion of the isthmian canal at a time when it was needed. The Panama Canal has remained an American enterprise, though it has produced a great residue of animosity. Given the transportation revolution and the lessening strategic importance of the canal in recent years, the time has come for United States internationalization of the Canal Zone, a step one can imagine Roosevelt supporting today, for he understood that various means existed to preserve a nation's interests and that it was necessary to avoid needless friction in international politics.

During Roosevelt's second term he continued to serve as policeman of the Caribbean, but, having established the principles of American policy toward Latin America, he allowed the State Department and Secretary of State Root (appointed after the death of John Hay) to handle day-to-day affairs. The result was improved U.S.–Latin American relations. America had established its determination to prevent European intrusion into the Caribbean, and

Root was now free to lessen difficulties with Latin American countries by treating their diplomats with dignity and by goodwill journeys to the south. The president was content to remain in the background, realizing he was an object of controversy in Latin America. As long as strategic and commercial interests were guaranteed and the duty of bringing order when necessary remained in U.S. hands, he allowed subordinates to carry out policy. Root did this well, earning the title of "the first Good Neighbor" from some historians. One can argue about Roosevelt's Latin American policy but, given more than sixty years of perspective, it does not seem altogether unreasonable, and the Latin American policy of Roosevelt's successors in the White House has not changed perceptibly.

Toward the Orient the president demonstrated flexibility, allowing a series of significant modifications over the years. Before 1905 he strove to erect a balance of power, which he achieved at Portsmouth. While voicing the thoughts of his first secretary of state about the Open Door, TR understood that the American people would not go to war to protect China or American interests in that country. He turned to the Japanese to protect American and world interests, recognizing that Japan would have special rights in China as did the U.S. in Latin America. He even talked to Japanese diplomats about a Monroe Doctrine for Japan in Asia.

After 1905 and the Treaty of Portsmouth the situation in the Far East changed dramatically, and so did the president's views. Japan moved to close the Open Door in Manchuria, and the Sino-Japanese rivalry, later to be one of the dominant events of the century, intensified. Roosevelt showed little interest in the former development and, like most Western politicians, little understanding of the latter. This resulted from his increased attention to European problems; his belief that Japan had special rights in China; his belief that the best protection of American interests in the Pacific, especially the Philippines, was avoidance of controversy with Japan; his realization that the American people would not resort to war to protect the Open Door; and the heating up of the immigration problem with Japan. It is true that Root and some of his subordinates in the State Department, such as Willard Straight, pressed hard for American rights in China and that, with TR's approval, they were able to salvage some guarantees from the Japanese. The president took no part in Straight's fierce anti-Japanese crusade, however, and seems to have had almost no knowledge of it. One fact is certain: there were practical limits to how far the State Department could go in its campaign to preserve Chinese sovereignty; its only useful instrument was negotiation with Japan. Although Root conducted relations toward the East Asian powers after 1905, there is little doubt that the president would have denied him the use of threats to protect China from the Japanese. Of course Taft, Roosevelt's successor, allowed the anti-Japanese prejudices of some State Department officials to become national policy; TR watched with great displeasure as the Taft administration scrapped his policies and blundered into difficulties in Asia.

Part of the difference between Roosevelt's and Taft's policies resulted from changes in the mechanisms for dealing with foreign affairs. As TR's interest in the Far East lessened, the State Department assumed more and more responsibilities. To handle them, Root set up the Division of Far Eastern Affairs in 1908, the first of the geographical divisions of the State Department. This new structure, as Charles Neu has noted, provided "an opportunity for policy to move upward from lower bureaucratic levels." While not particularly significant in the last years of Roosevelt's administration, this change proved decisive in the Taft years, when individuals such as Straight and Philander C. Knox exercised great influence; for, to be kind, President Taft had few definite ideas about foreign policy.

Even more important was TR's belief that the Open Door in China simply was not worth a war with Japan. One of the best expressions of this attitude appeared in a letter written to Secretary of State designate Knox on 8 February 1909, in which Roosevelt noted that relations with Japan were of "great and permanent importance." He said that it was most important for the Taft administration to understand that "Japan is vitally interested in China and on the Asiatic mainland and her wiser statesmen will if possible prevent her getting entangled in a war with us, because whatever its result it would hamper and possibly ruin Japan when she came to deal again with affairs in China." Since the Pacific coast of the United States was relatively defenseless and "we have no army to hold or reconquer the Philippines and Hawaii," war must be avoided.

TR's conclusion was that China and American interests in China were insignificant in the broader context of United States foreign policy; but Taft and Knox, prodded by subordinates and

American businessmen, thought they could isolate China and especially Manchuria from general Far Eastern problems and preserve the Open Door as they perceived it. Historians who have argued that there is essential continuity between Roosevelt's and Taft's policies toward the balance of power in East Asia have emphasized too much the attitudes of certain State Department officials and business leaders. At the top—TR and Taft—there existed differences with enormous consequences. As TR told his successor in late 1910, the Open Door in China was an excellent idea, "and I hope it will be a good thing in the future, so far as it can be maintained by general diplomatic agreement; but, as has been proved by the whole history of Manchuria, alike under Russia and under Japan, the 'Open Door' policy, as a matter of fact, completely disappears as soon as a powerful nation determines to disregard it, and is willing to run the risk of war." One such nation, TR believed, was Japan.

With these thoughts in mind, the Japanese immigration problem occupied almost all the attention TR gave the Far East after 1905. Immigration by Orientals had become a political issue in the United States by 1900. China was too weak to protest restrictive practices, but Japan, flushed with its magnificent victory over Russia, a white nation, was not. In 1906 the San Francisco Board of Education precipitated trouble between the United States and Japan by ordering Oriental students into a segregated school. Rhetorical and legislative excesses on the part of Californians irritated the president and weakened his position, revealing once again the limits domestic attitudes placed upon him. TR worked for peace with Japan but prepared for the worst. By means of the Gentlemen's Agreement and other negotiations and as a result of Japanese action, the flow of immigrants slowed, but not without a war scare. Japanese, dissatisfied with the Treaty of Portsmouth and blaming the president for preventing additional Japanese conquests at Russia's expense (incorrectly as history has shown), called for action by Japan to protect its citizens residing in the United States. Roosevelt decided to dispatch the U.S. fleet on a round-the-world cruise to remind the American people of their global commitments, strengthen his political position in western states, and stimulate pronavy sentiment in the Congress. He also assumed the Great White Fleet would have a sobering influence on Japan by demonstrating America's ability to defend its interests in the Pacific. Given these goals, the trip proved a success. More important was a decision by both governments to prevent the immigration issue from souring relations. When Roosevelt left the White House the two nations had returned to a status of respect, if mutual suspicion.

One area remains to be discussed: Europe. Bitter rivalries occurred there in the early twentieth century, Austro-Russian, Franco-German, and Anglo-German being the most important; but only the latter was of continuing concern to President Roosevelt. One idea dominated his European policy: conviction that Great Britain was a friend and Germany a potential enemy. With that in mind, he set out to clear away standing differences between the United States and Britain. He was disturbed about the Venezuelan crisis of 1902–3, approved the Anglo-Japanese alliance of 1902, was happy about solution of the Alaskan boundary dispute, and determined, after the death of the British ambassador to Washington, Sir Michael Herbert, to ensure good communications by securing the appointment of someone he trusted. During this time Roosevelt also tried to improve relations with Germany, but not at the expense of Britain. The German government never succeeded in gaining equality with the British, even though it enjoyed the advantage of having one of Roosevelt's closest friends, Baron Hermann Speck von Sternburg, as ambassador, and notwithstanding TR's repeated expressions of admiration for Kaiser Wilhelm II. The Germans alarmed TR. Their vigor, military skill, and aggressiveness were all traits he admired, but he considered them a menace to the peace of the world and to American security.

The Moroccan crisis of 1905–6 confirmed these images of Germany and had a lasting effect on Roosevelt's views regarding the European balance of power. After the German ruler's dramatic visit to Tangier, Morocco, in March 1905 challenging French control of that country, the president concluded that Wilhelm was most unreliable and possibly even dangerous. In the negotiations that followed this famous visit, TR, as he had done at Portsmouth, played a large role. The Germans sought support for an international conference on Morocco, hoping to weaken French control there. The French refused and war seemed a possibility. Once more working behind the scenes because of limited American public interest and using his wide contacts, Roosevelt persuaded the French and Germans to agree to a conference, gaining also a pledge from Ambassador Sternburg that Germany would accept whatever TR thought to be a fair solution. As it happened,

Sternburg unwittingly had misrepresented his instructions, giving Roosevelt a veto over German policy. Skillfully exploiting this inadvertent veto, the president moved to defuse an explosive situation.

The principals conferred at Algeciras, Spain, in early 1906 with Henry White representing the United States. After much difficulty Roosevelt brought about a compromise favoring the French, by placing the Moroccan sultan's police force under French and Spanish supervision. The Germans at first opposed this arrangement, but the president threatened to announce publicly that they had broken their word to him, and Berlin's resistance collapsed. Then, since he recognized and appreciated the need of nations to save face, he worked arduously to make the agreement appear to be something other than a great defeat for Germany. Because of TR's efforts, Europe in 1906 retreated from a world war.

By siding with the French, the ally of Great Britain, in the Moroccan crisis, as he had done with the Japanese, another British ally, in the Russo-Japanese War, Roosevelt demonstrated the pro-British orientation of his diplomacy. He continued this policy from 1906 until 1909 and, of course, even after he left the presidency. While some officials in London failed to appreciate the direction of American policy, Foreign Secretary Lord Lansdowne in particular, it was apparent to King Edward VII that friendship with the United States must be an essential part of any British foreign policy. After Sir Edward Grey succeeded Lansdowne, friendship with America indeed became the foundation of London's diplomacy. Throughout this period, Wilhelm struggled to bring Roosevelt over to Germany's side, at one point suggesting a German-Chinese-American alliance. Such schemes only persuaded TR that the kaiser was unpredictable and untrustworthy.

American diplomacy in Europe, except for the Moroccan crisis, was less active than elsewhere, for while American interests in Europe, especially commercial interests, were expanding, the situation there was not nearly as unstable as in Latin America and East Asia. As with other policies, however, TR based his European diplomacy on realism; his faith in Anglo-American cooperation was to characterize American foreign relations in the twentieth century.

The late Howard K. Beale has summarized the many successes of Rooseveltian diplomacy. Yet, after noting TR's extraordinary comprehension of foreign affairs, his ability to look into the future with regard to Russia and Great Britain, his understanding of the influence of internal events on the foreign policies of modern nations, his determination not to take stands he knew the American people would not back, and a host of other achievements, Beale wrote, "In the end, for all his activity, his tremendous influence on foreign policy, his surprising insights and prophecies, Roosevelt failed in his most important objectives." The stable world based on order for which he worked was not realized; Britain declined faster than expected; nationalism grew beyond all predictions. Beale believed TR should have grappled with these issues, that he had an opportunity to choose between "imperialism" and its alternatives; by selecting imperialism he created many of the problems of the present day. This criticism seems too harsh. There were certainly persuasive arguments against expansion; Fred H. Harrington and Robert Beisner have discussed the anti-imperialists, whose ideas Roosevelt dismissed too lightly. To suggest that he could have led America down a path other than that described by Beale as imperialism, however, is to miss an essential point about the nature of U.S. diplomacy. Given the tremendous changes in the United States and the world during his presidency, TR was in most cases either reacting to or anticipating the proclaimed interests of the American people. In some instances, rather than being the instrument of imperialism, he actually slowed the pace of expansion. As he came to understand the necessity and difficulty of defending colonial possessions, he steered clear of further territorial annexation, despite pressure to move in that direction.

Roosevelt never solved the problem of a democracy pursuing a course of expansion and imperialism; he never gave much thought to the subject. He did come to realize that there were great costs in imperialism that were at times not worth the benefits. While his rhetoric was often excessive, caution characterized his actions in foreign affairs, and he appears much less an imperialist than Taft, or perhaps even Wilson. Akira Iriye has suggested that Taft's diplomacy marked "the beginning of a moralistic diplomacy in East Asia." One wonders if that statement can be made more general—after TR left the White House the United States began to use moral arguments more and more to justify its acts and distinguish them from those of other nations; morality was no longer an end in itself. Eventually, American officials would begin to succumb to their own rhetoric and move on to such disasters as Vietnam. Roosevelt's model of foreign relations was that followed by the "most civilized" western European nations; to expect him to have invented another is perhaps to ask too much of one man burdened with the responsibilities of power.

Theodore Roosevelt made a major contribution by preparing his country for the international problems it was sure to face in the years after 1909. This was no easy task, for he had to work against many decades of tradition and apathy. Thus, he was an instrument of change. Almost as important is the fact that he increased the world's awareness of the United States. Because of his colorful personality, the policies he followed, and the successes he attained, America gained international recognition, though not yet concomitant respect. Roosevelt's policy was also one of continuity. In each of the major geographic areas of diplomacy, Asia, Latin America, and Europe, he dealt with existing ideas, refining them, using them to suit a changing world, but generally following long-held American traditions.

TR's stewardship of foreign affairs occurred at a critical time for the United States. Had the nation continued to ignore its relationship to world events perhaps the European war would have come sooner and turned out differently; it might certainly have turned out worse. There are many possibilities as to what might have happened had Roosevelt not been president between 1901 and 1909. There are also some certainties; one is that he served his country well.

BIBLIOGRAPHIC NOTE

A good deal has been written about TR, partly because of the abundance of primary materials. His own manuscript collection, the Roosevelt manuscripts in the Library of Congress, is extensive. An excellent published collection of primary materials is Elting E. Morison, ed., *The Letters of Theodore Roosevelt*, 8 vols. (Cambridge, Mass., 1951–54). The best general accounts of TR's life are John M. Blum, *The Republican Roosevelt* (Cambridge, Mass., 1961), William H. Harbaugh, *Power and Responsibility: The Life and Times of Theodore Roosevelt* (New York, 1961), G. Wallace Chessman, *Theodore Roosevelt* (Boston,

1969), and Henry Pringle, *Theodore Roosevelt* (New York, 1931). The two best general treatments of Roosevelt's diplomacy are Howard K. Beale, *Theodore Roosevelt and the Rise of America to World Power* (Baltimore, 1956), and Raymond Esthus, *Theodore Roosevelt and the International Rivalries* (Waltham, Mass., 1970). See also David H. Burton, *Theodore Roosevelt: Confident Imperialist* (Philadelphia, 1968), George Mowry, *The Era of Theodore Roosevelt* (New York, 1958), and David Healy's excellent "Theodore Roosevelt and the Sturdy Virtues," in his book *U.S. Expansionism* (Madison, 1970). An excellent article on Roosevelt's technique of diplomacy is Nelson M. Blake, "Ambassadors at the Court of Theodore Roosevelt," *Mississippi Valley Historical Review* 42 (1955).

For exact citations for the quotations from Roosevelt's correspondence and for a detailed analysis of the Treaty of Portsmouth and TR's role in it, see Eugene Trani, *The Treaty of Portsmouth: An Adventure in American Diplomacy* (Lexington, Ky., 1969). For a study of Ambassador George Meyer's reaction to Russian internal events during this time, see Eugene Trani, "Russia in 1905: The View from the American Embassy," *Review of Politics* 31 (1969).

A general treatment of TR's Latin American policy is in Samuel Flagg Bemis, *The Latin American Policy of the United States* (New York, 1943). There are a number of specialized studies; two of the best are on the interventions in Cuba. See David Healy, *The United States in Cuba, 1898–1902* (Madison, 1963), and Allan Millett, *The Politics of Intervention: The Military Occupation of Cuba, 1906–1909* (Columbus, 1968). An older account, still of some value, is Howard C. Hill, *Roosevelt and the Caribbean* (Chicago, 1927). There are a number of good recent studies on Roosevelt and the Far East. The best general account is Raymond Esthus, *Theodore Roosevelt and Japan* (Seattle, 1966). See also Charles Neu, *An Uncertain Friendship: Theodore Roosevelt and Japan, 1906–1909* (Cambridge, Mass., 1967). Both of these studies are based on Japanese as well as American sources. More general treatments of America's Far Eastern policy are Akira Iriye, *Across the Pacific: An Inner History of American-East Asian Relations* (New York, 1967), and Ernest May and James C. Thomson, Jr., eds., *American-East Asian Relations: A Survey* (Cambridge, 1972). The latter includes essays by Esthus, covering the period 1901–6, and Neu, covering 1906–13. In addition to some of the more general accounts, one should consult Charles S. Campbell, *Anglo-American Understanding, 1898–1903* (Baltimore, 1957), and Bradford Perkins, *The Great Rapprochement: England and the United States, 1898–1914* (New York, 1968), for treatments of Roosevelt's policy toward Europe.

Reprinted by permission of Cornell University Libraries, Department of Manuscripts and University Archives, Ithaca, N.Y.

WILLARD D. STRAIGHT

and the Great Game of Empire

Helen Dodson Kahn

Separating twentieth-century policy makers into "realists" and "idealists" has led to misunderstanding of the men, motives, and policies that have shaped the nation's foreign affairs. Such confusion is especially apparent in analyses of the turn-of-the-century period, the seminal years of United States involvement in the Far East. President Theodore Roosevelt was a "realist," some historians argue, because he appreciated the limits of American power in the Far East and subsequently ended American involvement in Manchuria, recognizing it as a Japanese sphere of investment opportunity. William Howard Taft is depicted, on the

The author gratefully acknowledges the financial assistance of a Herbert H. Lehman Fellowship and an American Association of University Women Fellowship which allowed her to complete this essay. Full documentation can be found in the author's doctoral dissertation, "The Great Game of Empire: Willard D. Straight and American Far Eastern Policy," Cornell University, 1968.

other hand, as pursuing an "idealistic" and "quixotic" Dollar Diplomacy in attempting to dislodge the Japanese from Manchuria, thereby placing the United States and Japan on a collision course. Wilson, according to the traditional analysis, was an "idealist" who, motivated by moralistic concern for the Chinese, withdrew from the international railroad consortium and renounced Dollar Diplomacy.[1]

Such an arbitrary division misses the important continuity of policy from Roosevelt through Taft and even Wilson. These three administrations shared an essential unity of goals. Although tactics shifted several times during those years, they did so mainly in response to changing conditions in the Far East and did not indicate altered goals among policy makers. All three administrations based their policies on a similar understanding of American national interests (regarding which moralistic considerations were not of primary importance), and committed themselves to preserving the Open Door in China.[2] Dedication to keeping China free

1. For this interpretation, see in particular Robert Osgood, *Ideals and Self-Interest in America's Foreign Relations: The Great Transformation of the Twentieth Century* (Chicago, 1953), and George Kennan, *American Diplomacy, 1900–1950* (Chicago, 1951). A. Whitney Griswold, *The Far Eastern Policy of the United States* (New York, 1938), Raymond A. Esthus, *Theodore Roosevelt and Japan* (Seattle, 1966), and Charles Vevier, *The United States and China, 1906–1913: A Study of Finance and Diplomacy* (New Brunswick, N.J., 1955) all draw a sharp dichotomy between the policies of Roosevelt and Taft. Harley Notter, *The Origins of the Foreign Policy of Woodrow Wilson* (Baltimore, 1937), and Li Tien-yi, *Woodrow Wilson's China Policy, 1913–1917* (New York, 1952), make a sharp distinction between the policies of Taft and Wilson.

2. The Open Door doctrine, with roots deep in the nineteenth century, became official American policy in 1899 and 1900 when the great powers were vying for position in China. The Open Door notes, issued by Secretary of State John Hay, announced to the world that the United States was vitally concerned with the future of China. Hay sought the concurrence of the strong Western powers not to challenge the sovereignty and integrity of the Chinese Empire through the establishment of spheres of influence. Instead, China's vast export market should remain open, without special privilege, to all world commerce. Admittedly fragile, this policy needed the agreement of the concerned powers to uphold its tenets, a consensus that never really was achieved. Moreover, the assumption that China would passively accept this Western penetration ignored the nationalistic fervor already stirring within the empire. Thus, in the twentieth century, the Open Door doctrine would face repeated challenges both from within and without China. A penetrating analysis of the formulation of America's Open Door policy is found in Thomas McCormick, *China Market: America's Quest for Informal Empire, 1893–1901* (Chicago, 1967).

from the domination of other powers and open to American trade
and influence became the keystone of American Far Eastern policy
for much of the twentieth century.

The activities of Willard Straight, a State Department officer
whose fascinating career spanned the Roosevelt, Taft, and Wilson
administrations, typify the essential concerns of United States
diplomacy toward East Asia. Straight was both artist and activist, a
dreamer of grandiose dreams and an ambitious achiever. He
thought in huge sweeps of time, planning fifty to one hundred
years into the future, molding history and shaping empires as the
British imperialists had done. Yet, after drafting these far-reaching
schemes, dreams that would have done justice to a Rhodes or a
Clive, he proved a prodigious worker and an excellent negotiator.
He labored long hours over the minutest details, changing words,
adding paragraphs, refurbishing and polishing long, detailed
arguments designed to effect accord among Peking, Washington,
and Wall Street and thereby provide structure and definition to his
plans.

Born in Oswego, New York, in 1880, Straight was the son of
two college teachers. Both parents died of tuberculosis before the
boy reached ten, leaving him to be raised by two old-maid friends
of his family. While enrolled as an architecture student at Cornell
University, he became a member of the Kipling Club. This
association changed his life. Straight became a disciple of Rudyard
Kipling and adopted the British poet's virile code of ethics as his
own. Kipling recognized the fragility of man's existence but,
unlike the *fin de siècle* authors who anguished over the meaning-
lessness of civilization, Kipling preached that reality was to be
found in the total involvement of man's energies in work. The
active life, Kipling explained, was the "bulkhead 'twixt despair and
the Edge of Nothing." Like his poet-mentor, Straight conceived of
all life as a game, a struggle carried on in a hostile environment
with the aim of surpassing or defeating the other contestants. He
first applied this grim philosophy to his own situation. Beginning
the fight without family, status, or material wealth, Straight
decided to use his abilities to gain the "most thought-of things in
the world": fame, riches, and position. Quitting or withdrawing

from the contest meant retreat from life and resignation to fate, a course that he deemed moral cowardliness.

Kipling's ideology also provided a framework for Straight's early understanding of the purpose of the Western presence in Asia. A self-avowed imperialist, Kipling viewed the British Empire as an engine of progress. The British, carriers of the "white man's burden," imposed civilization on backward peoples who were incapable of improving themselves. Straight wholeheartedly embraced this doctrine of racial superiority; the Anglo-Saxon's special genius for government imposed a duty to take civilization, enlightenment, and progress to those whom the poet called the "lesser breeds without the law." As an advocate of Kipling's view that the most fit should rule, Straight believed firm, orderly, and beneficial government to be more important than self-government. This view, tragically inadequate, later shaped his response to the growing antiforeign movements in China.

After graduation from Cornell University in 1901, Straight seized an opportunity to reach the Far East by accepting a position in the Chinese Customs Service. Having lived in the East briefly as a child, he now intended to study the language, customs, and art of China and to employ his artistic ability as a journalist-illustrator, and hoped in time to become as famous as Kipling. After six months of intensive language training, Straight became the personal aide and private secretary to Sir Robert Hart, inspector general of the customs. Despite this auspicious start to his career, Straight craved a more exciting life than that of a customs official, and in 1904 he resigned to accept a position as a Russo-Japanese War correspondent for Reuters and the Associated Press; then, after the war, he became vice-consul and secretary of the American legation in Seoul, Korea.

Throughout his life, Straight exhibited a rare talent for forming deep, lasting friendships, an ability he consciously developed because he knew that friends could help him move along the road to success. In Peking, Straight became well acquainted with most members of the diplomatic community, with the newspaper correspondents, and with European financial and business agents. In Tokyo during the war he cultivated the friendship of the American minister and his secretary, Huntington Wilson (who would later head the State Department's Far Eastern desk), and many war correspondents. These friendships introduced him to people with wealth, social status, and business and diplomatic importance. By handling the arrangements for the 1905 Korean visits of E. H. Harriman, the railroad magnate, and of Alice Roosevelt and her entourage (and later arranging honeymoon plans for Alice and Nicholas Longworth), Straight established important friendships that led to meetings with President Roosevelt and a 1906 appointment, conferred directly by the president at Harriman's suggestion, as consul general in Mukden, Manchuria.[3] He was then twenty-six.

During these years in the Far East, Straight broadened and modified his views, gaining a new appreciation of American involvement in Asia. He read voraciously, a habit he maintained all his life; he studied in particular the ideology of expansionists such as Josiah Strong, Archibald Colquhoun, Arthur Smith, and Alfred Thayer Mahan. He accepted as accurate William H. Seward's famous prophecy that the Pacific region would be the "chief theatre of events in the world's great hereafter." Civilization had evolved ever westward; indeed, the Far East already had become the scene of a struggle for world power. Straight concluded that an American refusal to participate in this struggle would constitute a confession of its moral cowardliness and decadence.

Moreover, Straight accepted the argument forcefully advanced by Arthur Smith and many progressives that a fortunate coincidence existed between the needs of the United States, then seeking a new economic and perhaps spiritual frontier, and those of an awakening and Westernizing China. Trade and investment there could guarantee the viability of the American system and at the same time bring Western civilization, democracy, and progress to China, thus guiding its renaissance. Like Mahan, Straight was certain that developments in China would determine the future of the world. Within the next hundred years, he noted, China would either be "one of our most dangerous enemies or most powerful friends," depending upon which powers controlled its modernization. Straight wanted America to "reshape the East," an action he deemed "essential to the logical and inevitable growth of the United States into a world power."

At the outbreak of the Russo-Japanese War, Straight agreed

3. Straight's contacts also led to his engagement to Harriman's daughter, broken when her father refused to sanction the marriage. Straight eventually married Dorothy Whitney, daughter of William C. Whitney, Cleveland's secretary of the navy, and heiress to a Standard Oil fortune.

with Secretary of State John Hay, President Roosevelt, and W. W. Rockhill (the president's key adviser on Far Eastern affairs) that the Japanese represented the forces of enlightenment and progress, checking the Muscovite tide that threatened to exclude Western civilization from Manchuria. As a war correspondent, however, Straight found his admiration for the martial qualities of stoicism, bravery, patriotism, and efficiency of the Nipponese tempered by their condescending treatment of Westerners. His dealings with them during and immediately after the war produced in him an intense racial hatred of all things Japanese. Moreover, the discriminatory treatment of American commercial interests Straight witnessed in Korea aroused fear that the Island Empire intended to police the Far East solely for itself. If, after the victories over Russia, Japan determined to exclude Westerners from Korea and Manchuria, as seemed increasingly obvious by 1906, Japanese ambitions posed a dangerous new threat to American commercial interests.

Soon after Straight's arrival in Mukden in 1906, he became involved in a dispute with his superior in Peking, an argument based on a fundamental and irreconcilable difference in outlook on the Far Eastern situation. W. W. Rockhill, the American minister to China, thought that despite Japan's greatly strengthened position resulting from Portsmouth, it would cooperate in maintaining the Open Door in the former war zone. Rockhill had urged full diplomatic support of Japan during the Russo-Japanese War and believed that because of its dependence on foreign capital Japan would continue to respect the integrity of China. In contrast, Straight was convinced that, despite promises to the contrary, Japan's military and civilian administrations in Manchuria were willfully using the period of military occupation to secure a dominant position and extinguish United States trade in southern Manchuria.

Straight believed that Japan already had demonstrated unwillingness to work with American investors in Manchuria. At the close of hostilities, E. H. Harriman had negotiated with Premier Taro Katsura for the establishment of an international syndicate to control Japan's newly acquired South Manchuria Railway. The Komura Agreement of December 1905, however, limited control of the railroad to Chinese and Japanese shareholders, and thus canceled Harriman's plan for cooperative development. The pact also contained a secret pledge by China never to build any railroad prejudicial to the south Manchurian line, a commitment that

justified Japan's opposition to any non-Japanese railroad construction in Manchuria and threatened the future of competitive
investment in northeast China. Refusing to relinquish his vision of
an around-the-world railroad, Harriman asked Straight to watch
for an opportunity to secure the missing Manchurian link.

In 1907–9, when he first initiated proposals to secure an
American position in north China, Straight was young, enthusiastic, and fully convinced that his country was on the verge of
assuming an imperial mantle and fulfilling its mission and spiritual
destiny. Manchuria, he thought, would be the "key to all China";
cooperation with the emerging progressive leadership there
would enable Americans to mold the "Chinese renaissance." With
proper handling the task of empire shaping might fall to the
United States—and what a great work it would be! It was a golden
age, a time when one might believe he played a part in shaping
the destiny of nations. Straight had a "great dream," as his
vice-consul later recalled. "He might well have been—indeed he
was for the moment—a potential Rhodes or Clive of North China."

From Mukden, Straight proposed what was eventually treated
in Washington as an alternative to the bankrupt pro-Japanese
policy. Like George F. Kennan's "long telegram" forty years later,
Straight's recommendations reached the Department of State at a
pivotal juncture. China, he reported, was then engaged in a
promising postwar reform movement. In the three eastern provinces, newly appointed, capable, progressive officials, particularly
T'ang Shao-yi, the governor of Fengtien province, were fearful of
Japanese purposes and wished to secure foreign financial and
political support for the development of Manchuria under Chinese auspices. Rather than depend on the questionable goodwill
of the Japanese, or expect support from Great Britain or Germany
(powers that had omitted Manchuria from their Open Door
declarations), the United States should act unilaterally in China.
Such a policy would protect future opportunities for American
trade and investment in this region, which Straight now viewed as
the "new West," a "virgin territory" that needed only American
capital to become "one of the most prosperous districts in the
world."

In cooperation with T'ang, Straight worked out a proposal for
American financiers to fund a Manchurian bank, which as sole
fiscal agent of the provincial government would undertake the
development of the three eastern provinces. Straight approached

A STORY OF THE CHINA SHOP
An Artist's View Of The Complications In The Far East
By ALBERT LEVERING

1. *Uncle Sam. "Seems ter be a little trouble at the store to-day, boys."*

2. *Uncle Sam (to France, Germany, and England). "There he goes inside, boys; guess we'd better stay out fer a while."*

3. *Uncle Sam (to China). "Be careful you don't get mixed up in it."*

4. *China. "Hellup!"*
Uncle Sam. "Jinkys! they've pulled him inside too. Don't git too near, boys."

5. *Uncle Sam. "Never mind, boys. Don't go any nearer. We'll just wait a few days."*

6. *The Kaiser, et al. "Dot looks to usses like ve vait. Uncle Sammy was right, yes?"*

This cartoon aptly portrays the "wait and see" attitude toward China and American involvement there that Willard Straight sought to change.

Harper's Weekly, *5 March 1904*

Harriman for support of the bank, but the panic of 1907 rendered the railroad magnate's consideration of the offer impossible. Rather than await an improvement of the economic climate in the private sector, Straight tried to interest Washington in encouraging extensive American investment in Manchuria. At a 1907 meeting with Secretary of War William Howard Taft at Vladivostok, Straight proposed utilization of the Boxer indemnity remission as security for a Manchurian development loan.[4] Apparently, Taft accepted Straight's argument that cooperation with progressive Chinese would enable the United States to block Japan's attempt to control north China, an area that might become a vital frontier for ambitious Americans. Taft formally recommended that Peking seek State Department approval for the use of the Boxer indemnity to develop Manchuria. Buoyed by Taft's encouragement, T'ang made plans to visit Washington.

As the date of T'ang's visit approached, financial conditions in the United States improved enough to permit Harriman to negotiate with the Chinese, and he asked Secretary of State Elihu Root to recall Straight to Washington. The young China expert returned as acting head of the Division of Far Eastern Affairs, instructed by the secretary of state himself to assist Harriman and to interest key eastern businessmen in the commercial development of Manchuria. Straight found Harriman and his financial backers, Jacob Schiff and Otto Kahn of Kuhn, Loeb and Company, prepared to undertake T'ang's proposed Manchurian development bank and a Chinchou to Aigun railroad across Manchuria. Moreover, he secured their agreement to finance China's purchase of the Chinese Eastern Railway, which in the spring of 1908 Russian officials had expressed interest in selling.

In the course of the discussions, Schiff proposed that the purchase of the Chinese Eastern Railway be linked to an overture to the Japanese for sale of the South Manchuria Railway. At the banker's request, Straight drew up a memorandum regarding this purchase, which Schiff presented to an official of the Bank of Japan. He suggested that it would be desirable "if American capital could be made the stakeholder of the main line of communication and transportation both in Southern and Northern

4. The idea favored by many American officials, including Rockhill, was to use the $12.5 million remission for the education of Chinese students in the United States.

Manchuria." Russia intended to sell, he said, and if Japan did not, the possibility would always exist that the Chinese government might build a competing line. This proposal, presented by New York bankers to Japan in 1908 during the closing days of the Roosevelt administration, was essentially the same as the one Taft's secretary of state would present in 1909 as the Knox Neutralization Proposal. Instead of relying on American capital exclusively, however, Knox would advocate international control. In both instances Japan refused to consider the idea.

While Schiff was engaged with the Japanese, T'ang Shao-yi began negotiations in the United States. Officials at State were hopeful that T'ang's proposals might provide the United States the substantial position it required in Manchuria if the Open Door doctrine were to be upheld. When Secretary of State Root met with T'ang in December 1908 he agreed that the Chinese could use the Boxer indemnity remission as security for a Manchurian bank loan. Moreover, Root promised United States support for a second plan, the reform and stabilization of China's currency. Negotiations proceeded well, so well that a friend of Rockhill's, not in sympathy with T'ang's plans, complained to the American minister that Straight had been successfully "running things" from his desk in the State Department and had secured a favorable reception for T'ang's proposals both "in White House and Department circles." Unfortunately for the schemes of these shapers of empire, just as negotiations were nearing completion, events in China—the empress dowager's death and Yüan Shih-kai's subsequent fall from power—brought T'ang's sudden recall.

By authorizing the use of the Boxer indemnity remission as security for a Manchurian bank loan and agreeing to support a currency reform loan, Secretary Root initiated during the Roosevelt administration the policy that during the Taft administration would be derisively labeled "Dollar Diplomacy." Root unofficially supported American financial interests in China, cognizant that the successful implementation of their plans would make Americans codirectors in a bank empowered to oversee all development projects in the three eastern provinces. The vast implications of this project were certainly not lost on the astute secretary: the establishment of the Manchurian bank would create a solid financial interest in Manchuria from which the United States could challenge Japanese expansion. Indeed, if successfully implemented, it would make Manchuria a virtual sphere of investment opportunity for the United States.[5]

T'ang's negotiations with Root, Harriman, and the New York financiers regarding Manchuria occurred in juxtaposition to Root's 1907–8 negotiations with Japanese Foreign Minister Kogoro Takahira, which according to most historians constituted an American recognition of Japanese dominance in Manchuria.[6] If these contradictory negotiations could be attributed to a deep split within the State Department one could accept the interpretation that high officials such as Secretary Root, who supported the Root-Takahira negotiations, overrode lower-ranking staff members, such as Straight, Huntington Wilson, and William Phillips, who supported the T'ang-Harriman negotiations. This explanation is untenable, however, because the evidence indicates that both Secretary of State Root and President Roosevelt supported T'ang's proposal for a Manchurian bank to be financed by the Boxer indemnity. Root's support of T'ang's anti-Japanese proposals is solid evidence that in 1908 the Roosevelt administration had no intention of withdrawing from Manchuria. On the contrary, it saw an opportunity to implant a strong American influence there to end Japanese domination of the region and guarantee the future of the Open Door.

The Root-Takahira Agreement can better be understood within the context of a wide-ranging diplomatic offensive that the United States waged against the Japanese in 1907–8. Washington knew that Japan faced severe domestic economic difficulties and problems related to the prosecution of its postwar policies in Korea and Manchuria. Confident that Tokyo was anxious to avoid war with the United States, the Roosevelt administration attempted to convince Japan of its determination to uphold the

5. Historians have ignored or belittled the significance of Root's discussions with T'ang. Esthus argues that because Roosevelt and Root had recognized Manchuria as Japan's sphere of exclusive investment opportunity, they refused to support the Manchurian bank.

6. Griswold and Vevier state that Roosevelt gave Japan a free hand in Manchuria. Esthus explains that Root recognized Manchuria as a Japanese sphere of exclusive investment opportunity. Charles Neu, *An Uncertain Friendship: Theodore Roosevelt and Japan, 1906–1909* (Cambridge, 1967), goes so far as to argue that Roosevelt and Root also accepted Japan's infringement of China's territorial and administrative integrity, a view with which neither Esthus nor the present author agree.

Open Door in Manchuria. In 1907, TR ordered the fleet to display the "big stick" of United States naval power in the Far East. In another, somewhat puzzling move, he actively encouraged Chinese and German overtures for an entente designed to challenge the Japanese position in Manchuria. Moreover, the State Department quietly but firmly supported China's position in the Manchurian railroad dispute with Russia and Japan, a controversy that Root realized had great consequences for the Open Door and the territorial integrity of China. These American actions, coupled with Taft's Open Door pronouncements made while in the Far East and the support for the T'ang proposals, nourished persistent worldwide rumors of an impending clash between the United States and Japan.

Roosevelt's diplomatic offensive elicited a Japanese proposal for an exchange of notes with the United States concerning their respective Far Eastern policies. Although Washington believed that Japan was retreating from her aggressive policies in north China, Japan had other intentions. Tokyo was seeking to improve relations with the United States and quiet the speculations of war that adversely affected its position on the European financial exchanges. It anticipated turning the potentially threatening visit of the American fleet into a friendly visit by an ally. Most importantly, it hoped to undercut the T'ang Shao-yi mission and forestall the completion of an American-German-Chinese entente. Straight harbored deep reservations about the proposed exchange and expressed concern that the agreement might be misunderstood in China as constituting another in Japan's series of Far Eastern ententes. Indeed, as Straight warned, Tokyo successfully propagandized the completed Root-Takahira Agreement not as a mutual reaffirmation of the Open Door, but as an American recognition of Manchuria as Japan's exclusive sphere of investment opportunity. Straight believed that Tokyo used the agreement to undermine the pro-American progressives in Peking, particularly Yüan and T'ang, and thus defeat the American effort to obtain a financial position in Manchuria. The Root-Takahira Agreement was, Straight maintained, a "terrible diplomatic blunder," and he never forgave Roosevelt for his role in it.

Although historians generally overlook Straight's impact on Roosevelt's 1908 Dollar Diplomacy, most do recognize him as the principal architect of Taft-Knox Dollar Diplomacy. From the time of their meeting at Vladivostok in 1907, Taft had considered Straight a valuable Far Eastern adviser. President Taft shared Straight's concern for the future of the American position in Asia and believed American investment in Manchuria could thwart an imminent Japanese threat to the Open Door there. Therefore he continued Roosevelt's Far Eastern policy, particularly the support that Root and Roosevelt had given to Harriman and Kuhn, Loeb for the Manchurian bank proposal, the Chinchou-Aigun railroad plans, and the Chinese Eastern Railway purchase. Taft hoped eventually to resume negotiations with T'ang for a currency reform loan. Although after T'ang's recall Straight received routine orders to return to his post at Mukden, the new secretary of state Philander C. Knox canceled them at Harriman's request and kept Straight in the State Department where he might study the possibilities for introduction of American capital into China, particularly Manchuria. Knox was committed to maintaining the Open Door, but it was not, as he noted, "a quixotically altruistic task for China's benefit." Rather, he kept the ultimate purpose of the Open Door clearly in view, "a door open for us equally with all other nations."

The Hukuang Loan provided the first opportunity for the introduction of American capital into China. In May 1909, Straight learned that a new German-French-British syndicate was negotiating with Peking to finance construction of a railroad in the fertile Yangtze Valley. Through the blunt tactic of threatening the discontinuance of the Boxer indemnity remission unless American interests were included, the State Department wedged the newly formed "American group" of bankers into the Tripartite Consortium. The United States demanded, and eventually secured, one-fourth participation in the loan, equal provision for the purchase of construction materials in the United States, and equal consideration in all other particulars.

Knox's demand for equal participation by the United States in the Hukuang Loan constituted an extension of the Open Door doctrine as originally defined by Secretary of State John Hay in 1899, but not a radical departure from existing American policy. According to some historians, Hay recognized spheres of influence with special privileges in railroad and mining concessions, asking only that equality of commercial opportunity be maintained within such spheres. Hay had understood the close relationship existing between investment and commercial opportunities and between investment opportunity and Chinese sovereignty, however. In 1902, therefore, he had opposed Russia's demands for "the exclusive right and privilege of opening mines, establishing railroads, *or in any way* [italics added] industrially developing Manchuria," on the grounds that such a monopoly would jeopardize both the sovereign rights of China and the trading rights of other powers. "The inevitable result" of exclusive investment spheres, Hay informed St. Petersburg, "must be the complete wreck of the policy of absolute equality of treatment of all nations in regard to trade, navigation and commerce within the confines of the Empire." Accepting Hay's argument regarding the interrelatedness of investment opportunity, commercial opportunity, and Chinese integrity, Knox extended Hay's opposition to general and exclusive concessions to include specific contracts. Especially in the case of railroads, which by their very nature were monopolistic, specific as well as general contracts threatened the Open Door for commercial opportunity.

The Taft administration's Dollar Diplomacy did not push apathetic American bankers into China; the initiative lay with the bankers. Harriman and his financial supporters, not the State Department, initiated the Manchurian railroad projects. The International Banking Corporation first brought the Hukuang Loan to the department's attention when it asked support for its threatened interests. The relationship between business and government was, however, understandably close. The bankers were totally dependent upon Washington's diplomatic support to conclude negotiations, while the State Department needed the bankers' financial power to secure a foothold for future American trade. This interdependence was implicitly recognized when the group selected Straight as its Peking agent. Because of his association with Harriman and his backers, his experience with the diplomatic community, and his connections with T'ang and Yüan (the Chinese officials most likely to grant contracts to American interests), Straight was the natural liaison between the government and business leaders. He viewed his new position with the Wall Street financiers as temporary; once the banking group was functioning, Straight intended to return to government service.

Unfortunately for Straight's plans, negotiations did not proceed rapidly. Britain opposed Washington's Open Door strategy of cooperative investment, preferring to keep the Yangtze Valley as a British sphere. American purposes also clashed with a developing antiforeign movement in China demanding recovery of control of Chinese resources. Unlike American leaders, many nationalistic Chinese saw little difference between cooperative and unilateral foreign investment, for both resulted in increased foreign control over China. Opposition to Western imperialism was directed also against the increasingly ineffective central government that granted the concessions. Because Straight believed the Chinese were incapable of developing their resources without the guidance and tutelage of Westerners, he viewed the movement as reactionary. Whatever its ideological basis, rights recovery posed a serious challenge to successful implementation of the American Open Door strategy.

While Straight served as the American group's Peking agent, he disagreed radically with the philosophy underlying Taft's China policy. Washington sought to prevent spheres of interest by securing absolute equality of opportunity vis-à-vis all concessions and contracts. This policy depended upon agreement among the European powers to seek no special rights and privileges from a weak Chinese administration. Rather than conceding the fact of a weak China, Straight desired to strengthen Peking sufficiently to maintain its integrity and thus preserve the Open Door for American trade.[7] For him, the Hukuang Loan was a means to this greater end.

Straight's involvement in the Hukuang negotiations occurred while his attention was still focused primarily on Manchuria. In that region, not troubled by any "rights recovery movement," he believed the opportunities for American investment were great. Harriman, the guiding spirit behind the American group, also was uninterested in the Hukuang Loan and its underlying philosophy of creating an "international financial community of interests." To him, the American group would prove most useful by providing financial support for a unilateral American project in Manchuria.

---

7. In the back of his mind, Straight wondered if a strong China might refuse to hold the door open, but because that day seemed so remote, that possibility did not seriously concern him.

Even though his attempts in 1905 and 1908 to secure the Manchurian link for his worldwide transportation system had failed, Harriman was not discouraged and embarked on still another effort. In 1909, he proposed that Russia sell the Chinese Eastern Railway and grant him trackage rights over the Trans-Siberian Railroad. This scheme received the apparent approval of the Russian finance minister. At the same time, Straight obtained a preliminary Chinchou-Aigun contract from the Chinese, but at this promising juncture Harriman died, and fate deprived Straight of his major support. The American bankers did not understand the import of Harriman's secret schemes and refused to consider them before completion of the Hukuang negotiations.

Straight assumed total responsibility for the advocacy of the Manchurian proposals. Working zealously all through 1909, he tried to convince New York and Washington to shift their attention from the Hukuang Loan to Manchuria, Mongolia, and Siberia, which he characterized as "the most attractive field for the Group's Far Eastern endeavours." Straight expanded Harriman's neat, uncomplicated project, designed to increase American influence in Manchuria, into a grandiose scheme for rearranging the entire Far Eastern power structure. He linked T'ang's 1908 proposals for a Manchurian bank to direct the development of China's northern provinces (including the construction of the Chinchou-Aigun railroad) with Harriman's 1909 plans for the purchase of the Chinese Eastern Railway from Russia, and then joined them to ideas for British-American-Russian cooperation in Siberian, Mongolian, and Manchurian development projects proposed by J. O. P. Bland, the Peking agent for a British banking firm. To this grand design, he added elements of his own; he proposed, for example, the negotiation of a Russian-American entente to secure Russian support for the Open Door in Manchuria.[8] In addition, Straight advocated judicious manipulation of American and European attitudes toward the war loan conversion and treaty revision sought by Tokyo in exchange for Japanese acceptance of

8. Specifically, Russia would agree to recognize China's sovereignty and administrative rights over the Manchurian railway settlements. Then, under the terms of the 1905 Portsmouth treaty and Komura Convention, which granted Japan the same rights in southern Manchuria as held by Russia in northern Manchuria, Japan would be forced to do likewise. This alone would do much to restore Chinese control over Manchuria.

the Chinchou-Aigun line. If necessary, he recommended American recognition of Japan's ambitions in Korea in exchange for her withdrawal from north China. By ending Japanese domination in Manchuria, this complex plan would effectively neutralize the area and open it to American commercial interests.

Once again, more cautious policies prevailed in Washington. Knox saw Straight's Manchurian proposals, principally the Chinchou-Aigun railroad contract, as tools that might be employed to force American capital into the entire Manchurian railroad system. The secretary of state radically altered the philosophy of Straight's plan; instead of the Russian-American cooperation Straight advocated, Knox based his proposal on the cooperative principle implicit in the Hukuang negotiations. This principle, which he considered a "concrete statement" of the Open Door, meant that whenever China pledged its credit for railway construction, the powers pledged to the Open Door principles of equal trade opportunity in China and the preservation of China's political integrity possessed such a "direct interest" as to be entitled to equal participation in the loans. Knox proposed the purchase of the existing Manchurian railroads and the financing of the Chinchou-Aigun line by an international consortium. The establishment of such a financial community of interest would preclude the establishment by any one power of a sphere of influence.

The two controlling powers promptly rejected the Knox proposal. Japan's rejection did not concern Straight, for after Jacob Schiff's 1908 exchange with Tokyo bankers, Straight had abandoned hope of acquiring control of the South Manchuria Railway. Rather, he intended to countermand Japanese influence by cooperating with Russia to build a competing Chinchou-Aigun Chinese Eastern Railway system and by forcing Japan to relinquish its claims of administrative control over the railroad zones. He further believed that Russia's failure to endorse the Knox policy did not pose a major obstacle, since Straight still assumed that Russian-American cooperation in the Far East was possible.

In spring, 1910, Washington officials agreed to seek Russian support for Straight's neutralization plan. The State Department sent Straight to St. Petersburg in search of a pact that Washington hoped would secure Russian goodwill for future enterprises in Siberia and Mongolia, as well as support for the Open Door in Manchuria. The negotiations, however, demonstrated the extent to which the two countries' Far Eastern policies diverged. Russia refused to support projects inimical to the Japanese position in northeast China; indeed, while Straight talked in St. Petersburg, Russia was completing an agreement with Japan expressly designed to close the Open Door in Manchuria.

Bitterly disappointed, Straight claimed Washington had bungled this opportunity to secure Russian support for the Open Door.[9] His criticisms had point, but many other obstacles precluded Russian-American cooperation in the Far East. The czar's top political council was divided into two groups holding antagonistic views of Russia's Far Eastern interests. One group, headed by Vladimir Kokovtsov, the finance minister, believed Russia should pursue an active expansionist policy and responded favorably to the Straight-Harriman proposals for Russian-American cooperation. The other group, headed by Alexander Isvolsky, the minister of foreign affairs, believed Russia's primary objectives lay in Europe and urged the czar to consolidate Russia's remaining Far Eastern interests through an accord with Japan. Great Britain, whose support Washington needed, refused to press Russia to challenge Japan. Rather, with an eye on the impending European struggle, Britain encouraged a Russo-Japanese entente. Other difficulties arose. Once Japan learned of the Straight-Harriman plans in 1909 (and before Knox announced his proposal), Tokyo officials prepared to offer Russia an agreement that would effectively block American designs in Manchuria. For these reasons, virtually no possibility existed in 1910 for Russian-American cooperation in the Far East.

The Russo-Japanese entente dealt a serious blow to America's Open Door policy. Fearful that continuation of any plans for the Chinchou-Aigun railway might provoke Russo-Japanese reprisals and yet equally worried that retreat would be a complete admission that the Open Door in northern China was dead, State Department officials seemed immobilized, unable to decide on a course of action. A proposal made earlier by the Tripartite Consortium bankers finally suggested a new approach. They had suggested that the interbank cooperation for the still pending

9. Principally, he charged that the decision to combine the bankers' Chinchou-Aigun proposal with the Chinese Eastern–South Manchuria Railway neutralization scheme made it a diplomatic proposal and thus involved the anti-American foreign minister Alexander Isvolsky, rather than a financial proposal involving the more sympathetic finance minister Vladimir Kokovtsov.

Hukuang Loan be extended to include all Chinese business. The State Department hoped that cooperation among members of the proposed quadruple consortium in the Manchurian bank loan and later in the Chinchou-Aigun contract would create that international community of financial interests the administration had sought unsuccessfully via Knox's proposal.[10]

Straight dutifully negotiated formation of the Quadruple Consortium though he still disagreed with the administration's cooperative policy. He preferred unilateral American establishment of a Manchurian bank and construction of the Chinchou-Aigun railroad. In late 1910, however, as he struggled with the four-power negotiations over the Hukuang and currency reform loans, Straight came to understand that Washington lacked the financial power to complete the loans under consideration unilaterally. Because of the limited market in the United States for foreign securities, American financiers could not successfully compete against European banks for Chinese loans. Straight's belated realization of American financial impotence led him to discard all hope for an independent or semi-independent policy and to become a proponent of a cooperative approach to maintaining the Open Door.

The youthful enthusiasms of 1907–9 had disappeared. Instead, Straight complained that his taut nerves were likely to "snap like a guitar string," and the pressures to which he was subjected brought him close to a nervous breakdown. Two years later, he could still recall the horror and nightmare quality of that period. The deep despair which he experienced arose principally from growing appreciation of the deteriorating framework in which he sought to implement American China policy: the creeping weakness of the Chinese regime; the determination of Russia and Japan

10. Former President Roosevelt disapproved the decision to seek a consortium loan in Manchuria. He advised Knox to recognize Japan's paramount influence in Manchuria where American interests were "really unimportant" and where the United States lacked the power to stop Japanese expansion. This disagreement, which has been widely cited as evidence of policy differences between the two administrations that extended back to 1908, occurred not in 1908 but only in 1910, in the wake of the Russo-Japanese entente.

to secure control of Manchuria; the unwillingness of Great Britain and France to support an Open Door policy against their allies; and the financial, political, and military inability of the United States to pursue the Open Door unilaterally.

The Chinese revolution finally caused Straight to abandon all hope of creating a viable native administration that could guarantee the Open Door for American trade and investment in China. Ironically, the Hukuang contract ignited the revolution in Szechuan. To Straight, the Hukuang Loan symbolized his efforts to impose Westernization and progress upon China and provide rational, efficient development under the Manchus. Supporters of the rights recovery movement, however, opposed the railroad as an example of foreign financial domination and the extension of Manchu control over the provinces. Beginning in May 1911, when the central government issued an edict nationalizing some provincial railways as required by the Hukuang contract, a wave of civil disturbances flared in China. In September, when the Peking government attempted to put down the unrest in Szechuan, the outbreak there increased to a full-scale revolt.

In the early stages of the revolution Straight remained optimistic that, although the Manchu dynasty was crumbling, his friend Yüan Shih-k'ai would emerge at the head of a strong constitutional monarchy. Such a regime, for which Straight sought Western support, appeared to him to offer the best hope for "good government," one capable of maintaining conditions conducive to Western trade and investment. When a weak, decentralized republican government emerged in 1912 instead of the strong constitutional monarchy on which he had pinned his hopes, Straight concluded that continued support for Chinese control over Manchuria and Mongolia, which he had consistently advocated since 1906, amounted to "tilting at windmills." Preferring not to think of himself as a "visionary," Straight advocated negotiating an accord with Russia and Japan that would recognize their dominance in Manchuria and Mongolia in exchange for assistance in maintaining the Open Door in China proper. Such an accord might permit some United States participation in the development of Manchuria and, more importantly, the cooperative policy would keep weak China open to "the trade and investment of all powers."

The compromise he proposed never materialized. Straight's next task was to represent the American bankers at the meeting

called to admit Russia and Japan to the Four-Power Consortium.
Instead of recognizing Russo-Japanese dominance in Manchuria
and Mongolia, as he had proposed earlier, Straight had to carry out
his assignment of creating a six-power consortium based on
absolute equality of participation. The State Department hoped
that such an agreement would preclude any monopolization of
loans affecting particular sections of China; but the words of the
agreement belied reality. Because of its importance to Great
Britain and France in the European struggle for power, Russia
controlled the consortium and prevented it from functioning
while the czar's agents pressed the Chinese for concessions
regarding Mongolia.

The inability of Washington officials to dominate the consortium did not, however, cause them to consider withdrawal of the
American group. During this critical revolutionary period in China,
the threat of Western intervention, imposition of a foreign
financial protectorate, or perhaps the long-feared partitioning of
China loomed large. As in the critical 1899–1900 period, American
policy makers believed the only opportunity for controlling or
modifying the action of the other powers and influencing the
future direction of China depended on the maintenance of a
cooperative policy. Leading Taft administration officials and, with
the sole exception of Kuhn, Loeb, all the key Wall Street financiers
agreed that the preservation of the consortium, their chosen
instrument of international cooperation, was of paramount importance.[11] Despite this consensus, in the opening days of the Wilson
administration the new president renounced Taft's cooperative
policy and the diplomatic support for the group of Wall Street
bankers. Instead, Wilson promised an expanded policy of Dollar
Diplomacy, modified by the New Freedom, which he expected
would enable smaller financiers to operate independently in
China.[12]

11. Griswold, Li Tien-yi, and Roy Watson Curry, *Woodrow Wilson and Far Eastern
Policy 1913–1921* (New York, 1957), all argue that by the end of the Taft
administration, the American bankers wanted to withdraw from the consortium.
12. Wilson's withdrawal is an ideal example of Jerry Isreal's thesis, in *Progressivism
and the Open Door* (Pittsburgh, 1971), that the Open Door strategy debates
between competition and cooperation mirrored the domestic debates of the trust
versus the competitive tradition, with the same forces and pressures shaping both
domestic and foreign policy.

During the Wilson administration, Straight devoted himself primarily to the expansion of American trade and investment in the Far East. Through his connections with Colonel House, the president's closest adviser, Straight tried to secure a position in the State Department. His failure, he believed, was due to his close association with Wall Street. In 1915, after leaving J. P. Morgan, he became vice-president of the American International Corporation in charge of Chinese affairs. The corporation, then being formed under the direction of Frank Vanderlip, president of the National City Bank of New York (one of the members of the American group), was designed to merge a construction company and trading organization with the financial facilities of the National City Bank and the International Banking Corporation. Notably, its corporate structure was identical with the one Straight repeatedly had urged upon the American group of bankers. It provided a broad-based commercial mechanism to coordinate the efforts for acquisition and implementation of development loans. In its initial year of operation, Straight guided the corporation's completion of several contracts in China, principally the Huai River Conservancy Loan and the Siems-Carey Agreement for financing and building fifteen hundred miles of railroad.

Straight undertook these operations in China with the intention of resuming a cooperative approach to the Far East. Convinced that the United States could not successfully compete with the consortium or with Japan, Straight believed President Wilson would eventually be forced to reconsider his opposition to the consortium. In anticipation of a change in policy, Straight sought a position for the American International Corporation in the original American group. He used his friendships with Colonel House, Secretary of State Lansing, and State Department officials William Phillips and Frank Polk to lobby both for renewed American participation in the consortium and negotiation of agreements with Russia and Japan. Such accords would concede Russo-Japanese dominance of Manchuria and Mongolia in exchange for reaffirmation by those powers of the commercial Open Door in those regions and of the "neutralization of the eighteen provinces of China."

In 1916, increasing State Department concern about Japan's opportunistic encroachments on China's sovereignty brought the administration to admit the failure of its unilateral New Freedom policy. In June, the president approved the State Department's proposal, a plan formulated by Straight, for immediately reviving United States participation in the consortium. Although the State Department's efforts to implement this program stalled because of the financial interests' inability to reach an accord, they constituted the first step in the establishment of the Second China Consortium.

Willard Straight viewed himself as an empire builder, fighting to establish and maintain an American presence in Asia. Unlike Clive or Rhodes, his British counterparts, Straight envisioned an economic empire rather than a formal colonial system based on political control of the native population, for the former secured the advantages while avoiding the responsibilities of political control. He played the "Great Game of Empire," not in the manner of a friendly chess game or sporting contest, but as a deadly serious struggle among the world's great powers for the right to dominate China. Like other key American policy makers of this period, Straight honestly believed that access to foreign markets, in particular the China market, was crucial to the future industrial prosperity and to the political and social health of the United States: that is, to America's position as a world power. Because of the great power rivalry in the Far East, access to the vast China market had to be secured without delay. As Straight explained his objectives, he was staking a claim for the future when American trade in China would be developed. "If we don't make our position secure now," he said, "it will be difficult if not impossible to come back." Imbued with Kiplingesque ideology, Straight constantly talked about America's "great responsibility" to complete the tasks "vital to the regeneration of China." Nonetheless he clearly appreciated that the "white man's burden" had an intensely pragmatic object. China, he once said, must be saved so that the altruists (among whom he counted himself) might "reap the profits of her development." That, he argued, was what Western philanthropy really implied.

Based on his understanding of American national interests, which in this period of industrial growth and consolidation he framed largely in economic terms, Straight accepted the goals of American Far Eastern policy. Perhaps as well as any of his contemporaries, he understood that the problem confronting

American leaders was the conflict among the great powers for control of the undeveloped areas of the world. In any weak country in which the United States sought markets for its nationals, two options existed. It must "either acquire territory or insist on an equality of commercial opportunity. It must either stake out its own claim or induce other interested Powers to preserve the 'open door.' " There was no middle course. Securing a sphere of influence, which would have guaranteed access to part of the China market for the United States, was not a viable alternative. American public opinion, not to mention America's diplomatic, military, and economic weakness, would have prevented the establishment of a colonial regime in China.

During the difficult 1905–17 period, Straight was involved in the dilemma of implementing America's Open Door policy and did much to shape the twists and turns of his country's strategy. At the outbreak of the Russo-Japanese War, Straight agreed with the decision of Washington policy makers to support Japan in its efforts to check the Russian advance into Manchuria. After the war, however, Straight perceived Japan as the greater threat to commercial opportunity in Manchuria. From his position as consul general in Mukden, he devised a new Open Door strategy that gained the support of New York financiers and Washington officials. Building on Straight's proposals, Root reversed the pro-Japanese policy followed by the Roosevelt administration at Portsmouth and, initiating a policy later termed Dollar Diplomacy, attempted to use financial power to secure an American position in Manchuria.

Straight also devised the schemes that became the basis for the Taft administration's efforts to create an international financial community of interest in China. Knox's 1909 proposal of neutralization and the overtures to the czar for the abortive 1910 Russian-American entente were based on plans proposed by Straight. He served effectively during the Taft administration as the agent of the American group of financiers, negotiating the formation of the Quadruple Consortium, the Hukuang Loan, and the Currency Reform and Manchurian Development Loan, and was justly credited by the American minister in Peking as responsible for the success of the negotiations.

Despite his role in the formation of the Taft-Knox cooperative policy, Straight preferred to follow a unilateral American policy to support the Chinese against Japanese expansion in Manchuria.

Such had been the rationale of the Manchurian bank and his proposals to gain control of the Manchurian railroad system. Ironically, by the time Wilson adopted a unilateral Far Eastern policy, Straight had become a leading advocate of cooperation. The United States, he had learned, lacked the financial resources to compete with the European banks for Chinese loans. Furthermore, the revolution critically weakened China and destroyed all possibility of successfully supporting Chinese development, either unilaterally or internationally. Because of the great power rivalries in the Far East, unilateral competitive investment spelled almost certain conflict. An international financial community composed of former competitors offered the promise of rational, peaceful international commerce. Equally important was the fact that international investments, made by a consortium on the principle of equality, might challenge the existence of spheres of influence, reinforce the Open Door, and effectively neutralize China. It should be noted that the consortium structure that Straight helped to create formed the basis of United States economic diplomacy in the Far East in the twenties.

Straight's promising career ended in 1918 when, at the age of thirty-eight, as he was preparing to serve as secretary of the American peace commission at Versailles, he died of pneumonia. At the time of his death, Straight was involved in planning the peace and he foresaw the general course of American Far Eastern policy in the postwar period. Maintenance of an American position in the Far East depended upon reaching an accord with Japan, one that would recognize Japanese supremacy yet preserve the Open Door. Membership in an international financial combination, he still insisted, would provide the economically powerful United States with the opportunity to become preeminent in the Orient. If, however, Japan were to challenge that dominance, American policy makers would confront unfortunate alternatives. They would either have to revise their belief that America's future depended upon access to the China market or be prepared to shed blood for the preservation of the Open Door. The ferocity with which Straight played the "Great Game of Empire" strongly suggests what would have been his answer.

BIBLIOGRAPHIC NOTE

Primary source materials for the study of Willard Straight and

American Far Eastern policy are abundant. The Straight papers housed at Cornell University are a particularly complete collection. Papers of many State Department officials, including Root, Knox, Bryan, Lansing, and lesser figures such as Henry Prather Fletcher and Breckinridge Long are in the Division of Manuscripts, Library of Congress. The State Department records are in the National Archives. Paul Reinsch's papers are at the State Historical Society, Madison, Wisconsin; W. W. Rockhill's, in the Manuscript Division, Houghton Library, Harvard University; Huntington Wilson's, at Ursinus College; Frank L. Polk's, at Yale University.

Griswold's 1938 work, cited previously, laid the basis for the traditionalist interpretation of American Far Eastern policy. The works of Esthus, Vevier, Li Tien-yi, and Roy Watson Curry, all cited previously, offer the best traditionalist accounts of the Taft and Wilson Far Eastern policies. Jerry Israel's book is a contribution to the revisionist interpretation of American foreign policy originally argued by William Appleman Williams in several works including *The Tragedy of American Diplomacy* (Cleveland, 1959), and by Walter LaFeber, *The New Empire: An Interpretation of American Expansion, 1865–1898* (Ithaca, 1962), and Thomas McCormick, *China Market: America's Quest for Informal Empire, 1893–1901* (Chicago, 1967). Herbert Croly's sympathetic biography, *Willard Straight* (New York, 1922), offers insight into the young diplomat's career.

TO DO GOOD IN THE WORLD:
WOODROW WILSON

Reproduced from the collections of
the Library of Congress

and America's Mission

Ross Gregory

Seldom in American history has a president of the United States so
influenced foreign policy as Woodrow Wilson in the years before,
during, and after the First World War. It was a time when
impressing personal qualities upon policy, as Wilson did, was a
fateful endeavor. His presidency coincided with the greatest war
in history up to that time, and its more than four-year course in
Europe and throughout the world produced many changes, some
good and some extremely bad: the crumbling and collapse of old
attitudes and institutions, the upheaval of social and economic
activities, and the appearance of new problems that would mark
the subsequent event-ridden decades of the twentieth century.

It has been said that a man never forgets his past. Woodrow
Wilson not only did not forget but glorified the experiences of his

55

youth; if there had been defects in his upbringing he was blind to
them. He always recalled his childhood with fondness, and drew
eagerly upon his parents' teachings. Born in 1856 in Staunton,
Virginia, he grew up in a South conditioned by Civil War and
Reconstruction. Memory of the great internal conflict produced a
dislike of violence so intense as to border on pacifism. Although
he never acquired the sectional hatred that plagued many of his
fellow southerners, he easily accepted other attitudes characteristic of the South. Jeffersonian individualism provided the basis for
his economic thinking; white supremacy so pervaded local—and
national—psyche that he scarcely questioned the principle, and as
president he found nothing improper in placing nonwhite people
beneath the level of other Americans.

Of all the experiences of youth none left a deeper imprint
than the religious environment in the Wilson household. His
father was a Presbyterian minister, his mother, the daughter of
one. The God Wilson came to know was that of John Calvin—and
of the Reverend Dr. Wilson—a loving but demanding sovereign
who drew a clear line between good and evil and expected the
maximum of obedience and service. The Wilsons lived a comfortable, if detached, middle-class existence, enjoying the prestige
and respect afforded a minister's family. That he was a preacher's
son made the community expect more of young Tommy (he was
christened Thomas Woodrow) and his father, a firm disciplinarian,
made certain his children reflected the family's religious beliefs
and the community's expectations. Hearing God's word each day
of the week, the young Wilson moved easily toward the conclusion that he had privileged access to truth and a special obligation
to serve God and mankind. This moral tutelage had lasting effect,
inspiring him in later years not to intellectual rebellion but to
continued obedience to the Presbyterian creed. Many of the
features of personality that characterized him as president—detachment, activism, discipline, fondness for order, self-righteousness—originated in a childhood spent in a Presbyterian parsonage
in the post–Civil War South.

At a time when ambitious young men of education and social
status might have plunged into the industrial expansion of the late
nineteenth century, Wilson found a career befitting a minister's
son more suitable to his tastes. He wanted no long hours working
on a farm or in the factory, no risk of tarnishing his character in the
grimy competition of business. Even so, the choice was not

instantaneous, not without indecision and surely some self-doubt. He spent several years in study, which produced an undergraduate degree from the College of New Jersey, as Princeton then was known. He took some courses in law (enough to pass the bar) at the University of Virginia and earned a Ph.D. from Johns Hopkins in Baltimore. There followed a successful career in teaching and writing. He spent seventeen years as a college professor, eight more years as president of Princeton; he wrote nine books and many articles, mostly on American history. In the course of this long career Wilson showed exceptional ability as a teacher, a penetrating student of American institutions, and, as Princeton's president, an innovative manager of the university's affairs.

The academic experience also fostered personal tendencies that had appeared earlier. Years of professional study strengthened his qualifications for speaking on politics and government and seemingly confirmed an ability to discover and interpret truth. Wilson's responsibilities as professor and president left him master of his domain; he preferred making decisions with no outside interference and exhibited at times a disturbing intolerance toward individuals brave enough to challenge his will. He became involved in two huge power struggles at Princeton, the last of which (an unsuccessful contest for control of the graduate school) left him embittered and anxious to move on to new fields of endeavor. By that time he had become known in New Jersey as a reformist educator and worthy prospect for political leadership in the Progressive Era. After a two-year political apprenticeship as governor of New Jersey he undertook the campaign for the presidency in 1912.

Swept into office on a wave of Progressive reformism, albeit mainly because Theodore Roosevelt had split the Republican party, Wilson appeared a political novice, the eastern schoolmaster who had come to instruct and discipline. He looked the part: trim and fashionable, standing erect with firm jaw, straight mouth, and eyes staring through pince-nez. He wished to be for the people, not of them, and he never appeared with open collar and shirtsleeves performing tasks beneath presidential dignity. He could be charming and graceful; but he could also be stubborn and inexorable, and political cartoons of the day—perhaps the clearest indication of a politician's image—scarcely ever portrayed him with a smile. He brandished none of the cocksure bantering that Franklin Roosevelt was to perform in the presidential chair, none of the clowning the people had enjoyed with Theodore Roosevelt. Wilson was no pessimist, and he certainly did not lack confidence; he simply handled his office with the same determined seriousness with which he approached life.

The new president could not forget that he was the Reverend Dr. Wilson's son. Still the hard-headed Presbyterian, seeker of truth, doer of God's will, he continued to have trouble dealing with people. "His prejudices are many and often unjust," remarked his friend Edward M. House. "He finds great difficulty in conferring with men against whom, for some reason, he has a prejudice and in whom he can find nothing good." Driven by a disconcerting tendency to talk down, he preferred to communicate through his books or from the comfortable distance of the platform. In speeches he communicated extraordinarily well, and his presidential messages were notable for use of the proper adjective or noun, the memorable phrase, the inspiring urge to some high goal. The same qualities produced other less admirable traits, however. His keen mind and superb powers of analysis left an appearance of inteflectual arrogance; he did not take criticism gracefully, and turned small issues into large personal quarrels. Finally, the president's high-mindedness and oratorical talents so influenced his thoughts that he seemed to have trouble separating rhetoric from facts, the ideal from the real.

In his conduct of foreign affairs the president's personal characteristics shone through. He insisted upon taking charge. When large problems arose he not only supervised policy, but also concerned himself with minutiae, often writing dispatches on his portable Hammond typewriter with its wide-spaced letters and blue ribbon. Distrustful of professional diplomats and officials removed from his supervision, he preferred to deal directly with governments, or through unofficial contacts such as Colonel House. He appointed few strong men to advisory positions, and seldom followed their recommendations. Service in Wilson's State Department was no pleasant undertaking. The first secretary of state, William Jennings Bryan, resigned in 1915 in protest of the president's handling of the *Lusitania* crisis, hurt that Wilson had made so little use of his talents. Bryan's successor Robert Lansing fared better; at least he remained in office a remarkable five years, freely gave advice, and appeared as a dignified spokesman of policy. Lansing did not make the policy he articulated, however;

his influence rarely extended beyond opinions on international law, and even in this field he proceeded in gingerly fashion.

The person to whom Wilson turned most for help was his friend House. A quiet little man with a mouselike face ("Colonel Mouse," he sometimes was dubbed), he dabbled in politics and had mastered the art of human manipulation. He gained his greatest success with Wilson—an accomplishment all the more remarkable because the subject was Wilson—and soon became known as the president's "alter ego" and "second self." Wilson conferred regularly with this Texas colonel, confessed problems and frustrations, sent him on special assignments; yet rarely did he allow House to decide large matters. Knowing the president's temperament, House did not try, at least not directly; he catered to Wilson, flattered him, and in this tactful way maintained a remarkable friendship for many years. House surely helped relieve the oppressive loneliness of the presidency, but he did little to lighten the burden of decision making, one that the president showed no inclination to relinquish.

In some ways Wilson contributed timely changes to the conduct of diplomacy. His assertion of executive authority vis-à-vis legislative control was in tune with demands of the twentieth century; o..ly Theodore Roosevelt had done as much. With Wilson in the White House no one doubted who was in charge, and so allocation of praise or blame was a simple matter. He obviously carried the process of presidential domination too far; by limiting diplomacy largely to himself, he narrowed perspective, weakened morale in the State Department and foreign service, and even unknowingly prompted secret efforts at undermining and sometimes lowered consideration of important issues to a level of petty personal rivalry. In all his writings on government Wilson had exalted executive leadership, going so far in one book as to remark that presidential authority in foreign affairs was "virtually the power to control them absolutely." No president would learn better than Wilson the error in that statement.

Other than the emphasis on personal leadership Wilson's academic and political background gave little hint of how he would conduct foreign affairs. Elected on a program almost entirely concerned with domestic problems, he had taken little notice of foreign policy other than to express a vague intention to be honest and just and an even more remote and ill-defined desire to place the United States at the "service of humanity." His scholarly studies had touched upon foreign policy only in passing and he had given recent international developments no more attention than had the average educated American. The haphazard manner with which he approached policy appeared in his appointment of the secretary of state. Bryan had traveled around the world some years before, an experience that should have instructed him in some of the world's ways; but in fact he was more innocent than his chief—which was saying something. Such an attitude had not seemed unusual, given the character of American politics at that time. Had Wilson lived in a settled and peaceful world, he probably would have followed the pattern of most previous presidents: keeping watch on domestic matters and keeping his political house in order.

As it was he came to office during a momentous time in world history. For all the progress in technology—such remarkable new machines as the automobile and airplane had recently been invented—there had been a distressing slowness in development of human institutions. It was a world of kings, colonial empires, exploitation and oppression, class conflict, dreadnoughts and fleet pageantry, and then in 1914, little more than a year after Wilson took office, the rush into a great war. The United States had observed these developments with an air of interested but confused detachment. Half a century of industrial growth had drastically changed the nation, propelling it into first place among economic powers; but Americans still remained puzzled about their place in international affairs. The Spanish-American War and Theodore Roosevelt's zestful diplomacy had thrust the nation into global politics, but many individuals had expressed fear lest the United States come to resemble the greedy, jealous nations of the Old World. The success of Progressive reformism at home seemed all the more reason for America to find a new role in the world appropriate to national strength and yet consistent with American ideals.

Wilson appeared on the world stage when the nation could delay a decision no longer. Lacking a systematic philosophy of foreign relations, he acted in accord with his philosophy of life, and so diplomacy became an application to world problems of the president's thoughts about mankind, the United States, and himself. At the heart of the philosophy were Wilson's belief in man's ability to improve the world and his desire to make the

United States an instrument of global reform. With proper leadership—his leadership, as it developed—nations could find institutions to conquer hunger, oppression, and war and bring to fruition God's plan for an orderly world. Taken together, Wilson's responses, at least his rationale, had such scope and consistency as to comprise a new philosophy of foreign relations.

To many people Wilsonian diplomacy came to represent a typically American approach to foreign policy, for the president's ideas encompassed attitudes and institutions already at work in the United States. First and most important was Wilson's idealized faith in democracy. As with most Americans of his day and class the country's success enthralled him, and he attributed national greatness largely to political institutions that had allowed the United States to grow and prosper while avoiding domestic upheaval and wars of conquest. Wilson attributed most world problems to the existence of colonial masters and autocratic governments led by selfish, powerful men who owed no explanation to the people they governed. Democracy constituted the logical expression of the human will—even God's will—in politics. It replaced conflict with discussion, armies with parliaments; it represented the most promising device for promotion of peace and order. While some areas might require time and enlightened guidance, the president believed democracy to be ultimately within reach of all. "When properly directed," he once said, "there is no people not fitted for self government."

A democratic nation would probably also be capitalistic. While Wilson came to the presidency a spokesman for Progressive economic reform, he was at heart a nineteenth-century liberal who believed that capitalism, despite some minor flaws, constituted the most humane and dynamic economic system. Capitalism represented nothing less than freedom and democracy in economics, a system that allowed all people, not some elite alone, to determine a nation's destiny. What had worked in the United States should function in other nations and in economic relations between states. "Lift your eyes to the horizons of business," he once told some American businessmen. "Let your thoughts and your imagination run abroad throughout the whole world, and with the inspiration of the thought that you are Americans and are meant to carry liberty and justice and the principles of humanity wherever you go, go out and sell goods that will make the world more comfortable and more happy, and convert them to the principles of America." Even though Wilson understood the value to the United States, in terms of markets and places for investment, of international capitalism, national self-interest did not represent his only reason for urging economic expansion, probably not even the most important one. He envisioned a reformist, humanized capitalism, designed to serve entrepreneur, worker, and consumer; ably and justly managed, such a system could serve as the economic arm of democracy.

Above all stood a vision of the United States as a superior nation, admirably suited to lead. Not burdened with militarism, unentangled in Old World *Realpolitik* or the dirty competition for colonies, the United States stood alone as a shining example of national morality. Under Wilson's humane guidance America could offer to undeveloped nations capital for economic growth and tutelage to a high level of social and political development. To the European states, now busily destroying themselves and each other, the United States could provide leadership in a new system of international relations.

For much of Wilson's presidency his ideas reflected more a vague goal than a concrete plan. He had not come to office expecting to change the world in his generation, and at first he attended only to those foreign problems that were brought to him. He did not propose anything resembling a program until 1918, when some new structure had become imperative. There did occur early in his administration one problem, in Mexico, which gave an indication of the future. Convinced that brigands were depriving the Mexican people of liberty and jeopardizing the Western Hemisphere, he intervened, first with diplomatic pressure, later by sending troops, hoping to preserve order and open the door for stable government. Instead he aroused native resentment, enmeshed the United States in bewildering Mexican politics, and nearly brought the two nations to war. Intervention in Mexico and later in other Latin American states demonstrated the shortcomings of Wilson's idealism. It exposed the fallacy of applying a single American solution to vastly different problems, of one nation's leader purporting to know what was best for others. The president's policy revealed his ill-concealed feelings of racial superiority and self-righteous paternalism ("I am going to teach the Latin American Republics to elect good men," he once said) and contradicted his stated purpose of making government the object of popular will. Amid proclamations of goodwill and high moral purpose, Wilson sponsored military intervention on a scale never seen before in that region.

While idealism—some authors have called it missionary idealism—set the rhetorical tone for Wilson's diplomacy, there was a more traditional and practical side. Whatever he hoped to accomplish in world affairs, he frequently acted in accord with restraints imposed by local conditions or the demands of national interest. He was an internationalist, but he felt a sense of nationalism and an obligation to protect his own nation's interests. His Latin American policy, whatever its stated purpose, sustained American supremacy in the Western Hemisphere. In the Far East he expressed sympathy for Chinese independence and in fact attempted halfheartedly to discourage Japanese encroachment; but he did not commit the United States, and when he left office China was at best a semisovereign state. Even though these and other policies were steeped in practicality, he preferred not to defend them in terms of national interest, for he felt that simple pursuit of national goals, which one might equate with selfishness or greed, was in itself not worthy justification for the actions of a great moral nation. In most cases Wilsonian universalism, the propensity to evaluate problems by American standards, provided easy reconciliation between national interests and the interests of the world.

Even though Wilsonian diplomacy was identified as a new diplomacy, not everything the president proposed was unique. Economic expansion long had been an article of faith to presidents, business, and agricultural interest groups. For many decades spokesmen had expounded the uniqueness of America, its superior political and economic institutions, if not its world mission. The nation's largest foreign venture in nearly a century, the Spanish-American War of 1898, had come about partly because of a widely popular missionary urge to free Cuba from Spanish rule. Wilson did not originate idealist diplomacy; he simply carried it further than any previous American leader. With a deep-seated belief in its merits and his incomparable mastery of language, he gave it articulation such as the nation, and the world, never had heard.

Wilsonian diplomacy has little meaning unless it is seen in the context of the First World War. Shortly after he came to office, Wilson's world seemed to be falling apart. The Great War of 1914–18 overwhelmed his presidency, occupying his attention during nearly six of eight years in office, causing sleepless nights and presenting problems larger than any president had faced since Abraham Lincoln. By exposing the decadence of the old political system, endangering the United States and American principles, the war was the primary factor in shaping the president's thoughts about Europe, America, and the world. At the end it provided both reason and opportunity for development of his world plan.

It is sobering to observe how the United States moved from a safe, remote position in 1914 when the war started, a nation disclaiming concern about the war's causes and about how it might end, to some two and a half years later when American leaders felt compelled to send young men to die, like millions of Europeans before them, in the muddy trenches of France and Belgium. With hindsight one may argue that if certain decisions had been different the United States could have stayed at peace. Yet there seemed something almost inevitable about American participation, if the war lasted long enough, for it was impossible that a nation as rich and strong as the United States, with broad world interests and such national pride, could remain unaffected by a conflict of such magnitude. While Wilson acted as national leader and spokesman, made all major decisions, and absorbed responsibility for the fateful consequences, his influence appeared less in the decision to enter the war than in the rationalization of intervention and interpretation of a war the United States now had become obliged to fight. Another president probably would have led the nation to war at some time but probably would have explained the cause a different way.

As did the majority of his countrymen, Wilson expected that the United States would take no part in the conflict. Though he experienced a certain sympathy for the Allies, as did House, Lansing, and nearly all his advisers, he had no intention of supporting either group of belligerents, feeling that his responsibilities consisted of preserving neutrality and protecting American rights while holding himself in readiness should the combatants ask for his help as an impartial negotiator. For many months mediation seemed the best way to provide Christian service and assure that the United States would remain at peace. He made repeated overtures, and twice sent House on "peace missions" to Europe, only to conclude sadly that the belligerents wished to end the war their own way.

Meanwhile problems of commerce had begun to show the precarious nature of neutrality. Americans immediately put to sea to resume normal trade with Europe and take up what new business the war might bring. Wilson supported this activity, assuming it to be a legitimate, safe (not to mention profitable) expression of neutral rights. Whatever moral objections the president might have had to the sale of guns and ammunition—he seems to have had remarkably few—became submerged in the emphasis on legalism, and so contraband became an important part of the war traffic. Because of the prewar pattern of trade and Britain's renowned mastery of the sea it seemed only natural, and not at all objectionable, that the bulk of commerce would go to the Allies. What Wilson and everyone else failed to anticipate was the emergence of the submarine as Germany's primary means of economic warfare. The United States became caught between German and British efforts to strike at each other on the seas. Wilson strenuously protested the activity of both nations, but he threatened only Germany, in some measure because of a growing relationship with the Allies, in larger measure because only Germany used submarines, a means of warfare he thought illegitimate and a costly, savage, irreparable infringement of neutral rights.

In the course of the long struggle over submarine warfare, Wilson experienced some of the most trying times of his presidency. Torn between a desire to keep his nation at peace and the need to protect its rights and honor, he personally agonized over the decision regarding each submarine incident, unwilling to trust the judgment of advisers. While critics attacked his policies—almost equally, it seems, for being either too lenient or too harsh with Germany—the majority of the American people chose to follow his leadership. Unfortunately, Wilson alone could not determine America's fate. The nation had become so entwined in international politics and economics that each major disturbance affected its well-being, and any American decision, even a policy of absolute isolation, affected the course of the war. Wilson scored outstanding victories through his protests against submarine warfare, but each German concession further aligned the United States with the Allies, handicapped Germany's war effort, and made demands in Berlin for an unrestricted U-boat campaign more appealing. Given such circumstances, it is remarkable that intervention came so late. Pursuing a delicate middle course between belligerency and outright pacifism, Wilson preserved both peace and prosperity for some two and a half years. He did not keep the United States out of war altogether, but his policies allowed Americans to escape some of the war's most savage encounters and to avoid intervention until the conflict, measured in months of combat, was two-thirds over.

Wilson's style is evident less in his opposition to submarine warfare than in the way he opposed it. He faced impressive practical reasons—public opinion, economic needs, national prestige—for refusing to accept unrestricted submarine warfare. He had no desire to ignore these factors; but he would not justify policy on the ground of practicality, however justifiable, not when national selfishness had been responsible for the war. He much preferred to rest his argument on moral and legal principle. As he wrote in the second *Lusitania* note, 9 June 1915: "The Government of the United States is contending for something much greater than mere rights of property or privileges of commerce. It is contending for nothing less high and sacred than the rights of humanity." By couching policy in terms of international law and principle, lecturing the Germans and the British on their responsibilities as civilized nations, Wilson impressed European belligerents as a phrase-making evangelist who showed little appreciation of their problems.

These same policies produced practical results, however. They enhanced the theme of international economic liberalism, as manifested in Wilson's principle of freedom of the seas, upheld friendly and prosperous American relations with western Europe, particularly Britain, and helped prevent German domination of the European continent. By defining American interests in terms of international law, Wilson gave this policy the universalist tone that had become familiar in Wilsonian diplomacy.

War came to the United States not because Wilson and the American people pursued it—indeed, to the final moment the president searched desperately for a way to avoid intervention—but because events brought the nation to a point where no other choice seemed reasonable. Wilson reluctantly concluded that the United States would suffer less loss of life, property, commerce, national prestige, and influence by going to war than by remaining the victim of submarine warfare. He had become a prisoner of his policies; but perhaps such imprisonment was inevitable because of the nation's increased involvement in global affairs.

In characteristic fashion the president's war message of 2 April 1917 spoke of larger issues. In this most momentous of his presidential performances Wilson could not resist making a rhetorical appeal to truth and principle. He explained that the German government had provoked American intervention as it had promoted war in Europe, but that Germany represented only a recent example of an enduring evil of history: oppressive, aggressive, undemocratic government. Thus the first object of war should be to crush German military autocracy. Once the Allies had accomplished that task they could move on to larger goals. "We shall fight," said the president, "for the thing which we have always carried nearest our hearts—for democracy, for the right of those who submit to authority to have a voice in their own governments, for the rights and liberties of small nations, for . . . concert of free people as shall bring peace and safety to all nations and make the world itself at last free." An eloquent and stirring speech, the address evoked acclaim from liberals over the world. Therein was part of the president's shortcoming; he had been too eloquent and high-minded. He had interpreted the war in remarkably simplistic terms and established objectives that no peace settlement could accomplish. Perhaps there could have been no other way, given the emotion of the time and the way Wilson handled foreign policy; but the war message of 1917 laid the basis for generations of cynicism about the war "to end all wars" and to make the world "safe for democracy."

War in simplistic terms

Events soon showed that Wilson did not intend his speech as mere talk. He prosecuted the war with the peace in mind, making sure that as American military contributions increased political influence, his influence also increased. He insisted on a voice in all major decisions, kept the American army separate from the Allied armies, and in January 1918 outlined in fourteen points his ideas of a just and lasting settlement. He undertook major reponsibility for arranging the armistice, insisting as a precondition that Germany renounce its military government. In choosing a peace commission he paid virtually no attention to politics or public opinion, preferring to select men (such as House and Lansing) that he knew and trusted. To lead the American delegation to the Paris Peace Conference the president, not surprisingly, chose himself.

When the shooting stopped at last in November 1918, Wilson traveled to Europe and appeared before crowds almost wild with enthusiasm. Large portions of Europe lay in rubble; the monarchies, the symbol and much of the substance of the old order, were destroyed; war no longer seemed an acceptable device for settling disputes. The people were hungry and weary, and they longed for someone to lead them. It surely seemed that the president's moment in history had arrived.

Only with the start of serious diplomacy did Wilson understand the difficulty of his task. In Paris he came face to face with men who shared neither his perspective on the European war nor his thoughts about the perfectibility of human institutions. "I really think," wrote British Prime Minister David Lloyd George, "that at first the idealistic president regarded himself as a missionary whose function it was to rescue the poor European heathen from their age-long worship of false and fiery gods." European leaders looked upon Wilson as possessing not superior wisdom, but the wealth and power of the United States, and it was in terms of wealth and power that they wished to deal. There was Georges Clemenceau of France, seventy-seven years old, with droopy eyes and droopy moustache, practitioner of *Realpolitik*, pessimistic about mankind. He wanted reparations and a weakened, if not destroyed, Germany. Lloyd George, the "Welsh Witch," had come to Paris after promising Britain to make Germany pay heavily. Vittorio Orlando, the least prestigious member of the Big Four, demanded for Italy a full share of money and territory. Other national leaders put forth various financial and territorial claims. It became apparent that what Wilson thought to be an opportunity, Europeans thought to be a problem. They acknowledged the need for political change, but wanted no settlement that might further weaken their nations and above all wished to give first attention to immediate concerns. Their proposals represented no more than a fitting end to a long and costly war, practical efforts toward reconstruction and security.

Wilson's trip to Europe marked a culmination of his efforts to change American and world diplomacy. Convinced that isolationism had become obsolete, he was prepared to accept perpetual American involvement in world affairs. He had come to the peace conference asking no indemnity, no territory or other material benefit. While he planned a peace program with American interests in mind, a system in tune with American political and economic institutions, the president regarded participation in the settlement as largely an act of service, one that he could not perform, he believed, if nations reverted to the old political system. Traditional diplomacy had failed and so genuine security could come only through a new system of cooperative relations. The initial step involved creation of a community of democratic states in accord with the principle of self-determination. Wilson did not expect to see such regimes quickly established in all nations; neither did he anticipate immediate dismantling of the colonial empires, the most obvious obstacle to self-rule, however much he wished it. The peace conference could make a proper beginning by stripping the defeated nations, Germany and Austria-Hungary, of territory to which they had no ethnic claim, and by fostering self-government in new states created from liberated areas in central and eastern Europe.

One of the most perplexing problems of the conference grew out of complex and fluid conditions in Russia, where a group of Bolshevik revolutionaries asserted the right to speak for the Russian nation. Neither Allied military intervention nor conciliatory gestures had ousted the Communists or moved them from a radical ideological line. The rise of bolshevism was a shocking development, an indication of what could happen elsewhere unless the nations meeting in Paris could put the world in order. Wilson hoped that the Russian people, no less than any other, could enjoy peace and self-determination, and yet he could not believe that the Communist regime was a fit participant in a partnership of democratic nations. Lacking understanding of the Russian situation, and with no better alternatives, he decided to withhold diplomatic recognition from the regime of V. I. Lenin and await developments, hoping that the Russians in time would see the light.

The second and most important Wilsonian theme at the conference was the proposal of the League of Nations, a grand parliament of the world. American and European liberals had supported similar schemes for many years, though Wilson had not endorsed the idea until 1916. Once committed, however, he gave the league the prestige of his office and his incomparable powers of persistence and oratory. In the peace conference it became the focus of Wilson's plan for world settlement and a new diplomacy. The league symbolized his belief that wars resulted from nationalism, greed, and power politics, conditions fostered by autocratic

OVERWEIGHTED.

President Wilson. "HERE'S YOUR OLIVE BRANCH. NOW GET BUSY."
Dove of Peace. "OF COURSE I WANT TO PLEASE EVERYBODY; BUT ISN'T THIS A BIT THICK?"

General Research and Humanities Division, The New York Public Library, Astor, Lenox and Tilden Foundations

government. Nations had no forum for rational discussion, no device to stop the machines of war. Wilson proposed a council of nations, equipped and willing to deal openly with territorial disputes, commerce, and armaments, or any issue that threatened peace and justice. If balance of power diplomacy had embodied man's evil nature, the new diplomacy appealed to his inherent goodness, for while the league was to have access to collective action against recalcitrant members, as suggested in the controversial Article Ten, its primary instrument was to be discussion. Wilson doubted that force would often, if ever, be needed.

The weakness in Wilson's efforts at peacemaking rested not in his financial and territorial proposals, for most of them were reasonable, but in his belief that the victorious nations would sacrifice immediate national interest to a larger crusade for peace and justice. Success of the League of Nations depended upon uniformity of purpose, a common definition of right and justice, among members. Negotiations at Paris showed that states were most concerned with advancing national interests, and that what might constitute justice for one country was unjust to another. Not entirely opposed to a league, European leaders were practical men who remained convinced that power would continue to be the determining factor in international relations. Understanding Wilson's obsession with the league, they bargained and maneuvered, finally threatening to withhold support unless he yielded on certain issues. Though the president resisted some of the most severe Allied demands, he gave in on others. Most damaging to his prestige were compromises out of harmony with a liberal peace program. He accepted a financial and territorial settlement for Germany likely to incense its people and make it difficult to bring a liberalized Germany into the world community; he approved territorial concessions, such as Japanese retention of the Shantung Peninsula, that infringed upon the principle of self-determination and constituted outright surrender to traditional power politics. Although Wilsonian idealism did not collapse beneath the weight of national demands, the president's program had begun to sag, a poor omen of things to come.

Wilson did not interpret his efforts at Paris as failure. Despite the bickering and need for compromise he felt he had salvaged a workable treaty. Above all he had obtained approval of the League of Nations, and functioning as anticipated—as Wilson anticipated —the league could correct mistakes in the treaty and preside over a world of peace and orderly change. The president returned to the United States in July 1919 convinced he had laid the groundwork for a new era. "The stage is set, the destiny disclosed," he proclaimed in placing the treaty before the Senate. "It has come about by no plan of our conceiving, but by the hand of God who led us into this way."

The struggle for acceptance of the treaty was of course Wilson's last major battle and a sad ending to what in some ways had been an outstanding presidency. Opposition immediately arose among senators who disliked both the form and substance of Wilson's foreign policy. Using every tactic of parliamentary obstruction, Republican critics subjected the treaty to "pitiless publicity," hoping to expose the slightest discrepancy in the long and complicated document. In the course of the extended debate the American popular attitude changed from enthusiasm for the league to confusion, then skepticism, and finally weariness. Americans developed many differing opinions, some favorable, some unfavorable, about the League of Nations; but at the end most seemed disturbed about the obligations implied in Article Ten and the prospect that America could lose control of its foreign policy. Like their counterparts in Europe, Americans placed their national interests first.

For all its shortcomings, the treaty might have passed had Wilson handled his duties differently. He took personal charge of negotiations throughout, in almost total disregard of the Senate, the Republican party, even public opinion. The compromises in Paris had lessened his prestige, particularly with liberals; long absence from the country, nearly six months, had had a bad effect on American opinion. When it became apparent that he could succeed only through compromise, the president refused and allowed the treaty to be defeated. To be sure, Republican critics behaved little better, for such senators as Henry Cabot Lodge were also personal and partisan; but the president had fostered this attitude by making the treaty personal on his part. Politics and personality so muddled the debate as to discourage a rational assessment, at that time or in later years, of Wilson's program, and it is not yet clear to what extent some senators were opposing the league, and to what extent they were resisting Wilson himself. As it was, the president suffered a bitter defeat. He lived on until 1924, nearly five years after his physical collapse; but his spirit died in 1920 with his league.

Perhaps it is better to say that Wilson's league did not die because it never came to life, and that the Senate did not reject an organization as much as an idea. The league survived for a generation without American membership, but it never functioned as Wilson had hoped. Leadership fell to the war-weary nations of western Europe, particularly Britain and France, which looked upon the league as an agency for enforcing the treaty and preserving the status quo. Their idea of justice, which did not mean abandoning empires, was closely related to what suited their national interests. The most one could have expected from the league was prevention, at least delay, of another large war; but the European powers were so weak and disunited that they failed. The league's most memorable legacy seemed the fact that the Second World War came so soon.

Stronger leadership might have preserved the European settlement longer, but the league had little chance of acting as Wilson's parliament of the world. Nations found it difficult to agree on basic rules because they seldom had common interests; they experienced different stages of development, different ideas of fairness and justice. While the league's purpose was to promote peace, order, and justice, the world possessed problems not likely to be solved in an orderly way. Satisfied nations, such as the United States, stressed order while dissatisfied states stressed change. Colonies wanted independence and nations wanted colonies; France wanted reparation and security from Germany, and Germany wanted restoration of lost territory and relief from an intolerable financial burden; Americans were satisfied with the prospect of a capitalist world, which Soviet leadership believed to be the worst of all possible evils. Small wonder the league did not function as Wilson had planned; small wonder its successor has had only slightly more success. The United Nations has experienced longer life than its predecessor and served as a useful sounding board for national grievances, but such large issues as the postwar government of China, the political structure of Europe, the status of Indochina, and even disarmament have been handled outside its chambers. These problems would not vanish in the presence of appeals to man's rationality and sense of justice. Even so, had Wilson returned to life some fifty or sixty years later and surveyed world history since his death and the problems ahead, he probably would have remained convinced of the need for a vastly different method of handling world affairs.

◇◇◇

Wilson's death and the end of the world war inspired an outpouring of books and articles that has continued with little interruption to the present. Scholars continue to show interest in Wilson's complex personality and all aspects of his presidential career, but his foreign policy intrigues them most of all. An obvious reason is that Wilson was president during a time of national and world crisis. He dealt with foreign problems because conditions forced him to do so; many were so complex that any policy undoubtedly would have invited criticism. The president, moreover, was an activist and innovator; he sought to make his office and country agents of change, to give foreign policy a distinct style, to show the way to a peaceful and better world.

After arguing for years the merits of the League of Nations and Wilson's effect on large-power diplomacy, historians during the tumultuous 1960s turned to new areas of concern. The important themes of that decade were not world order and parliamentary procedure but change and social justice. Wilsonian diplomacy seemed out of step with these movements, in view of the president's opposition to revolution and radicalism and his admiration for American capitalism. According to this new outlook, Wilsonian diplomacy did not fail; rather it had been all too successful. The president had provided a rationale for a dubious American policy in coming years; at worst he had encouraged suppression of social change and the construction of an American economic empire, thus contributing to making the United States the most conservative, perhaps the most greedy, nation in the world.

The argument has some measure of truth even though it rests on the questionable practice of applying contemporary values to conditions of another era. Wilson devoted much of his attention to finding order among the powers, to settling one war and preventing another, and not to the undeveloped—what many people then called "backward"—areas, where revolution came to be considered the only effective method of change, where capitalism could mean exploitation more often than economic betterment for the native population. Lacking a sophisticated understanding of the "third world," he viewed these areas with racial and national prejudices, and with belief in the universal acceptability of American institutions.

Wilson had made no secret of his fondness for capitalism. He encouraged American businessmen to seek markets abroad; his resistance to submarine warfare, whatever its tone, had the effect of protecting wartime commerce. He looked upon capitalism as economic reformism, a means of supplying goods and capital to areas without funds, a vast improvement over previous devices of outright colonial control or the old-type foreign concession, through which investors were nearly sovereign within technically independent states. He expected the system to function with advantage to buyer and seller, investor and citizen of the place of investment, and occasionally attacked concessionaires in China and Mexico who exercised excessive power. Wilson dreamed of a community of liberal democratic states willing to practice a system resembling free trade, and while he knew the United States would prosper in such a system he did not anticipate creation of an American order. The world was to have no overlord other than the League of Nations, which was supposed to handle all large matters of trade as well as politics. The flaw in Wilson's economic thinking came not from a desire to control the world, but from concern with the philosophy of capitalism rather than its application to given circumstances, and from his tendency to think in universal terms.

Some of the same observations applied to Wilson's attitude toward revolution and radicalism. An heir to the Civil War's violence, a product of middle-class upbringing (he might have thought differently had he worked, let us say, in Elbert Gary's steel mills), he had enduring faith in evolutionary democracy. In his mind revolution developed when an armed minority, unable to win popular support, sought to seize control. The object in all cases was to suppress the masses. As he told an audience in 1919: "If you have disorder, if you have disquieted population, you are going to have autocracy, because the strongest is going to seize power, as it has seized it in Russia. I want to declare that I am an enemy of the rulership of any minority, however constituted. Minorities often have been right and majorities wrong, but minorities cease to be right when they use the wrong means to make their opinions prevail. We must have peaceful means; we must have discussion." As recent scholars have stressed, Wilson opposed revolutionary socialism, but he also hoped to see the world free of militarism, monarchy, and dictatorship. Most revolutions of his day had been rightist efforts to seize power; until the

Bolshevik Revolution of 1917–18 he faced no major upheaval from the Left. From what he understood that revolution seemed no different, except perhaps in being more oppressive, from dictatorships in Latin America. Wilson's shortcoming was not a desire to prevent change, but a failure to appreciate ways by which change might take place.

Whatever the president's purposes, he left a powerful legacy that future generations might apply in different ways, some admirable, some of dubious wisdom. It is doubtful that Wilson would have approved all the policies the United States was to follow in later years, but his successors, in fighting the Second World War as in establishing global policies during the cold war, could believe they were following the true spirit of Wilsonianism.

No student can read the major expressions of Wilsonian diplomacy—the speeches and proclamations, the private messages to leaders abroad or individuals in the United States—without concluding that here was a well-meaning man promoting the cause of human dignity. He rejoiced at signs of success, brooded over indication of failure. One of his most difficult decisions at the peace conference permitted Japanese concessions in Shantung, an unwanted settlement that fostered imperialism in the Far East. Speaking to a friend a short time afterward, Wilson expressed his feelings: "He said that he had been unable to sleep the night before for thinking of it . . . [but that] the settlement was the best that could be had out of a dirty past. . . . The only hope was to keep the world together, get the League of Nations with Japan in it and then try to secure justice for the Chinese not only as regarding Japan but England, France, Russia, all of whom had concessions in China. . . . He knew his decision would be unpopular in America, . . . that he would be accused of violating his own principles, but nevertheless, he must work for world order and organization, against anarchy and a return to the old militarism." As a result of his efforts to reform world politics, Wilson became the symbol of American diplomatic idealism.

Unfortunately he also helped identify shortcomings of that approach. Good intention and moral purpose are admirable and often necessary in one nation's dealings with another, but alone they are not enough. Good intention lends itself to misinterpretation, can impede more practical if less high-minded efforts, and perhaps can lead to an inflexible self-righteousness. Supported with abundant treasure and an activist temperament, idealism can lead nations to take sides in factional disputes, even to impose one nation's standards on another. Wilson intervened in Latin America to relieve the masses of oppression, and in so doing sponsored oppression of a different sort. Perhaps governments cannot, nor should they always, refrain from moral judgments about their neighbors, but they should act only after careful consideration of what is the nation's business. The lesson applies acutely to large nations, such as the United States, with strength to impose their will. They otherwise stand the risk of justifying on grounds of moral correctness what in fact was only a matter of power.

It is not fair, however, to think of Wilson only in negative terms—the problems he did not solve, his lack of thoroughness in thought. Almost lost amid controversy over his ambitious plan has been the fact that he performed capably in the primary presidential function of protecting the security of the United States. His diplomacy preserved relations with western Europe and helped prevent European encroachment on the Western Hemisphere. He guided the nation through its greatest foreign war at that time, and without that effort Americans might have had to face a Europe dominated by the German army. When he left office the United States was more powerful than when he entered it in 1913. His league failed and its successor fell short of being a true parliament of nations, but the world refused to reject the idea of supranational authority. If it is true that power continues to be central in relations between states, it is no less true that those dealings often have been unsatisfactory to everyone concerned. Should the world advance beyond the nation-state to some higher political order—to, let us say, a federation of nations—the president at the time probably will lay a wreath at the grave of Woodrow Wilson.

BIBLIOGRAPHIC NOTE

Individuals who wish to study the Wilson period will find no shortage of published and unpublished materials. The files of the State Department at the National Archives in Washington are massive, as are Wilson's papers in the Library of Congress. Other valuable manuscript collections include the papers of Edward M. House in the Yale Library, the papers of William Jennings Bryan and Robert Lansing at the Library of Congress, and the papers of Walter Hines Page (the ambassador to Great Britain) at Harvard. One also can find much information about American policy in the records of the British Foreign Office and in private collections of such British officials as Sir Edward Grey, Lord Robert Cecil, Sir Cecil Spring Rice, and Arthur Balfour, all in the Public Record Office in London.

The student fortunately has easy access to many of the important papers through the State Department's excellent published series, *Papers Relating to the Foreign Relations of the United States*. The regular series, one volume per year, deals with normal diplomatic relations; the nine-volume *Supplements* cover the diplomacy of neutrality and war; and the thirteen volume *Paris Peace Conference* deals with peacemaking. A special two-volume supplement, *The Lansing Papers*, includes many private messages passed between members of the American government.

Of the many biographies of Woodrow Wilson the best brief studies are John Morton Blum, *Woodrow Wilson and the Politics of Morality* (Boston, 1956), and John A. Garraty, *Woodrow Wilson* (New York, 1956). Easily the most comprehensive coverage is Arthur S. Link's *Wilson*, 5 vols., (Princeton, 1947–65), a study that has several volumes yet to come having reached only to 1917. Marked by extensive research and scholarly objectivity, Link's work tends to give a balanced yet generally favorable treatment of its subject. Books focusing on Wilsonian diplomacy include Harley Notter's old but still useful *The Origins of the Foreign Policy of Woodrow Wilson* (Baltimore, 1937), Link's series of interpretive essays, *Wilson the Diplomatist: A Look at His Major Foreign Policies* (Baltimore, 1937), and N. Gordon Levin, Jr., *Woodrow Wilson and World Politics* (New York, 1968). Levin's volume is a penetrating and provocative analysis of Wilson's search for a liberal world order. It is questionable, however, whether Wilson would have agreed with the author's conclusion that America's global policies after 1945 constituted a "complete triumph" for "Wilsonian values." The multivolume publication of Wilson's papers, edited by Arthur S. Link, has not yet reached the presidential years.

For Wilson's secretaries of state the best studies are Daniel M. Smith, *Robert Lansing and American Neutrality, 1914–1917* (Berkeley, 1958), and Paolo E. Coletta, *William Jennings Bryan: Progressive Politician and Moral Statesman, 1909–1915* (Lincoln, Nebr., 1969). There is no good biography of Colonel House, but one can follow Wilson's relations with his friend in Alexander I. George and Juliette George, *Woodrow Wilson and Colonel House: A Personality Study* (New York, 1956), and in the important collection edited by Charles Seymour, *The Intimate Papers of Colonel House*, 4 vols. (Boston, 1926–28). A study by Ross Gregory, *Walter Hines Page: Ambassador to the Court of St. James's* (Lexington, Ky., 1970), discusses efforts by Page and Lansing to undermine the president's neutrality policies.

The period of neutrality has attracted a great amount of attention, much of it focusing on whether Wilson's neutrality policies were practical or idealistic. The realist point of view, which questions less the necessity for American intervention than the hopelessly moralistic tone of policy, comes out in George F. Kennan, *American Diplomacy, 1900–1950* (Chicago, 1950), Hans Morgenthau, *In Defense of the National Interest* (New York, 1951), and Robert E. Osgood, *Ideals and Self-Interest in American Foreign Relations* (Chicago, 1953). Recent volumes that have found considerable realism in Wilsonian diplomacy include Ernest R. May, *The World War and American Isolation, 1914–1917* (Cambridge, Mass., 1959), a book that first made extensive use of German documentary materials; and portions of the three most recent volumes of Link's huge biography. Examples of older "revisionist" criticism, a viewpoint that challenges both the tone and purpose of neutrality policy, are Walter Millis, *Road to War, 1914–1917* (Boston, 1935), and Charles C. Tansill, *America Goes to War* (Boston, 1938). Two recent brief accounts that find Wilson moved by multiple factors, some practical, some idealistic, are Daniel M. Smith, *The Great Departure: The United States and World War I, 1914–1920* (New York, 1965), and Ross Gregory, *The Origins of American Intervention in the First World War* (New York, 1971).

Students unfortunately do not yet have a good, up-to-date, single-volume account of Wilson's handling of the Treaty of Versailles and League of Nations. Scholars thus have had to rely on older books, specialized works, or the brief coverage in general studies of Wilson. Still useful are the old books by Thomas A. Bailey, *Woodrow Wilson and the Lost Peace* (New York, 1944), and *Woodrow Wilson and the Great Betrayal* (New York, 1945). Lawrence E. Gelfand in *The Inquiry: American Preparations for Peace, 1917–1919* (New Haven, 1963) has investigated Wilson's extensive preparation for peacemaking. Much recent attention has been devoted to the attitude of the United States toward events in Russia at the end of the war. The volume by Levin and Arno J. Mayer's *Politics and Diplomacy of Peacemaking* (New York, 1967) focus on the conflict between Wilson's liberalism and Lenin's revolutionary socialism at the peace conference and in the world. William Appleman Williams in *American-Russian Relations, 1781–1947* (New York, 1952) has argued that American policies in Russia were concerned most with overthrowing bolshevism, and George F. Kennan, in *Soviet-American Relations, 1917–1920*, 2 vols. (Princeton, 1956–58), has found other factors more important. For the treaty in the United States one should consult Bailey's volume, such specialized studies as Ralph Stone, *The Irreconcilables: The Fight against the League of Nations* (Lexington, Ky., 1970), and general works on Wilson. The last volumes of Link's biography are much needed and awaited.

Courtesy, Carnegie Endowment
for International Peace

PEACE WAS HIS PROFESSION:

JAMES T. SHOTWELL

and American Internationalism

Charles DeBenedetti

The death of James Shotwell in his spacious Manhattan apartment in 1965 at the age of ninety-one set off a flow of tributes that he had seldom known in life. *Time* marked the passing of a "tireless advocate of international political co-operation," while the *New York Times* eulogized "a statesman without portfolio." Certainly Shotwell's career justified both judgments. Though a historian and foundation official by occupation, he was by temperament an indefatigable private diplomat. For some forty years he worked tirelessly to organize peace. Oscillating between government service and private action, Shotwell sought to rationalize international politics by involving the United States and other nations in cooperative ventures for world order. His campaign began in 1917, when Woodrow Wilson initiated America's massive involvement in European politics, and it crested in 1945 when America and its allies established the United Nations. In between, the Canadian-born historian undertook numerous individual actions that in their

entirety embodied a robust definition of the place of internationalism in American diplomacy. Long before the Strategic Air
Command pledged to stand ready to atomize the world for peace,
he and his fellow internationalists struggled to overcome the
irrational impulses within international politics through the creation of an orderly structure that promised peace with change.
Peace was their profession—a profession in faith, and a profession
in common action.

Shotwell's vision of world politics gained its focus from the
American internationalist tradition that evolved in the first two
decades of the twentieth century. Conjuring the dream of a world
order founded on cooperation and comity, assorted aspects of the
internationalist approach to world politics long had appealed to
members of the American policy-making elite. Legalists such as
former Secretary of State Elihu Root favored the extension of
international law in patterns cut by the American judicial experience. Arbitrationists such as William Howard Taft supported
treaties of binding conciliation, while the militant nationalist
followers of Senator Henry Cabot Lodge sought to build a league
to enforce peace. World War I exerted a transforming effect upon
internationalism in America. The shocking sweep of violence,
combined in 1917 with the reality of revolution and President
Wilson's feverish promises of a New Diplomacy, produced a new
internationalist faith evolving from two beliefs: that war was a
social evil vulnerable to planned elimination and that the most
disastrous kind of war—total war—invariably resulted from mal-
function of the unreformed European state system. More Europe-
anist than internationalist, Wilsonian internationalists after 1917
did not seek global activism for the United States so much as
American supervision of Europe's mismanaged politics through
the League of Nations system. Dreading the next war and
confident of the pacifying power of America's influence, progressive internationalists resolved to persuade the American people to
support the great work as independent supervisor of relations
among the European powers. Peace for the world would come
through the pacification of Europe, and that grand aim was
possible—if the great powers accepted the systematization of
their relations under America's independent direction as expressed through the league. Peace need not be enforced; it had
only to be managed.

As the leading exponent of Wilsonian internationalism in

interwar America, James Shotwell led the campaign for a managed peace. During this period he operated in numerous capacities. Trained as a medievalist, he began teaching at Columbia University in 1900. Twenty years later, still a Columbia faculty member, he assumed an official position with the Carnegie Endowment for International Peace. In addition, he acted from time to time as an adviser to governments, an organizer of international committees, a public speaker, a publicist, a poet, and the driving force behind several pressure groups and organizations. Shotwell also served as an observer and occasional participant in the crucial events of his time.

A man of incurable optimism and simple decency, Shotwell worked unceasingly after 1917 to effect the ideology of liberal internationalism that Woodrow Wilson had so rousingly proclaimed but had never defined. More than anyone of his time, Shotwell gave substance to the vision of orderliness, rationality, measured change, expert planning, and free trade through multilateral action that undergirded Wilson's hopes and still remains at the center of the ideal world of American liberalism. Shaken by the revolutionary effects of World War I, Shotwell set out to revive the components of the Wilsonian coalition that had disintegrated during the fight over the League of Nations. He welded internationalist ideology and its followers into a force that exerted strong appeal for those who conducted American foreign relations in the years between 1920 and 1945. Liberal internationalism survived not because of lingering regard for Wilson, but largely because of Shotwell's work.

Shotwell's internationalist vision emerged from concern with what he identified as the most stubborn conflict of his time: the clash of scientific and industrial dynamism against entrenched social habits. Portraying himself as a concerned social scientist, he insisted that the power of scientific discovery constituted "the greatest revolution in all human history from the Ice Age down." He felt, however, that its ramifications were lost among peoples encased in prescientific habits. Although awed by the force of the scientific and industrial revolutions, Shotwell never forgot the frustration of flying from London to Paris in two hours in 1919 and then having to wait for five hours while government officials cleared him through customs. The experience impressed him as a classic example of the enormous cost that resulted from the failure to adapt social practices to scientific advances.

Preoccupation with the conflict between scientific dynamism and social-political *immobilisme* began early in Shotwell's tenure at Columbia. There he taught innovative courses in the history of the industrial revolution and formed close friendships with Charles A. Beard and James Harvey Robinson, two colleagues who shared his interest in the relationships among science, industrialism, and democracy. Before the war, Shotwell gravitated with them toward a group of "scientific progressives," New Yorkers who were united in the belief that the scientific mode of inquiry and planning offered the best hope for liberal democracy in an industrial America. Inspired by the philosopher John Dewey and the journalist Walter Lippmann, Shotwell and his friends held that cadres of experts, spreading the gospel of efficiency through instruments of technology, could guide American democracy through the stresses of spreading industrialization. Their message was gaining a respectable audience when the First World War suddenly intensified the complexity of their task and presented a challenging new forum for their plans. As a result, the dream of constructing a mass democratic order in industrial America expanded to embrace the world.

The formal basis of Shotwell's world view appeared between 1917 and 1920, when he enlisted his faith in the scientific approach to social issues in Wilson's crusade for reform of the international system. His guiding values were unspoken but explicit. Presupposing the existence of a universal moral order, he believed that peace, free trade, individual liberty, and free inquiry were hopes natural to all men. He further assumed that these hopes would flourish best through the global influence of the Anglo-American peoples. Certain that the advent of scientific warfare had finally ended America's isolation from the Old World, Shotwell demanded that the U.S. cooperate with England in pacifying Europe. This was to be accomplished through institutionalized reason, not force; through organized intelligence, not arms. He feared excessive American intervention abroad, and he opposed the idea of peace through deterrence, which meant threats of physical retaliation against aggressively ambitious states. While recognizing that lasting peace rested on material foundations, he pressed for a peace of conciliation that would thrive as people cooperatively sought more rational control over "those questions of economic and social justice which are the fundamental issues behind war."

Organized peace might begin in deterrence, but it could survive only through conciliation.

Beyond these basic assumptions, Shotwell's world view developed in response to practical experiences. In 1917 he proclaimed himself "an academic war casualty" and joined the National Board for Historical Services, a group of historians recruited to justify America's war policies by past precedent. He quit after four months to help Colonel Edward M. House and Walter Lippmann assemble the nation's top social scientists in the Inquiry, an organization intended to arm the president with an objective assessment of world conditions. Shotwell and other Inquiry leaders later assisted American negotiators at the Paris Peace Conference in the formation of the International Labor Organization. Fearful of mounting revolutionary sentiment throughout Europe, the Columbia historian identified the ILO as the liberal capitalist alternative to advancing socialism. Indeed, he characterized the infant organization as the prototype of a new line of functional institutions that would reconcile classes in industrial society and thereby maintain the social basis of international law and order.

The second phase in the development of Shotwell's world view occurred in the 1920s, as he gained fuller comprehension of the interdependence of industrial nations. For the Carnegie Endowment in 1920 he initiated the vast *Economic and Social History of the World War*, an attempt to determine the precise impact of modern war upon advanced societies. With an international staff of cooperating analysts, Shotwell directed the Carnegie project in gathering evidence that pointed toward the inescapable conclusion that war was no longer a viable instrument of national policy. The wizardry of science had transformed war into an enterprise whose incalculable destructiveness ended its historic usefulness as a means of national power. In an interdependent world of science and industry, unilateral violence jeopardized the well-being of every member state. It was imperative, Shotwell told an audience of German military and civilian leaders in 1927, for statesmen to realize "that *Machtpolitik* is no longer *Realpolitik*." The careless romanticism of power politics had to give way to the higher realism of cooperative action.

Shotwell also became convinced in the 1920s that social scientists were formulating a real methodology of international peace. He often compared the expanding science of peace studies with the state of economics in the 1770s, when Scotland's brilliant Adam Smith "transferred the science of Political Economy from the field of vague philosophy to that of an inductive science." In the same way, Shotwell argued, experts were beginning to demonstrate empirically that each nation shared vitally in the health and wealth of the entire international community. Shotwell's recurring references to Adam Smith likewise served as a striking reminder of his tendency to equate the development of "peace science" with the beneficent expansion of American business enterprise. Convinced that Washington officials opposed tributary colonialism, he believed that the American organization of peace depended in large measure upon the ability of other states to consume U.S. products, a problem that carried back "to the original problem of Adam Smith: how can the prosperity of our nation be increased through the increased prosperity of others?" Like Smith, Shotwell believed that the answer to that question lay in greater industrial productivity and free trade. The same forces that were sweeping advanced peoples toward fuller interdependence and shared material prosperity would someday "substitute for the passing armistice of nations an enduring peace."

Shotwell's interest in an operating science of peace subsided in the 1930s as Germany and Japan moved toward aggressive expansion. At first he responded ambiguously, urging America to cooperate with the league but at the same time advising Geneva to act with restraint in meeting threats to peace. Attributing expansionist impulses to economic factors, he called for international agreements on more equitable access for all industrial powers to overseas markets and sources of raw materials. A strong defender of the Open Door, he praised the preferences of Cordell Hull's State Department for free trade and worked closely with Thomas J. Watson, president of the International Business Machines Corporation and treasurer of the Carnegie Endowment, to promote "world peace through world trade." At the same time, Shotwell played a central role in fusing America's polyglot peace movement into a coherent political force. Joining pacifists Kirby Page and Ray Newton in 1935, he organized the Emergency Peace Campaign for the peaceful revision of the international status quo and reform of the world economic system. Increasingly, however, his revulsion against Nazi excesses and Japanese aggressiveness drove him to demand that America align with the Allied cause. By 1939 his attitude of scientific detachment in international politics had given way to a fear that the planet was split between authoritarian aggressors and peaceable Anglo-American democracies. A London-Washington axis became the new core of his liberal internationalism; peace depended on continued preeminence of that axis.

The final phase in the development of Shotwell's world view took place after the outbreak of the Second World War. He and his close friend Clark Eichelberger founded the Commission to Study the Organization of Peace, basically another attempt to mobilize experts in search of a rationalized peace. In addition, he helped the State Department in wartime to plan a postwar international organization. Shotwell functioned in these matters according to his old faith in the beneficence of rationalism, functionalism, organized expertise, expanding free trade, and guarantees of social justice; however, he strikingly emphasized the deterrent power of a peace-keeping agency in moments of urgent crisis. In the early 1940s, for the first time, Shotwell called for an American military commitment to a collective security system and for creation of a genuine international police force. The decade of world crisis left a remarkable imprint upon his approach to world order. The prevention of war had become as important as the preservation of peace.

Shotwell's acceptance of the need for American participation in the enforcement of peace was symptomatic of the larger shift among liberal internationalists late in the 1930s to interventionism. Wilsonians had long tried to straddle the contrary claims of cosmopolitan internationalism and nationalistic interventionism. Most recognized that slight—but profound—differences separated the two approaches to foreign affairs. Where internationalists viewed peace in a social and economic perspective, interventionists defined it as a military enterprise. Where internationalists urged American action through collective agencies, interventionists supported unfettered freedom of action for the U.S. Where internationalists saw the American interest in world order as conditional and specific to certain European developments, interventionists perceived the nation's interest as universal and immutable.

Friction between the two approaches flashed periodically. In 1918 Shotwell and his compatriots had organized the League of

Free Nations Association (parent of the present-day Foreign Policy Association) as a liberal alternative to the interventionist League to Enforce Peace and as the true defender of Wilson's ideals. Nine years later during the Nicaraguan crisis and again in 1931 over the Manchurian question, liberal internationalist forces behind Shotwell (who urged moderation in Washington) further clashed with interventionists such as Henry Stimson who were demanding forceful action by the United States. The violent and rapid crises of the 1930s, however, rallied Wilsonians behind demands for American intervention against the Axis. Confronted with Hitler's ambition, internationalists subordinated their pleas for American support of a collective order to the more immediate necessity of American intervention in the European war. Ironically, their short-term success was a long-term disaster. By pressing for intervention in the European struggle, internationalists converted the Wilsonian vision of America's world role into a new set of images. They began to urge the American people to become the guard and not merely the supervisor, enforcer and not merely manager, of a reconstituted global system. With that shift in emphasis there arose a self-justifying rationale for expansion that carried American physical power across western Europe and throughout former European colonial dominions at an economic and moral cost that may never be fully calculated.

Although his outlook and assumptions were fundamental to his work as a private diplomat, Shotwell's technique was equally important. As a professional peace seeker with solid intellectual credentials, he nonetheless confronted that perennial problem of the man of ideas in the world of politics. He had intellectual independence but no political base, influence but no power; he had attracted the attention of court patrons, but not the ear of the king. Lacking the support of a political party or powerful faction, Shotwell worked indirectly by building extrapolitical pressure groups and by filtering ideas into the policy-making process. This strategy enabled him to pursue three distinct but interrelated tactical approaches. He first organized and directed groups of experts in collecting data and proposing feasible alternatives to the use of force for consideration by policy makers. Secondly, he attempted to affect national policy through contacts with informal pressure groups and influential political figures. Finally, he assisted the internationalist wing of American business through groups such as the Council on Foreign Relations and the International Chamber of Commerce in forming economic ties across national boundaries.

A quietly persuasive man, Shotwell liked to lead informal committees in conducting research, gathering data, writing memos, formulating draft treaties, and issuing reports. Once his position was established, he tried to advance it through an informal network of contacts in Washington, New York, and foreign capitals. In a parallel way he recognized the importance of public support and worked assiduously through writings, speeches, and publicity mechanisms of the organized peace movement to energize popular sentiment behind the many causes he supported. Although Shotwell preferred to shape policy through private means, he remained always mindful of the imperative of sympathetic public opinion.

Shotwell, along with several groups of experts, gave continuing attention to the effort to form an international body of peace managers. As noted previously, his first ventures in this direction took place in 1917, when he collaborated with other scholars in the Inquiry, and two years later, when he helped establish the International Labor Organization as a voluntary international agency where technicians and specialists would propose standards for proper governmental behavior.

While setting up the ILO, Shotwell formed close and valuable friendships with international experts in other countries. He expanded this circle of connections between 1920 and 1937, while he was general editor of the *Economic and Social History of the World War*. Indeed, he had accepted that post with the intent of using it to erect a network of foreign policy experts who favored the League of Nations and more extensive international cooperation. He crisscrossed the Atlantic several times in the twenties to organize scholars and government officials for the Carnegie study and to build an embryonic community of peace scientists. His efforts brought him especially close to figures such as the French economist Jean Monnet, the German economist Albrecht Mendelssohn-Bartholdy, the Austrian historian Joseph Redlich, and the English journalist David Mitrany. Not one of these men exercised direct, decisive influence on policy within his nation, but all occupied influential positions within the governing circles of their respective countries. Further, all were men of rank and distinction within the larger European liberal community from which Shotwell hoped to draw the proponents and shapers of a world order.

Shotwell became director of the Division of Economics and History of the Carnegie endowment in 1924, a position that gave him great mobility and even larger influence. Three years later, he became chairman of the Committee on International Relations of the Social Science Research Council and director of research for the American branch of the nascent Institute of Pacific Relations. He participated in meetings of the institute in Honolulu in 1927 and in Kyoto in 1929, where he maintained that the calm discussion of critical Pacific issues offered new hope that past prejudices among peoples were giving way to a collective "strategy of peace." Though unfolding events mocked that hope, Shotwell refused to abandon his plans to organize the world's peace experts. In 1932 he accepted the chairmanship of the American branch of the Committee for Intellectual Co-operation. Quartered at the League of Nations, the CIC sought to unite scholars and intellectuals in the work of understanding the cultural and ethnic diversity that international organizations must respect. It was a unique, if increasingly isolated, center for rational dialogue in a world that was visibly sinking into a morass of renewed tribal hatreds.

Appalled by nationalistic excesses, Shotwell pursued various political activities in the 1930s that prevented him from engaging in any further organization of peace experts until November 1939, when he and Clark Eichelberger established the Commission to Study the Organization of Peace. Its membership ranged from former league officials such as Huntington Gilchrist and Arthur Sweetser to the financier Thomas Lamont and the historian Henry Steele Commager. Its members all believed that a lasting peace required a new international organization. To be effective and endure, this international agency had to be rational in structure, efficient in operation, resistant to forced change, and responsive to the universal human desire for social justice.

When it came to influencing issues of immediate national policy, Shotwell was not averse to involving himself directly in politics. The Inquiry had exposed him initially to the business of shaping policy at the highest level, and he never forgot its seductive pleasures. In 1924 he reorganized his former Inquiry associates into the American Committee of Disarmament and

Security, an informal effort to help the league powers deal with Europe's two most intractable problems. The committee drafted a formal Treaty of Disarmament and Security for the league's consideration, hoping "to supplant emotion by intelligence where intelligence is most needed." Some of the group's proposals were attached to the abortive Geneva Protocol of 1924, but Europe generally ignored this unofficial exercise in applied intelligence. Undaunted, Shotwell took advantage of the situation to create four cooperating committees of experts overseas. More importantly, the committee experience led him to conclude that U.S. neutrality constituted the largest obstruction to European disarmament. With neither Britain nor France willing to move without at least tacit U.S. support, America's hands-off attitude checked any hope of meeting Europe's overriding need for disarmament through the league system. A neutral and indifferent America, Shotwell concluded, posed the main barrier to organizing European peace and a saner world order.

For the next eight years, Shotwell struggled to revise neutrality and align American power with the league system. The most memorable incident in his campaign for neutrality revision came in March 1927 when he persuaded French Foreign Minister Aristide Briand to call for a Franco-American treaty to "outlaw war." For Briand, a joint renunciation of war with the U.S. promised to bolster French security by discouraging France's enemies. For Shotwell, the French bid provided an opening wedge in the close alignment of American neutrality with France and the league. Neither anticipated the imaginative resilience of hostile Republicans. Instead of rejecting Briand's olive branch openly, a decision sure to be unpopular, the secretary of state, Frank B. Kellogg, shrewdly channeled the French offer into the innocuous Kellogg-Briand Pact of 1928, a peace pact that joined sixty-two nations in a dual pledge to renounce war as an instrument of national policy and to use only pacific means to settle disputes. At Secretary of State Kellogg's insistence, however, it contained no distinction between covenant keeper and covenant breaker and thus no framework for the alignment of America with the league. Still, Shotwell continued the fight. He claimed that America's renunciation of war in the Kellogg pact bound Washington not to abet aggression through neutrality. He worked closely with Republican Senator Arthur Capper of Kansas and the League of Nations Association to convert the peace pact into a usable link between America and the league. That connection would come, he believed, as soon as Washington vowed never to permit its neutral trading position to assist a state that had broken the Kellogg pact by unilateral use of force as an instrument of national policy.

Shotwell's attempts to unite the U.S. and the league through the Kellogg pact persisted until 1933, when the continuing crisis in Manchuria and Hitler's rise to power gave greater immediacy to the management of conflict. While urging American cooperation with the League of Nations, he criticized Geneva for its censorious attitude toward Japan's actions in Asia. "The implication of force to police the world toward agreement will not succeed," he declared. "We must try to find that measure of agreement which substantially coincides with the belief of both parties. That is the basis of permanent peace." He helped organize two successive peace coalitions to generate American support for international economic reform and the collective preservation of order. He attacked the powers for abandoning the league as an organized means of peaceable action, and he urged league leaders to reorganize the Geneva system in a realistic way that reflected the varying interests of the powers in the maintenance of global stability. In order to survive, the league had to recognize that each state held a specific place on the "rim" of concentric circles that encompassed the "abyss" of a new European war.

Throughout the thirties, Shotwell's political activities were conducted at a discreet distance from official Washington. Though known to Secretary of State Cordell Hull and familiar with presidential advisers Norman Davis and Sumner Welles, he did not possess direct access to the corridors of power when President Roosevelt maneuvered warily in the face of powerful isolationist forces. Shotwell's reputation as an outspoken proponent of fuller American responsibility for world order excluded him from a visible place of influence in New Deal Washington. Yet, he did not permit Roosevelt's anxieties to interfere with his private efforts. In 1935 he inspired an unsuccessful attempt by Senator James Pope of Idaho to align America with the league on the condition that Geneva accept the Paris peace pact as the touchstone of its policies. In the same year, he assumed the presidency of the League of Nations Association and for the next four years led the fight to revise American neutrality. In the spring of 1940 he joined the Policy Committee of The Committee to Defena America by Aiding the Allies. Formed by Clark Eichelberger behind the

AN UNFORTUNATE OMISSION AT THE INTERNATIONAL REGATTA.

Morning Post (London), 1933

nominal leadership of the journalist William Allen White, the committee worked to build public pressure on behalf of U.S. assistance to beleaguered Britain. For Shotwell, the decade that began with a crusade to preserve peace in Europe through American cooperation with the league ended in a battle to propel the United States into a European war.

After Pearl Harbor, Shotwell's respectability rose appreciably in Washington. He was named to the State Department's Advisory Planning Committee which was responsible for planning the postwar organization of international peace keeping, and he contributed substantially to the work of the committee. Then, Shotwell worked toward mobilizing public sentiment behind administration plans for a new international organization. He attended the founding of the United Nations at San Francisco in 1945 and took understandable pride in this confirmation of America's leadership in internationalism. At the same time, he worried about the sincerity of Washington's commitment to the new world organization, for there was little evidence of a true internationalist spirit among top figures in the Truman administration. Shotwell's doubts multiplied in August 1945 when the atomic destruction of Hiroshima and Nagasaki fulfilled his fear of the apocalyptic power of modern science in an immature international system. Within weeks of the dawn of the atomic age, Shotwell was busily organizing new groups of experts in an effort to internationalize America's atomic secrets and make real the UN's potential for global leadership.

From his concern for the power of science and industry, Shotwell fashioned a third tactical approach to influence policy making: cooperation with the internationalist wing of American business. Between 1919 and 1921 he played a central role in forming the Council on Foreign Relations, the dominant private influence on foreign policy for the next half-century. Also in 1921 he figured in the calling of the Porto Rosa Conference, a meeting of those Balkan states concerned with the economic revitalization of southeastern Europe. When the conference began to flounder in ancient animosities, Shotwell arranged with friends in the International Chamber of Commerce to intervene with a plea for economic efficiency in the Danube Basin. The ICC intervened too late with too little to salvage the conference, but its presence highlights Shotwell's multifaceted operations. Convinced that capitalism meant peace, he collaborated with business groups in continuing attempts to advance a world system in which "diplomacy instead of being geared to the army and navy will be linked into the great structure of international business."

Instead of shaking his faith in the existing order, the Great Crash and Depression reinforced Shotwell's belief in the costliness of world war and in the need for fuller trading opportunities for all peoples. He worked closely with Thomas J. Watson and contributed periodically to the IBM journal, *Think*. With Watson's encouragement, Shotwell supported Secretary of State Hull's efforts to negotiate reciprocal trade agreements and headed extensive investigations into the weaknesses and needs of the international trading community. In 1938 he headed a study of "World Economic Co-operation" which detailed the interrelationship of freer world trade and a stable peace. Six years later he wrote a report for the Committee on International Economic Policy, a distinguished group of business leaders, which repeated the demand for a more open world trading community and cooperative planning toward international reconstruction. Like all Wilsonians, Shotwell believed strongly that freedom for business meant freedom from strife.

To all of his endeavors, James Shotwell brought conviction, enthusiasm, and a determination to build world order because it was necessary and right. He had tremendous appeal within the country's internationalist constituency, a large and potentially powerful group. A smooth writer with a convincing style, he produced several books and scores of articles for journals ranging from *Foreign Affairs* to *The Christian-Evangelist*. Also a popular public speaker, he exerted particular influence among church groups and women's organizations. Informative but not didactic, inspiring but not obscure, he succeeded as an extraordinarily able advocate of the causes he championed. At the same time, he operated as an effective private negotiator and an active force in committee sessions. A master of planning and publicity, organization and agitation, he pursued a dual career: one private, one public; one behind the scenes, one on center stage. This dualism was in practice complementary and vital to the policy alternatives that he so energetically sought. A firm but gentle crusader, he thought carefully before he acted; yet he acted forcefully when necessary.

Shotwell never defined or implemented any one foreign policy decision for the United States. Nonetheless, he contributed richly to the American diplomatic experience. A liberal in the tradition of William Gladstone and Woodrow Wilson, Shotwell was the most active and articulate exponent of the credo—consisting of reason, service, orderliness, benevolent capitalism, and cooperative progress beyond class conflict—that constituted the Wilsonian legacy in post-Versailles America. Wilson had proclaimed the beatitudes of world order and American international activism; it was left to Shotwell and his associates to give strength to the unsteady body of principles that the president had suggested. To a much greater extent than most have appreciated, the internationalism of Woodrow Wilson was more the work of the disciples than of the master.

As Shotwell and others advanced the faith after 1919, Wilsonianism signified the call for an organized peace that was anchored in Anglo-American power, rationalized by scientific experts, and couched in the rhetoric of democratic liberalism. It was thus a liberal prescription for a peace founded on expert knowledge and reasoned reconciliation. Shotwell believed that new techniques of planned cooperative diplomacy had to replace balance of power politicking and was convinced that the productive power of modern industrialism demanded a manageable world order supervised by experts and functioning through "the machinery of discussion." Opposed to European colonialism and military adventures, Shotwell sought an international system that would preserve order with prosperity; he wanted liberalism to function as "an instrument of liberation" instead of "an apology for things as they are." He looked mainly to America to bring about, through rationalization of industrial society at home and abroad, a cooperative international system that would minimize disorder and spread the material basis of a lasting peace.

Shotwell and other liberal internationalists assumed that their model world organization would control the momentum of the two most explosive forces of modern times: egotistic nationalism and interlocking science. As international observers who took pride in their realism, these men understood clearly the attractions offered by modern nationalism. In addition, they were proudly nationalistic in their own right and convinced that the United States had a special responsibility to extend its brand of progress. Wilson's greatest achievement, Shotwell said, was to issue a global challenge "which accepted nationalism but turned it against itself." In the same way, Shotwell and his associates sought to generate from the diversity of nationalism a collective force that defined the common good through calm analysis and rational action. Organized in a consensual structure and linked to advancing science, nationalism would thus become the principal means to attain a liberal, cosmopolitan world of general order, economic stability, and individual freedom. Nationalism and science, joined through the rational adaptability of pragmatic liberalism, would provide twin engines of progress within a new, dynamic, and reliable international order.

Shotwell's continuing fascination with nationalism and science equipped him at once with a sense of realism and a yearning toward idealism. Hardly a befuddled utopian, he perceived science as the most potent force for transforming international politics. Often his perception enabled him to view matters with the kind of striking prescience that he exhibited in the dark spring of 1941, when he declared, "The greatest fact in the world today is not to be found in the European war, vast and portentous as that war is, but in those laboratories where the atom may yield potentialities utterly beyond the control of any master of military powers." Yet, Shotwell's respect for facts and reality was juxtaposed with an abiding faith in the beneficence of science and human reason. Throughout his life he consistently refused to concede that man was bound to distort the power of science for antihuman ends. An irrepressible optimist, he insisted that progress was advancing in his own time as science joined liberalism, democracy, and intelligence in a structure of peace that promised order with justice: "The increasing mastery of time and of space and of human conditions makes us more and more dependent upon each other, and this process will go on increasingly from now until the end of time. With science we are turning a corner on the long road of human evolution. It is the newest thing since the ice age and the most potent. It is intelligence in action. But intelligence cannot achieve its true purposes under the iron compulsions of war; its vital need is freedom, without which it withers and dies no matter what material resources are placed at its command. For this fundamental condition of life, it will

atom bomb

sacrifice everything, face all odds. Seen in this light, science is the final, and invincible, ally of peace, and scientific war is destined to be a contradiction in terms." If Shotwell and other internationalists sounded naïve, it was because hope in the future and faith in their fellow men infused their beliefs.

In most ways, Shotwell's hope sprang from his devotion to the tenets of Anglo-American liberalism. He was plainly a reformer, a working pragmatist who proposed to adjust the existing international system to those massive displacements brought about by the collision of war, science, and social change. A tinkerer by temperament, he hoped to establish institutions that would allow for controlled change in the belief that peace flourished in an environment of liberalism (which he defined as "the upbuilding of fair dealing and fair thinking between nations"). Liberalism and liberal institutions offered the best tools for nations' attempts to deal in a scientific and organized way with a world of daily change. Like other internationalists, Shotwell had little confidence in popular control of diplomacy. He clearly preferred expert over democratic direction and feared that popular ignorance of world politics formed the chief breeding ground for mindless jingoism. Only expert analysis by an international "creative scientific mind" could educate the masses to awareness of the world's complexity.

Unfortunately, the power of expert analysis failed Shotwell and his friends when it became necessary to penetrate the fundamental content and direction of American diplomacy. Though he often criticized specific national policies, the Columbia scholar never attacked the American diplomatic establishment or the cluster of ruling groups that establishment represented in world affairs. He and his colleagues much preferred dabbling in institutions of world order to questioning the policy-making process and the distribution of authority within the United States. Satisfied with the domestic structure of power, liberal internationalists were incapable of mounting a fundamental challenge to this system, though to have done so might have compelled American policy makers to forego the politics of unilateralism and to seek the nation's highest interests in international cooperation. Shotwell and his friends elected to work as the servants and not the critics of power; it was a choice that would cost them their distinctive status and ultimately their cause.

The failure of liberal internationalists to analyze the structural deficiencies within American diplomacy reflected their tendency to view the world through the distorting lenses of American liberal nationalism. Shotwell and his associates too often identified the needs of humanity with the interests of the American political economy. Deceived by their own nationalistic and class biases, they badly underestimated the abiding unilateralism of most followers of Wilson and grossly overestimated their commitment to the principle of international organization. This compound error was tolerable in the years to 1938, when the Wilsonian faith was formally excluded from policy considerations that were basically isolationist; but their misjudgment was disastrous after 1938, when Washington grafted the old faith onto a policy of renewed global activism. This Wilsonianism was not the flexible formula that Shotwell had advanced for meeting changing international conditions through a consensual order; rather it represented a stiffening determination to apply the power of the United States unilaterally throughout the world against expansive authoritarian nations. Successive administrations in Washington adopted the Wilsonianism of liberal interventionism, not that of liberal internationalism. This legacy of Woodrow Wilson bespoke the moral universalism of such imperial proconsuls as Henry Stimson, and not the rational interdependency of James Shotwell.

The modern creed of liberal interventionism, which Stimson and his successors have disguised since the late thirties as liberal internationalism, assumed that peace among nations was not interdependent and regionally segmented but rather a fabric that was one and indivisible. Other tenets grew quickly from this central conviction, each rooted in the implicit belief that the Western powers could have prevented the Second World War and consequent Soviet expansion through early cooperation under America's militant direction. By the formula of liberal interventionism, revolutionary states that rejected American influence were authoritarian; authoritarian states consumed with ideological fervor were totalitarian; totalitarian states were aggressive; aggressor states were insatiable, and they inevitably menaced the integrity of peace. The preservation of American security through order therefore depended upon containment or elimination of hostile revolutionary governments anywhere at any time. Although more universalist than internationalist, this reasoning came to appear self-evident to those who matured amid the ugly events of the 1930s. The completion of the circle ironically vitiated the dream of true internationalism, the dream of an organized peace

realism
?
neglect
U.N.
league
of Nations

of interdependent powers. Once Washington equated its security with an indivisible global order, "realism" demanded neglect of those interdependent agencies that had already proven their incapacity to maintain order after Versailles. A peace based on cooperation was inadequate to the fears of Wilsonian interventionists, even those who professed to seek such a system. Only an armed America could be relied upon to protect *world* law and order.

Because of his nationalism and pragmatism, Shotwell contributed in some measure to the interventionist credo of the "national security liberals" who have militarized American foreign policy out of a determination to prevent a repetition of the disastrous events of the thirties. Yet the essential spirit of Shotwell's contribution to the American diplomatic tradition was contrary to the unbending unilateralism that successive liberal interventionists, running in a bipartisan line from Henry Stimson to Dean Acheson to Richard Nixon, have tried to disguise as a fulfillment of the nation's commitment to the ideals of collective security and international cooperation. Open, intelligent, sensitive, and cosmopolitan, Shotwell was genuinely concerned with the unity of all the industrial peoples in a commonwealth ensuring freedom, prosperity, and order. He responded energetically to countless challenges, but he believed that the largest question before his generation was whether industrial man could employ organized political intelligence to establish global institutions that could control the awesome physical power uncovered by organized scientific intelligence. James Shotwell approached this question in ways that were often superficial and frequently wrong; nevertheless, he was more successful than any other diplomatist in preatomic America in posing and pursuing what has surely become the paramount problem of our time.

BIBLIOGRAPHIC NOTE

Of available published studies, *The Autobiography of James T. Shotwell* (Indianapolis, 1961) provides the most comprehensive survey of the internationalist's life. Harold Josephson's unpublished dissertation, "James Thomson Shotwell: Historian as Activist," University of Wisconsin, 1968, is a thoughtful and critical work and includes a valuable bibliographical essay on Shotwell's many writings.

Scientific Progressivism is a notion described in Ronald C. Tobey's

The American Ideology of National Science, 1919–1930 (Pittsburgh, 1971). The milieu that shaped this concept is brilliantly analyzed in Morton G. White's *Social Thought in America: The Revolt against Formalism* (New York, 1949) and Charles G. Forcey's *The Crossroads of Liberalism: Croly, Weyl, Lippmann and the Progressive Era, 1900–1925* (New York, 1961). Bernard Crick's *The American Science of Politics: Its Origins and Conditions* (London, 1959) succeeds modestly in examining a topic that deserves much wider consideration.

Internationalist thinking in America before 1920 is surveyed extensively in Warren F. Kuehl's *Seeking World Order: The United States and International Organization to 1920* (Nashville, 1969). Sondra R. Herman has provocatively portrayed varieties of internationalism in *Eleven against War: Studies in American Internationalist Thought, 1898–1921* (Stanford, 1969). N. Gordon Levin's *Woodrow Wilson and World Politics: America's Response to War and Revolution* (New York, 1968) presents an invaluable analysis of the ideology of liberal internationalism, while Robert Divine's *Second Chance: The Triumph of Internationalism in America during World War II* (New York, 1967) engagingly describes the second great internationalist crusade.

The story of the interwar peace movement and the idea of collective security are examined in Robert H. Ferrell's *Peace in Their Time: The Origins of the Kellogg-Briand Pact* (New Haven, 1952) and Roland N. Stromberg's *Collective Security and American Foreign Policy: From the League of Nations to NATO* (New York, 1963). Ferrell expresses the same jaunty skepticism toward the work of peace seekers in "The Peace Movement," an essay that appears with Richard N. Current's helpful "The United States and 'Collective Security': Notes on the History of an Idea" in *Isolation and Security: Ideas and Interests in Twentieth-Century American Foreign Policy*, edited by Alexander DeConde (Durham, 1957). In a more sympathetic spirit, Charles Chatfield, Jr., explores the stark dilemmas faced by peace leaders between the wars in *For Peace and Justice: Pacifism in America, 1914–1941* (Knoxville, 1971). Finally, Richard J. Barnet tracks the formative effect of the years 1937–45 on the national security managers of cold war America in *Intervention and Revolution: The United States in the Third World* (New York, 1968) and *Roots of War* (New York, 1972).

U.S. Office of War Information

HENRY L. STIMSON

Republican Internationalist

William Kamman

When Henry L. Stimson died on 20 October 1950, he believed a lifelong dream had been realized: the United States had accepted the "active duty of world membership." Stimson was confident that most Americans in the ten years after Pearl Harbor understood that the free security so long enjoyed by the United States no longer existed. Isolationists who had misgivings about the League of Nations and World Court and had supported neutrality legislation to circumscribe presidential action in foreign relations were no longer intellectually fashionable. Membership in the United Nations had little opposition in 1945. Congress extended the selective service legislation that Stimson had championed, voted massive aid to Western Europe for economic revival, and in 1949 approved a military alliance to contain Russia's advance. Only a few months before Stimson's death President Truman ordered General MacArthur to defend South Korea with American troops.

Stimson welcomed these developments in United States

policy. During his long public career he had urged similar changes in American foreign relations: acceptance of world responsibility and United States leadership in preserving order and stability. How Stimson thought the United States could achieve this role is seen in his service under seven presidents, spanning some forty years. He was United States attorney for the Southern District of New York, secretary of war twice, soldier, special representative of President Coolidge in Nicaragua, governor-general of the Philippines, and secretary of state. He believed in a strong federal government with aggressive presidential leadership that would assert control over contending interests in the country and guide the nation's domestic and foreign policies. In his younger years he supported Elihu Root's army reforms, moved to strengthen the general staff, and infused a feeling of movement in the army. When the First World War came he sympathized with Britain and France and was an early advocate of preparedness but not of intervention, at least not until unrestricted submarine warfare became German policy. In the quiet years after 1918, dealing with colonies or small Caribbean republics, Stimson had accepted the burden of the white man to advise, teach, and direct. As secretary of state from 1929 to 1933 he came to feel that peace was indivisible and that aggression should be stopped early, an idea that dominated the rest of his public career. The United States, he believed, had an international duty to support the Monroe Doctrine, the Open Door, and the European balance of power, all in the name of national safety and democracy. His views on these questions were not always original, but the positions he held and the decisions he influenced were important, sometimes determinant, in the foreign policy of his country.

The long-lived Stimsons, an energetic, middle-class lot, arrived in America in the seventeenth century. They fought in the French and Indian War and the Revolution, and a great-grandmother told young Henry of conversations with George Washington. Stimson's father fought in the Civil War. The family imparted a sense of history and duty to its members and Henry L. Stimson was no exception. By the time he was born in 1867 the family was comfortably established in New York City. Henry spent a few years in Europe while his father studied medicine. Then his mother died, leaving a maiden aunt to raise Henry and a younger sister in their grandparents' house in New York. When the city lacked appeal for the boy and his schooling proved unsatisfactory, his father sent him to Phillips Academy at Andover where rigorous training prepared him for Yale. In New Haven he felt his most important educational experience was election to Skull and Bones, a secret society. After college he went to Harvard Law School and eventually with his father's aid entered the prestigious New York law firm of which Elihu Root was senior partner.

Stimson once remarked that as a young boy blessed for some time with four grandparents and four great-grandparents still living, he thought an individual's normal life-span was at least a hundred years. He did not achieve the expected centennial, but his life was long, though not exceptionally so when compared with such contemporaries as Root, Cordell Hull, Herbert Hoover, or Charles Evans Hughes.

Probably more than most of the nation's leaders who spanned the nineteenth and twentieth centuries Stimson had to confront peculiarly twentieth-century problems. He had known the western frontier before the Census Bureau officially declared it closed. He had roamed the wilderness, exploring and mapping portions, and had a mountain named after him. He once witnessed an Indian uprising. The outdoor life appealed to him as it appealed to his older friend, Theodore Roosevelt; this was one of the bonds between the two men. For Stimson a frontier America populated with Indians and cavalrymen was as real as the atomic weapons and mechanized warfare of the mid-twentieth century. The American wilderness left its mark on him as he handled twentieth-century problems; for him the frontier cleared away moral confusions and emphasized "courage, truthfulness, and frankness."

Stimson's early physical and intellectual environment produced a man in many ways similar to the Progressive profile as described by the historian George E. Mowry. As a lawyer, he was economically secure, well educated, and a member of the white-collar class that was "restless, sensitive, and troubled." He once told an audience at a class reunion that the legal profession never completely satisfied him because the ordinary New York lawyer was usually devoted to making money. That was not enough for Stimson, who wanted to work for a good cause. When Roosevelt, with Root's encouragement, offered him such an opportunity, a job defending the public interest, Stimson unhesitatingly accepted. He described service as U.S. attorney for the Southern District of New York, his first public office, as going from a dark place out to where he could see stars and get his bearings once more. He hammered away at wrongdoers until it was clear that their offenses would be consistently punished just as he would later try to hammer away at international aggressors.

Stimson shared with many Progressives an abiding patriotism and love of "rural" values, evident in his frontier and hunting adventures and in his attachment for Highhold, his Long Island estate. Highhold was a place of peace and beauty that provided refreshment and happiness during many trying periods. There Stimson played the role of country squire, taking proprietary interest in the community, associates, and friends. He was of the gentry who supplied the Progressive movement with important leadership, who offered service but were not servants, who sought power as a source of progress and improvement.

Stimson's second opportunity for public service came in 1911 when President William Howard Taft asked him to become secretary of war. The appointment, influenced by the tangled political situation in the Republican party, surprised Stimson. Taft had almost decided on another candidate when Secretary of the Treasury Franklin MacVeagh suggested Stimson. The idea appealed to the president. Stimson accepted after consulting family and friends including Roosevelt, who thought Stimson's future would be better served as an ex–secretary of war than as merely a defeated gubernatorial candidate (he had run unsuccessfully for governor of New York in 1910). Stimson viewed his appointment as a move to lessen Roosevelt's criticisms of the administration.

When Stimson took office the army was not large but it offered opportunities for continuing the modernization begun by his mentor Root. The new secretary of war also gained experience in administering colonies and working with Congress. His service in the War Department and later as a colonel of artillery in the First World War confirmed his natural sympathy with regular army officers.

Before 1914 Stimson's interest in political affairs concerned primarily domestic issues. He aimed at undercutting the machines and bosses, and he worked especially to reform the Republican party and the New York State constitution. He had some success in these areas, but as a vote-getting politician he was a failure. He was not good on the hustings; his speeches were lifeless and his demeanor not such as to instill warmth or devotion. He was a patrician with much ability and a strong moral sense to correct evil. If his America had inequities, if its democracy was deficient, Stimson felt it was his duty to change it through better laws and the election of strong leaders. He had read Herbert Croly's *The Promise of American Life* and accepted the author's faith in America's future; it was a land of promise and he yearned to leave his mark on its development.

In 1914 a century of peace came to a saddening end. For the United States, although this was not clear at the time, it meant that the choice to dabble or not in world politics would be constricted. Stimson's opportunities for public service reflected this change. As he took on new tasks involving diplomatic relations with other countries he may have pondered a passage in Croly's *The Promise of American Life*: "The American nation, just in so far as it believes in its nationality and is ready to become more of a nation, must assume a more definite and a more responsible place in the international system. It will have an increasingly important and an increasingly specific part to play in the political affairs of the world; and, in spite of "old-fashioned democratic" scruples and prejudices, the will to play that part for all it is worth will constitute a beneficial and a necessary stimulus to the better realization of the Promise of our domestic life."

Stimson met these new challenges in much the same way he had met earlier ones: with a sense of propriety and honor, faith in the law, and acceptance of responsibility both for himself and his country. These views along with his admonitions in later years that "gentlemen do not read each other's mail" and that "the surest way to make a man trustworthy is to trust him" were personal convictions and also reflected the code of his class.

At the beginning of the First World War in 1914, Stimson supported a neutral position for the United States, although his sympathies were with England and France. In 1915 he told a veterans' group that America stood for humanity and justice and that the country would betray its birthright if it went in any direction but toward those goals. He gradually came to believe that his nation's concern in World War I transcended protection of neutral rights; the real enemy was a way of thinking that led to military aggression, what he and his generation called Prussianism.

Early in the war he came out strongly for preparedness, a matter of great concern since his years as secretary of war. Stimson supported preparedness beyond the immediate crisis. He urged defense training in the public schools and later advocated a program of universal military training, which he thought would develop initiative and an understanding of what American citizenship meant. A strong military also had diplomatic benefits. He once asked rhetorically, "Is there a man who doubts that Wilson's note to Germany would receive more attention if it were known that our navy was in readiness and that our 'free people' in the language of Washington were 'disciplined and trained in arms'?" Interestingly he opposed woman suffrage during this period in part because he thought women might very well hinder preparation for self-defense.

When war came in 1917 Stimson hailed the decision and volunteered for service in order to "feel comfortable in his mind." His view of the struggle was idealistic. The future of free institutions was at stake; if the tide of battle went against the Allies "the cause of democracy—even here in far-off America—would go down with them." Czarist Russia confused Stimson's neat delineation of the war as a conflict between democracy and autocracy, but the March Revolution led him to say in the oratory of the hour that "out of the caldron of war has issued another great democracy vindicating its position on the side of freedom. Into such a struggle a man may well go with a lofty faith and burning ardor." Later reflection on these events caused him to recognize that in his zeal he had probably overlooked difficulties in defining the war. Yet the penchant for easy division between right and wrong, which he retained when he faced later problems, in this case had not produced a tragic error, he believed. The tragedy came with peace, when the United States failed to "remain a member of the team."

Stimson's views on the League of Nations paralleled those of his friend Root. Both men favored a world organization with American participation; but they believed that Wilson had gone too far too fast, and that a more general covenant would have allowed a gradual development more acceptable to the American people. Even before the opening of the peace conference Root had told Stimson he opposed any agreement binding a nation to go to war on the order of a league. The world was not ready for such a proposition and it would not win public support. After publication of the league covenant in February 1919, Root and Stimson went over it in detail; later Stimson urged his friend to expound his objections, which Root did. He objected to Article Ten, the clause providing for collective security, because it seemed to perpetuate the status quo as established at Paris. For Senate consent of the treaty he proposed three conditions: Article Ten should be excluded, the United States should have the right to withdraw from the league and determine for itself whether its obligations were fulfilled, and there should be no interference with America's freedom to act in purely American questions. These reservations also expressed Stimson's position. They provided a middle way for American participation, between Wilson and the irreconcilables.

The end of all hope for American participation in the league was slow in coming, for even after adverse votes in the Senate the 1920 election provided opportunity for renewing the debate. During the campaign Stimson was among the thirty-one prominent Americans who signed a statement urging Harding's election as the best way to advance the cause of international cooperation. He thought a Republican president would gain the consent of the Senate with reservations on Article Ten. Looking back in later years he regretted his participation in this effort, recognizing that in 1920 he had been self-deceived.

The years immediately after the election of 1920 were not the happiest of Stimson's life, for he was disappointed with America's role in the peace settlement and was also back in private law practice, which did not satisfy him. Since the Republican administration in Washington dominated (he noted) by westerners was not congenial, he shared, according to his memoirs, an oblivion that overtook many younger eastern Republicans during this period. Yet while he may have fretted about life as a private citizen as he approached threescore years of age, unbeknownst to him the best part of his public career was in the future. President Calvin Coolidge retrieved him from exile and President Herbert Hoover offered him the secretaryship of state.

Henry L. Stimson's first important work in foreign affairs and in dealing with alien peoples was in a proconsular role, in response to the United States' particular interest in Central America. In 1927 President Coolidge sent him to Nicaragua where he spent a month settling a revolutionary situation that was fast involving U.S. troops. For years Nicaragua had attracted United States attention because of its closeness to the Panama Canal and its own possible canal route, and because one of the nation's dictators, José Santos Zelaya, had disturbed Central American peace early in the century. The first American intervention to stabilize Nicaragua began during Taft's administration and ended in 1925. When the hoped-for peace and stability evaporated a few weeks after the departure of U.S. Marines, Nicaraguan affairs embroiled the United States more than before; when considered in conjunction with Mexican problems in the mid-1920s the situation appeared serious. Stimson's task was to restore order.

The Nicaraguan situation was not untypical for the United States in the Caribbean, particularly just after the turn of the century. A paternalism had developed to which Roosevelt, Root, Taft, Philander C. Knox, and Woodrow Wilson all contributed, and Stimson, greatly influenced by Roosevelt and Root, continued the pattern. It was a tradition in which phrases like "Roosevelt Corollary" and "Dollar Diplomacy" conveyed interest in stable political conditions to ensure safety for foreign lives and property, and concern that economic and financial matters be handled in such a manner that there would be no foreign complaints or intervention. Intertwined with these policies was a belief that the small republics could best fulfill their obligations if their governments were democratic. Watching over everything was the United States, claiming predominant interest in the area and a right to intervene. When Stimson went to Nicaragua, American power was part of his baggage.

The month spent in Nicaragua was a profitable occasion for Stimson, one of the best of his life. In his "pilot biography" published in 1948 he reflected that the big lesson from his work there was that "if a man was frank and friendly, and he treated them as the equals they most certainly were, he could talk turkey with the politicians and other leaders of Latin America as he could with his own colleagues." This view was similar to that of his old friend Root who in trying to improve Latin American relations undertook a campaign of "considerate friendship." While the

Root and Stimson approach was an improvement over all-too-fre-
quent assumptions of superiority by North Americans, there was
still a certain condescension and no small measure of a big-broth-
erly attitude. Stimson described the policy as one of avoiding
Scylla and Charybdis, of sailing between timid aloofness and
selfish exploitation. It was a righteous exercise that did not
recognize these countries as capable of independent existence.
For Stimson the upright course was supervision or intervention,
provided that intervention were based upon the welfare of the
country in question and not upon selfish interests of the United
States. The earlier intervention in Nicaragua had been simply
naked American interference from Stimson's point of view because it had done nothing to promote self-government. His offer
of supervised elections during his mission was the constructive
difference, for it would lead the country nearer to self-government.

The months and years after Stimson's departure revealed
weaknesses in his Nicaraguan proposals. One obscure liberal
officer, Augusto C. Sandino, refused to lay down arms; with a
handful of men in the jungles and mountains of northern
Nicaragua he conducted guerrilla warfare against Nicaraguan and
American forces. While the enigmatic guerrilla leader failed to
disrupt the program of election supervision and formation of a
nonpartisan national guard, he underscored the pitfalls of intervention. In large part because of him, Coolidge's successor Hoover
and Stimson, his secretary of state, had to rethink policy toward
the Caribbean. Stimson believed that the American record in
Nicaragua, Cuba, and the Dominican Republic had been credita-
ble, but that local nationalism made retrenchment necessary.

For Stimson this belated concession to nationalism was not
the chief lesson of the Nicaraguan affair. The important result was
development of a regular procedure for overcoming disorder and
instability for the well-being of all. In his mind international
society was not far different from a community where the
policeman, the sanitary code, and compulsory school had developed to guide and protect those with less knowledge and power.
The same law of evolution worked among nations; Stimson felt
America must be its brother's keeper with an obligation to be
helpful and responsible for the Central American countries in their
progress toward democratic self-government.

When Stimson went to the Philippines as governor-general in

early 1928 he revealed the same willingness to accept the burdens of the white man. For him the Philippines, which resembled Latin America more than its surrounding Asian neighbors, offered an opportunity to develop democracy and self-government but not necessarily independence. The Philippines' connection with America protected the islands from overpopulated adjacent lands with greater industrial and military capacity. When Stimson had first visited the islands in 1926 he had found great progress, under supervision. For people who urged more Philippine autonomy he noted developments during the tenure of Governor-General Francis B. Harrison, which allowed Filipinos greater self-government at the expense of financial and sanitation reforms. He approved a reversal of this trend after General Leonard Wood became the chief administrator of the Philippines, and when he succeeded Wood in that post he continued to think of a long-term role for the United States in the islands.

For Stimson the islands offered more than just a chance to evolve an imperial relationship. They were important as an outpost in the Far East, or as he and Wood said, a "spearhead of the great Christian effort." In addition, many persons who like Stimson approved the Open Door policy believed that United States presence in the islands strengthened America's position in the Far East. When in the 1930s Japan threatened Chinese territorial integrity, Stimson argued against giving up the Philippines; he thought such action would indicate that America was getting out of the western Pacific, thereby encouraging the Japanese and greatly reducing United States prestige in Far Eastern countries. The argument was consistent with his world outlook and acceptance of American responsibility, but if carried out logically it was fraught with danger of war, a danger present in both Nicaragua and the Philippines. In Nicaragua Stimson ignored nationalism and American marines confronted guerrilla combat; in the Far East where Stimson desired to strengthen the Open Door and increase American influence, America confronted Japan in the Philippines.

◇◇◇

Stimson enjoyed his tenure in the Philippines, his "experiment in responsible government," and when word came that President-elect Hoover was considering him for a cabinet post he reacted with mixed feelings. He refused to consider appointment as attorney general but would, if approached, become secretary of state. Hoover, after being refused by his first choices (including Senator William E. Borah and Charles Evans Hughes), offered the post to Stimson, a man who had a reputation for service to his party and country and who was supported by Root, Hughes, and Taft. The new president and his secretary of state had known each other since World War I, though not well. Working together closely from 1929 to 1933 was not always easy for either man. Their work patterns were dissimilar (Hoover worked much harder than Stimson), but perhaps more important was the president's growing preoccupation with economic matters, which may have increased his natural inclination toward cautiousness in foreign policy. For Stimson, disposed toward strong leadership of the Theodore Roosevelt type, the Hoover administration was a disappointment. Hoover thought his secretary of state too militant, and had he been reelected would not have retained Stimson in the cabinet.

It is an interesting commentary on American politics and ideology that Hoover offered the top job at the State Department to both Borah and Stimson, the first an isolationist and anti-imperialist, the other an internationalist and imperialist. Stimson directed many of his efforts in United States foreign policy toward mitigating what he considered to be the mistakes of 1919 and 1920 when the Senate—Senator Borah had been an irreconcilable—refused to approve membership in the League of Nations. After that there was no chance of American acceptance of the league covenant, but Stimson pushed for cooperation. Seeking other ways for international cooperation in the preservation of peace Stimson seized upon the Washington treaties of 1921–22, which supported the status quo in the Far East and gave international recognition to the Open Door, and upon the Kellogg-Briand Pact, a multilateral renunciation of war as an instrument of national policy. For Stimson these pacts became the basis on which to stigmatize aggression and to take some sort of collective action against violators.

The first test of the Kellogg pact was in Manchuria in July 1929. For several months Chinese nationalists had acted to remove Russian influence in Manchuria and particularly to end their control of the Chinese Eastern Railway. When the Soviets broke diplomatic relations and news reports indicated the possibility of an armed clash, Stimson sought a solution by reminding China and Russia, both signatories of the Kellogg treaty, of their obligations.

He also urged other signatories to encourage a peaceful settlement because, as he said, the efficacy of the treaty depended upon the sincerity of the nations party to it; their attitude would in turn strengthen world opinion in support of peace. Stimson later recognized that his use of the Kellogg-Briand Pact might have had little to do with settlement of the Sino-Russian differences, but he believed there was at least outward success in this first invocation of the treaty that encouraged "believers in the new order of peace." Stimson had faith in marshaling world public opinion, but in this episode, the Japanese and Russians thought his approach suspicious. How thoroughly Stimson understood the intricacies of Far Eastern politics is doubtful; his main concern was that even in the most difficult portions of the world in which the Kellogg treaty might be challenged, the United States had acted to organize public opinion against war makers. Although Stimson had invoked provisions of the antiwar pact during the Sino-Soviet conflict, there was no real test of those principles. Russian troops had evacuated Chinese territory in short order, and, as now seems clear, Stimson's use of the pact had little positive effect.

Extension of Japanese control in Manchuria beginning with the Mukden incident provided a greater challenge that allowed Hoover's secretary of state an opportunity to extend by several steps his thoughts on the keeping of peace. United States–Japanese relations had been satisfactory for some time when on the evening of 18 September 1931 an explosion tore up a few feet of track along the South Manchuria Railway near Mukden. The event triggered a Japanese occupation of south Manchuria and led to strained relations between Tokyo and Washington. Stimson reacted slowly to the Manchurian crisis of 1931 because there was hope that the Japanese government could regain control of its Kwantung army which was apparently acting independently, and he had no desire to make the affair even more difficult by arousing Japanese nationalism. Hopefully, direct Sino-Japanese negotiations would restore the status quo; if not, Stimson told the Japanese ambassador, the affair would create a bad impression and force consideration of treaty obligations.

Meanwhile Stimson looked toward the League of Nations. Cooperation with the league was a delicate problem for Washington, but he was glad the league had shown interest in the crisis. The United States could carefully support the league, and if any controversy arose with Japan it would be against the world rather

The Bird in the Gilded Cage

Wilmington (N.C.) Morning Sun, *14 July 1936*

than the United States. The United States thus could avoid taking the initiative and (as President Hoover put the case in a cabinet meeting) avoid having the baby dropped on its doorstep.

As the Manchurian crisis evolved, Stimson overcame his early reluctance to be actively involved. Through the autumn of 1931 he kept pressure on the Japanese government, for he wanted Tokyo to know it was being watched. What he saw and heard became increasingly distressing. When diplomatic pressure and watchful waiting seemed to have little effect Stimson suggested to Hoover some form of collective sanctions, but Hoover preferred a more cautious approach. Stimson himself was not sold on an embargo; there were so many complications, not least of which was popular support. If the league had imposed sanctions he would have been delighted and would have promised no interference, but there would be no unilateral American sanctions.

After the collapse of Chinese resistance in Manchuria Stimson took another approach to the Far Eastern crisis: nonrecognition. The United States would uphold the Open Door and refuse "to recognize any situation, treaty, or agreement which may be brought about by means contrary to the covenants and obligations of the Pact of Paris." For Stimson, Japan's lack of respect for repeated admonitions to observe the spirit and letter of international promises was a moral outrage. He wanted to record that his government would not recognize these violations and wanted to set a standard to which others might repair. While acting for the United States alone, because he did not want the delay or equivocation that joint action might bring, he hoped for sympathetic, if not similar, responses from other signatories of the Nine-Power Pact, one of the agreements signed at the Washington Conference of 1921–22. In this he was disappointed.

Nonrecognition was a policy that most Americans could support because it voiced revulsion for Japanese aggression but made no promises to the victim. In this respect it reveals the dilemma American leaders faced in the 1930s. Although it was probably the only course open, Stimson was not happy with it, for he wanted the treaties to be more than scraps of paper. Yet the state of American preparedness, the pacific inclination of the president, and the preoccupation of public opinion with the depression made anything more than verbal action impossible. Stimson did not consider his diplomacy of January 1932 the last word. His faith in the treaty structure as a basis on which

international law could evolve, as common law had, precluded
approval of aggression. Nonrecognition did not roll back the
Japanese occupation of Manchuria; it did not prevent the occupation of Shanghai a few weeks later, nor beginning in 1937 would it
stop the invasion of China; but it did set a proper if not very
forceful precedent.

international

Thus the lines were drawn in 1931–32 for a conflict with Japan.
Stimson had carried on the policies of his predecessors John Hay
and Charles Evans Hughes in the Far East. Early in 1933 he passed
them on to a receptive Franklin D. Roosevelt and his new secretary
of state Cordell Hull. Obsessed with the Open Door and strongly
influenced by the arguments of missionaries in China and Chinese
students in the United States, Stimson believed that education and
Christianity could exert a profound influence on China's progress.
Also, the enormous potential for United States commerce dazzled
him. He emphasized political and humanitarian idealism, which
he compared with the colonial effort in the Philippines to "train
an Oriental people in the art of self-government according to the
American model."

moralizing

Japan threatened those concerns, and especially the treaty
framework of European and world peace, which Stimson believed
would preserve American interests and at the same time prevent
another world war. As matters turned out, his goals were contradictory. Preservation of the status quo as supported by the league
covenant, the Nine-Power Treaty, and the Kellogg pact was one
hope. These agreements, he recognized, were "initiated by Western nations, and especially designed to fit the exigencies of the
industrialized world of Europe and America"; while they might not
be taken seriously in the Orient, they did exist. As for the other
goal of peace, Stimson noted that for better or worse the treaties
expressed the "earnest hopes of our part of the world," and if the
Western nations gave in and allowed the treaties to be treated as
"scraps of paper," then the hope of peaceable development in the
world would "receive a blow from which it would not soon
recover." The Japanese did not see China as he saw it; conditions
there were not satisfactory to Japan. When the military, which had
gained greater influence in policy, decided to make changes in
China, and when the United States refused to recognize the results
of Japanese aggression, Stimson worked, not always successfully,
to present a common front against Japan, and the hope for peace,
while not impossible, lessened. China remained the stumbling

issue of rt & wrong over peace & war (handwritten margin note)

block in Japanese relations; the break came ten years after the Mukden incident. Stimson continued to believe that the issue of right and wrong—by that time in Europe as well as in the Far East—was more important than the choice between peace and war.

On inauguration day, 1933, Stimson returned to private life. The law took some of his time; he traveled to Europe; he wrote (*The Far Eastern Crisis*); perhaps more importantly, he was an elder statesman who kept abreast with people of influence and power through conversation and correspondence. He had a friendly relationship with President Roosevelt and Secretary Hull whose views on foreign policy were not far from his own.

After seven years as a private citizen Stimson returned to public service. This, his last appointment to office, resulted in large measure from the mounting Eastern challenge to isolationism. Increasing dissatisfaction with Secretary of War Harry Woodring, in part for his opposition to foreign military commitments that might interfere with America's rearmament, culminated in June 1940 when President Roosevelt asked for Woodring's resignation and named Stimson as his successor. Stimson first met Roosevelt during the changeover of administrations in 1933. They had gotten along well and in the following years there were other meetings. Stimson's immediate support came from Grenville Clark, a founder of the Plattsburg Training Camps during World War I and a strong advocate of military conscription in 1940, who arranged for Felix Frankfurter, an associate justice of the Supreme Court, former protégé of Stimson when he was U.S. attorney for the Southern District of New York, and friend of FDR, to propose Stimson's name to the president. The arrangement included Robert P. Patterson as assistant secretary of war, later undersecretary, to serve with Stimson, who was almost seventy-three years old. Patterson was the first of an excellent staff brought together by the new secretary.

Political implications surrounded Stimson's appointment, but his views on foreign affairs had also been attractive to the administration. At the end of the Hoover presidency Stimson's advocacy of collective security and use of economic sanctions against aggressors had intensified. He deemed traditional neutral-

ity no longer appropriate; he wanted to warn aggressors and
would-be aggressors that America's moral and material resources
would be on the side of their victims. On the eve of his
appointment he emphasized the importance of the British fleet to
American security and called for compulsory military service. After
taking office he did not disappoint those who pushed his
nomination. The destroyers-bases deal with England in 1940 and
evidence that same year of greater cooperation with Canada and
Britain encouraged him. The Lend-Lease Act of 1941 making
America the great arsenal of democracy had, of course, his
wholehearted approval.

In the Far East Stimson urged the utmost firmness; he assumed
that the Japanese did not want a war with the United States, a
belief not shared by officials who feared that Japan might move
southward while avoiding a direct attack on United States territory. The administration's concern was to maneuver the Japanese
"into the position of firing the first shot"—which meant, according
to Professor Richard Current, convincing the American people that
expansion into Southeast Asia was as great a threat to the vital
interests of the United States as an attack on the Philippines,
Guam, or Hawaii. This concern became academic on 7 December
1941, and Stimson and others were relieved of their dilemma.
Stimson had feared that Americans were not alert to events in
Manchuria, Ethiopia, Spain, the Rhineland, Austria, Czechoslovakia, and Poland and had tried to strengthen America's peace and
security through neutrality legislation rather than cooperative
action. Now there was unity. "The self-imprisoned giant was set
free."

As secretary of war, Stimson contributed to major diplomatic
and military decisions, but none of the questions arising during
the Second World War has led to as much soul-searching and
historical analysis as the use of atomic power. Some writers have
questioned use of the bomb and have asked whether victory
would not have come as quickly through a demonstration,
warning, or description of the weapon, especially if the Americans
had been explicit about the future status of Emperor Hirohito.
Others put the bomb in the context of developing conflict with
the Soviet Union and explained its use as an attempt to force
Russian acquiescence to American plans for Europe.

For Stimson the decision was a military one and the logical
consequence of his thinking for fifteen years. In 1932, when

Japanese forces were having some unexpected difficulties overcoming the Chinese around Shanghai, Stimson pondered whether
the higher the price militarists had to pay the better for the
ultimate reign of law in the world. He hoped that Chinese
resistance would give pause to the Japanese militants and allow
moderates a chance to regain control in Tokyo. Events proved
otherwise, but he saw another chance later when other nations
and eventually his own challenged Axis expansion in Europe as
well as Asia. He accepted the value of power and war; the atomic
bomb gave the United States awesome power in the summer of
1945. At that time Stimson concluded that to gain Japanese
surrender their leaders had to experience "a tremendous shock
which would carry convincing proof of our power to destroy the
Empire." It seemed that only the complete destruction of Japanese
military power would open the way to lasting peace. The United
States after 16 July 1945 had the means to stop what had started at
Mukden on 18 September 1931.

When the Second World War ended in early August 1945 with
the mushroom clouds over Hiroshima and Nagasaki, new military
and diplomatic problems had already arisen. Of these Stimson was
remarkably aware; yet he, like other American leaders, faced them
with some uncertainty. He had misgivings about approaching
Russia with the bomb "rather ostentatiously on our hip," but soon
recognized that his old maxim from Yale days in the 1880s about
"the surest way to make a man trustworthy was to trust him" was
not always appropriate. His advice was patience and firmness.
These were not to be his problems, however. He retired in
September 1945, leaving a legacy of commitment to a world
community in which he hoped his country would be the leader.

Henry L. Stimson's role in American foreign policy carried on
the tradition of power and responsibility championed at the
beginning of the twentieth century by his friends Theodore
Roosevelt and Elihu Root. His ties to Root were particularly close.
During that statesman's long life (Root died in 1937) Stimson
frequently conferred with him, for, as he once told Justice Oliver
Wendell Holmes, many people depended on Root and his advice
to be the most valuable they could get in the world. Root's
influence was evident in Stimson's attitude toward the League of

Nations, the World Court, development of international law, and
Latin American diplomacy. In Far Eastern affairs, although there
were some differences, his approach generally followed Root's
ideas. During his years in the War Department in 1940–45 Stimson
kept in his office a bound set of Root's collected papers, often
relying on them to provide the guiding principle for a decision.

Root's views on international law had a particular effect on
Stimson. An abiding hope for an evolution of international law
had influenced Stimson's thinking increasingly during 1931–41,
and was evident in his interpretation of the Kellogg-Briand Pact to
which he frequently referred when considering Far Eastern problems. He did not agree with some contemporaries that the pact
was only a voluntary and simultaneous declaration of which each
nation remained the sole and independent interpreter, and he
disputed the claim that the treaty gave no rights and imposed no
obligations. He emphasized the phrase in the treaty's preamble
stating that powers resorting to war should be denied benefits
furnished by the treaty, and, mirroring Root's faith in the world
community's interest in violence against one member, Stimson
believed that the Kellogg-Briand Pact made international conflicts
a legal concern of all nations connected with the treaty. This
covenant he believed to be the foundation for a new order.
Positive construction of its provisions, expressed and implied,
could strengthen the treaty. During the increasingly anarchical
decade before Pearl Harbor he urged these views on Americans
and in 1939–40 encouraged revision of the neutrality laws to allow
this country to support victims of aggression, at least with
measures short of war. When the surviving leaders of Germany
were tried at Nuremberg in 1945 after the war's end, Stimson
likened the proceedings to the common-law tradition. The trials
were natural and proper; they were "a great new case in the book
of international law."

As the years passed and Stimson, through experience, the
precepts of Elihu Root, and the saddening course of .human
events, sought to gather his ideas, he gradually fastened on a
strong president as the key figure in American foreign policy. For a
long time, from his days as a Roosevelt Progressive until his last
service as FDR's secretary of war, he had argued for greater
executive power. In 1913 he had criticized government by congressional committee, which he termed wretched and impossible,
prompting selfishness and corruption. He wanted to grant the

president power to introduce a budget and proposals for revenue; he proposed forbidding Congress to add items to the budget without presidential consent. At another time he advised that a man or government could not be held responsible for doing wrong unless he were given the power to do right. He once told Root that international relations were different from domestic questions because greater leadership was required. "Americans know pretty well about their domestic affairs but they are ignorant as babies about their foreign relations; therefore, it was a much greater duty to lead and guide public opinion in international relations than in domestic relations and the attitude of the ear-to-the-ground statesman was far less justified in the former than in the latter." He was not satisfied with President Hoover's approach to foreign policy. Hoover was a Quaker and an engineer, which made Stimson believe he did not understand the psychology of combat. One should press ahead, not vacillate or give the appearance of timidity, discouraging followers while encouraging enemies. Stimson the lawyer had found the military maxim "In case of doubt march to the front" effective in law cases and true in other ventures as well. In human affairs requiring joint action one could not foresee or plan very far in advance for what was going to happen; it was not like building a bridge where one could calculate the stress and know mathematically the power and strength of it all. When he was urging modifications in neutrality legislation he inclined toward vesting complete and unlimited discretion in the president. He did not fear that the president would abuse this discretion, for he had observed that in no sphere of political action did the sobering effect of responsibility so affect a man as in relations with other nations. The man who "honestly and fully enjoyed the exercise of power" carried the mark of presidential greatness. The Roosevelts filled the bill.

Bold leadership and willing use of power in the conduct of foreign policy were signs of strength; men would follow a clear demonstration of duty and brush aside those who opposed. Too often, Stimson thought, there were lapses in presidential leadership: in the preparedness movement before entrance into the First World War, in the hesitation to support American participation in the World Court, in the initially weak stand against Japanese and German aggression. Too often presidents, fearing opposition, were timid or moved too gradually. Stimson was a man of action, and when blocked by his chief or the American people he was not happy. His proconsular service in Nicaragua and the Philippines had been agreeable; his years as secretary of state were disappointing; his tenure in the War Department, particularly after Pearl Harbor, was rewarding because hesitation and inaction had ended. Moral condemnation of aggression, as a sufficient policy, was over. The country could face, as he said in the postwar years, the second part of the question: an obligation to catch the criminals, which meant war. Stimson was not as reluctant to accept war as many Americans. He agreed with Theodore Roosevelt, who put peace above everything but righteousness, and believed that the final issue of policy was not peace and war but right and wrong.

In the intellectual milieu of American foreign policy Stimson was not original. He purveyed a traditional sense of destiny and power accompanied by preachments of law and morality. In the interwar period he had participated in one of the great debates of American diplomatic history, and events seemed to vindicate his position. Earlier than most Americans he was aware of the implications of Japanese expansion, and looking back from December 1941, his fellow citizens could well consider whether economic sanctions and closer cooperation with other nations might have nipped Japanese plans and, as he had hoped, prevented war. Perhaps the references to law, righteousness, morality, and the emphasis on Chinese territorial integrity may have made difficult a *modus vivendi* with Japan that would have entailed a compromise on China until a more propitious time for settling Far Eastern affairs. After all, China was lost to communism anyway, after the Second World War. Perhaps Stimson's position on aggression was more appropriate in Europe.

In the longer view of American foreign policy, with retrospect of a generation and more, questions arise about whether an act of war in any part of the world injures the United States, whether it is wrong to set limits to American activity as a member of the world community, whether it is true that the United States has an unlimited liability in the peace and freedom of the world, and how much discretion a president should have in foreign affairs. Stimson's words about peace and war, right and wrong, and his hope for a trumpet call to save freedom throughout the world seem a little jaded in the 1970s; his faith in international law does not have the appeal that it once had for many Americans. Perhaps he did represent a tradition that has brought the United States to the brink of catastrophe; but hopefully the architects of change in United States foreign policy will not exaggerate the virtues of withdrawal, weak executives, and the lack of idealism, thus creating an even more unfortunate condition.

BIBLIOGRAPHIC NOTE

Events during Stimson's public career, spanning almost a half-century and including two world wars, have attracted much commentary. Fortunately for historians Stimson provided an extensive record of his place in American history. The chief source is the large collection of Stimson papers and diary volumes at the Yale University Library, but there is readily available for students a sizable amount of printed material by and about Stimson. Frequently during his career he explained his role in important events. After his retirement Stimson, with the son of an old colleague in the State and War departments, McGeorge Bundy, wrote a "pilot biography," *On Active Service in Peace and War* (New York, 1947), which allowed him to explain and assess his public service. He wanted to forestall, as he said, other volumes that might be written without benefit of his papers or his counsel.

Earlier, after completing his mission in Nicaragua for President Coolidge, Stimson had published a slim volume, *American Policy in Nicaragua* (New York, 1927), in which he outlined his efforts in that nation. American policy, he believed, had a proper regard for Latin American independence although he recognized special geographic interests in Central America that made necessary particular regard for how these countries fulfilled their responsibilities. For him this condition derived from broad principles of self-defense.

Stimson chronicles his Far Eastern policies arising from the Manchurian incident of 1931 in *The Far Eastern Crisis: Recollections and Observations* (New York, 1936). More than a record of his activities during the "crisis" it is the testament of an American who in the mid-1930s strongly urged collective security, world order under law, and greater Anglo-American cooperation. In 1934 he gave the Stafford Little Foundation lectures at Princeton which were published as *Democracy and Nationalism in Europe* (Princeton, 1934). He was hopeful and optimistic about democracy in the face of European problems.

The Council on Foreign Relations and its quarterly *Foreign Affairs* provided a regular outlet for Stimson's views. "Future Philippine Policy under the Jones Act," appeared in *Foreign Affairs* 5 (April 1927), 459–71; "The United States and the Other American Republics," *Foreign Affairs* 9 (April 1931), Special Supplement; "The Pact of Paris: Three Years of Development," *Foreign Affairs* 11 (October 1932), Special Supplement; "Bases of American Foreign Policy during the Past Four Years," *Foreign*

Affairs 11 (April 1933), 383–96; "The Nuremberg Trial: Landmark in Law," *Foreign Affairs* 25 (January 1947), 179–89; and "The Challenge to Americans," *Foreign Affairs* 26 (October 1947), 5–14. One may also trace Stimson's views in news stories of the *New York Times* and particularly in his letters to the *Times*.

The best coverage of Stimson's diplomacy is Robert H. Ferrell's *American Diplomacy in the Great Depression: Hoover-Stimson Foreign Policy, 1929–1933* (New Haven, 1957), and his book on Frank B. Kellogg and Henry L. Stimson, volume 11 of American Secretaries of State and Their Diplomacy series (New York, 1963). Richard N. Current has been critical of Stimson for emphasis on law and morality in diplomacy and for interpretations and applications of policies that could mean a policeman's role for America in the world. See Current's *Secretary Stimson: A Study in Statecraft* (New Brunswick, N.J., 1954), his essay on Stimson in Norman A. Graebner, ed., *An Uncertain Tradition: American Secretaries of State in the Twentieth Century* (New York, 1961), his essay "Consequences of the Kellogg Pact" in George L. Anderson, ed., *Issues and Conflicts: Studies in Twentieth Century American Diplomacy* (Lawrence, Kans., 1959), and his article "The Stimson Doctrine and the Hoover Doctrine," *American Historical Review* 59 (April 1954), 513–42 in which he notes two separate doctrines. In the mind of Hoover nonrecognition was final and sufficient; for Stimson it was the first step toward stronger sanctions. For an explanation of Stimson's remark on maneuvering the Japanese into firing the first shot which does not support the contention that Roosevelt and his advisers were planning for an attack on Pearl Harbor, see Current's "How Stimson Meant to 'Maneuver' the Japanese," *Mississippi Valley Historical Review* 40 (June 1953), 67–74. Elting E. Morison has published an excellent biography of Stimson: *Turmoil and Tradition: A Study of the Life and Times of Henry L. Stimson* (Boston, 1960).

Some "New Left" historians see Stimson as the example in American leadership of the corporate lawyer and supporter of international peace and order who emphasizes American overseas economic expansion; see William Appleman Williams, *The Tragedy of American Diplomacy* (New York, 1962). In *The Contours of American History* (Chicago, 1966), Williams refers to Stimson as a descendant of the old feudal gentry. By the end of Stimson's career in 1945, Williams believes, he had broken with Theodore Roosevelt's conception of world power and come close to abandoning what the author terms the "frontier-expansionist outlook" when he advised greater cooperation with Russia on the atomic bomb. Gar Alperovitz in *Atomic Diplomacy: Hiroshima and Potsdam* (New York, 1967) traces Stimson's part in the decision to use the bomb, noting the dilemma between desiring to use the bomb as an instrument of diplomacy and fearing that such use would be disastrous.

Many writers have given attention to Japanese expansion in China in the early 1930s and America's response. Students of Stimson may consult Armin Rappaport, *Henry L. Stimson and Japan, 1931–33* (Chicago, 1963), who believes that at times Stimson may have acted rashly in handling the problem, but he ponders whether results would have been different had Stimson remained silent. Note also Herbert Hoover's *Memoirs*, vol. 2 (New York, 1952). Sara R. Smith, *The Manchurian Crisis, 1931–1932: A Tragedy in International Relations* (New York, 1948), regrets the failure of Anglo-American harmony in the affair and lack of greater United States cooperation with the League of Nations. For an account of New Deal views on Stimson's Far Eastern policy see Bernard Sternsher, "The Stimson Doctrine: FDR versus Moley and Tugwell," *Pacific Historical Review* 31 (August 1962), 281–89.

U.S. Office of War Information

THE OPEN DOOR IN PERSPECTIVE:
STANLEY K. HORNBECK

and American Far Eastern Policy

Russell D. Buhite

During the Second World War, when a Japanese official was asked if he knew of Stanley Hornbeck, he remarked, "Yes, he is the one responsible for war between the United States and Japan." Although that was a simplistic assignment of blame, Hornbeck, as a high State Department official and professional diplomat, did thrust himself into the vanguard of those in the government who opposed Japanese expansion. He was clearly more responsible than any other single individual for the application of economic sanctions against Japan, an act of great consequence in the coming of war. Indeed, beginning in 1928 and continuing for a period of sixteen years, few questions of America's Asian policy

This sketch is based in part on Kenneth G. McCarty, "Stanley K. Hornbeck and the Far East, 1931–1941," Ph.D. dissertation, Duke University, 1970. Professor McCarty is currently working on a full-length study of Hornbeck's career which promises to shed important new light on both Hornbeck and American foreign policy.

escaped his attention and few policy makers exerted such direct influence on the course of affairs. The dominant element in Hornbeck's view of the Far East was that he saw the area essentially in strategic terms and expressed greater concern for the larger picture than for any of its component parts. China was not so much the object of policy as it was one in a row of dominoes, the fall of which would eventually threaten American security. Hornbeck deserves attention especially because his views of the Open Door and of China made him the embodiment of the basic principles, strategy, and tactics of United States Far Eastern policy.

Stanley K. Hornbeck was born on 4 May 1883 in Franklin, Massachusetts, the son of Marquis and Lydia Hornbeck. His father was a Methodist minister just out of seminary. In 1883, not long after Stanley's birth, the family moved to Illinois, where the elder Hornbeck served several churches before accepting the presidency of Chaddock College, a small Methodist school located in Quincy. When Stanley was ten the family moved to Colorado, where he received much of his education. He attended a preparatory school in Boulder, was a student at the University of Colorado for two years, then transferred to the University of Denver, completing his B.A. degree in 1903. A classics major, Hornbeck was a good student and a hard worker but by his own admission no scholar. Notably, he did not acquire grounding in either history or political science. After graduation he accepted a teaching position in Golden, Colorado, but pounding Cicero into the heads of bored high school students quickly palled, and at the end of his first year Hornbeck decided to cast his sights higher.

In 1904 he applied for, and much to his surprise received, a Rhodes Scholarship, the first given to someone from Colorado. That scholarship wrought a major change in young Hornbeck, for the years at Oxford broadened his horizons, helped him develop a world view, and provided him with a sense of confidence about his ability to compete in a larger setting. Moreover, through his Oxford studies in modern European history he developed an interest in scholarship that was to be vitally important later.

Hornbeck returned to the United States in 1907, having decided to enter graduate school, and he enrolled at the University of Wisconsin. In 1909, after intensive study under the direction of Paul Reinsch, a specialist on the Far East and world politics who was later to become President Wilson's minister to China, he earned a Ph.D. in history and political science. During his years at

Wisconsin, Hornbeck came in contact with some of the best minds in the academic world, men like Richard Ely, John Commons, and Frederick J. Turner, though the precise degree of their influence on him is impossible to determine.

After the completion of his graduate study, circumstances led Hornbeck to an assignment that affected his career far more than his academic training. Unable well into the summer after graduation to secure a good teaching position in an American college, he came across a newspaper advertisement for a position in China, which, with the blessing of Professor Reinsch, he ultimately accepted. Later that year, Hornbeck went to China to assume the position as teacher of history and international law at Hangchow Provincial College. If Hornbeck's years at Oxford were critical, those in China were even more so; he spent four years traveling about the country, observing China's politics and learning its history. These were important times there. Hornbeck's stay coincided with the overthrow of the Manchu dynasty and the establishment of the republic. Also during this period he met Nelson T. Johnson, E. T. Williams, and John V. A. MacMurray, who were later to become chiefs of the State Department's Far Eastern Division.

After returning from China in 1913, Hornbeck's career took several turns before he settled into the policy-making structure of the State Department. When Reinsch was appointed United States minister to China he recommended that Hornbeck take his place at the University of Wisconsin, and the young scholar became an instructor in political science. His work in the position was apparently satisfactory, as he published several articles and one book during his tenure; but for reasons of his own, Hornbeck decided to leave teaching in 1917. He accepted an appointment to the U.S. Tariff Commission but he soon resigned, and in 1918 joined the army where he served as a captain in the army ordnance corps. Then he was detailed to the Inquiry,[1] an assignment that lasted until after the war when he became one of Wilson's advisers on Far Eastern questions at the Paris conference. In the twenties Hornbeck was a lecturer at Harvard and sometime

1. The Inquiry was a group of social scientists gathered under the direction of Woodrow Wilson in 1917 for the purposes of keeping him informed of international conditions and making policy recommendations.

adviser to the State Department until, in 1927, Nelson Johnson was promoted to assistant secretary; Johnson recommended his friend Stanley Hornbeck for the vacated departmental post, and in early 1928 Hornbeck became chief of the Far Eastern Division. From 1928 until his assignment in 1944 as minister to the Netherlands Hornbeck dealt primarily with Far Eastern questions, after 1937 as special adviser on political affairs in the State Department and in 1944 as director of the newly created Office of Far Eastern Affairs.

Like a number of men active in United States–Far Eastern relations during the first half of the twentieth century, diplomatic figures such as W. W. Rockhill, E. T. Williams, Paul Reinsch, John V. A. MacMurray, and J. Leighton Stuart, Hornbeck was a scholar-diplomat in the truest sense. He was an excellent lecturer and spoke often on Far Eastern topics before learned and academic societies. He also wrote several books and numerous articles. The University of Wisconsin published Hornbeck's dissertation, *The Most Favored Nation Clause in Commercial Treaties*. In 1916 Appleton published his most successful book, *Contemporary Politics in the Far East*, and his articles appeared in *Foreign Affairs, Annals, Current History*, and other journals. Later as a State Department official he did a good deal of public speaking, and he spent his retirement years after 1947 writing on the China question, sometimes in the editorial pages of the *New York Times*.

Neither Hornbeck's appearance nor his personality would have inspired poets. He was of medium build and height and could not in any sense be termed handsome. Extremely quick intellectually and possessed of a caustic tongue, he was an unwelcome and formidable foe in argument, and he had a scholar's eye for the ill-reasoned memo and poorly drafted dispatch. His precise and colorless demeanor stamped Hornbeck, in the eyes of some of his colleagues, as a kind of "fuddy-duddy." He also possessed the puritan's distaste for indolence. A hard worker who drove himself unmercifully, Hornbeck expected others to measure up; when they failed, he let them know. Accordingly, foreign service officers and subordinates often referred to him as "the old autocrat." Though he could be charming and a generation of scholars remembers him as friendly and helpful, Hornbeck did not have many close friends. The old China hand, Nelson Johnson, was probably the closest, in part because the two men were in substantial agreement and also because of Johnson's amiable spirit.

Personally, politically, and philosophically, Hornbeck was a conservative. Man, he often said, was a selfish, scheming creature and he once remarked to this author that in his view the most gracious act of generosity was simply selfishness turned around. His views on diplomacy accorded well with his view of man. Diplomacy, he once said, was not, as so often described, a game of chess. "Chess is played on an open board, with no chance of deceit or lying; diplomacy is not." Diplomacy was more like "a game of cut-throat auction bridge." This, he often stated, was not the way he wished it to be but the way it was.

At the same time, Hornbeck had no doubt that American statesmen generally followed a superior code of conduct and that both the goals and the methods of American policy transcended those of other states. Similarly, United States policy in the Far East, while of course designed to serve American interests, accorded with the basic principles of fair play to which much of humanity subscribed. Except for brief periods at the beginning and at the end of his career, Hornbeck was as staunch a supporter of that Far Eastern policy as he was a firm adherent of nationalism.

It was during his first participation in policy formulation at Paris in 1919 that Hornbeck found himself in opposition to established policies, because he believed the United States was needlessly sacrificing its moral and practical position in the Far East. As an adviser at the Versailles conference he worked against a pro-Japanese settlement of the Far Eastern question and opposed President Wilson's final commitment on the matter. The major Versailles discussions on the Far East focused on the interests and aspirations of Japan arising out of its participation in the war against Germany. In fall 1914, Japan had entered World War I on the Allied side and had taken over German possessions, in particular Shantung on the China mainland. Shantung, a northern Chinese province jutting into the Yellow Sea, had become a German-dominated area after the orgy of concession seeking in 1898; the Germans had acquired control of the coastal area of the province, known as Kiaochow, and mining, railroad, and other rights in the interior. Japanese quickly replaced the German officials in the concession and began running it as their own. In the famous Twenty-One Demands of 1915 and again in 1918 by treaty, the Japanese forced Chinese acceptance of the changed status of Shantung, and in a series of secret agreements made to secure Japanese naval assistance against Germany, Japan obligated the British, French, and Italians to support its postwar claim to the region. At Versailles Japan wanted formal recognition of its interests in that province. Tokyo also asked acceptance of two other points: acknowledgment of its right to annex certain formerly German Pacific islands and support for an international declaration of racial equality.

The question of the Pacific islands received much attention at the conference because of Japan's demand for annexation of the Marshalls, Carolines, and Marianas, and the West's fear of Japanese expansion. At length, the conferees devised a mandate system under which the league powers would administer the Pacific islands; the three island groups were placed under Japanese authority. Hornbeck favored American or British control but was willing to accept the mandate system; however, he was thinking ahead, for if the United States made concessions to Japan on this question, the Japanese might be brought to withdraw their claims of a "special position" in Shantung.

The Japanese were also thinking ahead. Hoping to strengthen their position on Shantung by making themselves the injured party on another issue, they pressed for a statement on racial equality, knowing they had little chance of getting it. Although President Wilson personally favored such a declaration, his own advisers and the British warned him of the proposition's political dangers. The British dominions, in particular, were bitterly opposed. Accordingly, the president did not vote for the measure and it was defeated.

Shantung was the major issue. Based on the Twenty-One Demands, the secret treaties, and the agreement of 1918, the Japanese claim to that region was difficult to dispute, and they pushed it vigorously. The Chinese, on the other hand, argued that the agreements were only temporary, that they had been forced upon China, and that in view of China's participation in the war, concessions that Germany had earlier extracted ought in justice to revert to China. The American position, on which Wilson's advisers were in unanimous agreement, was to support China, but because the Allies would not support the American position, and because the Japanese threatened to refuse to sign the treaty and withdraw from the conference unless they got their way on

Shantung, Wilson relented. Italy had already withdrawn over the Fiume issue, and the loss of Japan might imperil the treaty and league. Hornbeck, who had worked hard for the Chinese cause, believed, however, that the Japanese would eventually compromise and were simply using a technique they had learned from the Italians; in short, they were bluffing. He deplored the president's decision as neither just nor wise. It did not conform to "President Wilson's 'fourteen points' nor with the spirit and principles of American Far Eastern policy," the disappointed diplomat complained.

Although Hornbeck took the Chinese side in the Versailles deliberations he possessed little sentimental or romantic attachment to China. The blind sympathy for things Chinese exhibited by some "old China hands" was not what he meant by the "spirit" and "principles" of American Far Eastern policy. His concern about China, though genuine, was directly related to the position of Japan and the matter of present and future American interests. The overriding aim was to check Japanese imperialism, and Hornbeck hoped that China would develop into a stable, unified nation, one to which the United States would have free access. He deplored political chaos and refused to accede to the "whims" of Chinese nationalism if American "rights" were threatened thereby. Thus, when China in the twenties challenged the American position, the limited nature of Hornbeck's sympathy became clear. He supported the status quo in Sino-American relations and emphasized China's obligations as well as its rights.

In the 1920s China experienced the concurrent phenomena of unsettled political conditions and burgeoning national consciousness. The failure on the part of the great powers at both the Versailles and Washington conferences to make more than a gesture toward lifting the burdens of the unequal treaties from China created a sense of outrage in that country. Young Chinese workers and students, who were more aware of the outside world and some of whom were infected with Western Socialist and Communist ideologies, pressured their leaders to expel the foreigner or limit his prerogatives. Anger and frustration stemming from China's submissive role had burst forth in the May Fourth Movement of 1919 and in other antiforeign demonstrations. At the same time, China possessed no unified government for much of the twenties. The Kuomintang or Nationalist party of Sun Yat-sen, revitalized with Russian assistance, became the center of power in south China while the recognized government held power in Peking. In addition, countless warlords exercised more power at the local level than either of the two principal claimants to national authority. Finally, in the spring of 1926 Chiang Kai-shek led a Nationalist military drive northward, expelled the Communists from Kuomintang ranks the following year, and in 1928 secured nominal control of the country.

These conditions brought about direct clashes with the treaty powers. In May 1925, strikes in Japanese-owned cotton mills led to antiforeign marches, to sloganeering, and ultimately to bloodshed as foreign police fired on Chinese demonstrators. The following year, Chinese strike pickets attacked British nationals working at Canton; in November Chinese Nationalists attacked the customhouse at Hankow in an attempt to immobilize the customs administration; and in March 1927, a group of soldiers in Nationalist uniforms attacked foreign nationals living in Nanking, killing several, and inflicted considerable property damage.

American policy makers now tuned the China question into sharper focus than at any time since the Boxer Rebellion. There were two reasons: conditions created great and immediate concern about American lives and property in China, and Chinese demands forced the United States to consider its long-range policy on treaty revision, particularly with regard to the issues of the tariff and extraterritoriality. For years the United States had equated its own interests with those of the Chinese, assuming that the inviolability of Chinese sovereignty would provide the best chance for success of the two main goals of American policy, equal commercial opportunity and the right to carry on missionary activity. When the Chinese began to assert their independence, the United States found itself in an awkward position.

As events transpired, the United States occasionally used force in the defense of lives and property, as in the Nanking incident. Treaty revision posed more of a problem. The United States supported the cooperative policy agreed upon by the powers at the Washington Conference, but cooperation in using force to defend the treaty structure was not possible. Yet to give in to China was to act unilaterally and invite others to contravene the cooperative policy in their own way. In view of China's instability, it also risked damage to American interests.

The United States finally resolved the dilemma by taking a measured step toward meeting China's wishes, though not without considerable debate among State Department officials. Nelson Johnson, as Secretary of State Frank Kellogg's major Far Eastern adviser, desired conciliation to as great an extent as practical. John V. A. MacMurray, the American minister in China, wanted to stand firm because he believed that to give an inch would be to yield a mile, and he also feared the influence of bolshevism in China.

Although not in an official departmental position until 1928, Hornbeck leaned throughout toward support of the status quo. The problem as he saw it was that "none but a politically organized people, a state, can at once enjoy the rights and fulfill the obligations of sovereignty," and China did not meet that test. "There is now in China," he wrote in 1927, "no person or group whom a majority of the Chinese people, or a majority even of the leaders, recognize as having authority to make commitments on China's behalf or to accept commitments made by the Powers in China's favor." More than this, the treaty system had developed "not without cause and reason." Whatever its flaws it rested upon law. "It has been the legal basis upon which many foreigners and more Chinese have ordered their lives, made their investments, created and carried on their business . . . ; it cannot be abolished suddenly. . . ." Hornbeck was, however, willing to discuss extra-territoriality, but only if the United States went slowly and agreed only to a gradual relinquishment of that right, and he disdained the use of force to defend anything but lives and property. As he explained the cooperative policy, when the issue was peculiar to another country and China, when little U.S. interest was involved, or when the use of force was anything but defensive, the United States would not cooperate. While the United States might resist treaty revision, it could not cooperate in "aggression" against China; to do so would violate the principles of the Open Door to which the United States was irrevocably committed. Because Secretary Kellogg was generally predisposed toward a liberal approach, he worked closely with Johnson and in 1928 the United States granted China tariff autonomy and began negotiating on extraterritoriality.

If Chinese nationalism in the twenties brought American China policy into sharper focus, Japanese actions in the succeeding decade created greater apprehension about the larger questions of America's Far Eastern approach and the future of world peace. Japan's aggression in Manchuria and later in China proper consumed more of Hornbeck's time and that of his colleagues than any other question. American policy makers spent the decade assessing U.S. interests, debating alternative actions, and reacting to Japan's initiatives.

The story of the Manchurian crisis has been told many times. Japan attacked in Manchuria on 18 September 1931, proceeded to occupy strategic points, expelled foreign influences and interests, and in 1932 made it a puppet state called Manchukuo. In the process of securing control of this province Japan also attacked Chinchow, for the first time using air power against innocent civilians, and later waged pitched battles against Chinese troops in Shanghai because of anti-Japanese boycotts and other activities in that city. In spring 1933, Japan signed the Tangku Truce with China, giving the Japanese time to digest the heady potion they had just consumed before resuming the feast.

The Japanese blitz occasioned surprise, uncertainty, and chagrin among American officials. At length, the United States and other interested powers decided to pursue a policy of moral remonstrance and diplomatic pressure. Secretary of State Henry Stimson first tried conciliation, wishing to allow the Japanese civilian government time to rein in the military. When this did not work and the aggression continued, he invoked the Kellogg-Briand Pact, a multinational renunciation of the use of force as an instrument of policy. When this failed, he called his advisers together to consider economic sanctions, but the opposition of President Hoover and depressed economic conditions precluded their use. In January 1932, Stimson revived a policy utilized by Secretary of State William Jennings Bryan in the crisis of 1915 over the Twenty-One Demands: nonrecognition of any agreement between Japan and China contravening U.S. treaty rights in China. In February as the Japanese established "Manchukuo" he sent a letter to Senator William E. Borah pointing out the interrelatedness of the Washington treaties and suggesting invocation of the U.S. right to reject the Five-Power Naval Limitations Agreement.[2] In

2. The Washington Conference of 1921–22 had produced several agreements dealing with naval and political issues in the Pacific. Taken together these treaties could be considered a comprehensive program to sustain the status quo in the Far

parallel action dating back to October 1931, the League of Nations also invoked the Kellogg pact and then in December sent an investigating team known as the Lytton Commission to the Far East. None of these efforts, either American or league, deterred Japan.

No less than others in the State Department, Hornbeck agonized over the proper response to Japan's moves; and the metamorphosis of his thinking in the 1931–32 period is of considerable interest. The day after Japan's initial move in Manchuria he prepared a memorandum for the secretary of state in which he stated that events in Manchuria would intensify the struggle between the civilians and the military in Japan's government. External factors would determine who would win. Therefore, the United States should act to strengthen the hand of Foreign Minister Kijuro Shidehara. American concern, Hornbeck believed, should not be expressed in terms of American interests in Manchuria, nor should the United States at this point invoke the Kellogg pact. The latter option should be left to the World Court. In October when Stimson invoked the pact as a means of acting, Hornbeck acquiesced in the move, though he thought it little but an irritant to Japan and was never very sanguine about its effect.

This did not mean that Hornbeck was not willing to "get tough" with Japan under the proper circumstances. When the State Department discussed the possibility of applying economic sanctions, Hornbeck favored the move if the United States could act in conjunction with the other powers. "If the boycott is not given serious consideration," he wrote in early December, ". . . historians will attribute to the United States no small share of the blame for its failure." Sanctions would cripple Japan and could force an early end to its aggression. Any action, however, must be multilateral. In particular, Hornbeck did not want the British to push the United States into the lead on this matter, because American interests did not warrant such a position. Fear of European deviousness also governed his reaction to the question of American coorperation with the league in fall 1931. Britain and France "controlled" the league and would "use" the United States in the Far East. When the league decided in

internat.

East. Successive American administrations accepted this interpretation; the Japanese did not.

December to send the Lytton Commission to the Far East,
Hornbeck saw the move as meaningless; moral condemnation
would do no good, and unless the powers did something
concrete, Japan would stay in Manchuria.

Similar skepticism underlay Hornbeck's position during the
discussion of the nonrecognition proposal; consequently he was
of two minds about its utility. In this he differed with Secretary
Stimson. Aware of the slight effect of Bryan's nonrecognition
policy in 1915, Hornbeck saw little chance that the same policy
could be any more effective in the thirties. Yet he realized that
neither the United States nor the league could use force and that
sanctions were out of the question. Nonrecognition was one of
the few alternatives open to the United States; it would keep the
American legal record clear and had the advantage of flexibility
since it could later be canceled. In the fall of 1932 he went so far as
to describe nonrecognition as a "positive policy."

Stimson's letter of 23 February 1932 to Senator Borah accorded
with Hornbeck's views in that it suggested naval rearmament; in
fact, Hornbeck himself had written the first draft of the letter.
Actually, by early 1932 his views had begun to crystallize: Japan, he
believed, would stay in Manchuria; economic sanctions as well as
force were out of the question; the United States did not have
sufficient interests at stake to warrant a confrontation with Japan;
Japan had violated the Open Door and the treaty structure built
up since 1919; the United States ought not to take the lead against
Japan in defense of the treaty structure. Hornbeck concluded that
the best way to avoid war in the Manchurian affair and the most
sagacious course for the United States in its future relations with
Japan was for America to look to its broader Far Eastern interests
and increase its naval strength in the Pacific.

Once he purged himself of his anger over Japan's action and
had time to reflect on the situation, Hornbeck began to see
American Far Eastern policy in essentially the same perspective in
which it was nearly always viewed. When the powers began
dismembering China at the turn of the century the United States
responded with the Open Door notes, which comprised a
restatement of some long-cherished principles and a formalization
of its pre-1900 approach to the Far East. The Open Door represented an attempt to do something about the China situation
when the alternative of force was an impossibility. As Japan
gained ascendancy in Manchuria during the Theodore Roosevelt

administration, the American response was to call attention to the Open Door and concentrate on the protection of the Philippines but to avoid conflict with Japan, since no vital interests were involved in Manchuria. With the exception of President Taft (who tried Dollar Diplomacy as an alternative to force in an attempt to neutralize Japan and promote the Open Door), subsequent administrations based their actions on rather realistic assessments of American interests. The basic fact governing American policy was that the United States had a vital interest in the broader area of the Far East and Pacific but not in China.[3] Notwithstanding the Nine-Power Treaty, no administration was willing to go very far to support China's territorial integrity.

American policy and Hornbeck's own ideas in the 1933–37 period reflected this same "realism." In early 1933 the Far Eastern situation seemed improved because of the truce signed by Japan and China. As Nelson Johnson, American minister to China, put it, the Japanese needed a respite and were simply putting their diplomatic foot forward; in any case they had additional objectives. Proving the U.S. minister's contentions, a spokesman for the Japanese Foreign Office in spring 1934 enunciated a doctrine for eastern Asia that specifically forbade foreign interference in China. Then in 1935 Japan demanded a wide range of concessions in north China south of the Great Wall, including the right to comment on the appointment of Chinese officials in that area, and by the end of the year had secured the creation of an autonomous zone in Hopei and Chahar provinces. The Roosevelt administration, largely on the advice of Hornbeck, changed tactics in dealing with Japanese expansion. It did so not because Stimson's approach was out of accord with U.S. principles but because concern about possible war with Japan led to questioning the wisdom of further protest.

Hornbeck's recommendations in these years hammered at the point of avoiding friction with Japan, ruling out both irritating protests and statements of support for China. When the spokesman of the Japanese Foreign Office Eiji Amau issued a statement on the question of foreign interference in the Sino-Japanese

3. See the essay in this volume on Willard Straight for a contrasting view of United States policy. It should be noted, however, that three decades, reflecting great change in the situation and American attitudes, had elapsed since Theodore Roosevelt and Willard Straight enunciated the goals of American policy.

What About China's Rights in China?

Richmond Times-Dispatch, *1938*

quarrel, Hornbeck drafted an exceedingly mild protest which Secretary of State Cordell Hull ultimately issued. The message stated simply that the United States wanted to be a good neighbor but it was the American view that no nation could "rightfully endeavor to make conclusive its will in situations where there are involved the rights, obligations, and legitimate interests of other states."

In response to suggestions that the United States assist China or even mediate the conflict, Hornbeck took a firmly negative position. In the first place it was impossible to work with a nation like China which in its foreign relations spoke "through a multiplicity of mouths." In the second, to get involved was to risk offending Japan over the wrong issue. When the Chinese requested a loan in 1933 Hornbeck, though not averse to a revival of the consortium idea, advised against a United States loan. The Chinese had not "fulfilled past obligations." Later, as other requests came in, he said that China was a "gimme" country and advised telling the Chinese that the United States was tired of "playing the role of Santa Claus; that we want evidence of a real inclination on the part of debtors to meet their obligations." Hornbeck was clearly not prepared to allow China to become the dominant issue in Japanese-American relations, a principle that became the basis of the Roosevelt administration's policy, demonstrated by the paucity of its assistance to China and the mildness of its response to Japan's actions.

In the period from 1937 to 1941 American policy underwent a transformation from passivity to active opposition to Japan, because Japan's actions in extending the conflict beyond the confines of China and related events in Europe brought vital American interests very much into play. Once he perceived the threat to these interests, Hornbeck, who had long believed in naval preparedness and the futility of anything but force in confronting Japan, took the lead in counseling a more vigorous stance.

When the undeclared war between China and Japan erupted in 1937 American policy makers responded with extreme caution. They refused to mediate the conflict; they refused to give the Chinese any aid and cautioned them not to expect any; and they refused to invoke the Nine-Power Treaty. Secretary of State Hull invoked vague principles and attempted a continued "impartial" approach. Hornbeck was not in substantial disagreement with the

American response. The major debate in the early period of the crisis occurred over application of America's neutrality laws, passed in 1935–37. Hornbeck, who had opposed enactment of this legislation in the first place, advised against its use and was pleased when the administration accepted his point of view.

As fighting in China continued, President Roosevelt in October 1937 gave his famous "quarantine" speech, stating that aggression was like a disease requiring isolation. Soon afterward, in mid-October, the United States consented to attend the Brussels Conference; however, the former sentiment was quickly tempered, and the U.S. delegation at Brussels, which included Hornbeck, was not permitted to commit the United States to the use of economic sanctions. Although a constant element in U.S. Far Eastern policy was protection of American lives and property, in September 1937 the State Department warned Americans that they stayed in China at their own risk, and in December the Japanese sinking of the U.S. gunboat *Panay*, a brutal and wholly unwarranted attack, occasioned what was under the circumstances only a mild response from the Roosevelt administration.

Not long after the *Panay* affair, however, the United States began to alter its attitude; Hornbeck perhaps foreshadowed the change. By the time of the Brussels Conference he began to consider the need to take some action with regard to Japan, "not for humanitarian reasons, not for the sake of American property and interest in China, but because she threatens or will in the long run threaten our security." This is an important point in understanding American policy in the interwar period. Beginning in 1938 the United States began to aid China and stiffen resistance to Japan for reasons closely approximating those mentioned by Hornbeck.

Two areas were of primary concern to American officials after 1938: China and Southeast Asia. Because China became so intertwined in the fabric of American diplomacy, historians have concluded that the United States went to war with Japan in defense of the Open Door there. China, however, was important to Hornbeck, allegedly the most pro-Chinese of all of Hull's advisers, because China could tie Japan down, deplete Japanese resources, and exhaust its will to fight. In short, it would be in America's interest for China to fight Japan. While Japan's aggression was limited to China, moreover, the logical way to confront Japan was through assistance to China. "Better to have Chinese

soldiers continue to fight Japan and take now the small risk,"
Hornbeck stated in 1938 in arguing for a loan to China, than for
the United States to confront a stronger Japan "using the resources
of China in support of her onward march of conquest."

As Japan continued the conquest of China and in November
1938 proclaimed the New Order in East Asia, the United States
considered appropriate responses. Hornbeck recommended several related steps. He continued to promote the naval building
program. "For us, investment in a strong navy will be an investment for peace. Possessed of a strong navy, our position will be
such that no other country will venture to attack us." Reflecting a
harsher view of the situation than in 1932, he also advocated
stopping the flow of all war materials from the United States to
Japan, boycotting Japanese goods, and granting loans and credits
to China. In pursuing the course of economic sanctions, the
United States should also abrogate its 1911 commercial treaty with
Japan. By the end of 1938, in one form or another, most of
Hornbeck's suggestions were adopted: the United States began
a rearmament program, it purchased Chinese silver in large
amounts, and it authorized a Chinese loan of twenty-five million
dollars.

In the following year the Japanese made clear what Hornbeck
and other American policy makers had already begun to discern:
that they planned to extend their aggression beyond the borders
of China. In February they occupied Hainan, an island off the coast
of Indochina, and in March they took the Spratly Islands. These
actions, signaling that a more deliberate southward thrust would
follow, acutely alarmed the State Department. Hornbeck by this
time firmly believed that an "infantile" expansionism possessed
Japan, and no domestic developments would divert Japanese
leaders from this course; therefore, nothing would be lost by going
ahead with the policy best suited to American interests. He
personally favored a program "the opening number of which
would be application of economic sanctions," and, if need be, the
closing number of which "would be use of armed force."

Events in Europe gave Japan unprecedented opportunities in
1940. As Hitler swept through the Netherlands and defeated
France much of the resources-rich Southeast Asian area was
opened up for exploitation. Because of its growing interest in the
war in Europe and because of economic and strategic facts related
to its own existence as an independent nation, the United States

could not view with disinterest the fate of Southeast Asia. Hornbeck grasped this immediately. As a scholar who tried to keep abreast of works relevant to the Far East, he read as widely as time would permit and he frequently informed his colleagues of items of interest. In 1940 he circulated an article within the State Department that reflected his own views and revealed the great significance of the Southeast Asian region. The article, written by Professor Robert Burnett Hall of the University of Michigan and published in the April 1940 issue of the *Geographical Review*, stressed two points: that Southeast Asia possessed more than 90 percent of many raw materials vital to the United States, and that it was the one area of the world to which the United States could not be denied access. "Only on the lands west of the Pacific," Hall concluded, "and especially on Southeastern Asia, is our dependence so vital and complete that our very existence as a great industrial power, and perhaps even as an independent state, is threatened if the sources should be cut off." To Hornbeck, this was "the most interesting, incisive, and concise exposition that I have seen anywhere of the tremendous economic importance, especially to the U.S., of the Far Eastern Area."

Whatever the accuracy of this assessment, the threat posed by Japan's move southward in 1940 created great apprehension about U.S. interests, brought about stringent sanctions, and eventually led to war. In the summer of that year Japan sent a military mission to Indochina, closed the Burma Road, and threatened to move into the Netherlands East Indies; in September it signed the Tripartite Pact with Germany and Italy. Throughout the year Hornbeck continued to press for economic sanctions, including the embargoing of oil. Five years earlier, in fact, he had written his friend Nelson Johnson in China that oil "was the weak point in Japan's strategy," suggesting that when the United States chose to respond, cutting off oil would be a good tactic. With regard to the Netherlands Indies, he later pointed out that not only would a Japanese occupation be particularly harmful to American economic interests but it would allow Japan to obtain oil there, thus weakening the ability of the United States to apply pressure on that country through an embargo. While he advocated sanctions, he also fought vigorously to prevent shifting the fleet from Hawaii to the Atlantic. In sum, Hornbeck in 1940 worked extremely hard for an anti-Japanese policy, which included economic sanctions and, if Japan attacked Singapore, the use of force. So militant did

Hornbeck become in fall 1940 that his colleagues sometimes sought to exclude him from their discussions and Assistant Secretary Breckenridge Long called him a "dangerous man." [4]

The history of United States–Japanese relations in 1941 is a record of recrimination, statement and restatement of conflicting positions, and, because Japan's drive for empire did not abate, progressively applied American sanctions. Hornbeck did his part. Believing now that no chance of real peace existed until Japan had either exhausted its resources or was defeated, he actually opposed any further negotiations. He opposed the Hull-Nomura discussions; he rejected the idea of a meeting between Prime Minister Fumimaro Konoye and President Roosevelt; he disdained any attempt at compromise over the Japanese presence in China in late November. The best course, he believed, was to increase aid to China, which would tie Japan down and drain its strength, and add to the American embargo. As one of the first to advocate freezing Japanese assets, Hornbeck believed that these steps, if properly applied, were likely to bring Japan to its knees.

In the meantime Japan would not attack the United States. As late as 27 November 1941, Hornbeck offered five-to-one odds that the United States and Japan would not be at war on or before 15 December, three-to-one odds that the two countries would not be at war on or before 15 January, and even money that there would be no war on or before 1 March. "The undersigned," he wrote further, "does not believe that this country is now on the immediate verge of war in the Pacific." In a rather hastily conceived analogy, he stated that Japan was like an ass grazing in a field full of rocks and thistles. To the north and south of the field were haystacks, but between the ass and the haystacks were barbed wire fences. The animal had a choice of staying where he was or going against the barbed wire toward the haystacks. Japan, thought Hornbeck, would not go against the barbed wire. Unfortunately, as any country boy would have known, he was as wrong about asses as he was about Japan.

Once the United States became involved in World War II, the focus of American Far Eastern policy, for both military and political

4. Though Secretary Hull was not as militant he was willing to embargo some strategic goods, such as aviation gasoline, and to agree to grant China loans and military aircraft.

reasons, again shifted to China. The optimum hope militarily was
that China would develop an effective fighting force and inflict
heavy casualties on the Japanese; the minimum was that it could
at least remain in the war and continue to tie down over a million
Japanese troops. In the beginning, the United States also thought
that China would be a staging area for bombing and eventually for
an invasion of the Japanese home islands. Politically, the United
States wanted a strong, united, and democratic postwar China able
to take its place as the dominant country in Asia. These objectives
led President Roosevelt to include China in major wartime
conferences, to refer to Chiang Kai-shek as leader of a world
power, and, in short, to assign China a higher status than
warranted by the facts. Several conditions prevented the realization of these goals, among them inefficiency and corruption in
Chiang's government, the internal struggle between the government and the Communists, and the wartime priorities that allotted
most American resources to the war in Europe. The result was that
the effort in China contributed only marginally to the winning of
the war, and that, once the war ended, conflict between the
Communists and Nationalists culminated in a Communist victory.

The tangled situation in China forced consideration of difficult questions in the State Department during the war: how best
to aid Chiang, how to pressure him to reform his government and
his armies, and to what extent the United States should help
compose the differences between his government and the Communists. A basic element in these discussions was the growing
strength of the Communists and concern regarding how to fit
them into American policy. Some officials argued that the United
States ought to support only Chiang's government while encouraging the Communists to cooperate with and accept a place in it.
Others suggested that a more flexible policy would be better,
including aid to the Communists. The administration opted for the
former, though not without some genuine effort at compromise.

As usual, Hornbeck left little doubt where his sympathies lay.
He advocated increased and virtually unconditional support of
Chiang Kai-shek. To those who argued that Chiang's government
was corrupt, he replied that the United States did not scrutinize
the internal workings of other Allied governments. Moreover, the
Chinese had been fighting Japan alone for years and there were
bound to be problems; in any event, support should be given on
the basis of China's engagement of Japanese troops and on the

logic of aid to the legitimate government in power. To those who argued that Chiang's government was dictatorial, he responded that so was Stalin's.

Hornbeck therefore bristled at reports by American Foreign Service officers that detailed elements of decay in Chiang's regime and extolled the comparative virtues of the Communists. In response to one of these messages, he commented, "Seldom if ever have I seen any document prepared by a responsible officer of the Department or of the Foreign Service, of no matter what age or length of experience, expressive of such complete self assurance on the part of the author that he knew the facts, all of the facts . . . and that he could prescribe the remedy. . . . Never before have I encountered so sweeping a charge that almost everything . . . is wrong with China." He went on to point out that he considered the dispatch "irresponsible" and that he had taken time "to refresh my knowledge of its author," an ominous observation.

As events turned out, a military crisis in China in 1944 prompted President Roosevelt to demand that Chiang accept an American as full commander of his armies and that he carry out needed reforms. In sum, the administration now applied the pressure, though as it developed not terribly successfully, that Hornbeck so long remonstrated against. A simultaneous development in Hornbeck's career, perhaps because of his dogmatic insistence on arguing a contrary view, was his appointment as U.S. ambassador to the Netherlands. This position, which Hornbeck held until his retirement in 1947, took him away from Far Eastern problems for the first time in his career, but it did not eradicate his deep and continuing concern about the region. Indeed, assignment in Europe during the critical postwar years imbued Hornbeck with an even deeper hatred of communism and its portents for Asia. Recurring themes in his later lectures and articles were to be the mistakes in American policy during and after the war and the need to maintain a constant vigil against the Communist threat.

Until his death in 1966, Hornbeck remained an active observer of world politics and consequently spent most of his retirement in the study of his Washington apartment researching and writing essays on American foreign policy. Hornbeck deplored the Yalta decisions, opposed postwar American China policy, and supported war in Korea and Vietnam. In the case of Roosevelt's Yalta agreements on the Far East, he believed the United States "bought with Chinese coin unneeded Russian action and worthless Russian pledges." Later, American statesmen "caused the Chinese to buy, with their confirmation, a made-in-Moscow trojan horse." U.S. policy, moreover, accounted in part for the success of the Communists. American leaders, he believed, foolishly accepted certain faulty assumptions: that the Communists were agrarian reformers, that Russian pledges would be honored, and that Chiang's government was corrupt and therefore not worth saving. These assumptions, particularly the last, led to the termination of American aid and the Truman administration's verbal condemnation of Chiang Kai-shek.

Hornbeck believed China should have been included in America's effort to contain the Communist menace. What the Nationalists lacked "were the very things which but for the United States the Greeks also would have lacked, the things but for which Greece would have been overrun by the Communists." This failure to respond to the threat in China was the more deplorable because "a Communist China . . . will be a highway by which . . . Soviet influence will move and Communist armed force be able to strike southward and eastward." As one might expect, Hornbeck later defended support of the Nationalists on Taiwan and opposed the recognition of the People's Republic as "inconsistent" and "damaging" to America's effort "to contain Communism and achieve security." In a 1955 article defending nonrecognition he seemed to be reviving the Stimson Doctrine. The United States could not insist that other states do as it wished or subscribe to its principles; often it had to tolerate conduct it disapproved. "It is, however, under no compulsion to give assent to such. It certainly can refuse to authorize, it can decline to sanction, and it can withhold endorsement."

Just as Hornbeck believed the United States should have resisted Communist expansion in China so he also thought it essential that the United States respond in Korea and Vietnam. In the case of Korea, he thought President Truman's decision to intervene was wise (though it would not have been necessary had the United States prevented the fall of China). Although Hornbeck was no longer as certain of the monolithic nature of communism

by 1950, the expansion of Chinese power and Communist intrusion into Southeast Asia had to be denied. Because Southeast Asia
and the Pacific region constituted vital American interests, it was
as important to prevent the domination of the region by a hostile
power in the 1960s as it was in the late thirties and early forties. To
Hornbeck, therefore, Vietnam, like Korea, was a necessary war.

The focus of Hornbeck's concern with the Far East continued
to be its strategic implications. In the years immediately after
World War II, he had envisaged the Soviet Union replacing Japan
and, using China as an agent, extending its domain in Asia. Later,
he perceived Chinese power as an independent threat. While
Hornbeck was among the staunchest proponents of the Open
Door in public life, he was unwilling to back the principle with
force in its specific application to China until after the Second
World War and even then thought that assistance to Chiang would
achieve U.S. aims. Moreover, in the late forties and fifties
Hornbeck became concerned less with the traditional Open Door
and more with thwarting Communist expansion and maintaining
American access in a broader sense. As an internationalist, he
believed (along with most of his generation) that the major lesson
of the thirties was that democracies could not allow "aggression"
to succeed.

Patrick Gallagher of the *New York World* once said of
diplomat Henry White that "his heart beats for the Open Door."
He may well have said the same of Hornbeck, though it is doubtful
that Hornbeck's perception of the concept would have accorded
with Gallagher's. In any event, an assessment of Hornbeck's career
offers insight into the real meaning and significance of the Open
Door, indicating that it was more an ideal than a policy. As Philip
Moseley once observed, "hope divorced from power is not a
policy." In its application to China Hornbeck thought the Open
Door simply "a declaration of intentions" in support of the
principles of equality of commercial opportunity and a necessary
corollary, respect for China's territorial integrity. These principles
had not been discovered on the spur of the moment. "The
doctrine of equality of commercial opportunity had behind it a
century and a quarter of American diplomatic expression and
effort; it required no explanation to the American people; it was
representative of the average American's conception of justice
and of his own and other countries' rights." American policy was
shaped by the belief that "free states should remain free." In this

respect, Hornbeck believed, "the Far Eastern policy of the United States has sprung from the same root in American thought from which sprang the Monroe Doctrine in relation to the Western Hemisphere." The United States opposed "imperial adventure or partition" and possessed the right to make clear its opposition.

As the foregoing suggests, Hornbeck saw the Open Door not only as it related to China, but as the expression of a broader dimension of American foreign policy. The Open Door to him was a perfect reflection of the American system, way of life, and approach to foreign affairs; its roots were deep in the nation's past. "In the realm of formulated effort," he wrote, "the principal major objective of American policy since the earliest days of the Republic has been to ensure for American nationals and for American trade equality of opportunity. . . . The 'open door' doctrine in its two phases, equality of opportunity and the integrity of the state in regard to which it is applied, is the cornerstone of American foreign policy." On another occasion, Hornbeck cited Secretary of State Charles Evans Hughes's statement to the effect that the broadest principles of American foreign policy were simple. The United States did not covet territory, special economic influence, or control of others. "We wish to protect the just and equal rights of Americans everywhere in the world. We wish to maintain equality of commercial opportunity; as we call it, the open door." Because the Open Door policy was an extension of and was so closely tied to America's institutions, moreover, it could not be altered or changed lightly, not even in the face of Japan's thrust in the thirties.

This view of the Open Door is especially interesting in light of a provocative interpretation of that policy currently accepted by some scholars, that the functional needs of the American economic system have forced the United States to pursue an expansionist course, and that this expansionism has been expressed not in the acquisition of colonies or formal empire but through a persistent policy of demanding access to markets and raw materials and freedom of enterprise. Thus, America's twentieth-century world objectives, as manifested in the Open Door, have been hegemonical in nature and are equated with the interests of capitalism. With regard to China and other underdeveloped states, the policy dictated insistence on commercial and investment opportunities and opposition to nationalism and revolution.

There are some similarities and many differences between Hornbeck's Open Door and the one constructed by this interpretation. Clearly, Hornbeck believed that the Open Door had roots deep in the American domestic system. He also considered it a perfect expression of American commercial policy everywhere in the world. Moreover, in terms of policy recommendations, his interest in Southeast Asia and the Pacific in the late thirties and early forties partially reflected a concern for the continuing access and freedom of enterprise on the part of the United States. The same could be said about his postwar response to Communist power in both Europe and Asia. One can find numerous statements in Hornbeck's articles and speeches that reflect his fear of a world closed to American commercial activity; these help explain his support of U.S. actions during the cold war.

Further examination of Hornbeck's views, however, suggests the inadequacy of defining the Open Door simply as an expression of policy growing out of the needs of capitalism. No one was more devoted to the concept than he; yet he was willing to acquiesce in some of the demands of Chinese nationalism in the 1920s. At any rate, other American policy makers did go a considerable distance in implementing a liberal approach to China. In the thirties he refused to consider confronting Japan as long as the Japanese limited their activity to China. In short the Open Door in China was not important enough to warrant a fight. What this suggests is that because he refused a priori to sanction the means necessary to back the principles he so admired, to Hornbeck (and in fact the conclusion extends to nearly all American statesmen) the Open Door in the case of China existed at the level of aspiration rather than policy.

It could be argued that once Japan threatened to move southward Hornbeck counseled the use of force rather than acquiescence in Japanese take-over of a region vital to U.S. economic interests and that after World War II he advocated forceful action for similar reasons. The significant point, however, is not that he proposed to get tough rather than suffer limitations on U.S. access, but rather the reason for his concern. A study of Hornbeck's career reveals only a limited regard for American economic interests. These interests did not lead him to advocate action in China, and they were only partially responsible for his apprehensions about Southeast Asia. There is little evidence that such considerations determined his anticommunism or his post-

World War II demand for an open world. Hornbeck believed open access and a congenial world to be important to the nation's economic well-being, but far more vital was the guarantee of U.S. physical security and the defense of liberal democratic principles.

The basic element in understanding Hornbeck's conception of American foreign relations is national pride. The United States was morally and politically superior to other nations, for its domestic institutions manifested fair play, equity, and the freedom and dignity of the individual. Because the Open Door arose from these ideals, it in fact constituted the alignment of the United States with principles of fairness and equity in international relations. Notwithstanding the sophistication of his specific recommendations or the complex analyses he sometimes presented, Hornbeck's views were essentially simple, they were consistent, and they flowed directly from his deep faith in and love of his country.

BIBLIOGRAPHIC NOTE

The Stanley K. Hornbeck papers are available to scholars at the Hoover Institution, Stanford University. The Nelson T. Johnson papers, Library of Congress, are an important source for a study of Far Eastern policy in the twenties and thirties, as are the Henry Stimson papers at Yale and the Cordell Hull papers at the Library of Congress. All of these have been instrumental in this interpretation of Hornbeck. The *Foreign Relations* volumes are vital to a study of any phase of American foreign relations as are the State Department records located in the National Archives. For the forties, materials from the Franklin D. Roosevelt papers at Hyde Park and the Patrick J. Hurley papers, University of Oklahoma, were also useful. Hornbeck made his views public from time to time through speeches, journal articles, and books, many of which are cited in the text of the essay. These provide a fairly comprehensive statement of his beliefs and concerns.

Because Hornbeck's career coincided with an eventful period in United States–Far Eastern relations, the secondary literature is abundant and continues to grow. For the deliberations at Versailles two of the most substantial studies are Roy Watson Curry, *Woodrow Wilson and Far Eastern Policy, 1913–1921* (New York, 1957), and Russell Fifield, *Woodrow Wilson and the Far East: The Diplomacy of the Shantung Question* (New York, 1952). On the twenties one should consult Thomas Buckley, *The United States and the Washington Conference 1921–1922* (Knoxville, 1970), Dorothy Borg, *American Policy and the Chinese Revolution,*

1925–1928 (New York, 1947), and Akira Iriye, *After Imperialism: The Search for a New Order in the Far East, 1921–1931* (Cambridge, Mass., 1965).

The Manchurian crisis has received considerable scholarly attention. The best books on this phase of United States Far Eastern policy are Robert H. Ferrell, *American Diplomacy in the Great Depression: Hoover-Stimson Foreign Policy, 1929–1933* (New Haven, 1957), Armin Rappaport, *Henry L. Stimson and Japan* (Chicago, 1963), Richard N. Current, *Secretary Stimson: A Study in Statecraft* (New Brunswick, N.J., 1954), and Elting E. Morison, *Turmoil and Tradition: A Study of the Life and Times of Henry L. Stimson* (Boston, 1960). Dorothy Borg's excellent study, *The United States and the Far Eastern Crisis, 1933–1938* (Cambridge, Mass., 1964), is the authoritative book on the mid-thirties.

For Japanese-American relations and the approach of war, two standard works are Herbert Feis, *The Road to Pearl Harbor* (Princeton, 1950), and Paul Schroeder, *The Axis Alliance and Japanese-American Relations* (Ithaca, 1958). Waldo Heinrichs's *American Ambassador: Joseph C. Grew and the Development of the United States Diplomatic Tradition* (Boston, 1966) provides an excellent account of an important figure in American Far Eastern policy during the same period.

There have been several studies of Sino-American relations in the forties. Those dealing most satisfactorily with the complicated aspects of American policy are Tang Tsou, *America's Failure in China, 1941–1950* (Chicago, 1963), and Herbert Feis, *The China Tangle* (Princeton, 1953). Barbara Tuchman's *Stilwell and the American Experience in China* (New York, 1971) is a superb biography of a controversial figure. Russell D. Buhite's *Patrick J. Hurley and American Foreign Policy* (Ithaca, 1973) adds insight into the activities of Hurley in China.

THE MASKS OF POWER:

FRANKLIN D. ROOSEVELT

Reproduced from the collections of the Library of Congress

and the Conduct of
American Diplomacy

Theodore A. Wilson and Richard D. McKinzie

Almost three decades after his death, the personality of Franklin D. Roosevelt still broods, sphinxlike, over the landscape of United States diplomacy. Few contemporary problems and achievements can be explained without recourse to the decisions of America's thirty-second president. During Roosevelt's tenure in the White House from 1933 to 1945, the United States shrugged off traditional restraints of indifference, isolation, and insecurity; by April 1945, when death swept FDR from office, the nation had assumed a stance in world affairs more consonant with its economic, military, and political strength. Franklin Roosevelt himself set in motion some, and presided over all, of the decisions that moved America from a position of relative unimportance in world politics to one approaching global domination.

FDR was a focus of controversy throughout his brilliant career; however, after his death the partisans in an enduring

155

historical debate assigned greater significance to his actions than either admirers or critics attributed to them during his lifetime. Some historians have credited President Roosevelt with almost superhuman abilities, arguing that, had he lived, he would have avoided the errors—of omission, commission, and suspicion—that blighted wartime Allied cooperation and ultimately generated the cold war. Others, equally credulous, have asserted that FDR was solely responsible for divers misguided or evil acts, such as luring Japan into the Pearl Harbor attack and selling out Eastern Europe to the Soviet Union, to cite but two examples.

The intellectual community did not seriously question the view of FDR as a bold, farsighted president for nearly two decades. Only in recent years have scholars attacked the judgment that Roosevelt was a dynamic leader. While asserting that FDR was the principal architect of U.S. policy during his tenure, some have concluded that he was indecisive and excessively cautious, even timid. As Robert Divine has written: "Franklin Roosevelt's claim to greatness must rest on his achievements in domestic affairs. His conduct of foreign policy never equalled his mastery of American politics and his ability to guide the nation through the perils of depression and war." Divine's widely read book emphasizes Roosevelt's flexibility and sense of realism rather than the personal qualities stressed in earlier accounts. Many recent studies (on such topics as neutrality, lend-lease, unconditional surrender, and foreign economic policy) have virtually ignored the factor of presidential influence, because of ideological presumptions or bafflement as to the workings of FDR's mind, "that heavily-forested interior." Even in works with such pervasive themes as American economic expansion and national interests, FDR figures only as an unknown or neutral factor.

It would seem that victory in the long debate has gone, perhaps by default, to proponents of the view that Franklin D. Roosevelt was "an accidental hero." Many years ago, in his brilliant analysis of individual responsibility, *The Hero in History*, Sidney Hook disqualified FDR as a "true" hero. Instead, he was a man whirled to the surface by events, who for a time circled in the vortex of history and whose lasting influence was an accident of time and location rather than an individual reordering of historical forces.

Beyond that insight, a generation of scholarship has left almost untouched the central mystery of FDR's influence. The dominant explanation in foreign affairs—and, to a lesser degree, domestic politics—today is about what it was during Roosevelt's lifetime; the essence of this explanation is dichotomy. FDR was at once "both lion and fox," a man possessing an unclouded, realistic grasp of human weakness and capacity for error, and also a passionate awareness of humanity's potential nobility. In simple terms, FDR was both pragmatist and idealist; he was a remarkably skilled politician and a functioning idealist. To an amazing extent, discussions of Roosevelt's beliefs and actions boil down to a simple equation: FDR = TR + WW; that is, he combined the political skills and realism of his cousin Theodore Roosevelt with the visionary idealism of Woodrow Wilson, under whom he had served and whose portrait he kept in the Oval Office in the White House.[1]

FDR's "success" or "failure" in any circumstance thus depends on his "batting average," the number of times he correctly identified a situation as demanding a practical response (and, conversely, the frequency with which he hit away for idealism). Some have judged his batting eye well-nigh perfect. FDR's sense of timing occasionally deserted him, because he misread signals from his manager, public opinion (for example, during the court-packing fight of 1937 and the debate over intervention in 1940–41), because he accepted bad advice from teammates (such as the decisions on unconditional surrender and the second front), or merely because advancing age dimmed his eye and slowed those marvelous reflexes. Still, he remains the "Sultan of Swat" in American diplomacy, and the suspicion persists that, if he had not been abruptly yanked from the game, the United States would have swept the world series of postwar negotiations.

Unhappily, the pragmatist-idealist hypothesis does not contribute much to understanding this complex man and the decisions he managed. Though not a false issue, a Dr. Jekyll–Mr. Hyde explanation (success being assessed in terms of the observer's definition of good and evil) is superficial and misleading.

---

1. This interpretation has been revived and glitteringly refurbished by James McGregor Burns, whose two-volume biography, *Roosevelt: The Lion and the Fox* (New York, 1956) and *Roosevelt: The Soldier of Freedom* (New York, 1970), is the most perceptive study of FDR. For an insightful critique of the Burns thesis, see Robert Dallek, "Franklin Roosevelt as World Leader," *American Historical Review* 76 (December 1971), 1503–13.

In common with the vast majority of human beings, FDR wore not two faces but an infinite variety. These masks reflected good intentions but at the same time obscured and delineated other less rational and amorphous feelings. He changed these masks for reasons he himself may not have understood clearly.

In the case of presidential motivation, James Barbour has written: "Like any person facing extreme uncertainty, the President seeks within himself some ground of continuity, some identity he can recognize as his way of being. That identity is inseparable from his personal history; he senses what he is in large measure by what he was and by what he hopes yet to be. A moment's introspection will confirm that we tend to respond to new challenges with old habits—of belief, of feeling, and of action." Political leaders are extraordinarily skilled at concealing their inner feelings, so disciplined that the masks they wear appear to be and may become reality. This makes analysis of their psychological development necessary; indeed, if it is valid to say that political ambition is grounded in a need for ego gratification so great as to be compulsive, understanding the psychology of men such as Franklin D. Roosevelt is essential.

The screens President Roosevelt erected around his motives have proved remarkably durable, and few historians have endeavored to penetrate the elaborate network of rhetoric, jocular remarks, and obfuscation. Obviously, in common with his generation and his class, he held convictions about the nature of American society and America's proper role in world affairs; however, these beliefs did not comprise a rigid, all-encompassing definition of the limits within which he functioned. If, indeed, FDR possessed a *Weltanschauung,* it was only one of various factors shaping his response to men and events. For him, it seemed that each day brought a new world to conquer; each day a different FDR arose to begin the conquest.

One could arrange the facts of Franklin Roosevelt's life to conform to a mechanical formula for becoming president and contend that from birth he was destined for the White House. He certainly had numerous advantages: wealth and social position, physical attractiveness, an engaging personality, family influence in national politics, an "Eastern Establishment" education, and a dramatic struggle with disease that earned him sympathy and admiration. Superficially, at least, the progress of his career—New York state senator, assistant secretary of the navy, Democratic vice-presidential nominee, two-term governor of New York, landslide victor in the presidential election of 1932, and subsequent reelection to an unprecedented four terms—bespeaks a rendezvous with destiny. Nonetheless, such a construction is too facile. It misrepresents FDR's personal goals and the manner of his emergence as a figure of national and international importance. Doubtless the ambition for power always existed, but, as Roosevelt himself often admitted, his political successes were largely a matter of accident.[2]

Franklin D. Roosevelt was born 30 January 1882 at the family estate on the east bank of the Hudson just outside the quiet village of Hyde Park, New York. His father James, a comfortably fixed Dutch patrician, was a fifty-two-year-old widower at the time he married Sara Delano. The bride, exactly half his age, had overridden the vehement opposition of her doting father to wed his neighbor and business associate. This late autumn–early summer union, one may speculate, greatly affected the psychological development of FDR, the marriage's only issue.

The Hyde Park Roosevelts were as close to "country gentry" as America could provide, having possessed modest wealth and high social status for several generations. James Roosevelt, a man of stern mien and unimpeachable dignity (muttonchop whiskers, top hat, and cane), considered himself above all else a gentleman farmer. He served as vice-president of the Delaware and Hudson Canal Company, which had investments in anthracite coal, and as director of several other companies. Except for the panic of 1873, speculative ventures might have won him domination of the eastern coal industry. After this reverse, he settled down to be the squire of Hyde Park. He was "wealthy enough to have his own railroad car, eccentric enough to keep five hundred dollars in gold always handy, established enough to refuse an invitation from the *nouveaux riches* Vanderbilts." His was a life of family dinners,

---

2. Biographers have emphasized various factors, but no one as yet has explained how and why FDR aspired to high political office. Notably, James Barbour, whose recent work *Presidential Character* (New York, 1972) contains an interesting essay on Roosevelt, labels him an "active-positive" president but does not attempt to plumb the wellsprings of his ambition.

clubs, quickly consummated business deals, and quiet participation in community and philanthropic projects. Sara Delano Roosevelt, excluded from much of her husband's life, found satisfaction as mistress of the household and in molding the development of her only child. She was a formidable person on many counts, but on none was she more dogmatic than the code of "proper behavior" she imposed on her son.

The environment in which "little Franklin" grew up was that of upper-class Victorian America at its zenith. "In the long shelf of the biographies of American Presidents," a Roosevelt scholar asserted some years ago, "one searches in vain for the story of a childhood so serene and secure." Both James and Sara Roosevelt doted on their only child, though FDR's mother assumed principal responsibility for his welfare. Young Franklin never lacked material things; there were elaborate toys, hobbies, a pony, a twenty-one-foot sailboat on his sixteenth birthday. The Roosevelts kept an apartment in New York City and a summer place on Campobello Island, New Brunswick. FDR first visited Europe as a two-year-old and returned several times before reaching his teens.

By all accounts he was surrounded with love and companionship, but for most of his formative years it was adult love and adult companionship. As a result, he learned early to respond to grown-ups in ways they preferred, to act mature beyond his years. Sara Roosevelt's protectiveness of her "little man" was suffocating. She kept her son in dresses until he was five, shielded him from "common" children, and schooled him at home. FDR's dependence on his mother survived his marriage and even his accession to the presidency. The story is told that when a local politician came to ask thirty-two-year-old Franklin Roosevelt whether he would run for the state assembly, FDR responded with enthusiasm.

"But," he said, "I'd like to talk to my mother about it first."

"Frank," his visitor replied, "there are men back in Poughkeepsie waiting for your answer. They won't like to hear you had to ask your mother."

FDR gulped and said, "I'll do it."

There were, of course, minor and major rebellions—his decision to marry Eleanor Roosevelt, a love affair with his wife's social secretary, Lucy Mercer, reentry into politics after a nearly fatal bout with polio—but they were in a sense irrelevant. FDR was accustomed to having his way; he gained it by adjusting his wishes to the stronger will of others or by persuading others, less determined than he, that satisfying his wishes was what they really wanted. The point is not that FDR possessed a domineering personality (which he did) or that he allowed others to protect and fawn over him (which he did); it is rather that his relationship with Sara Roosevelt (and to a lesser degree his father) conditioned him at an early age to rely upon a unique repertoire of responses and methods with which he dealt with the world. His upbringing seems to have given him no interest in ideas as contrasted with people, extreme flexibility, reliance on indirection and postpone- ment, and tolerance of disorder. Above all, he became accus- tomed to seeing himself as the center of his universe.

The demands placed on FDR by his parents were social and familial. Beyond good manners and respect for one's elders, little was asked, though much was assumed. "Study law as I did," his father advised. "It prepares a man for a profession." FDR's profession was to be that of gentleman. Anything else was extra. Sara Roosevelt inculcated a sense of *noblesse oblige,* a recognition that "from those to whom much is given, much is expected"; but what this meant was never explained, and the future president apparently interpreted it to mean that he should play the role of plain citizen whenever appropriate. It was certainly a simple part to master, much less challenging than most of the numerous other roles he would be called upon to play.

FDR's childhood passed without apparent trauma in this atmosphere of benevolent authority. The first break came at age fourteen when he left home for Groton, best known of that peculiar New England institution, the "prep" school. Groton's founder and headmaster, the Reverend Endicott Peabody, preached and taught a life of active, responsible Christianity, and he laced the school curriculum with heavy doses of competitive athletics and Episcopalianism. His credo was service to God and mankind, tinged with a genteel brand of Social Darwinism. Peabody set out to make his charges the agents of social betterment. His "was the faith of a man of action, a spiritual athlete, rather than a contemplative scholar, and Roosevelt came to accept it as his own," Frank Freidel has written.

Because Roosevelt was two years older than his classmates (his mother had held him back), he found adjustment difficult. He encountered problems with "interpersonal relationships," which he resolved by trying to become a stereotypical Grotonian, singing in the choir, debating, taking his lumps on the scrub football team, even rejoicing over black marks for deportment. He worked hard at being accepted by his peers, adding yet another role to his repertoire, though this was not his best performance. The courses he took at Groton were dull when not stultifying, and FDR found no reason to achieve above the level of a "gentleman's C."

In 1900 Roosevelt went on to Harvard, where he performed competently in academic work, but devoted more attention to social opportunities and extracurricular activities. "Am doing a little studying, a little riding, and a few party calls," he wrote his mother. It does not appear that Sara Roosevelt cramped her son's style when she took an apartment in Cambridge after James Roosevelt's death during FDR's freshman year. He enrolled in the liberal arts program, but his instructors never fired him with intellectual curiosity. He complained that the curriculum was "like an electric lamp that hasn't any wire," and later remarked, "I took economics courses in college for four years and everything I was taught was wrong." Harvard's defects combined with Roosevelt's lack of interest yielded a mediocre education. To the extent that FDR took away from Harvard any social and political philosophy, it was "a mixture of political conservatism, economic orthodoxy, and anti-imperialism, steeped in a fuzzy altruism and wide ignorance." The same might be said of his views thirty years later, after he became president.

Roosevelt was active in the Harvard Glee Club and worked on the undergraduate daily, *The Crimson*, becoming editor in chief during his junior year. His greatest disappointment, which some biographers identify as the root cause of his political ambition, was not being tapped for Porcellian, the leading social club on campus, to which his famous cousin Theodore Roosevelt had belonged. For once, family connections and geniality failed to smooth the way. Eleanor Roosevelt later stated that this rebuff gave FDR an inferiority complex, and another relative termed it "the bitterest moment of his life." Its effects upon his personality and social views is unclear, though one may speculate that the experience, in combination with the insecurity caused by the difficulties he encountered at Groton and Harvard, drove him to shield his desires and encouraged a habit of not risking his self-esteem except on the safest of bets.

The characteristics of FDR's personality, the "repertoire of habits" with which he dealt with life, were formed by the time of his graduation from Harvard in 1904. He attended Columbia Law School, passed the New York bar in 1907, and joined an old Wall Street law firm. These were years of drifting, during which almost his only independent act was the decision to marry his fifth cousin Eleanor Roosevelt in spite of his mother's outraged and tearful objections. Sara lost this battle for her son's affection, but appears, ultimately, to have won the war.

FDR drifted into politics in 1910, by chance discovering his true vocation. He won election to the state senate from Dutchess County by ignoring partisan issues and playing up his relationship with "Uncle" TR. His swift rise to a position of leadership in Albany, despite his having the appearance of a "political prig," resulted from hard work, humor, lack of concern about issues and party lines, and a large element of luck. He seemed to be auditioning for "dynamic young politician," and since it brought him to center stage, even if in a provincial theater, he enjoyed the part.

In 1913, as payment for his energetic support of Woodrow Wilson's presidential campaign, Secretary of the Navy Josephus Daniels offered Roosevelt the position of assistant secretary. Always fascinated by the sea and aware of the parallels to be drawn with TR's career, he accepted enthusiastically. "I'd like it bully well," he told Daniels. This decision propelled him into a world vastly different from the one he had known, leading to broader perspectives and new challenges.

FDR sought out kindred spirits in Washington, members of old families who were beginning to accept government service as a civic duty, rather than as a function of *noblesse oblige*. The ingrained feeling of superiority natural to a Hyde Park Roosevelt continued to be present. When war broke out in Europe, FDR no longer could control himself. "I am running the real work" of the Navy Department, he wrote his wife, "although Josephus is here! He is bewildered by it all, very sweet, but very sad!" Between 1916 and 1919 he concentrated on improving the navy's efficiency, tinkering with administration but not proposing serious reforms. He was competent, visible, and accessible to the press, which was intrigued by this quotable, photogenic young man, especially since he was a Roosevelt.

When a few voices raised his name as a presidential candidate in 1920, Roosevelt moved to squelch the movement. It was not that he rejected the idea of becoming president, but rather that the possibility of his nomination and election was a long shot. "I can tell you . . . perfectly frankly," he wrote a friend, "that I do not propose to make an early Christian martyr of myself this year." Less stigma attached to a losing vice-presidential candidate and Roosevelt happily accepted the offer of the second place on the ticket when the Democratic party held its convention. During the campaign he proved more popular than the lackluster standard-bearer, James M. Cox. He spoke eloquently for U.S. participation in the League of Nations and for a return to prewar progressivism; but his voter appeal was personal. Reporters described him as "almost the poster type in public life" and "the figure of an idealized football player." They conceded that people were more taken with the man than with anything he said. That the Republicans won the election of 1920 was much less the result of candidates' actions than it was of the actions of President Woodrow Wilson.

In any case, before FDR had much time to brood over his party's defeat or plot his next move, physical catastrophe struck him. Vacationing with Eleanor and their five children at the family retreat on Campobello, FDR was suddenly seized with chills and stiffness. Within hours docors had diagnosed his affliction as poliomyelitis. Roosevelt, who prized physical strength and virility, had lost muscular control of his legs. All his biographers have described his mental and physical agony over the next few years, though they make light of his mother's insistence that he renounce public life and live out his days in genteel seclusion at Hyde Park. Some insist that the tragedy had beneficial results. Frances Perkins, later his secretary of labor, stated: "Franklin Roosevelt underwent a spiritual transformation during the years of his illness. I noticed when he came back that the years of pain and suffering had purged the slightly arrogant attitude. The man emerged completely warmhearted, with humility of spirit and a deeper philosophy. Having been to the depths of trouble he understood the problems of people in trouble." One could as easily argue that the changes others saw in FDR resulted from greater maturity, the adjustment of his public facade to conform to the expectations others had of a cripple, or a calculated appraisal of how he could use his infirmity to further his political career.

Roosevelt never seriously considered a future as a pampered invalid, and he slowly reentered political life. Perhaps the most important effect of his illness, recuperation, and slow return to politics was that the currents of the 1920s passed him by. FDR was preoccupied with his own problems; *The Wasteland*, the KKK's nativism-run-amok, or the vacuous hedonism of flappers and jellybeans never challenged his amorphous beliefs in the old ethics and values. The public demonstration that his handicap would not deter his career came at the Democratic convention in 1924. Clenching the rostrum to support his upper body and relying on eleven pounds of steel bracing to steady his legs, Roosevelt placed in nomination his fellow New Yorker, Alfred E. Smith. By 1928, he was ready to run for governor of New York. Though indebted to Alfred Smith for his victory, FDR set his own course in Albany. In some areas he acted boldly, assembling a "brain trust" to deal with the problems the depression rained on New York in 1929. Yet every decision was made with an eye to its national implications, for FDR and practically everyone else considered his two terms as governor an apprenticeship for the presidency.

FDR won the Democratic nomination on the first ballot in 1932. Running against Herbert Hoover, he took the safest course, giving voters a chance to vote against the man who had failed to end the depression. In large part he relied on his personal magnetism. Arthur M. Schlesinger, Jr., has noted that "people began to look for the Roosevelt characteristics; the upthrust head; the confidential look with eyebrows arched when he let fly a gibe at the opposition, followed by the slow grin as the audience caught on; the sly mockery; the biting scorn; the righteous wrath." Roosevelt promised a "New Deal" to the American people, but he rarely talked about specific changes; these could be criticized. (Another reason for vagueness was that no New Deal reform program existed.) He evaded sensitive questions and sometimes contradicted himself. The champion of the League of Nations in 1920 told an audience in his home state: "American participation in the League would not serve the highest purpose of the prevention of war and a settlement of international difficulties in accordance with fundamental American ideals. . . . I do not favor American participation." Driven frantic by the shifting views of his opponent, Hoover labeled FDR a "chameleon on plaid"; and so, within a limited spectrum of political colors and ethical motifs, he was.

James McGregor Burns has posed the central question about Roosevelt: "Was there then no hard center, no core personality, no final commitment in this man?" Burns concludes that a nexus of deeply held beliefs did exist under that "bright, smooth flow of talk," that President Roosevelt, for all his deviousness, was "basically a moral man. . . . He believed in doing good, in showing other people how to do good, and he assumed that ultimately people would do good. By 'good' he meant the Ten Commandments and the Golden Rule as interpreted by Endicott Peabody." It is possible that when Roosevelt voiced these teachings of his youth he was merely assuming another role, putting on another mask. Even if a compulsion to "do good" lay at the center of his being, was that a sufficient guide for a man faced with a devastating economic depression, the complexities of global politics, a shattering war? FDR was not and did not pretend to be an original thinker. He possessed in abundance a gift for using men and their ideas to his own advantage and for expressing in simple language the complicated arguments of others.

The absence of commitment and of logically derived views was especially apparent in his approach to foreign affairs. FDR, as noted, possessed no "world view," no inner world of ideas and assumptions, except perhaps in the most general sense. His ideas regarding foreign affairs justifiably may be termed unsophisticated, and on some vital issues he had no opinions at all. When he entered the White House, his views on foreign affairs were a mishmash of "family tradition," half-assimilated theories picked up at Harvard and Washington cocktail parties, and conversations with fellow politicians. The touchstone was belief that the United States must take an active role in world affairs. From Theodore Roosevelt he inherited faith in a strong navy and all that implied; yet Democratic forebears instilled in him an emotional rejection of "imperialism" and colonial regimes. Those views he did advocate tenaciously were almost all taken from childhood experiences and impressions. A summer spent in a German *Volksschule,* along with bicycling excursions through the countryside, persuaded FDR that he knew everything required to deal wisely with Germany; during the Second World War, almost every person who raised with the president the thorny problem of Germany's future was subjected to an involved reminiscence about FDR's youthful adventures, capped by a claim of presidential omniscience on the basis of these experiences. Similarly, Roosevelt based his assertion of superior knowledge about Asian policy on recollections of his grandfather Delano's participation in the China trade in the mid-nineteenth century.

Attachment to "internationalism" was another of Roosevelt's convictions, though he refused to define—either for himself or others—what that implied for the nation's foreign policy. Although he much admired the dream of Woodrow Wilson, FDR faulted him for his failure to make the dream reality. Apparently, FDR concluded that the earlier president had tried for too much too fast, had been too trusting, not hard enough, too fuzzy headed. According to one scholar, he believed that "war must still be the touchstone of policy in foreign affairs. At thirty Roosevelt was a worshiping Wilsonian. Into middle age he espoused a world order under a union of nations; but unlike Wilson, the evangelist, while pursuing peace, he never neglected military preparedness." He came to advocate what he termed "realistic" methods of achieving world order, scoffing at the Kellogg-Briand Pact, refusing to support the World Court, and arguing that the United States must go its own way in meeting the Great Depression. Not surprisingly, his attitudes regarding international relations were egocentric, nationalistic, and paternalistic. Other nations should accept the moral leadership of the United States, because it was right, necessary, and "realistic" for them to do so. Internationalism for him, as for many other American leaders in this era, became a justification for U.S. activism in world affairs, and not a program of specific measures to attain lasting peace.

Oddly coexisting with this "realistic approach" were several secondary Wilsonian principles. One was faith in the efficacy of disarmament. As he told Adolf A. Berle, Jr., in June 1941: "Don't forget that the elimination of costly armaments is still the keystone—for the security of all the little nations and for economic solvency. Don't forget what I discovered—that over ninety percent of all national deficits from 1921 to 1939 were caused by payments for past, present, and future wars." He held similar opinions about the theoretical desirability of an economic open world, a return to that "golden age" of free trade invented by classical economists.

One might pile up a list of particulars to prove that the president held opinions on various issues in U.S. foreign policy, that "FDR said X," "FDR supported Y," "FDR read Z" (though that would be more difficult); but it would be a meaningless exercise. His mind essentially was a *tabula rasa*. Compelled to play roles, Roosevelt seems to have been incapable of carrying out prior analyses of problems and taking stands on the basis of his conclusions; nor did he wish to do so. A well-meaning friend once told him that the New Deal was analogous to a great painting; therefore, like a great artist when his best work was almost finished, he should retouch the painting here and there, perfecting it, and then offer the masterpiece to posterity. The president rejected the analogy: "There 'ain't no such thing' as a masterpiece of permanence in the art of living or the art of government. That type of art catches a mood, fits the method of expression into the emotions of the day and mingles oils with watercolors, and steel engraving with dry point." On another occasion Eleanor Roosevelt brought up the question of religious education for their children. FDR replied that they should attend church and learn what he had learned.

"But are you sure you believe in everything you learned?" she asked.

"I really never thought about it," he admitted. "I think it is just as well not to think about things like that."

To analyze his own beliefs might inhibit the flexibility he so valued, and, besides, action resulted from responses to people, not abstractions. Roosevelt trusted his intuition to grasp what others wanted of him, and he was confident of his ability to satisfy their perceptions. He could be TR or Wilson or John Q. Citizen. His enormous versatility and dramatic skill, after all, had brought him to the presidency. Why should he concern himself thereafter with finding and projecting an "authentic" Franklin Roosevelt? Not only would it be a tiresome exercise, it might well flop.

Had the international scene remained relatively quiet during FDR's presidency, it is possible that isolationism would have characterized American diplomacy. This might have occurred in spite of the deeper forces pushing the United States toward world leadership and despite President Roosevelt's distaste for a less than preeminent role for himself and the country. The incoming president looked out on a world in political and economic disarray. The global depression in some ways had increased the importance of the United States in international affairs. Economic disaster forced the admission in European capitals that American participation was essential in efforts to restore a viable world economy and political stability. Yet the depression also turned the

AND COMPANY ALREADY ARRIVING

J. N. Ding Foundation. First published in Des Moines Register

American public inward and restricted the freedom of action of those responsible for foreign policy.[3]

Lacking a consensus, FDR attempted to ignore foreign affairs for much of his first term. He concentrated on domestic problems, where a consensus did exist, where individuals and groups across the spectrum of American politics were begging him to act boldly. Nothing comparable existed in the realm of foreign affairs. FDR confessed in early 1934: "In the present European situation, I feel very much as if I were groping for a door in a blank wall. The situation may get better and enable us to give some leadership." As a result, the United States swung to and fro between partnership in and boycott of the world community. Decisions such as the Roosevelt-Litvinov Agreements, ending America's paranoid refusal to recognize the existence of Soviet Russia, were in keeping with a sort of passive pragmatism. FDR's own opinion of the Soviet experiment reflected skepticism and disdain, but as always political calculations outweighed his personal views.

In May 1933 the president stepped forward with a plan to assure peace, a forthright appeal to world leaders to sign a nonaggression pact, renounce all weapons of offensive war, and curb arms production. Violent opposition abroad and in the Senate caused him to back down. Concluding that any attempt to realize other Wilsonian dreams, such as American enrollment in organizations for international cooperation, would similarly arouse the isolationist coalition, he opted for another Wilsonian trademark, watchful waiting. He deferred to Congress in the question of war debts, cooperated with the Nye Committee's investigation of arms trade and manufacture, and acquiesced in the passage of neutrality legislation that implicitly blamed Woodrow Wilson for American entry into the First World War. It may be, as Robert Divine has argued, that Roosevelt did these things from conviction and that until 1937 he believed isolationism was the only practical course for the United States. More likely, however, this "foreign policy by makeshift" stemmed from the inability of the public to cue him to any other response and to the fluctuating influence of his ideologically diverse advisers.

3. Whether the situation in foreign affairs would have been susceptible to aggressive leadership is moot. The pressures affecting U.S. diplomacy at this juncture are well described in Robert H. Ferrell, *American Diplomacy in the Great Depression* (New Haven, 1957).

FDR's penchant for indirection and his peculiar style of administration militated against a consistent foreign policy. The president's compulsion to hold power securely in his own hands led to the creation of overlapping administrative empires in competition with each other and with access to information and power linked to Roosevelt's personal survival and authority. FDR apparently thrived in the resulting atmosphere of confusion and Byzantine intrigue. Antagonistic to the rigidity and mechanical processes of bureaucracy, he preferred to act himself or to use personal agents to conduct sensitive negotiations. Though the dispatch of special diplomatic missions was as old as the Republic, FDR institutionalized the practice. He heartily distrusted the "striped-pants boys" in the Department of State and soon wearied of their dignified, hypercautious chief Cordell Hull. After trying various methods of getting around Hull, in 1937 he engineered the appointment of Sumner Welles, a fellow Grotonian and Harvard man who had been a page boy at his wedding, as undersecretary of state. Thereafter, he used Welles as his chief diplomatic counselor and confidant, avoiding any need for boring consultations with his secretary of state. By 1940 the strained relations between Hull and Welles were common gossip, and the secretary was threatening to resign, "because the President very obviously seeks Sumner Welles' advice in preference to his own." Later, the versatile Harry Hopkins assumed a similar function.

Presidential scorn for established procedures served merely to immobilize State, not to purge and restructure the chaotic foreign affairs bureaucracy. Weakened by internal divisions, competition for primacy with other agencies, deep-seated malaise and elitism, and other problems, the department bumbled on, still conducting the great bulk of the nation's diplomacy. Mutual lack of respect and communication between the White House and the inhabitants of the ornate State-War-Navy Building next door was to prove unfortunate, for it inhibited the president's ability to exercise leadership when he chose to do so.

Roosevelt's actions with regard to two issues soon after he assumed office—the Reciprocal Trade Agreements program and the Good Neighbor policy—clearly revealed his style of diplomacy. Democratic administrations traditionally had supported efforts to reduce tariffs and remove barriers to the freer flow of international trade. For some, that effort had become a crusade, which embodied mankind's best hope of achieving prosperity and lasting peace. Cordell Hull, appointed secretary of state largely because of his political standing with Congress, had fought for tariff reform since he delivered his maiden speech in the House of Representatives on the subject in 1905. An assistant once said of the secretary's obsession with trade issues: "Of course that is Hull. That is his . . . *raison d'être.* . . . His trade agreements . . . are the base on which rests his whole foreign activity." Having been assured during the campaign that FDR supported his principles, Hull expected to gain realization of his life's dream.

The route to trade reciprocity proved extremely circuitous. The president, whose understanding of international economics did not extend much beyond glittering generalities learned at Harvard, was captivated by the economic nationalism of his domestic advisers. In late 1933 he appointed a committee to coordinate trade policy and designated George N. Peek, a dogmatic opponent of tariff reductions, as its chairman. Hull was apoplectic. When neither side could amass clear evidence and public support, the president suggested a bastard compromise. He invoked a principle that had served him well in the past: when in doubt, postpone. Hull eventually brought such pressure that Roosevelt sponsored the trade agreements program. Although the Reciprocal Trade Agreements Act proved remarkably effective, it was only a beginning of the economic open world which Hull and a dedicated band in the State Department sought. Hull found himself struggling ever after to maintain FDR's allegiance.

In contrast to the crusade for trade reciprocity, the reordering of relations with Latin America, immortalized by President Roosevelt's reference in his inaugural address to the necessity for the U.S. to be "a good neighbor," was negative in purpose. It was designed to remove from the Roosevelt administration's list of potentially embarrassing issues the always ticklish problem of Latin America. The Good Neighbor policy resulted more from concern for U.S. purposes than from a new recognition of the sovereignty of Latin American nations. Further, Roosevelt only confirmed the trend toward disengagement inaugurated by his Republican predecessors. Hoover had quietly shut down military protectorates in several countries, and the "Clark Memorandum," written in 1928 but not made public until 1930, virtually repudiated the Roosevelt Corollary to the Monroe Doctrine.

Before the Second World War, Good Neighborism proceeded through two stages. The first reflected Washington's almost total concentration on domestic problems. The depression made FDR anxious to avoid awkward and costly entanglements abroad, such as were threatened by intervention in Latin America. Secretary Hull was deputized to work out the details. The U.S. refrained from intervention in Cuba when several revolutions shook the island, long a ward of the United States and land of opportunity for American investors. A year later, in April 1934, the Platt Amendment was abrogated, and soon thereafter the U.S. Marines withdrew from Haiti. Hull had anticipated these decisions by attending the Pan-American Conference at Montevideo. A second stage opened with the Buenos Aires and Lima conferences. It reflected U.S. anxiety about developments in Europe and Asia— and the immediate fear that Nazi Germany might obtain footholds in the Americas.

President Roosevelt's role in these events was that of publicist and conduit for policies conceived in the State Department. He never devoted serious effort to understanding Latin America's problems and always dealt with Latin American affairs, when the subject arose, from a viewpoint of kindly but smug paternalism. Ultimately, the efforts to achieve hemispheric solidarity produced treaties for collective security; but such acts as the Declaration of Lima (1938) and the Rio Pact (1947), milestones on the road to hemispheric cooperation, also derived from negative impulses— the depression, fear of German penetration, and the later obses- sion with communism—rather than acceptance of the need for mutual assistance. Untouched by these acts were the economic difficulties separating the Americas: the vast disparity in standards of living between North and South, the dependence of much of Latin America on one-crop economies and the power of North American investors and businessmen in many of these countries, the refusal of the United States, because of political calculation and scruples about economic theories, to assist in the diversifica- tion and reform of Latin America's economies. In this sense the present is not much different from 1932.

Franklin Roosevelt cannot be blamed for centuries of neglect and deprivation; however, his administration's indifference to the economic and social problems assaulting Latin America (and Asia and, in different ways, Europe as well) and the assignment of responsibility for those matters to a State Department that was backward looking and lacking in direction amounted to an abdication of leadership. FDR believed that the state of public opinion and the critical problems at home dictated a passive role in foreign affairs. Above all else, there impended the absolutely essential goal of his reelection in 1936. As a result, when the president gave serious attention to foreign affairs, the world had changed, and for the worse.

The president's awakening to the ominous situation in Europe and Asia most often is identified with his Chicago "quarantine" speech of 5 October 1937. This address, which shocked his countrymen and official Washington when delivered and has puzzled historians since, unveiled a new FDR, the statesman who would protect civilization against international lawbreakers. Demonstrating belated concern about conflicts then flaring in Spain and China, the president warned that America could not isolate itself from "a breakdown of international order and law." He then said, "When an epidemic of physical disease starts to spread, the community approves and joins in a quarantine of the patients in order to protect the health of the community against the spread of disease." If he was advocating, via this medical metaphor, collective action against aggressor nations, he soon backed off, even asserting after his return to Washington that the speech was an expansion rather than repudiation of neutrality.

The "quarantine" speech has been interpreted as a "trial balloon," a puff of hot air, the first shot in a battle to convince the American people of the growing threats to their security, and as FDR's public conversion to internationalism. Quite possibly, it represented all or none of these. Roosevelt himself was confused about his motives. Asked by journalist Ernest R. Lindley what he meant by the speech, he said: "I can't give you a clue to it. You will have to invent one." It did reveal that FDR once more was shifting roles. The repertoire of devices and tricks available to him in domestic matters was pretty well exhausted. Although he won reelection in 1936 by an unprecedented margin, this personal victory had not sparked a consensus such as he had enjoyed in 1933–34. The evidence seemed irrefutable. Dr. New Deal had lost his ability to mesmerize. The attempt to pack the Supreme Court, in which he perhaps risked more of his personal prestige than on any other issue, closed out of town to rotten notices. The "Roosevelt Recession," looming over the country when he spoke in Chicago, posed a challenge that a fireside chat and exuberant confidence could not overcome. The Spanish civil war, outbreak of a full-scale conflict between China and Japan, and Hitler's bellicose maneuvers in Europe merged with the president's domestic difficulties to stimulate a search for a new consensus. This time FDR chose foreign affairs as the stage for exercise of his unique talents.

One may argue that the Second World War began in 1931, when Japan manufactured an excuse for sending troops into north China. Then and later the United States had appeared powerless to halt Japan's imperial ambitions. The American response to the Manchurian crisis, the Hoover-Stimson Doctrine, nonrecognition of any forced conquest, relied on the force of American and international public opinion. The Roosevelt administration did little better. There developed a pattern of U.S. moralism and Japanese contempt for American strength of will that took the two nations ultimately to war. By 1937, it may have been too late to reverse course and FDR never seriously tried, leaving the thorny problem of Asia to the legalistic-minded Hull.

The situation was no more encouraging with regard to fresh initiatives elsewhere in the world. The president soon discovered that the consensus that he deemed necessary for forthright leadership would prove more difficult to achieve than a compara-ble mobilization of opinion on domestic issues. There existed widespread popular indifference to events elsewhere in the world, and bitter hostility about the wisest course divided those who were interested in foreign affairs. His own uncertainties and the conflicting advice of associates militated against aggressive leader-ship. Furthermore, Neville Chamberlain, Adolf Hitler, and other foreign statesmen proved less malleable than the ward bosses with whom FDR dealt so skillfully.[4]

The period 1938–41 was a frustrating time for FDR. To be sure, it was also an exciting time. The president sent messages of

4. Historians differ strongly on the issue of popular attitudes in this period. Polls, newspaper editorials, the White House mail, and other indicators have been invoked to "prove" that the American public adamantly opposed intervention in any form—or to "prove" just the opposite. No one has explained fully how FDR viewed "public opinion," what sorts of information he considered most revealing of the public mood. It is clear that the isolation imposed by the office and his physical limitation had great influence on his reading of popular attitudes.

encouragement, cajolery, and warning to the heads of powerful nations, many of whom accorded him recognition as the leader of world opinion. He moved battleships from one ocean to the other, approved decisions that eventually gave the United States unimaginable military power. He played at strategy and plotted naval engagements. Once it became certain that the American public desired defeat of the Axis powers, the president renounced the spirit of neutrality and, using brilliant dodges to contravene the letter of the law, funneled aid—ships, munitions, raw materials, dollars—to Great Britain and other nations resisting aggression. Such acts as the agreement to trade American destroyers for British bases and lend-lease were stopgaps. They did not confront, and indeed allowed FDR to postpone confronting, the basic issue: whether the nation's security demanded America's participation in the war.

FDR struggled with this conundrum for two years, until Pearl Harbor released him from the paralysis it inflicted. Nothing in his background and grab bag of habits prepared him for this sort of crisis, which required patient self-analysis and leadership amid the din of conflicting views. As James McGregor Burns has observed: "Roosevelt, in a sense, was captive to himself as well as to his political environment. He was captive to his habit of mediating among pressures rather than reshaping them, of responding eclectically to all the people around him, of balancing warring groups and leaders against one another, of improvising with brilliance and gusto. Impatient of theory, insatiably curious about people and their ideas, sensitively attuned to the play of forces around him, he lacked that burning and almost fanatic conviction that great leadership demands." The strongest criticism of Roosevelt's conduct of foreign affairs is that at critical points he failed to provide leadership, to "give the cue the people needed." Those who have offered this criticism assume that FDR, by an effort of will, could throw off his subservience to public opinion and political maneuvering and issue a clarion call for American intervention in the Second World War. A contrary claim is that the president's restraint "showed excellent political sense," that he admitted U.S. entry into the war was necessary but decided only a carefully planned campaign to educate the American people would avoid cataclysmic divisions destructive of this purpose.[5]

5. The claim that FDR was carrying out a shrewd campaign of public education dominated the early literature on his conduct of foreign affairs. See, for example,

The fact is that FDR's outlook did not permit him to respond in ways other than he did respond, and his reaction had little to do with consistency or calculation. The situation was ambivalent; therefore, he had to be ambivalent. Brief examination of one of the many "events" with which Roosevelt dealt in the period before Pearl Harbor exemplifies the degree to which he was entrapped in the contradictions of that "puzzle within an enigma," his personality.

Only after the startling collapse of France in June 1940 did the American people begin to realize that a Nazi-dominated Europe threatened the security of the United States. At the same time, Japanese adventurism created concern for American interests, real and mythical, in the Pacific. A tidal wave of sentiment for preparedness swept the country, though a thoughtful few asked, "Preparedness for what?" Congress acted to create a two-ocean navy and two months later, in September 1940, approved the Selective Service Act, the first peacetime draft in America's history.

After his reelection in November 1940, FDR proceeded to make material aid available to the Allies, but he resisted pressures for direct involvement in the war. This policy reflected the contradictory opinions of the public: 75 percent approved helping the British, while 85 percent indicated a desire to avoid war at all costs. Roosevelt possibly believed that material aid would suffice and that it would not be necessary to send American boys to die on foreign soil. He knew by early 1941, however, that lend-lease alone would not ensure an Allied victory. The British simply did not have the resources to win the war by themselves. It also became clear that the conversion of the United States, in FDR's words, into "the great arsenal of democracy," could not take place without full-scale mobilization, which required a declaration of war.

These grim calculations plunged the president into a deep

Samuel I. Rosenman, ed., *The Public Papers and Addresses of Franklin D. Roosevelt*, 13 vols. (New York, 1938–50). Careful examination of the president's actions in the controversy over revising the neutrality statutes, the Russo-Finnish War, and the convoying debate suggest that he was not a teacher but a pupil, himself waiting to be educated.

depression. Apparently, he thought his magic touch no longer worked, that he faced a "new ball game" in which his ability to outguess the opposition and stir up his own team had disappeared. An assiduous student of public opinion polls, Roosevelt gained from these indicators in spring 1941 confirmation of the futility and foolhardiness of frank leadership. FDR had a singular perception of the *mésalliance* between the presidency and public opinion. While possessing allegiance to the abstractions of the democratic process, he had rather less confidence in the electorate's ability to reach mature judgments. He was often disturbingly paternalistic, fond of playing the kindly but firm teacher, giving his pupils (the public) precepts for right action. In 1941 his tutorship was in disfavor. FDR's reaction was to withdraw from direction of affairs. He used a series of colds and sinus infections to shut out visitors bringing pleas for deeper American involvement. The key to this period of withdrawal was frustration. Roosevelt concluded that his effort to push through lend-lease had "temporarily exhausted his credit both with Congress and the country," and he must remain passive until the public caught up.

Presidential intimates could not refrain from pleading for action. In May, Secretary of the Interior Harold L. Ickes was despairing: "In every direction I find a growing discontent with the President's lack of leadership. He still has the country if he will take it and lead it. But he won't have it much longer unless he does something. It won't be sufficient for him to make another speech and then go into a state of innocuous desuetude again." Henry Morgenthau noted that the president and his sickly familiar, Harry Hopkins, appeared baffled. "They feel that something has to be done but don't know just what." Hopkins had told him that "the President is loath to get into this war, and he would rather follow public opinion than lead it." FDR's inability to pull the nation along by his assertive self-confidence was a novel and fearsome occurrence, and his advisers did not know what to make of it.

Almost the only project in which the president took an interest in this period was the planning for a conference with the British war leader, Winston Churchill. As he worked on this project he began to grasp its potential for easing the pressures upon him. It seemed a marvelous pedagogical device, and such opportunities—since the Germans and Japanese refused to provoke hostilities—had been nonexistent in recent months. A Roosevelt-

Churchill conference, prefaced by some stirring call for unity in the confrontation between good and evil, could have bombshell effects on attitudes at home and abroad. Perhaps a secret meeting of the democracies' two great leaders was *the* event for which FDR had been longing.

It is testimony to the extent of the president's personal approach to problems that the meeting with Churchill became a means of rescuing him from his malaise. It also embodied most of the techniques that were characteristic of Rooseveltian diplomacy: secrecy, indirection, drama, careful timing, and personal participation. The Atlantic Conference was the first of a series of meetings in which Allied leaders dealt with the strategic issues of the war and sketched the outlines of the peace. This meeting, which took place on U.S. and British warships anchored off Argentia, Newfoundland, from 9 to 14 August 1941, did confirm military aid to Great Britain, produced a short-lived agreement on policy toward Japan, sanctioned that statement of high principle, the Atlantic Charter, and, perhaps most importantly, brought about the first encounter between two leaders of the triumvirate that was to manage the destruction of the Axis.[6]

The decisions reached at Argentia were embryonic and temporary. The conference produced only one formal agreement, a statement of war and peace aims, which survived American entry into the war; the Atlantic Charter, ironically, was one matter to which President Roosevelt gave little importance. The meeting was most revealing about the president's style of diplomacy and established a pattern of behavior that was to dominate wartime negotiations. Demanding that the conference transpire in total secrecy, FDR limited the U.S. delegation to military leaders and members of his personal entourage. He brought along Sumner Welles to handle the details of any diplomatic conversations. Roosevelt excluded Secretary Hull from preparations for the meetings and did not even inform him of its existence until the conference was almost over. One effect of the insistence on haste and secrecy was that the Americans were poorly prepared for substantive discussions with their British counterparts. The president apparently preferred it that way.

6. For a full description of the Atlantic Conference and the issues summarized here, see Theodore A. Wilson, *The First Summit: Roosevelt and Churchill at Placentia Bay* (Boston, 1969).

Released from his imprisonment in the White House, FDR proved a patsy for the large dollops of flattery laid on by the British and for Churchill's sweeping expositions on politics and grand strategy. By meeting's end the president had agreed to a virtual ultimatum to Japan (later emasculated by the State Department), indicated support of the British strategy of bombing, blockade, and subversion, and approved a clause in the Atlantic Charter that subverted the foreign economic policy of his administration. Only on the question of a declaration of war did FDR resist British blandishments; however, Churchill soon learned that presidential commitments were as stable as shifting sand. Roosevelt really had not committed either himself or the country.

In retrospect, the meeting's significance lay in the relationships established (proof that Roosevelt and Churchill, each having gigantic egos, would be able to work together; the introduction of U.S. and British officials) and for the informal alliance between the English-speaking nations that it affirmed. Less clear at the time was the transfer of power that Argentia symbolized. Thenceforth, as America's gigantic industrial and technological resources were applied to the war, the United States became the senior partner, taking from Britain's faltering grasp the glories and obligations of world leadership. FDR came to relish that role more than any he ever played.

The meeting at Argentia did not resolve the immediate problem facing the president. Far from easing his difficulties, the conference pinned FDR tightly between the horns of isolationist denunciation and interventionist outcry. After his return to Washington, he chose to ward off accusations that the meeting meant war. This sacrificed a large part of the impact. How the American people might have responded had Roosevelt confessed that he had met with Churchill to deal with a desperate crisis and then proclaimed that the country must endure whatever sacrifice was required is idle speculation. Such a risky act of leadership was precisely what he hoped to avert; to him it would have been inconsistent with every dictate of experience.

The nation's drift toward war abruptly terminated with the shock of Japan's attack on Pearl Harbor. For Roosevelt, it was as if a great weight had been lifted from his heart. "They have attacked us at Pearl Harbor," he calmly informed a jubilant Churchill. "We are all in the same boat now." A new role, commander in chief, had opened for him. During the next four years, in the guise of Dr.

Win the War, he made brilliant use of all the enormous resources at his command. He led, cajoled, and maneuvered the United States toward the single goal of total victory and, it may be said, sacrificed his life in that cause.

It is regrettable that the limits President Roosevelt accepted and imposed on this last and greatest role in order to win the war were to destroy much of his achievement in diplomacy. The tragedy of Pearl Harbor, aside from lives lost and ships sunk, was that it did not resolve but merely papered over the debate about America's real interests in the conflict. America was at war, but beyond the motive of survival there was little understanding of why the United States was fighting, what interests were at stake, and what might be gained. Unrealistic hopes about the future blossomed and the American people mistook idealistic rhetoric for national goals. Perhaps even more tragically, they and their leaders miscalculated the nation's ability to achieve both ideals and self-interest.

The president, who now had the undivided attention of his audience, chose not to engage in any further educational efforts about the world and America's place in it. He concentrated on prosecution of the war and shunted aside difficult questions: the nature of the postwar world, the relationship between national sovereignty and a viable world peace-keeping organization, basic conflicts among members of the Allied coalition. Invoking the Wilsonian principle of "no predetermination," FDR refused to engage in political deals, or, indeed, to make any arrangements on postwar political matters. He insisted that such questions as the status of Germany and the future of colonial peoples be left to a "universal peace conference" that would be convened at war's end and over which he intended to preside.

The president did not lack awareness of the antagonisms beneath the surface of Allied cooperation. Nor did he ignore entirely the factors that limited American capacity to overcome these antagonisms. In fact, at times he minimized U.S. ability to influence the course of events. Because of his addiction to "the vice of immediacy" during the first part of the war, American diplomacy reflected a conscious acceptance of *Realpolitik* and *Machtpolitik*. Certainly, no desire to "make the world safe for democracy" was discernible in U.S. dealings with Franco's Spain, the tortured history of American relations with Vichy France, Roosevelt's self-serving treatment of the Nationalist Chinese, and Washington's cynical acceptance of the Badoglio regime after Italy's surrender. Similarly, the unconditional surrender policy, the administration's callous policy toward small nations, especially its cobelligerents in Latin America, and its adoption of "modern" techniques of warfare—population bombing and unrestricted submarine operations—betrayed easy acceptance of the principle that might makes right. President Roosevelt was not directly responsible for all these acts, but he set the tone: winning the war took precedence.

Overshadowed by the emphasis on wartime necessity, American diplomacy was riddled with inconsistency and crippled by lack of understanding about the purposes it was to achieve. The president's administrative style, founded on improvisation, proved inadequate to the demands of wartime diplomacy and postwar planning. FDR retained control over all diplomatic matters affecting strategy, and the confusion as to what was "diplomatic" and "military" ensured that little was done without presidential authority. He dealt with political questions affecting the great powers, mostly at the conferences with Churchill and Stalin. The wartime summits followed the script written at Argentia, often with unfortunate results.

The final meeting between the Big Three—Churchill, Roosevelt, and Stalin—took place at Yalta, a seaside resort in the Russian Crimea, in February 1945. Yalta later became a synonym for FDR's supposed "sellout" to the Soviet Union, with critics asserting that the agreements negotiated there amounted to deliberate treason. In fact, the Yalta Conference mostly confirmed decisions reached earlier, and any unfortunate effects of FDR's actions stemmed from application of those beliefs and behavior patterns, intensified in this case by physical (and perhaps mental) debility, with which he had always operated.

As at the Tehran Conference in November 1943, President Roosevelt assumed the role of mediator between Churchill and Stalin. By treating complex issues as personal matters that he and his two great colleagues could decide, FDR often found himself out of his element, unable to respond with anything more than genial optimism and assurances of mutual esteem. Although he brought a large entourage to Yalta, including his new secretary of state, Edward R. Stettinius, and although the U.S. delegation was well briefed, FDR did not use his advisers in any systematic way, preferring to extemporize and react to British and Soviet proposals.

The conference opened in an atmosphere of impending victory, with Germany toppling into defeat and Japan reeling. For the first time, however, the Allied leaders had to confront directly questions relating to the postwar world. Discussion of the occupation of Germany and reparations, the status of Eastern Europe, the United Nations, and territorial arrangements in the Far East brought to light vast differences in outlook and aspirations among the erstwhile allies. FDR struggled to maintain at least a facade of cooperation, even at the risk of appearing to appease the Soviet Union; but again he obtained amicable relations by glossing over some basic problems and postponing others. When the president, looking exhausted, returned to the United States, he pronounced Yalta a monumental accomplishment, and the public and Congress accepted this judgment. Within a few short months, however, the imprecise, unwarranted assumptions inherent in the Yalta Agreements were proving a source of mistrust and hostility.

Submerged in busywork and the construction of elaborate programs for global peace and prosperity, the State Department was swept along by the rising antagonism toward Russian communism. As a sop to Hull, who was kept away from the summit meetings by explicit presidential order, FDR assigned him to the supervision of State Department planning for American participation in wartime and postwar programs: the United Nations, its Relief and Rehabilitation Administration, the European Advisory Commission, the International Bank for Reconstruction and Development, the International Monetary Fund, and other agencies for international cooperation. This honor proved illusory, since Hull and his cohorts were permitted only to spin gossamer dreams. Meanwhile, war agencies that carried on foreign activities vied with State for power and prestige in foreign affairs. The Bureau of Economic Warfare, Treasury, Agriculture, the Foreign Economic Administration, and the innumerable boards and commissions controlled by the army and navy challenged the department's primacy. This bureaucratic warfare amused FDR, and he ignored the tangle of purposes and the enormous waste it produced.

The patchwork administration of foreign affairs somehow did not prevent the winning of the war, but it functioned at the expense of postponing consideration of vital issues. In this regard the president was depressingly shortsighted and lacking in confidence about his fellow citizens. By awarding his imprimatur to State's utopian proposals on economic and political internationalism, he committed the United States to participation in a vaguely conceived world organization, one presumably with power to maintain peace. Yet he himself always placed U.S. interest ahead of the aims of any supranational agency, and he was prepared to bypass or ignore the United Nations when vital interests were at stake. The international organization he envisioned would be dominated by the great powers—the "four policemen"—who would disarm everyone but themselves, victors and vanquished alike, and proceed to restructure the world according to a model of benevolent paternalism. Statements about the potential effectiveness of the UN were so optimistic, however, that many Americans were persuaded—and it may be that President Roosevelt convinced himself. FDR was fond of saying that he was a realist, that he was determined not to repeat the mistakes of Woodrow Wilson. If so, his was a curious sort of realism, based on two decidedly unrealistic assumptions: that the wartime coalition between the United States, Great Britain, and the Soviet Union reflected their basic interests and thus would continue, and that an economic and political environment for world peace and reconstruction could be created quickly after the war. More likely, though, FDR did not give serious thought to these matters, preferring to hope that some means of dealing with (or ignoring) them would present itself to him before they reached a critical stage.

A cerebral hemorrhage removed FDR before the defects in his diplomacy became obvious; a cynic would say that his timing once again was brilliant. He left an uncertain legacy. He had followed a cautious, limited policy in foreign affairs and had acted only when sustained by a popular consensus. Following patterns of behavior established in childhood and early adolescence, he responded to events instead of constructing a rational system of ideas and policies. The remarkable achievement of this essentially characterless man was his ability to immerse himself so completely in a particular role that it became *the* FDR and he became that character, faithfully reproducing the character's attributes and methods for the duration of its existence. Unfortunately, such an intensely personal approach to diplomacy relied upon political and dramatic gifts not likely to be duplicated for a long time, if ever.

It is doubly ironic that FDR's search for a solution to the difficulties facing the nation from 1937 to 1945 encouraged the emergence of a new consensus founded on popular enthusiasm, a jumble of stereotypes about other nations, and widespread ignorance about the world. Its dominant element was confidence in the American system. The enormous production rolling out of America's farms and factories, accomplished with comparatively small sacrifice and strain on the nation's political fabric, seemed to demonstrate the superiority of American institutions. Certainly, many Americans believed it did.[7]

These attitudes—especially faith in the transferability of American ideals and institutions and a blind confidence in the future—undergirded U.S. planning with regard to postwar problems. They formed the context within which occurred American responses to the development of a "cold war" with the Soviet Union. In the final weeks before his death, President Roosevelt appears to have attempted to launch a crash program of public education, deflating the optimism generated by administration pronouncements about the new world to ensue after war's end. If that is true, his efforts came too late; and his successor was to find little in FDR's diplomacy that informed him how to deal with the wreckage of war and blighted aspirations.

BIBLIOGRAPHIC NOTE

The documentary residue of Franklin D. Roosevelt's life is enormous. The Roosevelt Library at Hyde Park, New York, contains some ten thousand linear feet of presidential records alone, and the storage vaults

---

7. The shift in popular attitudes regarding America's role in the world is the most striking difference between 1933 and 1945. FDR mirrored this change but, like most of his countrymen, did not fully grasp its causes or its complications. The full effects of the changes in views and the realities of power they represented were obscured by the war and apparent survival of prewar diplomatic alignments; however, outside the normal channels of diplomacy, a floodtide of power and responsibility moved toward the United States.

of the National Archives and the Washington Federal Records Center hold hundreds of thousands of cubic feet of diplomatic-political-military records. Despite (or because of) this huge store of information, would-be biographers and monographers have been unable to find there much of FDR the president or the man. Furthermore, many pieces of the great puzzle of Rooseveltian diplomacy are only now becoming available because of State Department zeal (and the caution of the National Archives and Records Service) in applying regulations on access to diplomatic records. Of great assistance in the interim are the eighty-five volumes of *Foreign Relations of the United States* (Washington, D.C., 1861–) covering FDR's tenure. Edgar B. Nixon, *Franklin D. Roosevelt and Foreign Affairs,* 3 vols. (Cambridge, Mass., 1969), are an important supplement.

This is not to suggest that these obstacles have discouraged scholarly research. In fact, the volume and variety of works on the Great Depression and the Second World War is so immense that it seems to be approaching the state of fragmentation and interpretive chaos that now characterizes the literature on the American Civil War. Soon after FDR's death, Frank Freidel began an ambitious six-volume biography. By 1956 he had completed three volumes, *Franklin D. Roosevelt: The Apprenticeship* (Boston, 1952), *The Ordeal* (Boston, 1954), and *The Triumph* (Boston, 1956). A fourth volume, *Launching the New Deal,* which takes the story through summer 1933, appeared in 1973. Arthur Schlesinger, Jr., like Freidel a friendly critic, has yet to complete a projected four-volume study. The first three volumes are *The Crisis of the Old Order* (Boston, 1957), *The Coming of the New Deal* (Boston, 1958), and *The Politics of Upheaval* (Boston, 1960). The theses of James McGregor Burns's two volumes are contained in their subtitles: *Roosevelt: The Lion and the Fox* (New York, 1956) and *Roosevelt: The Soldier of Freedom* (New York, 1970). For an intriguing "psychohistorical" explanation, see the section on FDR in James Barbour, *Presidential Character* (New York, 1972).

Books by and about the people close to FDR have special value for understanding his personality. Eleanor Roosevelt's *This I Remember* (New York, 1949) is guarded but useful. Christopher P. Lasch, *Eleanor and Franklin* (New York, 1971), portrays FDR as incapable of deep personal intimacy. *The Roosevelts of Hyde Park: An Untold Story* (New York, 1972), by Elliott Roosevelt and James Brough, is a peculiar but informative book. Robert E. Sherwood's *Roosevelt and Hopkins: An Intimate History* (New York, 1948) remains in many ways the best biographical treatment. Also relevant are the memoirs and edited diaries of Frances Perkins, James Farley, Harold Ickes, Henry Morgenthau, Jr., Samuel Rosenman, Elliott Roosevelt, and Henry A. Wallace.

The aridity of Cordell Hull's *Memoirs,* 2 vols. (New York, 1948) offers evidence of the Department of State's isolation. The biography of Hull by

Julius W. Pratt, 2 vols. (New York, 1964) is respectable. See also Sumner Welles, *The Time for Decision* (New York, 1944) and *Seven Decisions That Shaped History* (New York, 1951), the egotistical but deeply perceptive *Memoirs: 1925–1950* (Boston, 1967) by George F. Kennan, and the writings and diaries of career diplomats and cabinet officials such as Adolf A. Berle, Jr., Breckinridge Long, Charles Bohlen, Pierrepont Moffat, William Phillips, Joseph Grew, and Henry L. Stimson.

The standard account on the coming of the Second World War remains William L. Langer and S. Everett Gleason, *The Challenge to Isolation* (New York, 1952) and *The Undeclared War: 1940–1941* (New York, 1953). The works of Herbert Feis, especially *The Road to Pearl Harbor* (Princeton, 1950), *Churchill, Roosevelt, Stalin* (Princeton, 1957), and *The China Tangle* (Princeton, 1953), are indispensable. Robert Divine, *Roosevelt and World War II* (Baltimore, 1969), is a thoughtful discussion of the president's role in foreign affairs. See Gaddis Smith, *American Diplomacy during the Second World War, 1941–1945* (New York, 1965), for an indictment of FDR's personal diplomacy. Postwar planning is treated in Harley Notter, *Postwar Foreign Policy Preparation, 1939–1945* (Washington, D.C., 1949), Robert Divine, *Second Chance: The Triumph of Internationalism in America during World War II* (New York, 1967), and E. F. Penrose, *Economic Planning for the Peace* (Princeton, 1953). Lloyd C. Gardner's *Economic Aspects of New Deal Diplomacy* (Madison, Wisc., 1964) and *Architects of Illusion: Men and Ideas in American Diplomacy, 1941–1950* (Chicago, 1970) offer challenging arguments. Among the critical accounts that emphasize the will to power and America's market imperatives are William Appleman Williams, *The Tragedy of American Diplomacy* (New York, 1962), David L. Green, *The Containment of Latin America* (Chicago, 1971), and the mammoth work by Gabriel Kolko, *The Politics of War: The World and United States Foreign Policy, 1943–1945* (New York, 1968). The most balanced account of Soviet-American problems is John L. Gaddis, *The United States and the Origins of the Cold War* (New York, 1972).

A good bibliography of printed material on FDR is in Burns's *Soldier of Freedom*. John E. Wiltz, *From Isolation to War, 1931–1941* (New York, 1968), is an excellent guide and analysis of the scholarship on foreign affairs. The Roosevelt Library has published *The Era of Franklin D. Roosevelt: A Selected Bibliography of Essays, Dissertations, and Periodical Literature, 1945–1971* (Hyde Park, N.Y., 1973), compiled by William J. Stewart.

National Park Service photograph,
Harry S. Truman Library

HARRY S. TRUMAN

and the Origins of Containment

John Lewis Gaddis

"Complete unbelief. That was first. . . . Then consternation at the thought of that Throttlebottom Truman." The words were those of David Lilienthal, but millions of Americans shared the same thought upon hearing the news of Franklin D. Roosevelt's death on the afternoon of 12 April 1945. At first, Harry S. Truman did seem to resemble Alexander P. Throttlebottom, the eminently forgettable vice-president in George Gershwin's musical *Of Thee I Sing.* The man who had just inherited the White House had been, up to that point, inconspicuous, one reason that Roosevelt, seeking a noncontroversial replacement for Henry Wallace, had chosen Truman as his running mate in 1944. During his brief tenure as vice-president, Truman attracted national attention only twice, by attending the funeral of a bankrupt political boss, Tom Pendergast, and by being photographed playing an upright piano with the sultry movie star Lauren Bacall perched on top.

As events quickly made clear, Truman was no Throttlebottom.

189

Few men have entered the presidency with less preparation, yet none have filled that position with less hesitation and self-doubt. Truman relished responsibility and thrived on decision making; he bore the burdens of office with a good-humored resiliency that never failed to impress those close to him. If he had second thoughts about the policies he followed, he kept them to himself. From the day he left office until his death almost twenty years later, Truman remained serenely convinced that he had done his best, and that his best had served the country well.

Scholars initially accepted that judgment, especially with reference to foreign affairs, which figured so prominently in the Truman presidency. In a 1962 poll, historians rated Truman a "near great" chief executive, largely on the basis of his decision to implement a policy of containment in dealing with the Communist world. The passing of the cold war and the trauma of Vietnam have altered perspectives, however. Revisionist scholars now argue that the cold war was unnecessary, and that Truman must bear a considerable share of the responsibility for having instigated it. It seems certain that Truman will occupy an important place in the history of United States foreign policy, though how historians will evaluate his role is by no means settled.

No man approaches power with a completely clean slate; policy makers invariably bring to positions of authority certain principles and practices, based upon previous experience, that influence their behavior. Harry Truman was no exception; indeed his abrupt accession to the presidency may well have reinforced for him the tendency present in all men to seek guidance from the past. Truman's prepresidential career shaped his approach to decision making in several ways: it provided him with a wide range of practical experience while impressing on him a sense of his own limitations; it taught him techniques of leadership in situations of crisis; it gave him familiarity with power without qualms over having sought it; and it furnished him with a knowledge of history from which he derived lessons for dealing with current problems.

Much was made of Truman's inexperience when he entered the White House, and in terms of factual information relating to foreign affairs, this concern was justified; yet Truman was hardly a neophyte when it came to experience in dealing with men and institutions. He had served ten years in the Senate, where his quiet but competent approach, particularly as chairman of the Special Committee to Investigate the National Defense Program, had won him the respect of colleagues on both sides of the aisle. Before his senatorial service, Truman spent twelve years as a county judge in Jackson County, Missouri, a job involving the administration of funds for the maintenance of roads and other facilities. Before entering politics, Truman had already dabbled in banking, farming, oil exploration, zinc and lead mining, and clothes retailing, and he had served as an officer in France during World War I. He would not likely have had such diverse experience if he had been able to attend college; lacking formal training for a particular profession, he had to move from one occupation to another as opportunities arose. In an age when most of the men who shaped United States foreign policy came from relatively narrow backgrounds in business and law, Truman brought to the presidency an unusually broad, if sometimes shallow, range of experience.

At the same time, these experiences gave him a keen sense of his own limitations and painful knowledge of failure. Truman's father had lost thousands of dollars speculating on grain futures, and Truman himself absorbed smaller losses on several of his own business enterprises. In 1922, the clothing store that he and a wartime friend opened in Kansas City went bankrupt. Politics seemed to be the only profession in which Truman did well, and even here his rise to national prominence stemmed more from the support he got from the Pendergast machine than from his own abilities. Persistent success, it has been argued, is intoxicating; it blurs objectivity and fosters an illusion of infallibility. This may be, but Truman's biographers have not had to worry much about the problem.

Military service during World War I taught Truman a great deal about leadership. Previous training in the Missouri National Guard earned him an officer's commission, and in France he commanded an artillery battery. Years later he recalled how he shaped his troops into line: "When I first took command of the battery I called all the sergeants and corporals together. I told them I knew they had been making trouble for the previous commanders. I said 'I didn't come over here to get along with you. You've got to get along with me. And if there are any of you who can't, speak up right now and I'll bust you right back. . . .' We got along." At one point, under German fire, Truman effectively rallied retreating troops by hurling streams of choice Missouri invective at them. The experience of command gave Truman confidence in his ability to lead men. It also reinforced a belief, which he may have inherited from his blunt and feisty parents, that the best way to deal with recalcitrant opponents was to "talk tough."

Despite his proclivity for belligerent rhetoric, however, Truman was a strong believer in the virtues of accommodation. His path to power was paved with compromises. He had to work through the unsavory Pendergast organization to succeed in Kansas City politics. Later, as senator from Missouri, he built an independent political base by winning the support of diverse interest groups, a technique that by its very nature required an ability to reconcile differences. Truman's nomination for the vice-presidency in 1944 was also a compromise, in this case between the liberal and conservative wings of the Democratic party. Conciliation and adjustment, Truman believed, were the lifeblood of politics; although he had principles they did not lead, as they have with other presidents, to inflexible policies.

One principle to which Truman attached particular significance was the importance of keeping one's word: a man who did not carry out his obligations was not to be trusted. It was characteristic of Truman that he did not approve of divorce because "when you make a contract, you should keep it. . . . When I say I'm going to do something, I do it, or bust my insides trying to do it." After the failure of his clothing store, Truman insisted on paying off his creditors, even though this took years and required a considerable financial sacrifice. Loyalty to friends he regarded as a sacred duty; one of the embarrassments of his administration was Truman's refusal to disassociate himself from some of his more disreputable Missouri cronies. Truman judged men by their reliability in keeping agreements, and it was the standard by which he, in turn, wanted to be judged.

As did many of his fellow Americans, Truman thought there was something corrupt about men with an appetite for power. He took pride in the fact that he had not originally wanted to hold any of the offices he subsequently occupied; power had sought him, rather than the other way around. Yet Truman's administrative experience taught him that an executive, to be effective, must not hesitate to use his authority and must jealously guard it from all challenges. The fact that he had not aspired to high political office may have helped Truman rationalize this seeming contradiction; had he actually wanted the presidency he might not have wielded its powers with such self-confidence.

Truman's knowledge of history, the product of extensive reading and a nearly photographic memory, continually astonished those around him; but his approach was a relatively unsophisticated one, as a recent biographer has noted. "He could conceptualize events only by means of the 'great man' idea of history, which he attached to a schoolboy notion that all problems had their parallels and precedents in the past." The fact that Truman drew many lessons from history affected his performance in the White House. Aware that successful presidents had usually been the strong ones, he resolved from the first to be an activist. He understood clearly the distinction between delegating authority and relinquishing responsibility, an important insight he had gained from studying Grover Cleveland's second administration. Knowing how Washington, Lincoln, and other predecessors had been vilified while in office, he was less sensitive to criticism than might have been expected given his inadequate preparation for the presidency. His belief that historical parallels offered reliable guides for dealing with current problems led Truman occasionally to make simplistic comparisons between past and present that did not always serve the nation's best interests.

Truman viewed international relations optimistically; harmony, he believed, was possible, provided there was an organization of nations to sustain and enforce it. World War I convinced him that such a structure was practical and that Woodrow Wilson had found the right formula for it in the League of Nations (a concept that went back to King Henry IV of France, as Truman delighted in pointing out). The failure of the United States to join the league had had tragic results. "I am . . . sure as I can be that this World War is the result of the 1919–20 isolationist attitude," he told the Senate in 1943, "and I am equally sure that another and worse war will follow this one, unless the United Nations and their allies . . . decide to work together for peace as they are working together for victory." Truman labored hard while in Congress to commit the United States to membership in the United Nations; after becoming president he never wavered in his support for the world organization. For most of his life he carried in his wallet a copy of the portion of Tennyson's "Locksley Hall" that predicted a "Parliament of Man, the Federation of the world." "We're going to have that someday," Truman once commented. "I guess that's what I've really been working for ever since I first put that poetry in my pocket."

Shortly after Truman's nomination for vice-president, an old acquaintance wrote of him, "He is a great man, but he doesn't know that he is great." In a way, this was true. Throughout his career Truman had remained unusually humble. His almost ostentatious self-deprecation may have reflected a degree of calculation, however, for Truman's reading of history had convinced him that humility was a prerequisite for greatness. On the eve of his announcement for the Senate in 1934 he had written a note to himself reiterating that belief. "Self-discipline with all [great men] came first. I found that most of the really great ones never thought they were great." Ten years later, on election night, 1944, Truman quietly predicted to a friend that Roosevelt would not survive his term and that he would become president. He worried about the prospect and thought he would need all the help he could get; yet he showed surprisingly little doubt regarding his ability to do the job if the need arose. Confidence, tempered with humility—it was not a bad attitude to have while waiting for lightning to strike.

Presidents who enter the White House upon the death of an incumbent face a peculiar problem. Respect and sentiment tie them to the policies of their predecessors, yet the exercise of power requires establishment of a separate identity if authority is not be be dissipated. Presidents have solved this problem in various ways; Truman's solution was to embrace the goals Roosevelt had sought but to alter dramatically their implementation.

The new chief executive had no difficulty in committing himself to carry out Roosevelt's policies because he sincerely believed in the wisdom of most of what the late president had done. Truman had been elected to the Senate as a New Deal supporter and, once there, had rarely deviated from the administration line. An ardent opponent of isolationism, the senator from Missouri had come out in favor of a postwar collective security organization even before Roosevelt. Significantly, his first act as president was to announce that the San Francisco Conference, due to meet in two weeks to write the United Nations Charter, would convene on schedule.

Roosevelt's loose operational style appalled Truman, who set great store by administrative efficiency. Bureaucratic jurisdictions overlapped, chains of command were poorly defined, organizational assignments bore little relation to functions performed. FDR himself had been notoriously evasive, as Truman privately complained before becoming vice-president. "He does all the talking, and . . . never talks about anything you want to talk about, so there isn't much you can do." Upon entering the White House the new president sought to establish a reputation for orderliness and decisiveness far removed from the careless habits of his predecessor. Subordinates noticed the change at once. One of them wrote: "When I saw him today I had fourteen problems to take up with him and got through them in less than fifteen minutes with a clear directive on every one of them. You can imagine what a joy it is to work with a man like that." This brisk approach to decision making enabled Truman to establish his own authority without repudiating the substance of Roosevelt's programs. It was also consistent with a lifelong habit: whether rallying frightened troops in France, dealing with recalcitrant politicians in Kansas City, or running for office in seemingly hopeless elections, Truman had always responded to difficult situations by taking the offensive. Now, in the biggest crisis of his life, Truman behaved characteristically by seizing the reins of power with vigor and authority.

The most pressing problem facing Truman was one that would plague him throughout his presidency: the Soviet Union. The new president had come to power at a crucial moment in the evolution of Russian-American relations. Conflicts over postwar objectives were surfacing with alarming frequency as the defeat of Hitler approached. Stalin's chief concern was security from future attack; he sought to achieve this by dominating Eastern Europe while keeping Germany weak. Roosevelt had recognized the validity of many of Stalin's demands, but had found it difficult to satisfy them without sacrificing objectives for which the United States was fighting, notably self-determination and world economic recovery. The Big Three had worked out delicate compromises on several of the issues that divided them at Yalta in February 1945, but these came apart almost at once as each side interpreted vaguely worded accords in line with its own national interests.

Truman knew nothing of these developments when he came into office because Roosevelt had not kept him informed. He quickly sought recommendations from FDR's advisers, most of whom had long favored a firmer policy toward the Soviet Union than the late president had been prepared to implement. Unsure of himself yet eager to appear decisive, Truman accepted their advice to "get tough," a course of action consistent with his own favorite method of handling crises. He was not afraid of the Russians, the new president told W. Averell Harriman, the United States ambassador in Moscow; after all, "the Soviet Union needed us more than we needed them." He would not expect to get 100 percent of what the United States wanted, but "we should be able to get 85 percent." He was going ahead with plans for the San Francisco Conference, and if the Russians disapproved, "they could go to hell."

The president's first opportunity to demonstrate his toughness came on 23 April 1945, when the Soviet foreign minister, V. M. Molotov, stopped off in Washington on his way to San Francisco. Truman lectured the Russian diplomat in a manner not unlike his handling of the unruly troops in Battery D. An agreement had been made at Yalta, he stated, and all that remained was for Stalin to carry it out. When Molotov tried to explain that the Soviet government was following what it considered to be the correct interpretation of the Yalta Agreements, Truman interrupted him. The United States wanted cooperation with Russia, he snapped, but not as a one-way proposition. Known for his usual imperturbability as "Old Ironpants," Molotov emerged from this experience badly shaken. "I gave it to him straight," Truman later bragged. "One-two to the jaw."

Some historians have seen this as the moment the cold war began. Certainly the new president's truculence upset the Russians, who had grown used to the smooth and slippery platitudes of FDR. In fact, though, Truman had no intention of reversing Roosevelt's Russian policy. He had reason to believe he was continuing it. Roosevelt himself had come to see the need for a tougher approach by the time of his death, and the new president's advisers were almost unanimous in urging a firm stand. In his eagerness to appear decisive Truman probably overreacted, as he himself later realized, but he did so in an effort to solidify his own authority, not to wreck chances for postwar accommodation with the USSR.

During this period Truman made other decisions that had the effect of avoiding, rather than encouraging, conflict with the

Soviet Union. He agreed to support Roosevelt's Yalta pledge that the Russians could have three seats in the United Nations General Assembly, even though he himself disapproved of this arrangement. He turned down Winston Churchill's proposal that Allied troops in central Europe remain in the advanced positions they had attained by V-E Day, not withdrawing into previously agreed-upon occupation zones until the Russians became more cooperative. He made no change in the Far Eastern agreement Roosevelt had concluded with Stalin at Yalta whereby the Russians would receive political concessions in return for entering the war against Japan.

By mid-May 1945, Truman had nonetheless begun to fear that the Russians had misunderstood his intentions. The fate of Poland remained unresolved. The San Francisco Conference seemed to be turning into a forum for the airing of differences instead of their resolution. Shortly after V-E Day, overzealous subordinates ordered ships transporting lend-lease supplies to Russia to return to port if the material they carried was not intended for use against Japan. Truman, who had intended a more gradual curtailment of lend-lease, immediately countermanded this order, but not before the Russians had complained bitterly. The incident convinced the president of the extreme anti-Soviet hostility that existed among some Washington officials, and of the need to make a new effort to settle differences with Moscow.

Truman entrusted this delicate responsibility to Roosevelt's favorite unofficial emissary, Harry Hopkins, who went to Moscow late in May. "I told Harry he could use diplomatic language or he could use a baseball bat if he thought that was the proper approach," Truman wrote. Hopkins's sympathetic attitude toward the Russians was no secret; Truman knew very well that his approach would be conciliatory. The Hopkins-Stalin conversations did much to clear the air. They worked out a compromise on Poland that preserved Soviet influence there but allowed the West to save face; Stalin reiterated his promise to enter the war against Japan and helped resolve a stalemate at San Francisco by accepting the American formula on voting in the UN Security Council; and, finally, the Russian leader agreed to meet Truman and Churchill in July at Potsdam, just outside Berlin.

Potsdam was the longest of the wartime summits—two and a half weeks—but it produced the fewest agreements. The Big Three did negotiate a complicated accord on German reparations, but had to refer other controversial issues to the Council of Foreign Ministers, which was to meet at regular intervals after the war. Truman found Potsdam a frustrating experience. "Churchill talks all the time and Stalin just grunts," he complained. "On a number of occasions I felt like blowing the roof off the palace." The president believed that disagreements stemmed from misunderstandings rather than basic conflicts of interest, however. This was to be expected, given language differences and the fact that discussion of so many issues had been postponed until after the war. "If there is complete understanding, there wouldn't be very many difficulties between us," he later commented, "because Russia's interests and ours do not clash, and never have. We have always been friends, and I hope we always will be."

Truman's initial months in office, therefore, offer little evidence to sustain the thesis that the new president deliberately set out to reverse Roosevelt's policy of cooperation with the Russians. Continuity, rather than change, was the keynote as far as the substance of policy was concerned. The difference was style: where Roosevelt had sought to woo Stalin by meeting his demands whenever possible, Truman, like a good poker player, tried to deal from positions of rhetorical, if not actual, strength. The new president's tough talk was designed to facilitate, not impede, negotiations. Any appearance of weakness, he thought, would only encourage the Russians to ask for more.

What Truman failed to take into account was the possibility that the Russians might also be bluffing. In retrospect, it is becoming increasingly obvious that insecurity, not self-confidence, motivated Soviet policy during this period. Severely weakened by years of war and internal upheaval, the Russians badly needed peace and the opportunity to rebuild. Truman's tough rhetoric, together with America's awesome demonstration of the power of the atomic bomb at Hiroshima, may well have reinforced Stalin's conviction that if *he* showed any signs of weakness, all would be lost. Both sides had learned too well that appeasement never pays. Prospects for an amicable resolution of differences suffered accordingly.

Truman soon realized that it would not be enough simply to carry out Roosevelt's policies. FDR had never formulated his ideas on the postwar relationship between Washington and Moscow with any precision; he had simply assumed that the alliance forged by the existence of common enemies would survive after those enemies had been destroyed. Roosevelt lived just long enough to see that this was not likely to happen but died before he could come up with a plan to meet the new situation. Truman listened carefully to the late president's advisers, but in the end it was he who had to decide what to do. Knowing relatively little about Russia but pressed by the need for action, Truman of necessity fell back upon past experience as a guide. The elements of his program were not always consistent, because lessons drawn from various experiences affected policy in different ways. The net result, though, was to bring about, by early 1946, a determination to make no further concessions to the Russians.

The experience of meeting Stalin at Potsdam did not sour Truman on the possibility of good relations with the Soviet Union; rather, it seems to have encouraged him. In common with most other Americans who dealt with the Russian dictator, Truman found him personally likable, despite his shrewd and tenacious negotiating tactics. Probably any Russian would have seemed gracious after Molotov. There were some tense moments at Potsdam, especially when Stalin refused to consider a pet scheme the president had concocted for the internationalization of strategic waterways; but Truman returned home with a grudging respect for the Soviet leader, in whom he sensed something familiar. "Stalin," he later told Jonathan Daniels, "is as near like Tom Pendergast as any man I know."

What the Kremlin autocrat would have made of this comparison is difficult to say, but Truman drew important conclusions from it. One was that Stalin was a fellow politician, with whom one could make a deal. If he and Stalin could only sit down with each other, the president told Joseph Davies in 1946, they could "get together on a fair basis that would support peace, at least for a trial. But it was impossible to make a deal with Molotov. He was not a 'big man' like Stalin. That was clearly shown at Potsdam. Without Stalin at the table, it would have been impossible to get anywhere with Molotov." Truman liked to say of Kansas City boss Tom Pendergast that, whatever his other faults, he had always kept his word. For a long time the president persisted in the belief that Stalin, had he been able, would have done the same thing; but the Russian leader, Truman regretfully concluded, was not a free

agent. "After all," he told C. L. Sulzberger, "[Stalin] is only
secretary of the Politburo and has his troubles with the other
thirteen members just the way I have my troubles here with my
Cabinet and the Congress." The president confided to a whistle-
stop audience during the 1948 campaign: "I like old Joe, but Joe is
a prisoner of the Politburo. He can't do what he wants to. He
makes agreements, and if he could he would keep them; but the
people who run the government are very specific in saying that he
can't keep them."

Truman's conviction that "you can understand the Russian
situation if you understand Jackson County" was perhaps naïve.
There is no evidence that Stalin's domestic constituency imposed
significant limits on his freedom of action. Truman drew another
analogy from his experience in Kansas City politics that was quite
revealing. The Russians, he believed, were negotiating from
weakness rather than strength. "A dictatorship is the hardest thing
in God's world to hold together because it is made up entirely of
conspiracies from the inside." This was a perceptive and largely
accurate insight into the nature of the Stalinist regime. Because of
it, Truman found it easy to accept the key point of George F.
Kennan's analysis of Soviet behavior, that internal problems
explained Moscow's hostility, not any blueprint for external
expansion.

Unfortunately, Truman failed to connect this conclusion and
his equally strong conviction that the best way to deal with an
opponent was to take the offensive. The possibility that a weak
and suspicious adversary might mistake bluffing for belligerence
seems to have escaped him. Thus, when Stalin made two tentative
efforts to increase Soviet influence in Iran and Turkey in 1946,
Truman responded by treating the situations not as defensive
probes by the Russians reflecting their own insecurity, but as
extremely dangerous threats which, if not contained, would bring
on World War III. The U.S. lodged a public protest in the United
Nations, Truman sent the fleet to the Mediterranean, and, in the
case of the Turkish episode, he actually resolved to go to war if
necessary to repel the Russians. Luckily, it was not necessary;
Stalin backed down both times. Because threats, not negotiations,
had produced results, these incidents reinforced Truman's penchant for the "tough approach" at the expense of his instinct for
compromise. They probably also reinforced the Russians' view
that Truman, unlike Roosevelt, had no interest in ensuring that the

Soviet Union satisfy what it considered to be its legitimate security needs.

The Iranian crisis also convinced Truman that the Russians could not be trusted to keep their agreements. Stalin had promised to have Soviet troops out of northern Iran (which they had occupied during World War II) by 2 March 1946. His failure to meet this deadline was no small matter. "I held [Stalin] to be a man of his word," Truman noted shortly thereafter. "Troops in Iran after March 2 upset that theory." By 1947, the president had come to believe that the Soviets had not kept any of the commitments they had made during the war. "I have tried my level best to get along with our friends the Russians," he observed, "and I still want to get along with them. But when I make straight out and out agreements with a government, in the name of the United States of America, and not a single one of those agreements is carried out, I have got to use other methods. They understand one language, and that is the language they are going to get from me from this point." There is no doubt that the Russians did have a cavalier attitude about meeting their obligations. In a report to the president in 1946 White House aide Clark Clifford counted some twenty violations of written agreements within the previous four years. Many of these accords were vaguely worded, however, and therefore were susceptible to varying interpretations. Truman's insistence that the Russians meet the same standards of behavior he expected from his personal associates made these discrepancies seem more sinister than they actually were.

Truman did not, interestingly enough, regard ideology as a motive for Soviet expansion. "There's no Socialism in Russia," he wrote in 1945. "It is a hotbed of special privilege." The only example of true communism, he liked to argue, was the Sermon on the Mount. In Truman's view the official ideology of the Soviet state was just a facade for totalitarianism. "Really there is no difference between the government which Mr. Molotov represents and the one the Czar represented—or the one Hitler spoke for." The Soviet Union constituted a threat, therefore, but it was not much different from that posed by Germany and Japan before World War II. Communism, in Truman's opinion, had little to do with it.

Despite his later rhetoric Truman did not—at least in the early days of the cold war—see the international Communist movement as monolithic. Russian imperialism was the real problem; aside from some 1948 campaign oratory there were surprisingly few references in his pre–Korean War speeches to the dangers of world revolution. Truman foresaw the possibility that Communist parties outside Russia's immediate sphere of influence might reject Moscow's leadership and thus was quick to take advantage of Tito's defection in 1948, despite the fact that Yugoslavia remained firmly Communist. He always doubted Moscow's control over China's Communists; one reason Mao Tse-tung's victory upset him so little was that he expected serious difficulties to develop between Moscow and Peking. "I think you will find . . . that the Russians will turn out to be the 'foreign devils' in China," Truman wrote to Arthur Vandenberg in 1949, "and that the situation will help establish a Chinese Government that we can recognize and support."

It has been argued that Truman was insensitive in his dealings with the Russians. To a degree, this was true; but his was an insensitivity derived from inexperience, not deliberate animosity. Despite his own repugnance for the Soviet regime, Truman wanted peace just as badly as Stalin. His perception of Stalin's policy convinced him, though, as it did many other observers at the time, that peace would be safe only if Russian expansion were resisted. The Soviet dictator perceived security *only* in terms of expansion; his probes around his borders, his tough negotiating tactics, his cynical attitude toward agreements he had made seemed almost calculated to drive a man like Truman to the conclusion that "force is the only thing they understand." Nor is it clear in retrospect that Truman was wrong. Stalin's aims do appear to have been limited, but there is no assurance they would have remained so had the West not resisted. The problem Truman faced was how to resist Soviet expansion without at the same time overextending American resources. It was a dilemma much on the mind of the president and his advisers as they began to formulate the policy that came to be known as "containment."

◇◇◇

Harry S. Truman arose before a joint session of Congress on 12 March 1947 to proclaim that "it must be the policy of the United States to support free peoples who are resisting attempted subjugation by armed minorities or by outside pressures." Four months later, George F. Kennan, head of the State Department's

Policy Planning Staff, wrote in the journal *Foreign Affairs* that "the main element of any United States policy toward the Soviet Union must be that of a long-term, patient but firm and vigilant containment of Russian expansive tendencies." Few statements in the history of American diplomacy have produced more confusion. Journalists immediately linked the two, assuming that it was now Washington's policy to oppose communism wherever it appeared. Historians reached similar conclusions, viewing 1947 either as the point at which the United States abandoned isolationism and took up its legitimate responsibilities as a world power, or, alternatively, as the point at which the United States became a world policeman, dispatching men and resources all over the world in a futile attempt to contain a mythical monolith, the international Communist conspiracy.

In fact, neither Truman's speech nor Kennan's article conveyed what their authors intended; both are excellent examples of the obfuscatory potential of imprecise prose. The Truman administration had no global plan for the containment of communism in 1947. Its goal was the considerably less ambitious one of restoring the balance of power in Europe; its choice of means for accomplishing this reflected a keen awareness of the limitations, rather than the omnipotence, of American power.

For American leaders throughout the twentieth century the most important requirement for a congenial international environment has been that Europe not fall under the domination of a single hostile state. Concern over the European balance of power goes back at least to the turn of the century; certainly such considerations influenced Woodrow Wilson's efforts to mediate World War I and his subsequent entry into that struggle. The totalitarian nature of Hitler's regime made Nazi Germany's threat twenty years later seem particularly ominous; it was clearly decisive in persuading Franklin D. Roosevelt that he could not allow the collapse of Great Britain after France fell in 1940. Japan's attack on Pearl Harbor actually thrust the United States into World War II, but the Roosevelt administration had decided a year and a half earlier to risk war in order to prevent the totalitarian domination of all of Europe. Truman, thus, was hardly breaking new ground when he described the world as polarized between democracy and totalitarianism; it can be argued that the American commitment to oppose threats to the balance of power in Europe goes back at least to 1940, and possibly to 1917. What was novel about the Truman Doctrine was not that it marked any fundamental shift in the basic objectives of United States foreign policy, but rather that it indicated the emergence of a new challenge to these objectives in the postwar behavior of the Soviet Union.

Truman and his advisers saw Moscow's threat to the European balance of power as political and economic, not military. Wartime devastation and natural calamities had so disrupted life in Europe that Communist parties in France, Italy, Greece, and elsewhere were thought to have excellent chances of coming to power through coups or even free elections. This prospect seemed dangerous, not because of the general repugnance these men felt for communism, though that certainly existed, but rather because the European Communist parties were, between 1945 and 1948, tools of the Kremlin. Their victory would have placed Europe under the domination of a single hostile power, the very thing Americans had fought World Wars I and II to prevent. United States policy in Europe from 1947 through 1949—the Truman Doctrine, the Marshall Plan, the Vandenberg Resolution, the North Atlantic Treaty, and the Military Assistance Program—can best be understood as an attempt, through political, economic, and, later, military means, to achieve a goal largely psychological in nature: the creation of a state of mind among Europeans conducive to the revival of faith in democratic procedures. As Kennan later put it, "It had been primarily the shadow, rather than the substance, of danger which we, in contemplating a European recovery program, had been concerned to dispel."

The president's advisers did more than he to shape this imaginative and, on the whole, successful policy, but it was Truman who selected these men. Well aware of his own intellectual limitations, Truman never let his ego get in the way of accepting recommendations from experts better informed than he. At the same time, he had enormous respect for the office he occupied; while he was prepared to accord subordinates large areas of responsibility, he insisted that they defer to his ultimate authority by keeping him informed at every stage of the policy-making process and by bringing all final decisions to him. Advisers who did this could expect confidence, a free hand on most issues, and intense personal loyalty.

The careers of Secretary of State George C. Marshall, from 1947 to 1949, and Dean Acheson, who filled that position from 1949 to 1953, illustrate this tendency clearly. Both men carefully kept Truman apprised of what they were doing; in return the president let them formulate foreign policy without White House interference. When Marshall objected to a hastily conceived scheme to send Chief Justice Fred Vinson to Moscow during the final days of the 1948 campaign, Truman immediately vetoed the idea, despite the fact that this required an embarrassing public reversal of policy on the eve of a hard-fought election. Acheson came under intense criticism from right-wing elements during his term of office but Truman doggedly defended him, even though Acheson's resignation might have considerably simplified the task of conducting foreign policy. Marshall and Acheson were both good judges of men; the subordinates they recruited implemented containment with a considerable degree of skill and ingenuity. Truman's wide grant of authority actually made the Department of State, for one of the few times in recent history, the government's chief policy-making agency in the field of foreign affairs. Its performance under this mandate was impressive.

There is no doubt that Truman's choice of advisers limited the range of options brought before him for consideration; but presidents must, in self-defense, restrict the number of counselors to whom they listen. Although the number of viewpoints Truman could consider were therefore limited, he himself was not narrow-minded. The White House staff did not screen options for this president; he generally insisted on hearing alternatives directly from their advocates and on deciding among them himself. Nor did he confuse disagreement with disloyalty; advisers whose recommendations did not meet with presidential approval usually continued to enjoy the chief executive's confidence as long as they met the requirements of deference, decisiveness, and disinterestedness upon which he insisted in his counselors. Comparisons between administrations are difficult to make, but it does seem likely that the relationship Truman established with his advisers provided him with a greater range of alternatives from which to choose than most of his successors have enjoyed.

The basic idea behind containment was a congenial one for Truman: that economic assistance, not military force, was the best way to resist Soviet expansion. "Communism succeeds only when there is weakness, or misery, or despair," he argued. "It cannot succeed in a strong and healthy society." Peace and prosperity went together in Truman's mind; as living standards increased throughout the world, he believed, chances of war would decline.

Like many former New Dealers, Truman was perhaps naïve in his passionate expectation that economic development would cure the world's ills. "I have been dreaming of TVAs in the Euphrates Valley, . . . in the Yangtze Valley and the Danube," he once told David Lilienthal. The president grasped the vital importance of economic recovery in the reconstruction of Europe, and he strongly supported his advisers who advocated this policy. He also played a major role in convincing the American people that it was in their interest to help finance that process.

Truman was keenly aware of the limits of American power, and of the consequent need to distinguish between peripheral and vital interests. "Our resources are not unlimited," he observed in 1947. "We must apply them where they can serve the most effectively to bring production, freedom, and confidence back to the world." Europe had first priority in his mind; he sought to minimize involvement in other troublespots, like China and the Middle East, which seemed less vital to American security. The administration quite deliberately channeled available funds into the European Recovery Program, despite the fact that this required such rigid ceilings on military expenditures by 1948 that the Joint Chiefs of Staff could promise only to defend Great Britain and the Western Hemisphere if war came. The assumption, of course, was that there would be no war, that restoration of the balance of power in Europe would be sufficient to ensure United States security. Confronted with a revived and confident Western Europe, it was believed, Stalin, or, more likely, his successor, would abandon plans for expansion and accept peaceful coexistence with the capitalist world.

Although Truman believed strongly in the virtues of military preparedness, he was equally convinced that the armed forces ought to be the instrument of the nation's foreign policy, not the other way around. Accordingly, he did not hesitate to hold the military to what was left in the national budget after domestic needs and the European Recovery Program had been funded. "The Marshall plan is . . . cheaper than a shooting war would be," he explained. Truman's arbitrary ceilings on arms expenditures during the 1947–50 period stemmed in part from the great significance he attached to balancing the budget; inflation, he feared, would set off a new depression, which was what the Russians wanted. These constraints also reflected a healthy skepticism on Truman's part about exaggerated military estimates. "The air boys are for glamour and the navy as always is the greatest of propaganda machines," he wrote in 1948. "I want a balanced sensible defense for which the country can pay." Secretary of Defense James V. Forrestal, the victim of many of Truman's budget slashes, later commented, "In the person of Harry S. Truman I have seen the most rocklike example of civilian control that the world has ever witnessed."

Despite the sweeping language of the Truman Doctrine and Kennan's containment article, therefore, the actual policies the United States followed between 1947 and 1950 hardly justify description as an all-out effort to contain communism everywhere. Rather Truman and his advisers appear to have been seeking a world in which several centers of power could exist, each exerting a restraining influence on the other. It is difficult, otherwise, to explain the administration's persistent enthusiasm for European unification and, after 1948, Japanese rehabilitation. It seems the only way to account for the almost desperate efforts of Truman and Acheson to keep their options open in dealing with Communist China. Even the administration's steadfast refusal to negotiate with the Russians on substantive issues was a holding tactic. It was never meant to preclude meaningful discussions once the "situations of strength" of which Acheson liked to speak had been established. Speculation about what did not happen is always perilous, but it does seem possible that the policies of Truman, Marshall, and Acheson, had they been allowed to run their course, might have resulted in the evolution of a multipolar world operating on balance of power principles, a world not too different, ironically enough, from what became the apparent objective, twenty years later, of Henry Kissinger and Richard Nixon.

It did not work out that way. By the end of Truman's administration the United States had moved from implementation of a restrained and cautious policy with limited objectives toward a new and far more sweeping program of action that posited the challenge to United States security as worldwide and made no real distinction between varieties of communism. Containment became globalized; it was at this point that the gap between Washington's commitments and its resources for meeting them began to widen. The reasons for this are many and complex. Certainly Truman's actions alone did not wreck chances for the emergence of the kind of world he wanted to see; the president was, to a large extent, at the mercy of circumstances beyond his control. As Truman would have been the first to admit, however, presidents cannot escape at least partial responsibility for what happens during their term of office. Two characteristics of Truman and his advisers—an inability to see situations from the viewpoint of other countries and a certain casualness about means employed to gain their objectives—contributed to the process by which the United States embarked upon a policy of global containment.

Leaders of great nations often see their own countries as the target of moves by potential adversaries while assuming that their actions could not possibly be interpreted by a rival as hostile. Truman operated in this manner. He consistently stressed the purity of American motives while assuming the worst of the Russians, then puzzled over why Moscow suspected sinister intentions on Washington's part. This tendency was particularly apparent in Truman's attitude toward the international control of atomic energy. The United States, he believed, had made the most generous offer in the history of the world by proposing to turn over control of nuclear weapons to the United Nations. When the Russians failed to view the Baruch Plan in the same light, Truman concluded that they were up to no good, ignoring their understandable reservations about United States retention of sole custody of atomic weapons until the control scheme went into effect. The administration responded in a similar manner during 1947 and 1948 to the creation of the Cominform, the Hungarian and Czechoslovak coups, and the Berlin blockade. It now seems clear, as Kennan pointed out at the time, that these were defensive responses by the Soviets to the unexpected psychological impact of the Truman Doctrine and the Marshall Plan. Truman and his advisers treated them as new provocations and responded by pushing formation of the North Atlantic Treaty Organization and creation of an independent West Germany, moves that stimulated further counter-escalation by the Russians.

In Truman's defense, it ought to be pointed out that Stalin was as prone to this kind of thinking as were Washington officials; he tended to regard every United States action as directed against him. In the case of the Soviet dictator, the problem was compounded by a paranoia so intense that he would not trust even his closest subordinates, much less leaders of the capitalist world. Roosevelt had tried to break through this barrier during the war by doing everything he could to meet Stalin's wishes, but in the end the effort failed; Stalin remained as suspicious as ever. There seems, in retrospect, little Truman could have done to overcome Stalin's paranoia, but he need not have exacerbated it to the extent that he did. A greater concern with how Moscow would interpret American actions might have prevented this.

Truman was also less careful than he ought to have been about the means he employed to gain his objectives; these backfired more than once. Upon the recommendation of his advisers, the president deliberately exaggerated the Soviet threat in his March 1947 address calling for aid to Greece and Turkey and in another appearance before Congress a year later in which he sought to assure final passage of the Marshall Plan, the revival of selective service, and the establishment of universal military training. There were good reasons for making all-out pitches in both of these situations—congressional purse strings were tightly drawn—but the imprecision of Truman's rhetoric made it difficult for Congress or the public to distinguish, as the administration sought to, between Soviet expansionism and international communism. This became painfully obvious with regard to the Far East, where Truman, fearful of impairing support for the European Recovery Program, did nothing to explain why communism was coming to power in China, or how it was that the United States was not resisting that development. The resulting backlash far exceeded in severity anything that would have occurred had Truman been candid about China from the first.

The administration's preoccupation with bipartisanship further encouraged this casualness about means. For men of Truman's generation, who had seen Woodrow Wilson's dream of a league of nations collapse because of partisan bickering, the idea that domestic political differences ought not to extend to foreign policy was close to sacrosanct. Nor were the president and his advisers unsuccessful. On most issues relating to international affairs during this period (China is the major exception), partisan politics did exert little influence; but this consensus, which was supposed to be a means of achieving an enlightened foreign policy, too often became an end in itself. The effect was to

Gib Crockett, Washington Star-News (24 September 1951), and Harry S. Truman Library

discourage public discussion of controversial subjects and to cause officials to employ greater resourcefulness in seeking unity at home than in obtaining a reduction of tensions abroad.

Early in September 1949 United States intelligence discovered that the Russians had exploded their first atomic bomb. Truman received this information calmly, for he had never expected the American nuclear monopoly to last indefinitely. Still, the Soviet explosion had come three years earlier than government experts had anticipated. News of it shattered one of the most cherished assumptions of the 1947–49 period—that even if war with Russia came, the physical security of the United States would not be at stake. Shortly after Truman announced that the Russians had the weapon, information leaked out that United States scientists were studying the feasibility of constructing a "super" or hydrogen bomb. Once this happened, Americans quickly fell prey to the illusion that development of a bigger weapon would regain for the United States the advantage it had lost.

In retrospect it seems that this might have been a good time to renew negotiations on international control and other unresolved issues, for the Russians had achieved a rough form of strategic parity, NATO was a fact of life, the Berlin blockade had been settled, and the depression that Soviet economists had been predicting for the United States had not come. Domestic politics, together with the tendency of Truman and his advisers to interpret Russian behavior as invariably offensive, prevented serious consideration of this option. In January 1950, Truman announced that the United States would build a hydrogen bomb. Not for another two decades would Washington officials come to realize that, in the area of nuclear weapons, parity offered greater security than superiority.

The decision to build the hydrogen bomb, in turn, forced reconsideration of the rigid budget ceilings Truman had placed on defense expenditures. Oddly, this reassessment originated in the civilian sector of the government, not the military. Truman's economic advisers had begun to argue that the nation could afford to expand its productive capacity, thus generating increased government revenue, without inflation. These ideas were put forward in support of the president's domestic program, but State Department planners, concerned over the Soviet atomic bomb, quickly seized on them as a justification for increased military spending. The result was NSC-68 (National Security Council

NSC 68

memorandum no. 68), the nation's first formal statement of national security policy. This document pictured the Soviet Union as aspiring to world hegemony, refused to rule out the possibility of war, and recommended a much broader, more energetic, and more expensive effort to counter this threat. The question of whether communism motivated Moscow's policy or was the instrument of it was left unclear, but by defining the Soviet challenge as worldwide NSC-68 encouraged the tendency to equate the interests of communism everywhere with those of the Kremlin. Coming at a time when the threat of communism appeared to have increased, and when domestic pressures for more vigorous efforts to contain it had intensified, NSC-68 indicated how a global policy of resisting communism could be implemented without bankrupting the country.

Truman still had not accepted the final recommendations of NSC-68 when the Korean War broke out late in June 1950, but that event could hardly have been better calculated to insure their approval. The administration assumed from the first that the Russians had sanctioned the North Korean attack, a conclusion that recent evidence from Soviet sources tends to support. By suggesting that Soviet ambitions were not confined to Europe or the Middle East, and that Stalin would risk war to attain them, the invasion seemed to confirm, in the most dramatic way, the basic premises of NSC-68. Truman had no difficulty in finding an appropriate historical parallel: "In my generation, this was not the first occasion when the strong had attacked the weak. I recalled some earlier instances: Manchuria, Ethiopia, Austria. I remembered how each time that the democracies failed to act it had encouraged the aggressors to keep going ahead. Communism was acting in Korea just as Hitler, Mussolini, and the Japanese had acted ten, fifteen, and twenty years earlier." After consulting with Acheson, Truman ordered the supreme Allied commander in occupied Japan, General Douglas MacArthur, to assist the South Koreans, first with air and naval forces, then, as the situation became more serious, with ground troops. Simultaneously, the United States convened an emergency session of the United Nations Security Council which condemned the North Korean invasion (the Russian delegate, for reasons still obscure, was absent) and endorsed the effort to repel the attack as a United Nations operation.

Had Truman stopped there it seems likely that the United

States could have resisted aggression in Korea without involving Communist China; but the inability of Truman and his advisers to see events from the opponent's point of view, together with their casual attitude toward means, led Truman to authorize two additional steps that in effect, by the end of 1950, involved the United States in an undeclared war with China. On 27 June Truman announced that the Seventh Fleet was patrolling the Formosa Strait; three months later, General MacArthur received permission to cross the thirty-eighth parallel and "liberate" North Korea.

Republican leaders in Congress had been pressing for a United States guarantee of Formosa's security since Chiang Kai-shek fled to that island late in 1949. Truman had resisted, partly because he considered the Nationalists mainly "grafters and crooks," partly because he and his secretary of state still hoped for a split between Communist China and the Soviet Union and did not want to jeopardize this possibility by adopting a "two China" policy. By sending the fleet to patrol the Formosa Strait two days after the Korean War broke out, Truman and Acheson sought to disarm domestic critics and at the same time reassure Peking that "neutralization" of Formosa was "without prejudice to the political questions affecting that island." The Chinese Communists refused to be reassured. Long suspicious of American motives because of the aid Washington had continued to dole out to the Nationalists (principally to placate Republican critics), Mao Tse-tung and his colleagues interpreted the "neutralization" of Formosa as United States intervention in the Chinese civil war on the side of Chiang Kai-shek. Truman intended so such thing, but in his search for short-term unanimity on the home front, he compromised the administration's long-term goal of playing off the Chinese against the Russians.

Much more damaging was the decision, made in September 1950, to change the objective of the fighting in Korea from defense of the south to "liberation" of the north by allowing General MacArthur to cross the thirty-eighth parallel. This followed MacArthur's brilliant landing at Inchon on 15 September which trapped most of the North Korean army in the south and gave Washington officials the illusion that victory was at hand. Unwilling to halt the momentum built up by a highly successful (and politically outspoken) general, Truman and Acheson authorized the move into North Korea despite the risk of Chinese Communist intervention. In doing so, they acted on two assumptions: that the Chinese would accept assurances that the move was not directed against them, and that MacArthur would follow orders not to deploy his troops in such a manner as to make intervention likely. Neither assumption held. As MacArthur's forces moved north, the Chinese, after warning publicly of their intentions, began infiltrating troops across the Yalu River. MacArthur gave them a tremendous opportunity by foolishly splitting his forces, and late in November the Chinese attacked in full force, bringing about the immediate evacuation of United Nations troops from North Korea. The United States was now involved in a limited war with China. The Truman-Acheson policy of playing Peking off against Moscow lay in ruins.

This was the darkest hour of Truman's presidency, but it was also, in some ways, the finest. The president wisely chose not to respond to the Chinese attack with a counter-escalation of his own which would have meant all-out war with Peking and the probable involvement of the Soviet Union. Instead, he returned to his original objective of driving invading forces from South Korean soil, even though this meant accepting a stalemate on the battlefield. When MacArthur publicly questioned this strategy, Truman relieved him of his command, a move that solidified for years to come the principle of civilian control over the military. At the same time the president authorized his diplomats to begin seeking a negotiated settlement of the war. The armistice took two years to arrange. By the time it was completed Truman was out of office; but it was he who kept the first hot war of the nuclear age limited. For this valuable precedent the world owes him a considerable debt.

By getting into an unnecessary fight with the Chinese Communists, the Truman administration encouraged the view that international communism was a monolith that had to be resisted wherever it appeared. From this it was easy for succeeding administrations to jump to the conclusion that there was no distinction between peripheral and vital interests, that threats to order anywhere endangered American security everywhere. Truman and his counselors never shared this view. Even during the most bitter fighting in Korea they kept their attention focused on Europe, which they believed to be the decisive theater of the cold war. The Far East, for them, was never of more than secondary significance.

The language the Truman administration used failed to reflect the caution its behavior demonstrated in practice. Statements of policy like the Truman Doctrine and NSC-68 are probably necessary; bureaucracies cannot function without broad guidelines establishing operating procedures. Men who draft such statements tend to forget, however, that they will not always be present to control implementation. Sweeping proclamations have a tendency to survive those who proclaim them; successors may not apply them as cautiously as their originators intended. Thus it was that the rhetoric of the Truman administration lived after it; but its restraint was interred in its archives.

"I have been asked whether I have any regrets about any of the major decisions I had to make as President," Truman wrote in 1960. "I have none. . . . There were many things that had to be done that might have been handled some other way. But considering the information available at the time and the circumstances prevailing when I had to make many of my decisions, I do not see how I could have acted very differently." This is not an unreasonable assessment. Policy makers are at the mercy of their own preconceptions and their perceptions of situations as they occur. Decisions do have to be made; action does have to be taken, often on the basis of limited information. "If you are going to walk the floor and worry yourself to death every time you have to make a decision," Truman observed, "then you are not suited for the job."

It did not take much agonizing to realize that, in the view of the overwhelming majority of informed Americans, the behavior of the Soviet Union after World War II did constitute a threat to the security of the United States. Stalin at no point made clear the limited nature of his objectives; what Americans saw was a progressive escalation of anticapitalist propaganda together with a pattern of action among Communist parties throughout the world too well coordinated to ignore. The Truman administration did not have to trick Congress or the public into initially supporting containment. The problem was rather to bring popular determination to resist the Russians into line with the nation's capability for doing so.

Truman and his advisers did this well. Their goal was to restrict the further expansion of Soviet influence by reinvigorating

European society in the shortest possible time with the minimum possible expenditure of American resources. They succeeded brilliantly, aided by the clumsy brutality with which the Russians cracked down on the Hungarians, Czechs, and Berliners in 1947 and 1948. The initiative in Europe had passed to the West by 1949; containment had worked, without war, inflation, or militarization.

There comes a time, though, when negotiation must replace confrontation if any settlement of differences is to be reached. The president and his counselors failed to make this transition. The difficulty was that continued public and congressional support for containment hinged upon the existence of an obvious threat to American security. Administration officials feared that prolonged discussions with the Russians, even if unproductive, might encourage complacency and a return to isolationism. That could be disastrous, because the whole objective of containment had been to instill confidence in the minds of those vulnerable to Soviet expansionism. The success of postwar American foreign policy had come to depend, in a curious and profoundly tragic way, upon the enduring credibility of the threat it had been designed to contain.

Security is an intangible; only after it has been lost can one estimate with any precision what would have been necessary to maintain it. It now seems probable that the Truman administration missed a promising opportunity to negotiate seriously with the Russians in 1949; after Korea, prospects for a mutual reduction of tensions were much bleaker. It ought to be kept in mind that Truman did not possess the advantage of hindsight; quite understandably he preferred to overestimate American security requirements, even if this helped perpetuate the cold war. Placed in his position, given what he knew at the time, not many responsible men would have acted differently.

BIBLIOGRAPHIC NOTE

Students of Harry S. Truman's foreign policy must, at present, rely chiefly upon printed materials since the pertinent documents at the National Archives and the Harry S. Truman Library are, for the most part, still closed to researchers. Truman's own memoirs, *Year of Decisions* (Garden City, N.Y., 1955) and *Years of Trial and Hope, 1946–1952* (Garden City, N.Y., 1956), provide a basic source, though they should be used with some care. A postpresidential memoir, *Mr. Citizen* (New York, 1960), is also useful. Truman's public statements while in office appear in the *Public Papers of the Presidents: Harry S. Truman, 1945–1953* (Washington, D.C., 1961–66), and there is also some information on Truman's views in the appropriate volumes of the Department of State's series *Foreign Relations of the United States,* which now covers the period through 1947.

Richard S. Kirkendall is writing a biography of Truman; until it appears the best accounts are Margaret Truman, *Harry S. Truman* (New York, 1972), Bert Cochran, *Harry Truman and the Crisis Presidency* (New York, 1973), Jonathan Daniels, *Man of Independence* (Philadelphia, 1950), Alfred Steinberg, *The Man from Missouri* (New York, 1962), Cabell Phillips, *The Truman Presidency* (New York, 1966), and William Hillman, *Mr. President* (New York, 1952), which reprints excerpts from Truman's fragmentary diary. See also two articles by Kirkendall, "Truman's Path to Power," *Social Science* 43 (April 1968), 67–73; and "Harry S. Truman," in Morton Borden, ed., *America's Eleven Greatest Presidents* (Chicago, 1971), pp. 255–88.

Biographies in the series American Secretaries of State and Their Diplomacy, edited by Robert H. Ferrell and Samuel Flagg Bemis, provide useful discussions of the Truman administration's foreign policy; see especially George Curry, *James F. Byrnes* (New York, 1965), Robert H. Ferrell, *George C. Marshall* (New York, 1966), and Gaddis Smith, *Dean Acheson* (New York, 1972). Also of value are Dean Acheson, *Present at the Creation: My Years in the State Department* (New York, 1969), George F. Kennan, *Memoirs,* 2 vols. (Boston, 1967, 1972), *The Journals of David E. Lilienthal,* 5 vols. (New York, 1964–1971), especially volume 2, Walter Millis, ed., *The Forrestal Diaries* (New York, 1951), Arthur H. Vandenberg, Jr., ed., *The Private Papers of Senator Vandenberg* (New York, 1952), James F. Byrnes, *Speaking Frankly* (New York, 1947) and *All in One Lifetime* (New York, 1958), and Charles E. Bohlen, *Witness to History, 1929–1969* (New York, 1973).

Important treatments of special topics include the following: Joseph M. Jones, *The Fifteen Weeks (February 21–June 5, 1947)* (New York, 1955), Warner R. Schilling, Paul Y. Hammond, and Glenn H. Snyder, *Strategy, Politics, and Defense Budgets* (New York, 1962), Alonzo L. Hamby, *Beyond the New Deal: Harry S. Truman and American Liberalism* (New York, 1973), Glenn Paige, *The Korean Decision, June 24–30, 1950* (New York, 1968), John W. Spanier, *The Truman-MacArthur Controversy and the Korean War* (New York, 1965), Barton J. Bernstein, ed., *The Politics and Policies of the Truman Administration* (Chicago, 1970), James David Barbour, *The Presidential Character: Predicting Performance in the White House* (Englewood Cliffs, N.J., 1972), and Richard E. Neustadt, *Presidential Power: The Politics of Leadership* (New York, 1960). A valuable collection of documents is Barton J. Bernstein and Allen J. Matusow, eds., *The Truman Administration: A Documentary History* (New York, 1966). Richard S. Kirkendall, ed., *The Truman Period as a Research Field* (Columbia, Mo., 1974), surveys opportunities for further research.

U.S. Information Agency

DEAN
ACHESON
Architect of a
Manageable World Order

Robert H. Ferrell and David McLellan

Throughout the history of the United States, since the beginning of government under the Constitution, the secretaryship of state has attracted individuals of intellect as well as action—this in opposition to the presidency, which has drawn men with the latter quality alone. Dean Acheson was no exception to this rule. Indeed, if compared with the other men who have held the first cabinet post, Acheson stands out as more intellectual, to use a word popular in our century, than most other secretaries. His was a special quality of intellect, in which he joined the power of logical thought with a talent in use of words; he was the author of eight books including a Pulitzer Prize–winning account of his secretaryship. The only secretaries of state who approached him in literary ability were Jefferson, whose writings appeared largely in the form of discursive letters, together with an occasional state

219

paper or philosophical utterance; and John Hay, whose poetry, so popular in his own time, is now happily forgotten.

To conclude, however, that Acheson was highly effective as secretary of state because he was so gifted with powers of analysis and prose is to venture upon only a portion of the reason for his greatness. A second factor was the president he served, a man of activity, of whom no one could contend that there was inability or unwillingness to make a decision. Acheson could never have worked easily or well with Harry S. Truman's predecessor, and the secretary's brisk judgment of Franklin D. Roosevelt, "admiration without affection," was more than just a personal appraisal. Roosevelt could twist and turn before making up his mind, and was not above or below allowing all sorts of confusion in administrative ranks before a decision at last was reached; not so Truman, who could weigh alternatives and take chances, serene in the belief that he had done his best. Even more fortunately for Acheson, the man of Independence possessed some of the same scholarly inclinations as the cultivated, articulate Washington lawyer. In the newspaper appraisals of Truman after the latter's death in the spring of 1973 one individual who lived in Independence said that he had watched, night after night, as he passed the iron-gated Victorian house, to see the light on in the upstairs study and the profile of the old president reading late into the evening. Acheson understood individuals such as Truman who were familiar with books; in a heartfelt letter to a librarian during the last years of his life he remarked that without books, without the experience of other individuals in other times gained through the printed page, there would have been for him "a sort of partial death—the death of all of me which extends beyond what I can see, hear, taste, or touch, pretty much the whole life of the mind."

The third factor that made Acheson an outstandingly successful secretary of state was of course the times, the dangerous era in which he exercised his power as the nation's leading official in the making of foreign policy. That era demanded greatness, and in cooperation with President Truman, Acheson made his now notable responses. This is not to say that circumstances alone always produce greatness, as a cynic might suppose; but the postwar period called for decisions of participation in affairs around the world, decisions of a sort that had concerned hardly any of the preceding secretaries of state. Acheson responded in ways that, taken together as a foreign policy, surely ensure his place among the memorable leaders of the nation.

The Middletown experience of Acheson's youth was especially important, perhaps even dominant, in the adult proportions of his life. The future secretary of state was born in that Connecticut town in 1893, the son of the Reverend Edward C. Acheson, the rector of the local Episcopalian church. His family background gave him a sense of identity that was to support him with an almost fatalistic serenity against the attacks later to be launched against him. From his father he acquired a stoic philosophy: "Much in life could not be affected or mitigated, and, hence, must be borne. Borne without complaint, because complaints were a bore and nuisance to others and undermined the serenity essential to endurance."[1] It was, perhaps, easy to practice such stoicism in his secure and privileged place. His status sometimes made Dean Acheson seem a little aloof, a little remote, even a little insensitive to the problems of more ordinary mortals. The feeling of compassion that led him to refuse to turn his back on Alger Hiss did not seem to extend as easily or as deeply to the man in the mass and could even lead to intolerance of those whose approach to problems seemed "sicklied o'er" by the pale cast of idealistic emotion. Still, there is a great deal to be said for a man who believed that the integrity of one's life was his most precious possession.

Academic writers, especially academic historians, are likely to maintain that, whatever the background, the experiences of college are important if not determinative. This was only partly true for Acheson. Yale College would always mean for him a place and time of enjoyment, and he earned only a "gentleman's C" average, presumably so that he would not stand out from the crowd of his fellows, but perhaps also because a C average was not that difficult to obtain. He would not have amounted to much beyond an elegant stockbroker or businessman of sorts had he not passed on from New Haven to Cambridge and attended the greatest law school of his time. At Harvard he came alive, rising

1. Dean Acheson, *Morning and Noon* (Boston, 1965), p. 18.

quickly to the challenge, perhaps in part out of realization that he had not done well at Yale. Among other faculty notables he encountered the still young Felix Frankfurter, who only a decade before had been assisting the U.S. district attorney in New York City, Henry L. Stimson. Already Frankfurter was weaving the web of friendships that would mark him off as one of the master maneuverers of the twentieth century in American politics. Upon seeing the stuff of which his student Acheson was made he arranged for him to clerk for Justice Louis D. Brandeis.

Frankfurter's decision was important to Acheson for two reasons. For one, it placed him under the tutelage of not merely a lawyer of competence but a man who was a Democrat and possessed a social conscience. It is true that Brandeis reinforced in Acheson the incipient strain of elitism; the Supreme Court justice believed that progress and civilization depended very much on the efforts of those few men in every society who have the will and intelligence to resist or overcome the ignorance and folly of the mass. Acheson certainly cultivated a similar outlook, which explains his manifest contempt for those in Congress and the press whom he thought should know better. From Brandeis, however, he also learned an anti–big business philosophy, sympathy for the underdog, and especially concern for the salvation of society.

After clerking for Brandeis it was easy for Acheson to enter a prestigious law firm, Covington and Burling, thereby exploiting his considerable intellectual qualities and his social agilities, becoming well known in the capital, making himself an ideal candidate for high appointive office when the time was right. For twenty years after serving Brandeis, Acheson pursued his law practice with Covington and Burling, a period broken only momentarily by appointment as undersecretary of the treasury in 1933 when the Democrats returned to power. This ill-starred arrangement lasted only a few months, when he got into a contention with President Roosevelt over the administration's monetary policies and with a commendable independence—a sort that was never far from any of his public positions—resigned. His behavior during his years in the Rooseveltian political wilderness, from 1934 to 1941, had a good deal to do with his return to presidential good graces. Roosevelt usually hated the people who quarreled with him. Few individuals were able to move out of the Roosevelt administration and then, years later, move back in again. Paradoxically, Acheson's commitment to New Deal philosophy and programs deepened in his years out of office.

Eventually, with the onset of the Second World War in Europe in 1939, it seemed clear to Acheson and to President Roosevelt that the country would have to help Britain and France, and Acheson joined with other Democrats in private life to speak publicly and otherwise sponsor support of the administration's pro-Allied moves. His help in arranging the destroyers-bases deal of 1940 was so notable that Roosevelt saw advantage in bringing him into the State Department; early in 1941 Acheson became assistant secretary in charge of economic affairs under Secretary Cordell Hull. During the brief secretaryship of Edward R. Stettinius, Jr., in 1944–45, he occupied the lightly regarded but important post of assistant secretary for congressional relations, after which he served as undersecretary for two years for Secretaries Byrnes and Marshall. Resigning in July 1947, he came back to the department as secretary in January 1949 and remained until the Democrats went out of office four years later.

Acheson's apprenticeship for the high office of secretary during these years was a time when the ideas of intelligent men changed rapidly, and there surely was a change in Acheson. Although his personal fortunes were barely touched by the Great Depression, its social ravages and its aftermath in the form of international lawlessness and aggression made a profound impression. He soon shared the view of Keynes and others that a better way of running the capitalist system would have to be found. As undersecretary he became a strong advocate of the International Monetary Fund and of lower tariffs against those individuals who would have returned to the dog-eat-dog days of the 1920s and 1930s. As the assistant secretary responsible for administering wartime lend-lease he became increasingly aware of the world's parlous economic condition. He frequently found himself opposed to Secretary of the Treasury Henry Morgenthau, Hull, Leo T. Crowley, who headed the Office of Economic Warfare, and even FDR in their attempts to use lend-lease to beat down Britain's imperial preference and economic defenses. His view was that the United States would need Britain's economic strength after the war both as a trading partner and as a force for political stability.

His years of apprenticeship were also a time when the Department of State was having organizational problems, which were compounded by the attitudes of President Roosevelt. FDR possessed a contempt for Hull, distrusted the Foreign Service, and preferred to rely upon the White House staff and a few friends in the department to decide most of the big diplomatic questions. Acheson shared the frustration of other department members at seeing their services treated so disparagingly; but he came to see that the department itself was not working well, for bureaucratic reasons of inertia, incompetence, and irrelevance. During the war the department had expanded from a small group of people, less than a thousand in all, to a vast bureaucracy of more than six thousand persons, only a few of whom were involved in the business of sending and receiving cables pertaining strictly to foreign policy of the old-fashioned prewar political sort. This bureaucracy was capable of good work, but it needed its motor overhauled. The big question that he asked himself when Byrnes offered him the undersecretaryship in 1945 was whether he could do that.

Late in 1944, when Hull resigned, Roosevelt chose the ineffective Stettinius to succeed him. Acheson was offered the post of assistant secretary for congressional relations in the expectation that he too would resign; instead he impudently accepted the post rather than quit, and an appointment that might have seemed a dead end turned out to have an important bearing on his career. It was his responsibility to pilot the United Nations Charter, the Bretton Woods Agreements, and other bills having foreign policy significance through the House and Senate. He came prepared to find dealing with politicians a degrading business, but he actually found it quite exhilarating. In the first place his gentlemanly style won him admission to the inner coterie of the Senate where, over ham sandwiches and bourbon, the important details of the legislative mill were decided. Secondly, he found that it tickled his vanity to be accepted as "one of the boys." Thirdly, since he was not the number-one man in the State Department, he was able to say some pretty harsh things against legislative critics and get away with it. Finally, he made the acquaintance of Harry S. Truman.

When Stettinius was propelled into the United Nations as U.S. representative in the summer of 1945 and replaced by Byrnes, the absence of the peripatetic "Jimmy" at a continuing series of international conferences (Byrnes was out of the country during almost half his tenure as secretary) gave Acheson, who meanwhile had been appointed undersecretary, a chance to get his hands on the administrative machinery. His administrative reordering of the department was an action of major importance. The device by which he brought the floundering bureaucracy into order was a simple one: the ordering of responsibility. He held a conference every morning of the work week during which he personally confronted the department's leading officers and asked for new business and disposition of the old. Everyone knew who was responsible for what, down to the lowliest desk officer. It was merely a matter of people to people, as a later administration described a different diplomacy; but a lot of dead wood had to be eliminated or circumvented, and the principal thing that made it work was Acheson's ability to impart to his immediate subordinates the conviction that what they were doing was important and therefore had to be done to the best of their ability. He detested committee meetings and especially committee decisions, which he believed always dropped to the lowest common denominator. He felt that the principal administrator of any office, bureau, or department needed to hear different opinions, even clashing opinions, but then had to make up his own mind and not take refuge in some group report. He believed most of all in clear lines of authority and responsibility.

During the Byrnes era, however, Acheson was not quite master in his own house, since it was Byrnes's house. This was an awkward arrangement; when Byrnes failed to keep the president informed, Acheson had to explain to Truman what was going on and report Truman's unhappiness to Byrnes. This unnecessary cleavage often put the president on the spot vis-à-vis the administration's critics, and even worse it permitted Senator Arthur H. Vandenberg, John Foster Dulles, and other Republican kibitzers to exert an unhealthy influence on the administration's diplomacy. For example, Truman made unduly hard-line promises to Vandenberg about atomic matters because Byrnes had not informed him of his own initiatives at the Moscow Foreign Ministers Conference of December 1945. Byrnes often undid the work the department had carried out at his own instruction. Perhaps the worst example of this was the fiasco over international atomic control. Before departing for Paris in early 1946 he instructed Acheson to prepare a comprehensive American plan for international control of atomic energy. After months of hard work by a committee led by the then head of the Tennessee Valley Authority David E. Lilienthal and the distinguished physicist J. Robert Oppenheimer, Acheson was able to present a brilliantly conceived plan for an international control system. Instead of adopting it as the basis of U.S. policy, however, Byrnes recommended that Truman appoint Bernard M. Baruch, a stuffed-shirt financier with a winter estate in Byrnes's home state of South Carolina, to head the U.S. delegation to the United Nations meeting on the subject. Baruch and several reactionary associates proceeded to burden the Acheson-Lilienthal Plan with unnecessary provisions for elimination of the veto in the UN Security Council and for all kinds of condign punishment for any state found guilty of cheating. The Soviet Union rejected the Baruch Plan out of hand.

In Byrnes's frequent absences from Washington it fell to Acheson as undersecretary and acting secretary to handle more and more of the day-to-day and month-to-month business of the department. Planning and decisions for the British and French loans, atomic energy, and the United Nations all came his way. At a time when squabbles over ending price control, settling coal and railroad strikes, and keeping harmony within the cabinet hurt the prestige of the administration, he succeeded in running foreign policy on a more efficient basis and in delivering a series of mildly impressive congressional victories—sufficiently impressive for James Reston to write that nothing could be more appealing to President Truman than Acheson's "gift of negotiation and debate. . . . He plugs away, with great powers of definition, for a steady, consistent policy based on the facts . . . and despite the limitations of his job, his intelligence, his knowledge, and capacity of definition are sufficient to be effective if they are not . . . decisive."[2]

Acheson found Roosevelt's successor a congenial leader. There is no need to repeat the many ways in which Truman's character and operating style appealed to him. Suffice to say that while he discovered that it was impossible to work directly with Roosevelt he found Truman's unpretentious, straightforward, and open manner of dealing with subordinates to be entirely accept-

2. "The No. 1. No. 2 Man in Washington," *New York Times*, 25 August 1946.

able. Acheson abhorred secrecy and deviousness in any superior; he could not stand to feel demeaned or used. Truman's personality took this repugnant element out of relations with subordinates. He believed in a strong presidency; he also set great store by administrative efficiency and was prepared to delegate authority without relinquishing responsibility. All these traits were congenial to Acheson's temperament. Seldom have two men from such different social backgrounds found the basis for an enduring partnership. Seldom have men in politics taken a deeper sense of pleasure and joy in a political relationship. It lightened both men's loads and made it possible for both to accept their differences easily and openly.

Acheson's ideas on foreign policy when he became undersecretary in late August 1945 were hardly what his later critics, the revisionists of the 1960s and 1970s, have said they were. He had not been associated with the earlier "tough" line toward the Soviet Union advocated by Averell Harriman and Admiral William D. Leahy that had gotten the president off to a bad start in the conduct of Soviet diplomacy. He arrived in a position to help make policy at a moment when Truman was becoming aware of the extreme anti-Soviet views of some of his advisers and of the need to make a new effort to settle differences with Moscow. As I. F. Stone recognized, Acheson was not identified with these anti-Soviet influences: "He has been pro-De Gaulle, anti-Franco, strongly opposed to the admission of Argentina to the U.N., and friendly to the Soviet Union. . . . Of all the men now in the department, Acheson was by far the best choice for Under Secretary, and it is no small advantage to pick a man who already knows a good deal about the [department's] inner workings."[3] In the minds of men like Adolf A. Berle and Patrick J. Hurley he was if anything identified as neutral on the subject of the Soviet Union and moderate in his whole approach to American interests. His principal preoccupation during his first year in office was with the mounting chaos and despair that threatened so much of the world. His principal lament was that if Americans would only do what had to be done—pass the British and French loans or agree to international control of atomic energy—threats and problems would take care of themselves. At that time he favored a serious

3. "Shakeup in the State Department," *Nation* 161 (25 August 1945), 171–72.

effort to reach agreement with the Soviet Union on international control of atomic energy as well as one last attempt to negotiate a German settlement before zonal differences sealed the split of Europe indefinitely.

Soon after becoming undersecretary, Acheson confronted evidence that the Soviets were using pressure on Iran and Turkey, which, if successful, would lower confidence in the United Nations and undermine the security of an area of the world strategically important to the West. Hundreds of cables poured into the department from Tehran, Ankara, and Moscow, all stressing the aggressive intentions of the Kremlin. Asked to comment on Soviet purposes in Iran, George F. Kennan—at that time the chargé d'affaires in the Moscow embassy—did not think Soviet leaders would risk war, but believed they were determined "to bring into power in Iran a regime prepared to accede to major immediate Soviet demands. . . . Soviet forces in Iran will serve this scheme by sheer force of intimidation." [4] Acheson agreed. Kennan attributed similar intentions to Soviet pressure on Turkey to give up control of the Bosporus. Whatever the real Soviet intentions, the practical implications of the Iranian and Turkish situations soon changed Acheson's view of the USSR. He advised the Iranian government to bring its case before the United Nations and recommended that the United States "let the USSR know that we are aware of its moves, but leave a graceful way out if it desired to avoid a showdown." In the case of the straits crisis he recommended that Truman send the U.S.S. *Missouri* to Istanbul and that the U.S. go to war if necessary to repel the Russians.[5] For Acheson and the president these episodes were a litmus test of Soviet intentions. Just as Russia had for its objective a security belt in Eastern Europe, so the American leadership believed that the best warranty of American strategic interests lay in a system of formally sovereign and independent states. Roosevelt had mentioned specifically that he regarded a strong and independent Iran as "something of a testing ground for the Atlantic Charter and the good faith of the United Nations." [6] Americans generally believed

4. *Foreign Relations of the United States, 1946,* vol. 7 (Washington, D.C., 1969), pp. 362–63.
5. Ibid., p. 347.
6. Gabriel Kolko, *The Politics of War: The World and United States Foreign Policy, 1943–1945* (New York, 1968), p. 309.

that the independence of all countries was a *sine qua non* for a peaceful international order and therefore viewed Soviet moves against Iran and Turkey with particular alarm and foreboding.

Acheson at this time began to use the United Nations to advance American ends, and perhaps this tactic was a mistake. Much of the justification for America's hard-line response to Soviet actions in 1946–47 was that by refusing to evacuate northern Iran and by threatening Turkey the Soviets were demonstrating a disregard for the United Nations. Acheson did not really believe in the United Nations, in frequent sharp contrast to Truman. He was willing to espouse its principles for want of a better justification and later sponsored the Uniting for Peace Resolution[7] which made the United Nations even more responsive to U.S. interests. This attitude, however, embodied the danger of employing the United Nations as a means without being committed to it as an end or endeavoring to make it work. This careful legalism in defense of power politics certainly contributed to the confusion that later reigned in many American minds between actions dictated by national interest and the belief that America was always behaving according to international principles of a higher order.

On the issue of whether American resistance to Soviet moves was blind and unthinking, without comprehension of the Kremlin's limited motives, Acheson's course probably was as good as any alternative. In the preceding essay John Gaddis has written that both Acheson and Truman came to believe that only resistance to Russian expansion would preserve peace. The possibility that Soviet probes might be limited and essentially defensive was not recognized at the time; as Gaddis notes, there was no guarantee that those probes would have continued to be limited if the West did not resist.

It was only a short jump from elaborating policy for the crises over Iran and Turkey to arriving at the conviction that something would have to be done to replace British efforts in Greece. Acheson—who after Byrnes left the department in January 1947

7. This was a resolution of the U.N. General Assembly on 3 November 1950 stating that if the Security Council, because of lack of unanimity of the permanent members, fails to exercise its responsibility for peace and security the General Assembly shall consider the matter and make recommendations for collective measures including the use of armed force if necessary.

remained as undersecretary for six months under Byrnes's successor Marshall—was now thinking of the American-Soviet conflict as
a duel between two fundamentally incompatible antagonists. "Not
since the clash of the Greeks and the Persians, the Romans and
Carthage have two such fundamentally opposed civilizations been
in the balance," he told a group of skeptical congressmen whom
the president and Secretary Marshall had failed to convince of the
need for aid to Greece and Turkey. For Acheson it was a typical
bravura performance designed to save a bad situation, but he
really did believe the situation would become that serious unless
the American people and Congress were willing to act. He did not
envisage the Truman Doctrine being applied everywhere. He
certainly did not believe it could work or should be applied in
China where the Communists were slowly gaining the upper hand,
and he certainly did not at that time or even as late as January 1950
believe it was necessary or could be made to work in Southeast
Asia.

Congress agreed to the Truman Doctrine, not without the
usual Vandenberg flourish in favor of the United Nations which
Acheson rather hypocritically acceded to. This constant invocation
of the United Nations Charter and legalism to cover an American
strategy of power not only confused in the American mind the
basis on which the U.S. was acting, but also veiled from Acheson
and the president the virtue of frankly exploring an alternative
approach to the Soviets: an approach of power, of spheres of
influence. If they had perceived the existence of that alternative,
the U.S. would not so quickly have embarked on the crusade of
defeating Soviet machinations wherever they appeared.

In judging American diplomacy for its failure to confront the
distinction between its emphasis upon legal and moral principles
and its essential practice of power, one cannot be blind to the
double standard of all states. Just as the Soviet Union preached
Socialist fraternity and practiced repression, so the U.S. can hardly
be stigmatized for taking advantage of its corner on the market of
international idealism. One of the Department of State's senior
officials, Loy W. Henderson, unconsciously expressed this point
very well in a memorandum to Acheson in October 1946: "The
moral strength imparted by high principles and the conviction that
the U.S. is defending not only its own cause but that of all free

nations is a tremendous factor in world affairs. . . ." [8]

Acheson remained as undersecretary long enough to see the Marshall Plan proposed, confirming his long-standing belief that future peace and security depended on the United States doing much more in the economic sphere than had ever been anticipated when Roosevelt, Hull, and Morgenthau were working to weaken the British Empire during the Second World War.

In analyzing Acheson's statecraft after he became secretary in January 1949, the distinction between the situation as it existed at that time and Acheson's response to it should be kept in mind. The possibility, increasingly discussed today, that Soviet policy was not rooted in self-confidence but in insecurity was not at all apparent then. The Berlin blockade was at its height. Nationalist resistance was crumbling in China. The Communist parties of France and Italy were still working to defeat the Marshall Plan. Most people in Europe as well as in America were convinced that Stalin really meant business. European Communists still hoped that was the case, and influential writers like Jean-Paul Sartre and Hubert Beuve-Mery, the editor of Le Monde, clearly felt that some form of Marxist regime was preferable to the reign of capitalism or to another war followed by another occupation and another American liberation.

Very few people thought of Soviet behavior as an expression of weakness; the prevailing mood was one of fear and desperation. In such a case Acheson may not have been so wrong in believing that only a renewal of Western strength could avoid the worst, which might be a Soviet political breakthrough followed by another war, for that is probably what would have happened had Europe succumbed at that time.

Although the Soviet Union was soon to lift its blockade of Berlin, Acheson had already resolved in his mind that there was little if any hope of Russia or America compromising on Germany. The barren results of the Foreign Ministers Conference of that spring in Paris convinced him that discussion would get nowhere.

8. *Foreign Relations, 1946,* vol. 7, p. 242. For the entire memorandum see pp. 240–45.

From then on, he said upon return, these conferences would be like the steam gauge on a boiler. They would indicate the built-up pressure, the gains and losses in position that took place between meetings. He said that the steam gauge's recording of the Paris conference was that the position of the West had risen greatly. Since there was no hope for negotiation, the West should simply ignore the implications for Russia of what it was doing and get ahead with the business of forging its own unity and strength.

Events of that year—the fall of China, the Soviet A-bomb, the seeming lethargy of the Western responses—only added to Acheson's somber view. The Soviet Union was like a force of nature, like a river; it could be dammed up or deflected, but it could not be kept from flowing. Although not unlike Kennan's metaphor about the inevitable tendency of Soviet policy to expand into the basin of world power, Acheson's metaphor had an even more deterministic cast to it. Gaddis Smith has expressed its implications very well: "If, as Acheson believed, the Soviet government was a force of nature propelled entirely by physical laws of expansion, then indeed it would have been foolish to attempt a mutual exploration of American hopes, fears, and attitudes." [9] Acheson took as his basic assumption that the distrust and differences between the USSR and the West were too great to be settled by negotiation. Stalin, of course, acted on the grim assumption that the future would witness a series of frightful clashes before socialism triumphed over capitalism. (Whether Stalin believed it is a moot point.) Under the circumstances Acheson did not believe that negotiations were worthwhile. The Soviets, he declaimed, respected only strength; the West should concentrate on making itself so unified, so strong, so prosperous that the relationship of forces that would emerge would give the Kremlin no choice but to cease and desist from pressure on the West. There would be no need for negotiation. The existing situations of strength would determine the lines of settlement.[10]

This was to be containment with a vengeance; but did it go beyond that? There were position papers prepared for Acheson's negotiations with Foreign Minister Robert Schuman of France and

9. Gaddis Smith, *Dean Acheson* (New York, 1972), p. 101.
10. This might work in Europe where there was a solid base to build on, but Acheson soon discovered that no such base existed in Asia or the Middle East where all was jungle and shifting sand.

Foreign Secretary Ernest Bevin of England that stipulated the withdrawal of Soviet forces from Eastern Europe as the ultimate goal of NATO policy; but neither the British nor the French were ever persuaded to accept that objective, and it seems to have been put forward more as an aspiration than as a practical objective.

Acheson did not believe that a "situations of strength" strategy would increase the likelihood of war; in any case he was convinced that such precautions were necessary if the West was not to remain at the mercy of Soviet threats and pressures. He believed that the men in the Kremlin were realists who would be restrained by the new relationship of power. He does not seem to have appreciated fully the fact that their realism might lead them to greater efforts to increase their situations of strength, or to new and even more dangerous adventures such as unleashing war in Korea. The West, he contended, was not strong enough under any circumstances.

This policy probably was not the most ideal. Although Acheson would have denied that he was imposing a zero-sum game on the Russians, it amounted to that. So long as negotiation from strength was all strength and no negotiation, it was all too likely to be seen as such by the Russians. Acheson was remiss in not tempering his strategic predispositions with some consideration of the possibility that the Kremlin's behavior might be subject to greater restraint and modification than appearances seemed to indicate. This led him to brush aside too readily Kennan's arguments against a rigid commitment to the reunification of Germany on exclusively Western terms, and against too exclusive an imputation to the Kremlin of expansionist intentions in drawing up the famous position paper known as NSC-68 (National Security Council memorandum 68).

Haunted by the seeming weakness and disunity of the West, and prompted by belief in the therapeutic value of action and organization, Acheson as secretary of state determined to bend all his formidable energies and skills to making the North Atlantic area so unified, strong, and prosperous that neither the Europeans nor the Kremlin would have any doubt of Europe's ability to survive. Even before the North Atlantic Treaty had been ratified he was determined to make it more than a guarantee pact. He understood French Premier Henri Queuille's remark that one more occupation would finish France, that America would be liberating a corpse. The Europeans wanted an American commitment.

Acheson had every intention of gaining it for them because he believed it was in America's interest to overcome the divisions of Europe and prevent a repetition of the last war.

By ruling out the need to allow concessions to the Soviet Union, he increased his potential for granting concessions to the Europeans. Since no acceptable compromise on Germany was possible he was free to offer maximum terms for Bonn's adherence to the Western alliance: the unification of Germany on Western terms at some unstated later date. The French were willing to accept this because it did not seem likely that the Kremlin would ever agree to German unification on those terms. This meant that future negotiations with the Soviet Union would be heavily mortgaged and America's room for maneuvering severely restricted by the absolute conditions of Acheson's NATO diplomacy. While it provided the U.S. with maximum support at the time it did not augur well for the future.

Acheson showed real authority in handling the rearmament of Europe, and it was an authority much appreciated at the time. It had its difficulties, but it had its results. As the secretary of state elaborated his European policy he pushed Congress to comply with his requests for military appropriations and authority. Most congressmen preferred to wait and see what the Europeans would contribute to the alliance before action, but Acheson insisted that the United States meet its share of the burden regardless of what the Europeans did or did not do. He then told the Europeans that unless they matched the American effort he could not hope to get the Congress to go along the next time. Painful though the experience was for European statesmen, Acheson's resolution and ability to deliver the goods profoundly impressed them. They were scarcely accustomed to someone who could make the balky congressional cow give such regular milk, and most of them fell all over themselves to accommodate Acheson's requests.

Despite the rigor of Acheson's diplomatic approach and the painful choices with which he frequently confronted European statesmen, the leaders of the European nations essentially liked to do business with him. He was notably free from moralizations and cant. He may have chastised them severely in private for their backsliding, and he put intense pressure on them behind the scenes to settle the nationalist claims of their colonies as quickly as possible, but he did not lecture them or pillory them in public. He always tried to be helpful. He was fertile in innovative expedients and compromises and fortunately able to do much to help them out with public opinion at home. Despite the shock to French relations of Acheson's demand that the Germans be permitted to rearm, it never came to the breaking point. The respect and sympathy between Acheson and Schuman was a remarkable interlude in Franco-American diplomacy.

Running NATO was no easy task. As Robert E. Osgood suggests: "In a multilateral alliance exacting extensive commitments and contributions [collaboration] is bound to be a delicate and exacting task, for the requirements of collaboration do not automatically coincide with the requirements of security. A viable alliance must permit material and political concessions to the requirements of cohesion." Beyond that, agreement on common military plans is difficult because the cost of modern military strategy "affects, and is therefore affected by, strong domestic, economic, and psychological pressures. . . . Then domestic pressures are especially marked where strategy infringes upon public expenditures, individual taxes, notions of fiscal soundness, the conscription of manpower, and the allocation of money. . . ."[11] In order to deal with these problems Acheson had succeeded in getting a system adopted whereby a NATO commission led by the so-called three wise men (Harriman for the U.S., Edwin N. Plowden for Britain, Jean Monnet for France) had been accorded the right to look into each member's finances and make recommendations for the most appropriate and equitable ways to allocate its national resources. This was an unprecedented abridgment of national sovereignty that only Acheson's personal standing and diplomatic skill made possible. It would be another decade before the Common Market achieved a similar authority to intervene in the domestic affairs of the European states. Anyone familiar with the magnitude of the sacrifice that European governments made to the success of NATO strategy during the Acheson years knows that a majority of Europeans were convinced, at least until 1953, that the Soviet Union constituted a mortal danger.

Even before the Korean War he had insisted upon passage by Congress of the Military Assistance Program. Once the war broke out in the Far East he was able to galvanize the NATO allies. He did not do it without some difficulties, for he received much

11. Robert E. Osgood, *NATO: The Entangling Alliance* (Chicago, 1962), pp. 18–19.

France

criticism from General Charles de Gaulle, then out of office. De Gaulle capitalized on the dissatisfaction of Frenchmen over their country's distinctly second-class place compared with the United States and the United Kingdom. France's sense of being treated as more of an object than a subject of the alliance enabled the difficult Frenchman to mount a campaign that would carry him a few years later to the Elysée Palace. Despite such opposition Acheson went ahead. It is a tribute to his talents of persuasion and improvisation that, especially after 1951, he was able to make steady headway even without the dramatic support of the Berlin blockade or the Korean War. Under his management NATO became more than a military alliance; it enabled the State Department to resolve many tangled and potentially divisive European situations as well as ease their withdrawal from empire by providing them with an attractive alternative in the form of an Atlantic community.

The Lisbon Conference of February 1952 constituted the high-water mark of American NATO diplomacy in Europe. In return for the presence of half a dozen American divisions and equivalent air and naval units on the line in central Europe, the Europeans contributed the equivalent of twenty divisions. Under the aegis of NATO and of the European Defense Community (which the French parliament eventually failed to ratify) the French and British had agreed to end their occupation of West Germany and permit West Germans to rearm. Unfortunately these feats of economic and military collaboration could not be sustained because they rested upon too narrow a base. Although a prodigious diplomat and institution builder, Acheson had a narrow preoccupation with collaboration for purposes of national security that made his edifice vulnerable once the threat that had prompted North Atlantic collaboration began to lose its grim and menacing visage.

tar spot

The one area of policy in which much confusion and uncertainty remained during 1949–53 was the Far East. Acheson had participated in the decision, in connection with the Marshall mission to China in 1946, not to permit the U.S. to become involved militarily in the struggles between the Nationalists and the Communists. He became secretary of state three years later when the fall of the Nationalist regime and the flight of Chiang to Formosa were becoming settled facts. Republican critics in and out of Congress had been pressing for a U.S. guarantee of Formosa's security. Despite the ferocity of Republican criticism Acheson refused to extend American protection to Chiang's Formosan regime. Pointing to the already existing Soviet gains at the expense of China he warned that the nation should do nothing toward mainland China that would "deflect from the Russians to ourselves the righteous anger, and wrath, and the hatred of the Chinese people which must develop." Instead of prolonging a futile involvement in the Chinese civil war he envisaged ending the occupation of Japan and restoring Japan, on the model of West Germany, as a counterweight against Communist expansion in Northeast Asia.

As for the future of Southeast Asia, there was great uncertainty in his mind. In his speech to the National Press Club of 12 January 1950, he addressed himself to the issue that would dog Americans for over a quarter of a century: what U.S. policy should be toward those countries whose governments lacked popular support and the means of preventing revolution and Communist take-over. Here ambivalence seemed in order. On the one hand Acheson told Ambassador Philip C. Jessup who was about to undertake a sweeping examination of Asian policy, "You will please take as your assumption that it is the fundamental decision of American policy that the United States does not intend to permit further extension of Communist domination on the continent of Asia or in the Southeast Asia area." On the other hand he told the National Press Club that the day of foreign domination was over in Asia, and the truth was that no outside nation and no outside people were "wise enough and disinterested enough very long to assume the responsibility for another people or to control another people's opportunities." The military security of the countries of Southeast Asia beyond the U.S. military perimeter guarding Japan and the Philippines "lay beyond the realm of any practical relationship" and he preferred, as he said later, "not to speculate" on what the United States "might do in the event of various exigencies in Asia." [12]

There undoubtedly was a dilemma involved in policy toward

12. Dean Acheson, *Present at the Creation* (New York, 1969), p. 356.

Southeast Asia, and Acheson should not be blamed too much for finding himself unable to choose and then dignifying this inability into a policy. A good approach might well have been noninterference, to allow natural forces, particularly Sino-Soviet antagonisms, to run their course. This policy required patience, faith in history, and restraint that the American public did not have; they could not accept such a course.[13] Acheson clung to it as best he could, but by May 1950 he had already sacrificed the principle to expediency by backing the French in Indochina. Then came the shock of Korea.

The attack in Korea could be interpreted in two ways: as demonstrating the prescience of NSC-68, the need to provide more effective military backing against the possibility of Communist aggression in other parts of the globe; or as demonstrating the limits of trying to dam up Soviet power and refusing to continue the search for some basis of negotiation and compromise that would reduce the compulsion on both sides to exploit every weakness possible against the other. Kennan earlier had called for some form of spheres of influence in Northeast Asia, and once again put forth this line of reasoning—to no avail. Acheson chose to view the Korean attack as proof of the wisdom of NSC-68. In a memorandum to Truman before a presidential press conference he wrote, "The attack upon Korea makes it plain beyond all doubt that communism has passed beyond the use of subversion to conquer independent nations and will now use armed invasion and war"—a threat in Asia as well as in Europe. [14]

His support of the president's decision to repel the North Korean invasion was rooted in what men of his generation had felt about the failure of democracies to resist German and Japanese aggression less than a dozen years earlier. It was also rooted in the conviction that if nothing was done it would undermine the confidence and trust of a Europe still uncertain of America's leadership, a belief reflected in Charles E. (Chip) Bohlen's report that when he conveyed word of the American decision to Foreign Minister Schuman the latter's eyes filled with tears. "Thank God," he said, "this will not be a repetition of the past." Europe in general, except for the Communists, applauded the American decision.

13. Smith, *Acheson*, pp. 136–37.
14. Ibid., p. 186.

Less praiseworthy was the alacrity with which Acheson recommended that the Seventh Fleet be put into the Formosa Strait and the relative insouciance with which Communist China's reaction to all this was viewed. In retrospect it appears that the purpose of the policy of hands-off-Formosa was to still the clamor of the China Lobby and also to bury the hatchet between Acheson and Secretary of Defense Louis Johnson in favor of administration harmony; but it is doubtful if Acheson would have so lightly sacrificed his China policy on the altar of domestic harmony had he not been largely insensitive to Communist China's interests in the whole affair—a failing all too quickly confirmed by his approval of the decision to permit General Douglas MacArthur to unify Korea even at the risk of advancing to the Chinese frontier on the Yalu. The carelessness with which he viewed Chinese interests stands in marked contrast to his concern in European policy to avoid provoking the Soviet Union and is principally explainable in terms of a monumental blind spot for what effect America's actions would have on China. Negligence bordering on criminal folly rather than hostility marked the administration's view of China's role during these critical months, as evidenced by Acheson's attempts to reassure Peking in the last desperate weeks of November. Unfortunately, by that time nothing could be done to call off the offensive, and the subsequent disaster must be ranked as one of Acheson's most grievous failures.

Some observers are inclined to rate his management of America's decision to enter the Korean War as the greatest demonstration of his ability to balance the needs of instantaneous reactions with the need to think through the long-range ramifications of those decisions. In retrospect it may well be that his greatest performance came in those desperate days of December 1950 and January 1951 with annihilation facing the United Nations army in Korea, with Prime Minister Clement Attlee and General MacArthur clamoring for evacuation of U.S. forces, and with still others denouncing the administration's countenancing of a Communist Chinese delegation being permitted to present an indictment of the United States before the UN. He steadied the administration, recommended against extending the war to China, and guided America into a winning diplomatic position in the UN debate. This was fully as important a test, both for world peace and for U.S. diplomacy, as the decision to resist aggression six months earlier. It took courage not to give way to the despair and unreason that swept the country and to reduce American goals in Korea to the single goal of holding once again a line at the waist of Korea along the thirty-eighth parallel.

Choosing to fight a limited war was a new experiment in twentieth-century statecraft, but it was the only alternative, given the logic of Acheson's strategy. Unfortunately it was not an experiment for which Americans were temperamentally prepared, and the failure to keep the war limited by bringing in China all but destroyed the administration. Only the greatest courage and responsibility on the part of all involved—Truman, Acheson, Marshall, who by this time was secretary of defense, and General Omar N. Bradley, who was chairman of the Joint Chiefs—kept it from becoming much worse.

The war on the Korean peninsula that might have been ended in October 1950 after the Inchon invasion[15] now dragged on for two more years over issues entirely extraneous to the original matter: namely, the terms for an armistice commission and the repatriation of Chinese prisoners of war. The long-drawn-out statement of these issues in the truce talks only allowed more casualties and was a devastating liability to the Democratic administration's political situation at home.

Events surrounding the Korean War reinforced Acheson's conviction that Communist activities everywhere had to be treated as an extension of Soviet and now, by implication, Chinese expansionism. This was most unfortunate, for it not only led him through his UN spokesman Dean Rusk to brand Peking as a puppet of Russian imperialism with which America could never entertain diplomatic relations, but it also led to abandonment of his previous skepticism about the French role in Indochina.

The disastrous unfolding of events in Korea had locked Acheson into a position on China and Indochina just the opposite of what he had held only a year earlier. He showed far less caution and sensitivity toward Communist China than toward the Soviets. He unwittingly invited disaster, from the trauma of which neither he nor the American people would emerge with a lucid view of the Asian situation. Although he was under heavy political pressure at home to oppose communism more resolutely in Asia

15. In September MacArthur had captured this port in western Korea, near Seoul, outflanking nearly all the North Korean troops in the South.

than had previously been his wont, this alone does not explain the reversal of his position. He had failed to foresee that the crude nature of the situations of strength strategy, which he had begun with such confidence in Europe, could not be extended to Asia where the U.S. was in a far less advantageous situation relative to forces in the area. The result was to freeze policy toward Asia into a rigidly moralistic and anti-Communist position far less favorable to such attitudes than was the case in Europe.

Acheson's thinking did not go anywhere near Senator Robert A. Taft's view that "now that a Communist assault in Southeast Asia is on the horizon it should be clear to our government that the only chance to stop it is by a Chinese Nationalist invasion of the Communist held territory." [16] Acheson was prepared to have America intervene directly in the war in Indochina should Chinese intervention in support of Ho Chi Minh require it. Fortunately, despite the expansionist intentions imputed to Peking, nothing of that sort occurred; but he was no longer willing to accept the distinction between the war in Indochina and the feud with China, and the escalation of aid to the French followed, despite the fact that Acheson knew the French were in a morally false and militarily well-nigh hopeless position.

Admittedly, in some Far Eastern developments Acheson scored well, as in his stand over the dismissal of MacArthur in 1951 and his management later that year of the Japanese Peace Conference that met in San Francisco. His support for Truman's dismissal of MacArthur was dictated by knowledge that MacArthur was not only challenging the president's authority but interfering in a dangerous way with the conduct of policy in the Far East. The decision having been made that it was not in the national interest to prolong or enlarge the Korean War, MacArthur's attempts to do so constituted an intolerable affront to civil authority. The subsequent Senate hearings into the Far Eastern situation permitted Acheson to defend the administration's efforts to keep the war in Asia limited. His success before the senators, and that of Marshall, Bradley, and the Joint Chiefs, was a welcome interlude in the generally difficult implementation of Far Eastern policy.

16. Quoted in Foster Rhea Dulles, *American Policy toward Communist China, 1949–1969* (New York, 1972), p. 124.

In the case of the Japanese Peace Treaty Acheson obtained almost a personal triumph. In a real sense he was the diplomatic father of the treaty, although John Foster Dulles was fond of claiming it and generally it redounded to the credit of the Truman administration. It had been an accident of the Second World War that MacArthur had been in command in the Far East, and his presence in that theater after the war had tended to keep Republican critics away from the administration's policy; a complaint about the Japanese occupation was an implied criticism of a Republican general. Acheson knew as well as anyone that it was highly desirable to maintain this state of affairs, and when the presidential elections of 1948 went against the Republicans he was quick to see the convenience of having another Republican foreign policy expert employed by the administration.

Dulles had attended international conferences since the end of the war and had proved a reliable adviser. At first President Truman, incensed by some of Dulles's campaign utterances, refused to appoint him; but Dulles eventually received appointment as special adviser to the secretary of state, and then special ambassador, to negotiate the Japanese treaty. Even at that time Dulles loved to travel, and his desire was put to good use by a series of trips to the capitals of nations intimately involved in the Japanese Peace Treaty. He secured their approbation in advance. The subsequent peace conference in San Francisco allowed Acheson momentarily to become a popular figure. In a very early televising of an international meeting—television was just "coming in" in those days—he forcefully, by occupying the rostrum, prevented the delegate of a Soviet satellite, Poland, from speaking beyond the allotted five minutes against the treaty; he first declared the delegate's effort to extend his remarks as out of order, and then took the microphone away from him, all visible to television viewers who could applaud this diplomatic victory for the United States. It was not exactly the way Acheson believed in "selling" foreign policy to the American people, but it worked.

In the Far East, then, one might say that there were some bright spots, but generally Acheson's policies did not work well there. He brought to his office a belief that man is capable of avoiding the worst fate in his struggle if he makes the effort to master the forces of human desperation. In Europe he succeeded in putting into effect, within the limits of the possible, the full means of doing this; but the shock of Asian events to American

Out Frisco Way

Buffalo Courier-Express, *1951*

expectations proved too powerful, and in the notable case of the Korean War mastery almost succumbed to a loss of control and near disaster.

In securing adoption of his costly situations of strength strategy Acheson had to pay a fearful personal price. He was not a popular figure at home. His dignified, aristocratic mien was alien to Americans, including most congressmen. He inspired enormous trust and confidence among fellow cabinet members (Secretary of Defense Johnson excepted) and within the department, and he had the respect of the members of the Senate and House committees, which was crucial to passage of so much enabling legislation. His stern and often minatory manner of holding Congress to the logic of containment and alliance building was an abrasive and often scarifying experience, however. As he said to Vandenberg when rejecting the latter's plea that because the North Atlantic Treaty had been passed there was no need for military assistance: "Intangibles do not impress. The Treaty is no substitute for substance." Congressmen and senators, more accustomed to horse trading and compromise, found him a difficult and frustrating figure to deal with. Republicans in particular found his stark and uncompromising positions on the North Atlantic Treaty, on troops to Europe, on Chiang's own responsibility for the fall of China, and on disentangling from the regime on Formosa hard to take. Frequently, if Truman had not intervened with a concession here and there or a little soothing balm, relations would have been even more strained. Of course, among many congressmen and many members of the public the hatred of Acheson reached pathological proportions. Not only was he a symbol of a worldly "Eastern Establishment" but he possessed a gentleman's code that forbade him to turn his back on Alger Hiss or to agree that his associates in the State Department were Communists. So long as he felt he had the genuine support and confidence of Truman, however, he had no intention of resigning. The two men were linked by adversity more closely than ever. Each knew that Senator Joseph R. McCarthy was a scoundrel and neither had any intention of knuckling under to his demagogic attacks.

Perhaps Acheson took some comfort in knowing that his

attackers—McCarthy perhaps excepted—objected far more to his policies than to his personality.[17] Given the source of the animus against him—rooted in the bitterness of Republican isolationists and China Lobby supporters and in the general frustrations connected with foreign affairs—it is doubtful that any other secretary of state would have fared much better. The same hard logic that led him to espouse situations of strength in Europe, which the public had accepted, also led him to oppose extending the war in Asia to include China.

Whatever the future was to reveal about the correctness of his views and the fickleness of much American public opinion during his tenure at the Department of State, his four years as secretary had been rigorous and difficult; the exit of the Democrats in 1953, after twenty years of national power, was a relief. He returned with joy to his Washington law practice, undertook a series of sessions (one weekend every month) at Princeton to tape his recollections together with those of his highest associates, and began to write occasional pieces for the public press and periodicals. The Eisenhower administration clearly was going to be in office for awhile, and Acheson enjoyed the opportunity to be on the outside poking criticisms at the "ins," especially when they were as vulnerable as the businessmen Eisenhower brought into the government.

The absence of the disciplining force of high office led him to espouse unnecessarily harsh and intolerant attitudes toward those individuals with whom he disagreed. He was yet able to distill the philosophy with which he had conducted American diplomacy in a series of distinguished and scholarly books, but his comments upon contemporary affairs sometimes suggested that he was not applying the principles of that philosophy with the same detachment and objectivity. Change meant scrapping the policies and attitudes of the past that were no longer relevant; this Acheson found difficult to accept. Another factor explaining what his critics decried as increasing conservatism, even a hard-line reactionary approach to both domestic and foreign problems, was undoubtedly advancing age. As the twilight years came upon him he

[handwritten marginalia: hawk but professional]

17. Glen H. Stassen, "Individual Preference versus Role Constraint in Policy Making: Senatorial Response to Secretaries Acheson and Dulles," *World Politics* 25 (1972–73), 96–119.

reacted to public issues somewhat in the way his older friend Truman was reacting. Whatever he said, as whatever Truman said, was good copy.

As the Republican years stretched on toward the denouement of 1960 it became clear to Acheson that his own chances of getting back into government were slight if not nonexistent. The young faces of the presidential campaign of the latter year meant new people in the cabinet posts, whoever won; and although President-elect Kennedy carefully consulted Acheson for names for the cabinet positions the retired secretary of state could be sure that his own name would not be considered seriously except for some honorific post he surely would not desire. This fact, too—that he was permanently out of public office—explains some of the statements made in his later years after leaving the secretaryship of state.

During the Democratic administrations of the 1960s his advice was frequently sought on foreign relations, and he never hesitated to give it. His advice on Berlin in 1961 (to hang on) was generally sound. His advice on the Cuban missile crisis (to bomb Russian missile sites) was fortunately rejected. Here was a perfect example of a suggestion that was highly inappropriate to the new state of affairs in the Kremlin. There was need to be firm, but also conciliatory.

Acheson's early advice to President Lyndon B. Johnson not to get involved in a land war in Vietnam was sound. He later went along, probably so as not to lose influence. Had he earlier supported Undersecretary of State George Ball, he might have halted the drift into the war. His role as one of the wise men who encouraged Johnson to reverse himself on Vietnam was highly important. At a critical moment he staked his reputation as a hawk and a hard liner against the military and the closed system of the bureaucracy, those who still wished to pursue that futile war. His opinion helped Johnson and Secretary of Defense Clark Clifford to reverse the ever deepening irrationalities of the war.

As Acheson moved into his later seventies he was ever more enjoying himself, appearing on television, lecturing college and university audiences, writing for the "op-ed" pages of the *New York Times*, but his writings, which always were vigorously interesting, alternated between points of policy, mostly foreign policy, and memories and invocations of the past. He recalled his youth in Middletown; *Morning and Noon*, as he aptly had entitled the first part of his reminiscences, was published in 1965. In *Present at the Creation,* he described the signal acts of his years in the Department of State, when a new foreign policy was produced for post-1945 America. He lived on in Georgetown, close to the scene of national action, but his heart, and usually his physical presence, was at his farm in Sandy Spring in nearby Maryland where he wrote and read. He died there one afternoon in October 1971.

BIBLIOGRAPHIC NOTE

Any account of books relating to Secretary Acheson must begin with the secretary's own eight volumes. The first of these was *A Democrat Looks at His Party* (New York, 1955), an argument for his party's stewardship of the federal government during the years from 1933 to 1953. There followed an analysis resting on Woodrow Wilson's *Congressional Government* (1885) entitled *A Citizen Looks at Congress* (New York, 1956), a distillation of the wisdom of Acheson's years of visits to the Hill. The William L. Clayton lectures at the Fletcher School of Law and Diplomacy, published under the title of *Power and Diplomacy* (Cambridge, Mass., 1958), defined his views about limited war, especially the need for caution during the age of nuclear power. *Sketches from Life* (New York, 1961) offered delightful vignettes of men he had known. Then came *Morning and Noon* (Boston, 1965), the first of what the secretary perhaps envisioned as a two- or three-volume memoir, unfortunately never finished; this book takes his life to 1941 when he entered the State Department. *Present at the Creation* (New York, 1969), a huge account of the department years, was completed at a time when his policies of 1945–53 were coming under sharp criticism from revisionist historians. Acheson was thoroughly aware of this criticism and considered it stupid; shortly before his death he told the *New York Times* reporter Alden Whitman, who (following a quaint procedure recently inaugurated by the *Times*) interviewed him for his obituary, that the revisionists were psychological cases. *Fragments of My Fleece* (New York, 1971) and the posthumous *Grapes from Thorns* (New York, 1972) were collections of essays. In the first of these he offered "these little fragments of my fleece that I have left upon the hedges of life." In the second he remarked that he and his longtime secretary, Miss Barbara Evans, had discovered that "among the thorns of the law and the thistles of politics and diplomacy we found some fruit that had retained its flavor and, in some cases, its tartness." Of secondary accounts there are thus far (1974) only two, the eminently readable and sensible book by Gaddis Smith, *Dean Acheson* (New York, 1972), a volume in the series *American Secretaries of State and*

Their Diplomacy, and *The Shaping of Foreign Policy: The Role of the Secretary of State as Seen by Dean Acheson* (Cleveland, 1969), by Ronald Stupak. See also the articles by David McLellan, "The Role of Political Style: A Study of Dean Acheson," in *Foreign Policy in the Sixties,* edited by Roger Hilsman and Robert C. Good (Baltimore, 1965); "The 'Operational Code' Approach to the Study of Political Leaders: Dean Acheson's Philosophical and Instrumental Beliefs," *Canadian Journal of Political Science* 4 (March 1971), 52–75; and (with Ronald Stupak) "The Statecraft of Dean Acheson," *Worldview* (March 1972), 32–38.

Both authors of this essay have read, reviewed, and/or employed in class most of the revisionist literature on the Acheson-Truman era in American foreign policy. A few among a mountain of books and articles critical of Acheson's diplomacy from the revisionist perspective are Lloyd C. Gardner, *Architects of Illusion: Men and Ideas in American Foreign Policy, 1941–1949* (Chicago, 1970), Joyce and Gabriel Kolko, *The Limits of Power; the World and United States Foreign Policy, 1945–1954* (New York, 1972), Walter LaFeber, *America, Russia and the Cold War, 1945–1971* (New York, 1971), S. E. Ambrose, *The Rise to Globalism: American Foreign Policy, 1938–1970* (Baltimore, 1970). Both authors have essays forthcoming in a new collection entitled *The Truman Period as a Research Field,* edited by Richard S. Kirkendall (Columbia, Mo., 1974), which will examine the literature from both the traditional and revisionist perspectives.

THE SEARCH FOR MEANING:
GEORGE F. KENNAN

Orren Jack Turner

and American Foreign Policy

Thomas G. Paterson

Scholars consider him a first-rate historian, Foreign Service officers rank him as one of their best, presidents and secretaries of state

This essay draws largely upon the Kennan papers at the Princeton University Library; Kennan's two-volume autobiography, *Memoirs, 1925–1950* (Boston, 1967) and *Memoirs, 1950–1963* (Boston, 1972); his prolific published works; official diplomatic correspondence; C. Ben Wright, "George F. Kennan, Scholar and Diplomat: 1926–1946," Ph.D. dissertation, University of Wisconsin, 1972; oral history transcripts at the John F. Kennedy Library and Princeton University; and numerous manuscript collections cited in Thomas G. Paterson, *Soviet-American Confrontation: Postwar Reconstruction and the Origins of the Cold War* (Baltimore, 1973). For an extensive bibliography of Kennan's work and critical commentaries, see Thomas G. Paterson, ed., *Containment and the Cold War* (Reading, Mass., 1973). The author is very grateful to J. Garry Clifford, Holly V. Izard, C. Ben Wright, Walter LaFeber, Thomas G. Smith, Theodore A. Wilson, and Eduard Mark for their helpful suggestions. The Harry S. Truman Library Institute and the University of Connecticut Research Foundation provided travel funds for the author's study of cold war diplomacy; the American Philosophical Society and the Rabinowitz Foundation provided additional financial aid in the preparation of this essay.

have tapped his expertise on the Soviet Union, a generation of college students has been weaned on his publications and prescriptions for a "realistic" foreign policy, and literally hundreds of thousands of Americans and foreigners have become familiar with his contemporary analyses of international relations. Soviet leaders went so far as to declare him *persona non grata* in 1952. Critics of the war in Indochina in the 1960s welcomed him as an ally, but dissenters from American foreign policy since World War II identify him as the masterful cold warrior who helped launch the global containment doctrine. George Frost Kennan has pursued a demanding and varied career as diplomat and intellectual, often at the center of policy making and public controversy; yet he claims for himself little influence over events, ideas, or individuals. The historical record certainly does not substantiate this denial of influence, but it does reveal, with the help of Kennan's anguished self-portrayal in his memoirs, an inner tension between the life of the professional diplomat and the life of the intellectual.

Throughout his career Kennan lived with two competing aspirations. One was the life of the bureaucrat, the Foreign Service officer, legalistic and precise, dedicated to a professional creed and style, enamored with tradition, distant from the winds of domestic politics, disciplined, moderating the opinions of the overzealous, and always eager to influence decision makers. Kennan liked being an "insider," for that role provided a needed sense of belonging, prestige, and access to power. Yet he never seemed comfortable in the foreign affairs bureaucracy; he found it too confining and encumbered, too tied to routine and menial tasks, too demanding of subservience to assigned missions. More than once he complained that his superiors, usually depicted as less able than himself, ignored his talents. He was chagrined that Foreign Service officers found themselves "tidying up the messes other people have made, attempting to keep small disasters from turning into big ones," instead of contributing fresh policy perspectives. He resented the intrusions of uninformed congressmen and a whimsical public and bemoaned the decline in stature and power of the Department of State. It seems fair to conclude that Kennan has felt frustrated because for most of his career he sought but was denied a role, to use a recent example, like that assumed by Henry A. Kissinger for President Richard M. Nixon.

Kennan's other aspiration propelled him toward the life of the *intellectual* [handwritten in margin]

intellectual, the scholar playful with ideas, speculative, independent of mind, skeptical and probing, the dedicated teacher, the moralist preaching his convictions, the oracle of reasoned vision, and the artist. This was a life of individualism and loneliness, opposed to the ordinary and routine, always suspicious of pat answers. Whereas the diplomat-bureaucrat attempts to be precise and methodical, the intellectual muses and experiments. Kennan's "irrepressible intellectual brashness," as he described it, found sustenance in the role of the "outsider." Kennan the scholar regretted that he could not interact more with his historical subjects: "They became part of my life. . . . But they were never able to see me, or to react to my interest. I wandered through their lifeless world like a solitary visitor through a wax museum. . . . My concern for them was not matched by any reciprocal concern on their part for me." The life of the intellectual, then, also had drawbacks for Kennan, not the least of which was isolation from the corridors of power and the awful possibility that his ideas would be misinterpreted. Since the 1920s, when he entered the Foreign Service, Kennan has essentially pursued two careers simultaneously, not finding complete fulfillment in either. Therein lies his self-image as a failure and the differing interpretations others have given to his conception of cold war diplomacy, as well as his alienation from the government he sought so faithfully to serve.

Throughout his life, Kennan nurtured remarkably consistent attitudes and values; as he himself observed, they were quite different from those of the Soviets, whose ideology and government he studied so closely. He has described himself as a "conservative person, a natural-born antiquarian, a firm believer in the need for continuity across the generations in form and ceremony. . . ." Indeed, he looked to the past for models after which to pattern ideas and behavior. Because he witnessed the deterioration of his revered values, he never seemed at home in the twentieth century (or in his own country). Words like honor, responsibility, efficiency, rigor, discipline, steady habits, perseverance, self-restraint, individualism, culture, tradition, decency, courage, cleanliness, order, and humility mark Kennan's reflections on himself and on others—as if he had torn a page from Benjamin Franklin's autobiography. These qualities added up to something he vaguely called "western civilization," rooted in morality, pride in work, competition, individualism, freedom of thought, and "social conservatism." In contrast, Marxism and the Soviet Union prostituted these values through collectivism, fanaticism, denial of individual rights, and a break with tradition. In the early 1930s, Kennan wrote that he "rejected the Communists because of their innate cowardice and intellectual insolence. They had abandoned the ship of Western European civilization like a swarm of rats when they considered it to be sinking, instead of staying on and trying to keep it afloat. . . ." The Communists "had called all their forefathers and most of their contemporaries hopeless fools," and that behavior was a "sacrilege." "I felt," Kennan explained, "that it [communism] must some day be punished as all ignorant presumption and egotism must be punished."

He visited his arrogance and contempt upon Americans as well. He lacked patience with people less bright than himself and held little respect for a political system that permitted the untutored to vote. He chided Americans for their lack of historical perspective, low level of knowledge about the country's problems, and emotionalism. Frequently emotional himself, he could not tolerate it in others, especially when in collective form, in the "masses." He seldom concealed his disdain for those who neither aspired to nor recognized his own quest for the attributes of the ideal diplomat: charming, brilliant, cultured, educated, self-confident, and respected. For much of his life he seemed out of touch with the country he served abroad. He observed and understood foreign countries much better than his own and when in the early 1950s he returned to private life, he had to "re-encounter" America. What he saw there as a drift away from the best in Western civilization repelled him.

Style and method were particularly significant to Kennan. It was crucial *how* one did what he had to do. "Let no one underestimate," he told a Northwestern University audience in 1951, "the importance in this life of the manner in which a thing is done. It is surprising how few acts there are, in individual life, which are not acceptable if they are carried out with sufficient grace and self-assurance, and above all with dignity and good manners. . . ." He believed that in foreign affairs the test for the diplomat was not just purpose, but also conduct. He was easily put off by the style of others, from the often rude, blunt Soviets in the 1930s and 1940s to the long-haired iconoclasts of college campuses in the 1960s. When German troops in 1939 were about to enter Prague, Kennan was "determined that the German army

Drawing by David Levine. Reprinted with permission from the New York Review of Books. *Copyright © 1972 N.Y. Rev. Inc.*

should not have the satisfaction of giving the American Legation a harried appearance," so he shaved "meticulously" before going to the office. Such behavior was impressive, but it also revealed a bureaucrat's obsession with style and routine and a pseudoaristocrat's concern with propriety.

These traits were evident long before Kennan emerged as a major architect of cold war diplomacy. He was born in 1904 to an Anglo-Saxon family in Milwaukee, Wisconsin. His father was a hard-working lawyer and his mother a self-conscious "aristocrat." By his own admission, young Kennan's life was "comfortable and safe." His family had no quarrel with a society that had rewarded it with a more than adequate income, and Kennan has reflected that his early experience refuted the Marxist image of the blood-sucking capitalist. "I could identify neither with the exploiter nor with the exploited." At age twelve he headed for St. John's Military Academy near Milwaukee. Its strict discipline and spartan environment left little time for frivolous pleasures, and Kennan learned to keep his room neat and orderly and to merge his personal preferences with those of the group. When he graduated in 1921, as if to illustrate that other aspiration, he was designated class poet.

A St. John's administrator advised the somewhat shy Kennan to go to Princeton University, an inclination already stimulated by his reading of F. Scott Fitzgerald's *This Side of Paradise* (1920), which was set in Princeton. He proceeded to flunk part of the entrance examination, but, given another chance, managed to pass the second round of tests. As the last student admitted to Princeton, he was assigned the least desirable room and his demeanor became as gloomy as his accommodations. He was, he later wrote, "an oddball on campus, not eccentric, not ridiculed or disliked, just imperfectly visible to the naked eye." He was a loner, knowing few people, distant from his instructors, always last in line, with no desire to join one of the university's prestigious clubs. Later he recalled that he sought a kind of "martyrdom" in those years, and in 1925 left college "as obscurely as I had entered it."

Not knowing what else to do, Kennan decided to apply to the newly formed Foreign Service. He had liked his limited study of international affairs at Princeton and he had always been impressed with the record of his grandfather's cousin, also bearing the name George Kennan, who had distinguished himself as an expert on Russia. Then, too, Ivy League graduates predominantly staffed the diplomatic corps at that time, so Kennan was following a path well traveled by Princetonians. After a rigorous oral examination conducted by Undersecretary of State Joseph Grew, Kennan was accepted into the Foreign Service School in 1926. He then spent several months in the consul general's office in Geneva, shedding his "introverted" self for that of a man of responsibility in a distinguished profession. He went next to Hamburg as a vice-consul and became absorbed in the intellectual life of that Social Democratic city, attending lectures and musing beside the famed harbor; but apparently stifled by his job, he decided in 1928 to return to the United States to undertake graduate study.

His superiors in the Foreign Service induced him to change his mind by offering him three years of graduate work in Europe, if he would study the Arabic, Chinese, Japanese, or Russian languages. Kennan chose Russian, in part because the elder George Kennan's "tradition" beckoned him and in part because he sensed that the United States would eventually recognize the Soviet Union and need experts. Area specialization was something new for the Foreign Service and Kennan became one of a handful (including Charles Bohlen and Loy Henderson) trained in Russian affairs in the 1920s. Already fluent in German and French, he departed for Estonia to study Russian. He learned fast and was assigned to Riga, Latvia, America's contact with Russia, where travelers to and from Russia were interviewed and Soviet publications collected. From Riga he was sent to the University of Berlin to study Russian history, literature, and language. During the two years there he became annoyed with American "liberals" tolerant of the Soviet experiment, because, as he wrote in 1931, "the present system of Soviet Russia is unalterably opposed to our traditional system, that there can be no possible middle ground or compromise between the two. . . ." It was a pessimistic prediction and adamant conviction, probably encouraged by his contact with anti-Soviet Russian émigrés.

Assigned again to Riga in 1931, now third secretary of the legation, Kennan eagerly threw himself into his work, and from his desk flowed economic reports, analyses of Soviet propaganda, and even an article, "Anton Chekhov and the Bolsheviks." He was less enthusiastic than many Americans about the prospects for Soviet-American commerce, because the Soviets would need American credit, and he advised that diplomatic recognition of the Soviet Union would not be a panacea for facilitating trade. Kennan was not pleased with the imprecision and irresolution of the Roosevelt-Litvinov Agreements of 1933. Later he chided the president for thinking that recognition would somehow curb Germany or Japan. As Kennan recalled, "Never—neither then nor at any later date—did I consider the Soviet Union a fit ally or associate, actual or potential, for this country."

On leave in Washington during the Litvinov-Roosevelt talks, Kennan was introduced to William C. Bullitt, soon to be the first American ambassador to the Soviet Union. They established an immediate rapport and Bullitt, impressed by Kennan's knowledge of the Russian economy and his fluency in the language, added Kennan to his staff. Kennan probably concealed his pessimism about Soviet-American relations from the more optimistic ambassador. The initially cordial Soviets were delighted with the young diplomat because they identified him with the anticzarist elder Kennan and because his mastery of Russian flattered them. The sluggishness of the Soviet bureaucracy exasperated Kennan, but the embassy staff, which included journalist-diplomat Charles W. Thayer and career officers Loy Henderson and Charles Bohlen, exhilarated him. In 1935 Russia entered the terrible period of the purges, and Kennan became an acute and outraged observer, personally attending many of the trials. It was "a sort of liberal education in the horrors of Stalinism." Stalin had eliminated "liberal" forces in favor of a "new gang of young and ruthless party careerists," who had abandoned "modern western civilization" for conspiratorial thinking, secretiveness, cruelty, unscrupulousness, and opportunism.

Kennan had no liking for the "proletariat" or for Marxism. His elitism and conservatism were apparent when he took a short trip to a Black Sea resort area in 1936. He was disgusted with the "simple people's" lack of grace; they made "pig sties" of the hotels and lacked appreciation for the scenery. For Russian Marxism there was intellectual distaste. He rejected its "stony-hearted fanaticism" and its contribution to the liquidation of groups of people like the bourgeoisie because of a rigid application of class distinctions. The Marxist "ideology" was "pseudo-science, replete with artificial heroes and villains. . . ." The new restrictions on diplomats during the purges exacerbated Kennan's intense disaffection. An aura of suspicion gripped Moscow and Soviet officials tried to isolate foreigners from the Russian people, with some of whom Kennan had built up rewarding relationships.

During the 1930s Soviet-American relations deteriorated over the failure to reach agreement on the payment of World War I debts, the purges, and the meeting of the Comintern Congress of 1935; Bullitt became increasingly disillusioned. Kennan liked the ambassador's sophistication and self-confidence, but found his impatience and contempt for the foreign affairs bureaucracy unbecoming to a diplomat. Yet as Bullitt soured on the Soviet Union and adopted the "hard line" so much appreciated by Kennan, the two grew close in their thinking. Bullitt resigned in 1936. His replacement, Joseph E. Davies, Kennan considered a political hack, ill fitted for the post, lacking in seriousness, looking too much after his "newspaper image." It was an exaggerated assessment, but Kennan chastised Franklin D. Roosevelt more than Davies, for the president was a politician and inadequately hostile to the Soviet Union. Kennan contemplated resigning from the Foreign Service but chose instead to make the best of a bad situation and departed for Washington in 1937.

The "hard liners," members of the Moscow embassy and the Division of Eastern European Affairs in the State Department, shared Kennan's views. This division, under the guidance of career officer Robert F. Kelley, had opposed recognition and seemed an anomaly in the Roosevelt administration. Its hostility was explicable, because, after all, the division had spent the 1920s finding reasons *not* to recognize the Soviet regime. In mid-1937 the division was abolished and its functions distributed to two desks (Russian and Baltic-Polish) in the new Division of European Affairs. Kennan suspected that pro-Soviet attitudes in the "higher reaches" of government governed the decision. Political consider-ations no doubt had some part in the decision, but Kennan's analysis was far too simple. The reorganization was one of several changes Secretary of State Cordell Hull initiated in 1937 after two years of study; at the same time he merged two divisions into the new Division of American Republics and created the office of counselor.

Despite his disappointment, Kennan accepted the Russian desk post and for about a year (October 1937 to August 1938) talked with businessmen, protested Soviet restrictions on the

Moscow embassy, and watched for violations of the Litvinov-Roosevelt Agreements. It was not a happy time for him—he felt
ignored and unappreciated—but his ideas about Soviet-American
relations jelled further. In May of 1938 Kennan spoke to a Foreign
Service School audience about the wellsprings of Soviet policy.
The Russians, he said, had been influenced by "Asiatic hordes"
during their long history and were thus conditioned to think of
foreigners as enemies. The Asiatic's "acute and abnormal sense of
'face' and dignity" compelled Russian leaders to claim infallibility.
Furthermore, the size of the country contributed not to a sense of
moderation but rather to "extremism." The Russian character took
on the traits of a "typical oriental despotism" and at the same time
an "inferiority complex," because the Russians were aware of their
own defects. Kennan called for "patience" in American foreign
policy: "We must neither expect too much nor despair of getting
anything at all." His conclusions were quite deterministic and
subjective, but he spoke with amazing assurance. Hostility toward
and deep suspicion of the Soviets, as well as the counsel of
patience, became the hallmarks of Kennan's thought. Yet Kennan's
hostility was often alarmist, contributing not to patience but to
urgency and exaggeration.

In mid-1938 Kennan asked to be transferred to the field again
and he was assigned to the American legation in Prague. When
German troops entered the somber city in March 1939, the
legation was shut down and Kennan moved to the embassy in
Berlin. He thought there was nothing the Czechs could do but
submit to German power; resistance would have been "romantic."
He seemed to accept the fall of Czechoslovakia as predestined,
because he believed the breakup of the Austro-Hungarian Empire
after World War I was a mistake, fragmenting power in the
Danube Basin and inviting international squabbles. In Berlin he
became bogged down in administrative tasks not to his liking and
watched Europe go to war. When Germany invaded Russia in June
1941, Kennan approved lend-lease aid in America's self-interest,
but warned against professions of friendship with or moral
support for the Soviet Union, which he considered hardly a fit ally.
From December 1941 to May 1942, the Germans interned Kennan
and about one hundred thirty other Americans. Kennan assumed
leadership and maintained discipline, but became bitter toward
Washington, believing his government had abandoned the group.
He expected the State Department to gain his early release

through Lisbon in exchange for Germans and was deeply annoyed when half of his group was ordered to wait for another ship so that some Jewish refugees could be transported to freedom first.

Back in the United States, he rested and thought. He soon identified himself as a moderate between the extreme anti-Soviet and pro-Soviet groups in the United States. In apparent anticipation of considerable Soviet influence in Eastern Europe after the war and in apparent contradiction to his stated views against self-determination for small nations in the area, he opted for the latter in the hope of curbing Soviet expansion. Before the war he demonstrated no such strong opposition to German expansion in that region and argued that small states in fact invited instability. In September 1942, Kennan was assigned to Lisbon as counselor. He did not go willingly. He complained to the State Department that his qualities were being ignored; he was a trained specialist, he had knowledge of ten countries and ten languages, and his departmental ratings were high. Kennan argued against wasting his time "plugging away at administrative jobs." He wanted to be assigned to a German desk or post in economic foreign affairs. Kennan the intellectual, impatient with the bureaucracy, was asserting himself.

In Portugal Kennan handled intelligence operations and negotiations for bases in the Azores. He depicted Antonio Salazar as "one of the most able men in Europe and a man of high moral principle," not mentioning that the dictator supported General Francisco Franco in the Spanish civil war and that he had gained power through the military. For the first time in his career Kennan became a negotiator as well as an observer; yet he felt handicapped because Washington did not keep him properly informed and he had to get much of his information from British officials. With some shock, he received a cable in October of 1943 instructing him to see Salazar to request a naval base, aircraft base, cable system, radar installations, and observation posts in the Azores. Kennan protested that this extensive military request, if granted, would compromise Portuguese neutrality and invite a German declaration of war. He was delighted when the president told him to deal with the matter in his own way, but suddenly he was recalled; he expected to be punished, because, against instructions, he had given Portugal assurances of sovereignty in the colonies before negotiating for the bases.

Shortly after arriving in Washington, he was whisked off to

the Pentagon for a high-level meeting with Secretary of War Henry L. Stimson and the Joint Chiefs of Staff. It was a humilating experience; military officers reprimanded him for not making demands on Salazar. Unceremoniously dismissed, Kennan "slunk away," but while eating lunch alone he grew indignant that he should have been so treated. He resolved, typically, "that if I was to go down, I would go down fighting," and went to the president himself. Roosevelt told him not to worry about the Pentagon people and sent him back to Lisbon, once more to handle the question of bases in his own way. Kennan acquitted himself well in discussions and secured the use of bases important to the war effort. Actually, a new minister had been sent to Lisbon to complete the negotiations and Kennan, wanting nothing to do with him, requested a transfer. He believed that the military establishment had sent the new envoy, because the State Department had become, as he wrote later, a "messenger boy for the Pentagon and accustomed to sneezing whenever the Pentagon caught cold. . . ." The whole affair soured Kennan further on the Roosevelt administration, the growing weakness of the State Department in the making of foreign policy, and the intrusion of the military into diplomacy.

Kennan was sent next as counselor to the European Advisory Commission (EAC) in London, where his disenchantment grew. Before he assumed the post he was admonished to give advice only when asked for it, a reflection on his independent behavior in Portugal and on the low regard with which Washington held the EAC. To aggravate matters further, Kennan became ill with ulcers. The EAC was supposed to draw zones for postwar Germany, but its authority was never well defined and the military seldom explained the zonal boundaries it sought. Again demonstrating his maverick tendencies, Kennan could tolerate no more than a few months (January to April 1944) in such a spineless institution and requested a transfer. He received an unexpected boost: Averell Harriman, ambassador to the Soviet Union, requested Kennan as an adviser and Kennan was appointed counselor of the Moscow embassy. He departed in July 1944 for the land he knew best, whose leaders and foreign policy he liked least.

The years before 1944 were pivotal to the formulation of George F. Kennan's ideas about foreign policy, as well as to his self-perception as a diplomat. In his view, the Soviet Union was aggressive, made so by a fanatical ideology, historical imperatives,

and ruthless leaders. The Soviets' disruptive influence in international relations stemmed largely from internal causes. Seldom did
Kennan consider that the external pressure on Russia from other
nations might have affected Soviet behavior. Furthermore, he held
a mechanistic view of Russian foreign policy, believing it to be
largely constant over time. There was little American diplomats
could do but be patient in the face of Soviet officialdom's
inveterate hostility toward the West. He never conceded that the
West's anticommunism, manifested by the Allied intervention in
Siberia and nonrecognition, as well as the unchecked rise of
Hitler's Germany and the delay in the opening of the Second
Front, may have aroused some of that hostility. This intense
distaste for things Soviet derived not only from Kennan's revulsion
against conspicuously reprehensible Soviet acts, but also from his
own conservatism and fascination with Western Civilization. His
general conclusion was that the United States was too conciliatory
toward Moscow.

In the period before 1944, Kennan's impatience with his own
lack of power and what he believed to be his superiors' ignorance
of his talents emerges clearly. He frequently felt neglected and
stymied; his ideas were rejected, and the tasks assigned him were
routine and uninspiring. He was the bureaucrat who had meritori-
ously learned his job, but felt inhibited and restless. He was an
intellectual who thought analytically, committed his ideas to
paper, and tried to convey them to higher officers, where they
received little attention. Kennan was a gifted man, but as his
colleagues recognized, he was also opinionated, headstrong,
conceited, and sometimes cranky. He could be quite emotional
and subjective, and his assessments of Soviet policy, although
informed by uncommon knowledge, were nevertheless largely
conjecture. In order to illustrate the speculative methods of
Sovietologists, Charles Thayer has recorded a story about a
Kentucky mountaineer asking a neighbor's boy about his parents:

"Where's yer paw?" he asked the boy.
"Gone fishin'."
"How d'ye know?"
"Had his boots on and 'tain't rainin'."
"Where's yer maw?"
"Outhouse."
"How d'ye know?"
"Went out with a Montgomery Ward catalogue and she can't read."
"Where's yer sister?"

"In the hayloft with the hired man."

"How d'ye know?"

"It's after mealtime and there's only one thing she'd rather do than eat."

As he prepared to go again to Moscow, George F. Kennan seemed equally certain about his answers to questions relating to the Soviet Union.

Kennan arrived in Moscow on 1 July 1944 and was soon assigned the rank of minister-counselor; but, typically, he became impatient because his duties were largely administrative, and because Ambassador Harriman, by necessity, talked more frequently with the head of the military mission, General John R. Deane, than with Kennan. He was chagrined, too, that the staff was not interested in listening to his reflections on embassy life in the 1930s. Kennan admired Harriman's efficiency, but he was not a career diplomat and did not hold the Foreign Service in sufficient awe. Still deeply annoyed with the Soviet conduct of isolating foreign diplomats, feeling personally neglected, and dissenting from Roosevelt's wartime diplomacy, Kennan planned to resign.

As Soviet-American conflict over Poland heated up, however, Harriman began to ask his Soviet expert for advice, and Kennan bombarded his chief with "protests, urgings, and appeals." Kennan, "running around with [his] head in the usual clouds of philosophic speculation," became more a political oracle and less an administrator, more an intellectual and less a bureaucrat. From 1944 until April 1946, when Kennan returned to Washington, he drew upon the ideas he had developed in the 1930s to comment pessimistically on prospects for postwar international relations. Harriman himself was reaching for a less conciliatory policy toward Russia. Kennan's advocacy of toughness, so eloquently articulated, probably accelerated the ambassador's conversion. In January 1946 Harriman left Moscow for good, leaving a now more assertive Kennan as chargé d'affaires. Truman administration officials read his thoughtful but alarmist cables to Washington with increasing favor.

During the 1944–46 period Kennan's writings carried several common themes. After the war, he predicted, Russia, yearning to be a great power, would build up militarily and could not be trusted to fulfill agreements. He did not believe the Soviet Union would attack Western Europe, but his cables did not suggest many limitations on Soviet behavior. Indeed, he sketched a picture of the self-confident, aggressive giant, uncompromising, flushed with power, responsible for most of the world's disturbances. In early 1945 he told Harriman that Russia would seek "maximum power and minimum responsibility" in China leading to possible "domination" and "control." Later that year he cabled Washington that "security and aggrandizement" constituted Soviet aims in the Near and Middle East, to be achieved through an "endless, fluid pursuit of power." Soviet tactics would include the support of nationalist groups, political intrigue, subversion, and military intervention. "One of the outstanding characteristics of Soviet foreign policy is its flexible multiformity." Kennan also foresaw problems. Moscow would have difficulty arousing its citizenry to postwar sacrifice. Its postwar empire would prove unmanageable. The question was whether the United States could exploit these handicaps.

Kennan recommended that Washington follow a policy of "political manliness" toward Russia. He shared the growing sentiment in the Truman administration that Russia should be denied postwar economic assistance until it conformed to American interpretations of treaties and proved more cooperative. Believing that Eastern Europe was lost to American influence, Kennan recommended that the United States concentrate its energies in Western Europe, building it up as a counter-sphere of influence, but letting no Soviet action stand without a frank rebuttal. Washington should avoid diplomatic agreements that in any way might suggest American acceptance of Soviet power in Eastern Europe; the United States should not attempt to negotiate the impossible, a rollback of Soviet influence.

Collaboration with Russia in postwar Germany, he thought, was a "pipedream." He looked upon the Potsdam Conference agreements of July 1945 with "unmitigated skepticism and despair," for though they sought to establish quadripartite control, the language was too vague. Russia could not be held to the provisions on reparations, because Moscow would take what it wanted from Germany regardless of an agreement. Dismemberment of Germany, he advised, should be accepted as a fact, and the United States should proceed independently. He feared that centralization, as provided for at Potsdam, would lead to the

Germany buffer against Russia [handwritten margin note]

"communization" of Germany, because Russia would use its zone as a "springboard for a Communist offensive elsewhere in the Reich." The United States should build up the Western zones economically, because the German economy was the backbone of the Western European economy. The Germans, the "strongest people in Europe," were crucial to European reconstruction. A peace settlement of revenge and punishment would only arouse German nationalism and make America's task in Europe more difficult. Kennan strongly disapproved of the Morgenthau Plan, de-Nazification and decartelization programs, as well as the war crimes trials.

In February 1946, Washington was eager to have an interpretive report on Stalin's election speech and Moscow's reasons for not joining the World Bank—to determine, in short, what made Soviet foreign policy tick. For years Kennan had been preparing himself for just such a request. "The more I thought about this message, the more it seemed to be obvious that this was 'it.' " He was tired of plucking people's sleeves to draw their attention to the Soviet menace. "Here was a case where nothing but the whole truth would do. They had asked for it. Now, by God, they would have it." On 22 February Kennan completed his "long telegram," an eight-thousand-word "elaborate pedagogical effort," which ultimately elevated Kennan to the heralded status of *the* expert on the Soviet Union and *the* intellectual in the Foreign Service.

The telegram began with a discussion of the "basic features" of the Soviet outlook on international relations. Placing heavy emphasis on ideology as the wellspring of Soviet behavior, Kennan pointed out that the Soviet mind was geared to capitalist-socialist conflict. Hostility to the capitalist outside world was not a Russian attitude, but a Communist one, a party line. Yet at the bottom of the Kremlin's "neurotic view of world affairs is traditional and instinctive Russian sense of insecurity." Marxist-Leninist dogma, argued Kennan, was the new vehicle for perpetuating this Russian tradition. The Soviets after the war, he predicted, would use Communist parties as an "underground operating directorate of world communism." Russia would seldom compromise; in fact, its foreign policy would be "negative and destructive in character, designed to tear down sources of strength beyond the reach of

Soviet control." In summary, "we have here a political force committed fanatically to the belief that with US there can be no permanent *modus vivendi,* that it is desirable and necessary that the internal harmony of our society be destroyed, our traditional way of life be destroyed, the international authority of our state be broken, if Soviet power is to be secure." Kennan closed his message with less alarmist language. He believed Russia would not risk a major war because it was too weak. America, furthermore, could counter Soviet expansion by constructive propaganda efforts at home and abroad and by maintaining a healthy and cohesive society in the United States as a model. Kennan seemed to emphasize that Russia was more a "political" than a "military" threat, but his statements could be variously interpreted.

Officials in Washington read the long telegram with relish and excitement, for Kennan seemed to have captured their own moods and fears. He later confessed that the telegram read "exactly like one of those primers put out by alarmed congressional committees or by the Daughters of the American Revolution, designed to arouse the citizenry to the dangers of the Communist conspiracy." Here was a document that was authoritative, convincing, and simple, demonstrating just how intransigent the Soviets were. Kennan's timely message helped persuade the administration to speak out more forcefully against Soviet foreign policy, to "get tough," in popular jargon. It had actually been following a "tough" policy before, but now it was more willing to follow it publicly. Administration figures chose to emphasize the parts of Kennan's message that described an uncompromising, warlike, aggressive, neurotic, and subversive Russia that somehow had to be stopped. Whether Kennan intended to or not, he fed exaggerated fears that an international Communist conspiracy, directed by Moscow, sought to subvert the world.

Kennan's ideas and recommendations in the 1944–46 period contain both merit and shortcomings. Russia *was* too headstrong and blunt, too suspicious and fearful. Ideology held a significant place in the Soviet outlook. Soviet propaganda attacks on the United States were crude and antagonistic. (Unlike many other contemporaries, however, Kennan recognized that the USSR was cautious and not militarily aggressive.) Soviet influence in Eastern Europe did block American influence and there was little the United States could do to change the arrangement of power in that area. Too many agreements were vaguely worded. The

Potsdam accords on Germany probably were wishful, especially given the obstructionism of the French (to whom Kennan gave scant attention). Germany did add significantly to the economy of Western Europe and, given the American perspective, had to be revived.

Yet the historian must conclude that Kennan simplified the complex, ignored contrary evidence, and indulged in a great deal of speculation. He placed too much emphasis on Soviet ideology and in so doing posited a mechanistic view of Soviet foreign policy: that it flowed not from interaction with other nations but from internal imperatives and that it was unchangeable over time. Rarely did he suggest that actions of the non-Communist nations influenced Soviet behavior, an omission glaring in its importance. Kennan relied heavily on *his* sense of what motivated Russia; he became the psychiatrist putting the Russians on the couch. What he found was a country endlessly creating world tension; what he disregarded were the instances of compromise over Poland, Iran, the United Nations, and Germany. He may not have thought the compromises significant, but they were compromises nonetheless.

Nor was communism the smooth-running monolith he depicted. Eastern Europe was not closed to the West before 1947. Soviet influence there was varied, uncertain, and perhaps defensive. There was no master blueprint for empire. Czechoslovakia held free elections in May 1946 and until the coup of 1948 retained a remarkable degree of independence. Hungary conducted elections in the fall of 1945 (the Communists managed to get only 17 percent of the vote) and did not fall to a Communist coup until 1947. Finland, although under the close scrutiny of the Soviets, affirmed its independence. Yugoslavia early squabbled with Russia, and under Josip Tito's independent communism, resisted Soviet subjugation. The exceptions were Poland and Romania, both tightly controlled by Moscow. The point is that Soviet policy was mixed, contrary to Kennan's description (which was not much different from Winston Churchill's account of an "iron curtain"). Tears in the curtain existed. Kennan exaggerated the Soviet presence, making it appear total and much more fearsome than it really was. He of course cautioned the United States to abstain from meddling in Eastern Europe, but his very description encouraged thinking that affirmative action had to be taken there. American diplomats attempted to use the one tool they had in the region: economic aid. They dangled loans before the Eastern

Europeans, alternately extending and withdrawing them, which only aroused Soviet fears of an American intrusion and stimulated further Soviet penetration.

In these early cold war years, Kennan seemed to have little faith in diplomacy itself. Since the Russians could not be trusted, there was no sense in signing agreements with them. Certainly some treaties were violated, but the issues were usually complex. Russia broke its treaty with Iran which required withdrawal of Soviet troops in early 1946, but only because Anglo-American influence in that country bordering Russia had grown through military and economic advisers, as well as oil concessions. Kennan was one of the few American diplomats who recognized that Soviet action there was designed to head off foreign penetration, but he nevertheless seemed to accept the American advances in Iran as a basic good. In most cases, agreements were not broken, but rather interpreted differently by both sides. Too often Kennan discouraged negotiations, and opportunities for accommodation were lost. One might ask, as did critic Henry A. Wallace, whether toughness does not simply beget more toughness.

The issue of a postwar loan to Russia, which Kennan vigorously and successfully opposed, is illustrative. Postwar reconstruction was a primary Russian goal, and as early as 1943 the Soviets inquired about a large American loan. American officials delayed the question until 1945 and then decided to use the loan as a diplomatic weapon *before* negotiations, to gain concessions on Eastern European issues, rather than as a bargaining tool at the conference table. Russia resented the rejection of its request and such overt economic pressure in 1946, especially after it agreed reluctantly to talk about Eastern Europe and a loan in conjunction. In this case, foreign aid was never given the opportunity to reduce tension because the United States, wielding its economic power, refused to negotiate. Kennan helped create that position.

Kennan's long telegram particularly impressed Secretary of the Navy James V. Forrestal. He circulated the message widely in Washington and required military officers to read it. The State Department sent it to American ambassadors, who responded with enthusiasm. Forrestal engineered Kennan's return to Washington and installed him as a lecturer at the National War College. "My reputation was made," Kennan recalled. "My voice now carried." In official Washington he became a recognized philosopher of United States diplomacy; but like most philosophers,

[margin handwritten note:] Post-war loan exacerbate tension

Kennan would suffer under the interpretations and emphases others gave to his ideas.

From September 1946 to May 1947 Kennan lectured at the National War College to high-ranking military officers, Foreign Service officers, and an occasional cabinet member (including Forrestal). On 24 February Undersecretary of State Dean Acheson asked him to participate in discussions of the Greek crisis, sparked when the British decided to withdraw troops from that country torn by civil war. After the first meeting, during which Kennan endorsed aid to Greece, he participated little. On 6 March he dropped in at the State Department and saw a draft of the president's message, soon to become the "Truman Doctrine" speech of 12 March 1947. Kennan complained about the sweeping language of the address and the seemingly open-ended commitments it implied. He also opposed military aid to Turkey, because he did not believe that country stood in danger of Russian attack. His complaints came too late; the message was delivered to Congress where it sounded a bell of panic at the same time it suggested that the United States would go anywhere on the globe to resist what it perceived to be a Communist thrust.

In late April Secretary of State George C. Marshall arrived in Washington from the frustrating Moscow Conference convinced that the Soviets had little interest in European cooperation. "The patient is sinking," he told a radio audience in reference to economic ills in Western Europe, "while the doctors deliberate." Marshall moved quickly. He called Kennan to his office on 29 April and ordered him to establish the Policy Planning Staff to study the European economic crisis, to make recommendations within two weeks, and to "avoid trivia." A harried Kennan scurried about to find personnel and with commendable speed his new agency produced an important memorandum dated 23 May. Communist activities, it began, were not at the root of Western Europe's problems, but rather the war, which had disrupted European life. American aid, then, should be aimed not at combating communism, but at correcting the economic maladjustment "which makes European society vulnerable to exploitation by any and all totalitarian movements and which Russian communism is now exploiting." In words to appear later in the "Marshall Plan" address by the secretary at Harvard University, Kennan's report suggested strongly that Europe itself initiate a cooperative program. Russia would not be permitted to block the new program and the Eastern European nations would have to accept American conditions before their participation could be allowed.

Kennan's memorandum and one by Undersecretary Will Clayton, which gave a moving account of misery in Western Europe, formed the nucleus for discussion at the decisive high-level meeting of 28 May. Clayton was emphatic that Western Europe did not economically need Eastern Europe, and as his memorandum put it, *"The United States must run this show."* Kennan said, "Play it straight," and they agreed that the plan should be presented in such a way as to let Russia and the Eastern European countries exclude themselves. The conditions would be difficult for Russia to accept: endorsement of multilateral, non-discriminatory trade practices and a reduction of Soviet influence in Eastern Europe. Few conferees thought the Soviet orbit would accept participation. Actually there was little possibility the Soviets would join an American-dominated program essentially aimed at them. Soviet hegemony in Eastern Europe had not been stabilized, and an influx of American dollars and influence could only be read as a challenge. Of course, Congress itself would probably never have funded a program that had Soviet membership, especially after congressmen had been aroused to new heights of anti-Sovietism by the message of the Truman Doctrine. In short, the decision to leave the door open represented diplomatic finesse rather than sincerity. Later, the United States reaped immense propaganda value by claiming that it had offered Marshall Plan aid to Moscow, which rudely had turned down a sincere invitation. Kennan's influence on this question, as well as on the American decision to undertake a major foreign aid program, was significant. His memorandum coherently synthesized ideas and provided core material for Marshall's Harvard address.

Kennan did not see Marshall often—it was not the general's habit to indulge in long conversations or interruptions—but their offices adjoined and the Soviet expert had unusual access to the highest officer in the State Department. Kennan also kept up his "intellectual" relationship with Secretary Forrestal, who was fascinated with a paper Kennan had presented him in January. Forrestal and the State Department gave Kennan permission to submit the paper to the editor of *Foreign Affairs.* Titled "The Sources of Soviet Conduct," the article appeared in the July issue of the journal under the name of Mr. "X." *New York Times* columnist Arthur Krock, who earlier had been shown a copy of the paper in Forrestal's office, soon dispelled the mystery of authorship, and Kennan was propelled to the center of national discussion. Commentators quickly assumed that the "X" article was government policy and Kennan was tagged the father of the containment doctrine. He seemed to provide the theoretical justification for the Truman Doctrine and the Marshall Plan.

The highly respected article repeated many themes expressed in the long telegram, but it emphasized ideology and left vague what the United States should do to combat Soviet expansion. Kennan wrote about the implacable Communist hostility toward the capitalist world, the doctrinaire fanaticism of Stalinist leaders, and the secretiveness, duplicity, suspiciousness, and basic unfriendliness of Soviet conduct. Russia would take its time beating down its foes abroad since Soviet leaders were confident that capitalism would collapse under its own contradictions. Moscow would accept short-run losses to ensure its long-term goal. "In these circumstances," Kennan wrote, "it is clear that the main element of any United States policy toward the Soviet Union must be that of a long-term, patient but firm and vigilant containment of Russian expansive tendencies." "Counterforce" had to be applied to "constantly shifting geographical and political points" in order to "promote tendencies which must eventually find their outlet in either the break-up or the mellowing of Soviet power." Kennan pointed out that Russia had serious internal economic and political weaknesses. In contrast, the United States could stand as a successful model of internal stability before the world.

Although largely responsible for implanting the containment doctrine as the commanding principle of American foreign policy in the cold war, the "X" article was not one of Kennan's best efforts. As he himself later admitted, it was too ambiguous, too imprecise; it failed to deal with Soviet power in Eastern Europe and the difficulties of ruling an empire; and it never defined what the tools of containment were to be. The article's imprecision led to years of debate and to a policy of global intervention as cold warriors borrowed those parts of the "X" article and the Truman Doctrine that fit their conception of the United States as a manager of international stability.

Kennan used words like "force" quite vaguely and the speculative article as a whole was cast in black-and-white, bad guys–good guys terms. He placed no limits, geographical or chronological, on containment, and thereby ignored the resources and will of the United States to undertake such a long-term program. Nor did he consider the constitutional system, especially Congress's role in foreign affairs, which might place some restraints on the continuous fulfillment of containment. Kennan did not distinguish between vital and peripheral areas, and as Walter Lippmann so aptly noted, containment could become a "strategic monstrosity," with the United States supporting a host of client states. Perhaps most importantly, Kennan never spelled out how the United States should implement containment, whether by economic, political, military, or psychological means.

Questionable was his statement that a mechanistic Soviet power "moves inexorably along a prescribed path, like a persistent toy automobile wound up and headed in a given direction, stopping only when it meets with some unanswerable force." Once again, he ignored United States power and expansion as contributing factors to Soviet behavior. Too simply, he applied one interpretive model to Russia and another to the United States. Russia's foreign policy derived from a response to internal needs, not to real or imagined threats from outside; America's foreign policy derived from a response to external challenges. In other papers Kennan had pointed out that both ideology and traditional Russian nationalist ambitions explained Soviet behavior, but in the "X" article the latter element is largely absent. Then, too, ideology can serve a government in several ways: it can be a driving force, but also a rationalization for other motives, a form of communication, a symbol of continuity, or simply an interpretive device to explain a troubled world. Kennan provided no such distinctions, nor did he supply any formula for the solution of issues; he betrayed considerable pessimism about the efficacy of diplomacy.

On numerous later occasions, Kennan claimed that he never meant that the United States should undertake global interventionism or emphasize military means. It is frankly difficult to know what Kennan meant. He did speak frequently of the Soviet Union as a political threat and did argue that Russia would not assault Western Europe. He did oppose the military emphasis in aid to Greece and Turkey and the seeming permanence of American occupation forces in Japan and Germany. He applauded the

Marshall Plan as the best means to fulfill containment. He objected to the development of the H-bomb in 1949–50 and called consistently for tactical military units for limited wars. He questioned the need for a military alliance like NATO, advocating a less formal arrangement, and complained that National Security Council paper 68, which recommended a stronger U.S. effort to meet the threat of Soviet expansion, was too militarily oriented. There is evidence, then, that Kennan did not agree with the Truman administration's movement toward an extensive military buildup.

Yet, at the same time, Kennan conceded a great deal to the military point of view. Forrestal, after all, was his initial patron, widely recognized as one of the most military-minded men in Washington. Kennan could not have been ignorant of the uses to which Forrestal was putting his ideas. Furthermore, it is a truism in international relations that to be effective politically and economically a great power must have a hefty military punch. Kennan himself had frequently spoken of an "adequate military posture." He also endorsed the Rio Pact, the need for some kind of military coalition in Western Europe, and intervention in the Korean War. In the 1947–50 period he wrote publicly on behalf of containment without clarifying what he meant. Indeed, he reprinted the "X" article without alteration in his popular *American Diplomacy, 1900–1950*, published in 1951.

Even if he did not intend or agree with all the means utilized by Truman to administer his cold war policies, however, Kennan seemed to offer a very broad doctrine and essentially to concede the basic notion that an aggressive and uncompromising Russia (and/or communism) was a threat that had to be dealt with through counterforce almost everywhere and at any time. Whether he intended to or not, Kennan helped to establish undiscriminating globalism and interventionism as permanent features of American diplomacy. Kennan the intellectual would henceforth suffer as others, less reflective than himself, used his ideas to support a multitude of interventions and a military establishment of enormous proportions. The father of containment would spend much of the rest of his life attempting to disown his offspring.

After the successful launching of the Marshall Plan, Kennan fixed his attention on three problems: Japan, Germany, and military defense. He believed that Japan was a strategic bastion in the Far East because of its industrial might, and its preservation in non-Communist hands was essential to a balance of power in that area. In early 1948, when Kennan departed for Tokyo for firsthand study, the questions of the duration of the American occupation and a peace treaty were still open. Kennan urged that the Far Eastern Commission largely be bypassed, so that the United States could act unilaterally to help Japan achieve economic rehabilitation, defense, and independence. Kennan questioned land reform, the busting of trusts, reparations shipments, and the purging of Japanese from positions in government, business, and education. These programs should be curbed and a peace treaty should be delayed until Japan was quite able to stand on its own non-Communist feet. New directives encompassing most of Kennan's recommendations and endorsed by the president were sent to Japan in 1949, and to Kennan's surprise, General Douglas MacArthur agreed. He was disappointed in 1949, however, when Secretary of State Acheson moved toward an early peace treaty, and Kennan attributed the outbreak of the Korean War to deep Soviet resentment that treaty negotiations were begun without Russia in 1950 and completed without Soviet signature in 1951.

Occupied Germany presented comparable problems and Kennan recommended similar solutions. He had long opposed a punitive peace. Although American policy contained as many constructive as corrective elements, Kennan wanted decartelization, dismantling, and de-Nazification to cease. With the coming of the Marshall Plan and the recognition that West Germany's rich deposits of coal and iron and industrial potential were vital to Western European recovery, the United States dropped most of the corrective measures in favor of full-scale reconstruction. In March 1949, with the Berlin blockade still operative, Kennan took a short trip to Germany and called for an agreement with the Soviets whereby American troops would gradually withdraw after unification. Secretary Acheson vigorously opposed unification, prompting Kennan to conclude that the United States was locking itself into the endorsement of permanent German division. Actually Kennan himself was partly responsible for this state of affairs; he had said more than once that cooperation with Russia over

Germany was a "pipedream." Acheson was essentially agreeing with Kennan's earlier view.

The disagreement over Germany reflected a growing division between Kennan and Acheson. When he became secretary of state in 1949, Acheson chose to use the Policy Planning Staff infrequently. The issue of military defense sharply widened the differences between the two men. Acheson, always seeking to work from military strength, wanted to enlarge NATO; Kennan thought the alliance unnecessary. Acheson seemed to be preparing for a major war; Kennan did not think Russia would attack Western Europe and advocated mobile tactical units. The secretary set in motion plans to rearm West Germany and to develop the H-bomb; Kennan strongly opposed both because they would close opportunities for accords with the USSR. Finally, during the Korean War, Acheson enlarged American objectives by sending troops across the thirty-eighth parallel, something Kennan had argued against as early as June 1950, fearful as he was of expanding the conflagration through Chinese entry.

Out of tune with the heavy military emphasis and apparent abandonment of diplomacy, and convinced that the secretary had no confidence in his staff, Kennan asked in late September 1949 to be relieved of his duties. He stayed on until August 1950, when he took a position at the Princeton-based Institute for Advanced Study. As an outsider, he seemed obsessed with explaining to others through numerous lectures and publications what he had learned on the inside. He lectured Americans that they were too emotional in their foreign policy views, too easily swayed by simple answers, too susceptible to stampedes of opinion. These themes he eloquently, if too simplistically, expressed in his still-influential book, *American Diplomacy, 1900–1950* (1951). In the midst of McCarthyism he protested strongly against mindless anticommunism and defended fellow Foreign Service officers against the senator's vicious attacks.

The Foreign Service continued to claim his talent. Ironically it was Acheson who called upon him for help. The secretary asked him in May 1951 to speak privately with Soviet Ambassador to the United Nations Jacob Malik about opening truce talks in Korea. The Kennan-Malik discussions were quite fruitful, for they agreed that negotiations should begin. Through such informal diplomacy Kennan spurred formal Korean talks, which began in July. In the fall of 1951 Acheson called again, this time to invite Kennan to become the new ambassador to Russia. Kennan was hesitant; after all, he disagreed with so much that Acheson and Truman were doing. Yet the appointment would represent a culmination of his career in Soviet affairs and he was a bureaucrat at the call of his government, so he dutifully accepted.

It did not take long for Kennan to discover that the appointment lacked meaning. He was not directed to undertake new negotiations nor to reassess policy; indeed, diplomacy was discouraged. He left for Moscow "empty-handed, uninstructed, and uncertain. . . ." His disappointments multiplied. In Moscow, the embassy was bugged, Soviet agents tailed him, and the Kremlin snubbed him. Stuck in the embassy, a "gilded prison," his bitter memories of the 1930s and 1940s revived. Now he argued that much of the Soviet hostility was due to America's overmilitarized foreign policy. He complained to Acheson that "it is not for us to assume that there are no limits to Soviet patience in the face of encirclement by American bases." His superiors did not respond to his analysis and Kennan decided it was time to leave his profession; but before he could, painful events intervened.

In September 1952 Kennan left Moscow for a conference in London. During a brief stop in Berlin, reporters peppered him with routine questions. One query about the relations between the embassy staff and the Russian people elicited an annoyed and terribly undiplomatic reply. Being isolated in Russia, he said, was not unlike his internment at the hands of the Germans in 1941–42. As a result, the Soviet government soon declared him *persona non grata* for comparing the Soviets with the Nazis. Actually he was happy to give up the ambassadorship, although the way he gave it up violated his sense of proper conduct. The appointment of John Foster Dulles as secretary of state reaffirmed Kennan's inclination to break permanently with the Foreign Service. Dulles wanted him out anyway; his stinging critique of containment and his espousal of "liberation" left no doubt about his differences with Kennan. Quietly and sadly Kennan once more left Washington for Princeton.

Kennan returned to the Institute for Advanced Study and took up his scholarly work. Articles and lectures poured from his typewriter. *Russia Leaves the War* (1956) and *The Decision to*

Intervene (1958), two impressively researched volumes on Soviet-American relations in 1917–20, were widely praised. As a public figure, of course, he could not escape public issues.

After Stalin's death in 1953 and an apparent thaw in the cold war, many prominent European leaders hoped to reduce military weapons and troops in Europe. In 1957, Polish Foreign Minister Adam Rapacki advocated a "nuclear free zone" comprising Poland, Czechoslovakia, and Germany. That same year, Soviet Premier Nikita Khrushchev called for a summit meeting to discuss "ruling war out as a means of dealing with international issues," and British Labour party leaders like Hugh Gaitskell formulated plans for a "disengaged zone" in Central and Eastern Europe. Washington demonstrated little enthusiasm for such ideas, openly rejected the Rapacki Plan, and indeed suggested that the United States might give nuclear weapons to West Germany to counterbalance alleged Soviet military superiority on the Continent.

A number of events stimulated these "disengagement" proposals. Stalin's death and Khrushchev's vehement denunciation of the dictator and espousal of "peaceful coexistence" in 1956 suggested that a less belligerent Soviet foreign policy had developed. Indeed, the peace settlement over Austria in 1955 and the subsequent withdrawal by the United States and Russia from that country seemed encouraging. Other events, however, seemed calculated to heat up the cold war. In 1956, the Soviets crushed the Hungarian revolution and Britain and France attacked Egypt over the Suez Canal controversy. To some observers the failure of the Hungarian uprising indicated that the only way to relieve Soviet pressure on Eastern Europe was the removal of Soviet troops, which a mutual withdrawal of American and British troops from West Germany could accomplish. Yet West Germany had entered NATO in 1955 and continued to expand militarily. The dramatic launching of *Sputnik* in October 1957 convinced disengagement advocates that talks had to begin quickly, before America responded with an accelerated emphasis on missile development and weaponry.

Evidence of the maturation of George F. Kennan's ideas was illustrated in November–December 1957 when he delivered six eloquent, if vague, lectures over BBC radio. Millions in Europe heard the Reith lectures, broadcast from London, and they were widely reprinted. The architect of containment, read the headlines, appeared to be abandoning his creation in favor of "disengagement." He called for a unified, nonaligned Germany, withdrawal of foreign troops from the "heart of the Continent" (Eastern Europe and Germany), and restrictions on the deployment of atomic weapons there. In these lectures, unlike in the "X" article of 1947, Kennan was much less willing to judge Russia. "Their world is not our world." Nor should the United States meddle in the "non-European world." Developing nations should be allowed to grow in their own way; foreign aid, complained Kennan, did more harm than good. Finally, he was critical of strengthening NATO, because in 1957–58 diplomacy rather than a "military fixation" was needed. Implicit in Kennan's speeches was a belief that the United States had overcommitted itself. He had not abandoned the containment of Soviet expansion; rather, he advocated disengagement as a way of "liberating" Eastern Europe and defusing any potential Soviet expansion. The Kennan of 1957, as a comparison of the "X" article and his Reith lectures suggests, had been educated by changes in the Soviet-American confrontation and his realization that unlimited containment stultified diplomacy itself.

A flurry of speeches, serial articles in such opinion magazines as *The New Republic* and *Foreign Affairs*, and heated retorts from Truman and Acheson greeted Kennan's lectures. Opponents of disengagement, like Henry A. Kissinger, asserted that Russia remained a military threat to Western Europe. Therefore, American troops should continue in West Germany as a deterrent; NATO should not be weakened. Others protested that Soviet *political* control of Eastern Europe would not end with the removal of Soviet *military* control. The people of Eastern Europe might attempt to throw off the Communist regimes. Critics predicted the return of Soviet soldiers. The Germans themselves might not accept disengagement and a reduced role in European affairs. Chancellor Konrad Adenauer vocally opposed disengagement and in fact called for more West German military growth. Professor Hans Morgenthau, a German émigré and distinguished political scientist, was equally cautious, suggesting that a united Germany could eventually become a new and threatening German empire and that Russia might prefer a divided Germany, partially restrained by the United States, to a strong one.

Dean Acheson delivered the most stinging and unremitting critique. Correspondent James Reston observed the Kennan-Acheson tussle: "Next to the Lincoln Memorial in moonlight the sight of Mr. Dean G. Acheson blowing his top is without doubt the most impressive view in the capital." Acheson charged that Kennan "has never, in my judgement, grasped the realities of power relationships, but takes a rather mystical attitude toward them." The "realist" appeared to be attacking the "realist." Acheson ridiculed Kennan for his vagueness and imprecision and dismissed disengagement as "new isolationism." The former secretary of state displayed an utter lack of faith in the Soviet Union, which might, he feared, reintroduce troops in Eastern Europe, threaten Western Europe, and sign an anti-American defense pact with the new Germany. Kennan hurled a private barb at Acheson in a letter, commenting that "rarely, if ever, have I seen error so gracefully and respectably clothed. One hates to start plucking at such finery; but I suppose that in one way or another I shall have to do so."

Kennan also received enthusiastic support. British Labour party and German Social Democratic party leaders applauded him. Senator John F. Kennedy wrote Kennan in early 1958 commending his lectures for their "brilliance and stimulation" and reproving Acheson for his "personal criticisms" of Kennan. Walter Lippmann was happy to point out that he had advocated disengagement as early as 1947, when he had criticized the "X" article; a decade later Kennan and Lippmann were struggling as compatriots against cold warriors like Acheson and Kissinger who were reliving the battles of the 1940s and who continued to resist diplomacy in favor of military might. Kennan now trusted in Russian rationality and insisted that despite the risks, disengagement was a viable alternative to a potentially explosive cold war confrontation. The West would not know what Russia thought without at least negotiating. In those days of rigid positions, however, the weight of opinion was against Kennan.

Beginning with the disengagement controversy, Kennan had intermittent contact with John F. Kennedy. While teaching at Yale University in January of 1961, Kennan received a telephone call from the new president and was offered an ambassadorship in either Poland or Yugoslavia. Kennan welcomed the opportunity to serve again, if only to be able to leave the Foreign Service with more honor and propriety than he had in 1952. He accepted the assignment to Belgrade and for two years cultivated contact with Yugoslav officials, gained unusual access to Josip Tito, absorbed the varied culture of the country, and put the embassy staff to work writing a history of Yugoslavia. He noted obvious contrasts between this post and his tour of duty in Russia. Tito was not suspicious and tricky like Stalin. Foreigners were welcome in Yugoslavia and travel was largely unrestricted. Yugoslavia practiced an independent communism, proudly rejecting dictation from Moscow.

What bothered Kennan most was not the Yugoslavian government but his own. In 1961 the Tito-sponsored Belgrade Conference of nonaligned nations triggered vociferous anticommunism in the United States. Congressmen reacted sharply to some anti-American speeches delivered at the conference and began seeking a way to punish Yugoslavia. America's ever-present, undiscriminating, and ritualistic anticommunism flared up again. Kennan blamed the response on Eastern European émigré groups and the American propensity to view world affairs emotionally. Congressmen first disrupted the sale of planes to Tito's government. Then, in 1962, they canceled the "most favored nation" provision in trade relations between the United States and Yugoslavia. It was a vindictive move against a country that had few grievances against the United States and vice versa. Kennan had tried to stop this action by flying to Washington and lobbying with legislators. His failure, and his belief that Foreign Service personnel were minor figures in the American political system, "took the heart out of any further belief in the possible usefulness of a diplomatic career."

Earlier, in 1961, he had asked Kennedy not to endorse the "Captive Nations Resolution" which called for the liberation of peoples living in Communist countries and which Congress mindlessly passed each year. Kennan interpreted it to mean that Washington was committed to the overthrow of the Yugoslavian government, a policy that placed an ambassador in an anomalous position. Kennedy submitted to popular clamor and declared a "Captive Nations Week." This action, combined with the restriction on trade, convinced Kennan that his helplessness as a representative of the United States had been publicly demonstrated to the Yugoslavs. In 1963, without bitterness and with great dignity, Kennan left the diplomatic corps. The Belgrade post was by his own estimation his most rewarding and enjoyable; however, the experience soured him further on the American political process, the intrusions of Congress in foreign affairs, and hysterical anticommunism. Domestic politics, he concluded, was an "intolerable corruption" of diplomacy's "essential integrity."

Yet George F. Kennan felt compelled to go before the Senate Foreign Relations Committee in 1966 to appeal for a gradual withdrawal from Vietnam. Again he acted as the reasoned dissenter trying to persuade public opinion and the Congress—against the president—that the morass in Indochina was an unfortunate consequence of globalism. Interventionists like Dean Rusk, Walt and Eugene Rostow, and Dean Acheson had been justifying the expedition to Vietnam by citing the precedents of anti-Communist containment in the 1940s. Kennan refused to permit himself and his ideas to be used in this way. Under the tutelage of Senator J. William Fulbright, the Foreign Relations Committee was in an early stage of rebellion against the war and was looking for respectable allies. The recognized father of containment was willing to testify. Students and faculties had been protesting and marching, but neither the committee members nor Kennan felt comfortable with their frank and iconoclastic style. Kennan once again thrust himself into the center of a major debate by testifying that the containment doctrine was inapplicable to Indochina.

"I find myself," he remarked, "in many respects sort of a neo-isolationist." By that statement he meant that the United States should be modest and discriminating in its commitments abroad, a view that has gained increasing respect and popularity in the 1970s. He insisted that China was not a military aggressor in Indochina, that a military solution to what was largely an internal political conflict was fantasy, that Vietnam was an area of secondary importance to United States security, and that the war was disrupting American relations with both Japan and Russia. Facile analogies with the 1940s did not face the new realities of the 1960s. Asia was not Europe; China was not Russia. Containment should not be universal. He envisioned Vietnam as an independent Communist country like Yugoslavia; but under vigorous questioning by Senator Frank J. Lausche, ambiguity crept into Kennan's presentation. He said that "if we had been able to do better in Vietnam I would have been delighted, and I would have thought that the effort was warranted. . . ." This note of pragmatism seemed to undercut his appeal to principle. Yet his message was clear: the United States must curb its role as world policeman.

The combination of protest marches, critical analyses by scholars, Communist victories in the hills and cities of Vietnam, and tempered dissent by public figures like George F. Kennan moved both the Lyndon B. Johnson and Richard M. Nixon administrations, however slowly and incompletely, to a de-escalation of military intervention in Indochina.

In early 1973, a still active and alert Kennan talked frankly during a television interview. "I've been gloomy lately," he commented, because America faced massive problems at home and abroad. He felt the United States should no longer try to be the dominant player on the world stage. Whether or not this was a neo-isolationist attitude (and the term should not be used in a pejorative sense), it meant limited commitments overseas, a reduction in the military establishment, more attention to domestic questions, and a frank realization that Washington had neither the duty nor the capability to establish a world balance of power. Kennan voiced skepticism about President Nixon's dramatically orchestrated trip to Peking in 1972. Kennan was not merely suspicious of Nixon's visions of grandeur as international peacemaker. He also nurtured serious doubt about close relations with the Chinese, a consistent position for him since the 1950s. He always preferred Japan as America's "friend" in Asia and had opposed recognition of the People's Republic of China. His views toward that regime were strikingly similar to his 1940s views on the Soviet Union. In 1964, for example, he depicted China as dominated by "embittered fanatics" wedded to an ideology that encouraged the "ruthless exertion of power." The Chinese were determined to destroy what Americans valued.

In the 1960s Kennan had begun to comment frequently on domestic issues such as overpopulation and the environment. In the 1973 interview he summarized his views toward America and its diplomacy, pointing out that the United States had no business meddling in other country's affairs until it had straightened out its own. America had become too commercial minded, too dependent upon the automobile. A self-perpetuating technology produced unneeded inventions that "whipsawed" the American people and made them waste their natural resources. A cab ride in New York City, he said, with a cynical cab driver living in an unhappy, polluted city, had brought his thinking into focus. Americans, Kennan implored, needed leadership and inspiration to alleviate their serious environmental disorder. Although his prescriptions derived from a conservative perspective, they were not far removed from more radical views on the importance of preserving individualism, curtailing the machine, respecting the environment, and giving priority to domestic ills. Both recognized that the quality of American life would ultimately determine United States influence in the world.

Having spent many years as a frustrated bureaucrat-diplomat, Kennan had become more accustomed to the life of the analytical intellectual. One of his aspirations had always been in that direction, for impatience with the foreign affairs bureaucracy marked his diplomatic career. He was never the typical obedient functionary. Americans will remember him more for his ideas on Soviet history and diplomacy, containment, disengagement, American emotionalism, the relationship between the political system and foreign policy, and the need for an elite Foreign Service than for his contributions as a diplomat in formulating the Marshall Plan, changing policy toward Germany and Japan, initiating peace talks during the Korean War, or in serving as ambassador to Russia and Yugoslavia. Whether one accepts or rejects his ideas, so eloquently and forcefully expressed since the 1920s, Kennan has persistently demanded that Americans give attention to them and that statesmen confront international problems with energy, integrity, and intelligence. His legacy will, for some time, claim an influential place in discussions of current and future foreign affairs.

BIBLIOGRAPHIC NOTE

Because George F. Kennan was such a prolific author and controversial public figure, the quantity of literature on his career is massive. A lengthy bibliography of Kennan's own articles and books, including his scholarly publications, can be found handily in Thomas G. Paterson, ed., *Containment and the Cold War: American Foreign Policy since 1945* (Reading, Mass., 1973). Kennan's own eloquent two-volume autobiography, *Memoirs, 1925–1950* (Boston, 1967) and *Memoirs, 1950–1963* (Boston, 1972), is indispensable for a surprisingly frank peek into his exciting life.

Although at this time Kennan's private papers are only partially open to scholars, the complete collection is housed at the Princeton University Library. He used many of the documents in the preparation of his memoirs, but many others have not been published. Letters to, from, and about Kennan and his ideas can also be found in other manuscript collections, many of which are cited in Thomas G. Paterson, *Soviet-Ameri-*

can Confrontation (Baltimore, 1973). Oral history transcripts of interviews with Kennan on topics covering the postwar years are open to research at the Princeton University Library (John Foster Dulles Project) and the Kennedy Library. The Department of State's *Foreign Relations of the United States* volumes include Kennan's influential cables from Moscow in the early cold war period and his advice on such programs as the Marshall Plan.

There is yet no full-length biography of George F. Kennan, but Professor C. Ben Wright has begun one based on his Ph.D. dissertation completed at the University of Wisconsin, "George F. Kennan, Scholar and Diplomat: 1926–1946" (1972). Analytical studies of Kennan and his prescriptions for American foreign policy, especially containment, can be found in Paterson, *Containment and the Cold War* (Reading, Mass., 1973). For stimulating interpretations see the following works: Jonathan Knight, "George Frost Kennan and the Study of American Foreign Policy: Some Critical Comments," *Western Political Quarterly* 20 (March 1967), 149–60; Marvin Kalb, "Vital Interests of Mr. Kennan," *New York Times Magazine*, 27 March 1966; Richard Powers, "Kennan against Himself?" Ph.D. dissertation, Claremont Graduate School, 1967; George Kateb, "George F. Kennan: The Heart of a Diplomat," *Commentary* 45 (January 1968), 21–26; Louis Halle, "George F. Kennan and the Common Mind," *Virginia Quarterly Review* 40 (Winter 1969), 46–57; " 'X' Plus 25: Interview with George F. Kennan," *Foreign Policy*, No. 7 (Summer 1972), 5–21; and Alfred Kazin, "Man of State," *New York Review of Books*, 2 November 1972.

Kennan's containment philosophy was spelled out in his famous "X" article, "The Sources of Soviet Conduct," *Foreign Affairs* 25 (July 1947), 566–82. Provocative commentaries include Walter Lippmann, *The Cold War* (New York, 1947); William Appleman Williams, "Irony of Containment," *The Nation* 182 (5 May 1956), 376–79; Lloyd C. Gardner, *Architects of Illusion* (Chicago, 1970), pp. 270–300; and J. William Fulbright, "Reflections: In Thrall to Fear," *The New Yorker* 47 (8 January 1972), 41–62. Kennan's disengagement proposals were published as *Russia, the Atom and the West* (New York, 1958). For debate see Dean Acheson, "The Illusion of Disengagement," *Foreign Affairs* 36 (April 1958), 371–82; and Walter Lippmann, "Mr. Kennan and Reappraisal in Europe," *Atlantic* 201 (April 1958), 33–37. Kennan's belief that the containment doctrine is inapplicable to Asia is well illustrated in his testimony before the Senate Foreign Relations Committee, *Supplemental Foreign Assistance Fiscal Year 1966—Vietnam* (Washington, D.C., 1966). David P. Mozingo, "Containment in Asia Reconsidered," *World Politics* 19 (April 1967), 361–77, is one of the best discussions of this crucial topic.

Kennan's *American Diplomacy, 1900–1950* (Chicago, 1951), an oversimplified survey that finds American foreign policy dominated by mindless moralism and legalism, is revealing about Kennan's self-defined "realism." Interpretive essays include Dwight J. Simpson, "New Trends in Foreign Policy: A Criticism of the 'Kennan Thesis,'" *World Affairs Quarterly* 27 (January 1957), 102–14; and Dexter Perkins, "American Foreign Policy and Its Critics," in Alfred H. Kelly, ed., *American Foreign Policy and American Democracy* (Detroit, 1954), pp. 65–88.

The secondary literature on the history of the cold war is, of course, prodigious. The best overviews, with differing interpretations, are Walter LaFeber, *America, Russia, and the Cold War, 1945–1971* (New York, 1972), Louis Halle, *The Cold War as History* (New York, 1967), Gabriel and Joyce Kolko, *The Limits of Power* (New York, 1972), and Adam Ulam, *Expansion and Coexistence* (New York, 1968).

POWER AND REALITY:
JOHN FOSTER DULLES

U.S. Information Agency

and Political Diplomacy

Herbert S. Parmet

John Foster Dulles's critics regarded him as Eisenhower's Rasputin. They understood neither his political mission nor his sophisticated analyses of power relationships and the dynamics of Communist expansionism. Along with much of the electorate, the administration's opponents agreed that he advocated a more aggressive cold war stance than previous secretaries of state. Those who feared the dangerous implications of his public statements thought he viewed the line drawn between East and West as the apocalyptic struggle between good and evil, a fight between thermonuclear powers that pitted capitalism, Christianity, and freedom against atheistic Communist materialism. He was an old Puritan who had insinuated himself into the favor of the well-meaning but naïve and politically inexperienced general who occupied the White House. Little wonder, then, that the president, widely regarded as a man of peace, called Dulles an Old Testament prophet. Indeed, few thought of him as anything other than a foreboding figure,

285

one of considerable intellect and convictions but with the vanity and rigidity of another era.

Even before the Republican convention of 1952, Dulles's position had been well publicized. His statements echoed the cold war militants, particularly those who believed that Truman and his administration had responded inadequately to international communism. Just before the convention battle between the moderates and liberals backing Dwight D. Eisenhower and the conservative supporters of Senator Robert A. Taft, publisher Henry Luce's cold war zeal led him to open the pages of *Life* magazine once more to Dulles's views. The Dulles article was bravely entitled "A Policy of Boldness," and it called for initiatives against Communist expansion. Truman's measures were depicted as mere reactions to Communist aggression, as willingness to "live with it, presumably forever," that condemned to permanent slavery the six hundred million people subjugated by the Soviets since 1945. Clearly, the Dulles prescription was a more vigorous approach.

"It is ironic and wrong," he wrote, "that we who believe in the boundless power of human freedom should so long have accepted a static political role," and "that we who so proudly profess regards for the spiritual should rely on material defenses while the avowed materialists have been waging a winning war with social ideas stirring humanity everywhere." The United States must not accept any "deal" that would confirm Soviet rule over alien people, he wrote. Task forces must be created to develop a "freedom program for each of the captive nations." Rather than meek acceptance of containment, political, economic, and cultural programs must be developed to achieve the liberation of all captive peoples. Although the United States must not resort to military tactics that would encourage bloody uprisings and reprisals, it must strengthen its defenses. Emphasizing his words, Dulles added that the free world must *develop the will and organize the means to retaliate instantly against open aggression by Red armies, so that if it occurred anywhere, we could and would strike back where it hurts by means of our choosing.*

The foreign policy plank of the Republican platform of 1952 confirmed the Dulles influence. Not only would "liberation" be an objective, but certainly the new administration would repudiate those agreements that condemned national groups to eternal "enslavement." That, of course, meant Yalta, where FDR had made concessions to Stalin in 1945. Moreover, the record of the subsequent Republican administration for the following six years was obviously his design rather than the work of the beloved and trusted general-president: McCarthyism not contained but unleashed in the corridors of the State Department building and Chiang Kai-shek unleashed in the Formosa Strait; "massive retaliation" with its implicit threat of substituting nuclear wars for local skirmishes fought by conventional armies; a disingenuous encirclement of Communist-held territory with a chain of mutual security treaties; recognition of the follies of policies that antagonized traditional allies.

It was Nikita Khrushchev who made what was perhaps the most revealing observation about the secretary of state. "I feel very sorry for Dulles," said the Russian leader to Dag Hammarskjöld. "I admire his intelligence, his wide knowledge, his integrity and his courage. Dulles invented brinkmanship but he would never step over the brink."[1] Others, with longer memories, may have recalled a contribution Dulles made to *Life* in 1946. The words he chose to begin a two-party analysis of the postwar outlook were: "No nation's foreign policy can be ascertained merely from what its officials say. More important are the philosophy of its leaders and the actual manifestations of that philosophy in what is done."

Dwight Eisenhower liked to say that Dulles's life until 1953 had been spent preparing to head the State Department. The president's hyperbole should not detract from the importance of his observation. The selection of Dulles was so obvious, so predestined, that at least once during the preinaugural period the president-elect seemed annoyed that he had no choice but merely to ratify the selection. Perhaps it is no exaggeration to say that at least three other Republican presidential contenders of that era, Arthur Vandenberg, Thomas E. Dewey, and Robert A. Taft, would have chosen Dulles.

If he possessed credentials that surpassed those of anyone else in his party, those qualifications were further enhanced by his

---

1. David E. Bruce to Dulles, 2 April 1959, Dulles papers, Princeton. Material in this essay from the Dulles papers and the Dulles additional papers is used with the permission of the Princeton University Library and the Dulles Committee.

political standing. Before 1952, however, his reputation required some rehabilitation before he could be acceptable to the party's right wing. At best, the Dulles background as a partisan was not strong. As a Republican foreign policy adviser with the Truman administration, he had been an advocate of bipartisanship; the consequences of the "fall" of China provoked a bitterly partisan denunciation of Democratic culpability. His closeness to Dewey, the man Senator Everett Dirksen condemned so theatrically at the 1952 convention for having twice led the party down the road to defeat, was a considerable liability among the anti-Eisenhower people. A still more serious blemish on Dulles's record was his expression of confidence in behalf of the subsequently convicted Alger Hiss. He lessened such liabilities by waging a strongly conservative campaign during his unsuccessful 1949 fight for the Senate against Herbert Lehman in New York. His connection with the Japanese Peace Treaty and aid in securing that country as an American ally against Far Eastern communism was also helpful, as was the obvious anticommunism, with pronounced spiritual overtones, that he expressed so strongly. His most recent state-ments, particularly the "Policy of Boldness" article, helped to dispel any remaining doubts about where he stood.

The son of a Presbyterian minister, Dulles was born in 1888 in the far-upstate New York community of Watertown. While he was a student at Princeton, fellow undergraduates found it difficult to consider him a congenial companion. Rather withdrawn, some-what of an elitist, he was a moralizer who lacked the qualities that contribute to personal popularity. Throughout his life, he main-tained a prominent association with the National Council of Churches. He stressed spiritual strength and expounded freely on the virtues of Christianity. French Foreign Minister Couve de Murville noted that his own Calvinism enabled him to detect the importance of religion in Dulles's thinking. One astute observer who sat with him at many meetings of both the cabinet and the National Security Council described his demeanor in the following manner: "When it is time for Dulles to speak or make a reply, he does not look at the person he is addressing but fixes his eyes on the ceiling. This creates an unfortunate impression of conscious superiority on his part, as though the people across the table are not as important as the ideas which represent Eternal Truth, and, therefore, must be addressed to the Cosmos."

Nevertheless, it was Dulles who made the Machiavellian

comment to a journalist that the "United States is almost the only country strong enough and powerful enough to be moral," a remark that reveals much about him. As important as piety was to his system of values, as ascetic as his behavior was, he was far too intelligent and sophisticated to ignore realities. "He had the reputation of being a pious man," George F. Kennan wrote, "but I, a fellow Presbyterian, could never discern the signs of it in his administration of the State Department."

Through family tradition, personal experience and study, his diplomatic background was outstanding. His maternal grandfather, John W. Foster, had spent eight months as President Benjamin Harrison's secretary of state. His Uncle "Bertie," Robert Lansing, was more prominent as the most significant of the three men who headed the State Department under Wilson. At the age of thirty, Dulles, trained as a lawyer, went to Paris with the president as counsel to the American commission to negotiate the peace treaty. He also served with the reparations commission and in 1933 was the American representative at the Berlin debt conferences.

The consequences of post–World War I diplomacy did much to mold his thinking. He became convinced that adequacy of power alone had been demonstrably inadequate, that failure to provide for change had created inherent obstacles. Power, Dulles believed, was energy that defied mere containment. Outlets, or safety valves, had to be provided. In his first book, *War, Peace and Change* (1939), he complained that "most political treaties do not seek to create a condition of elasticity, which will be adaptable to changes in the balance of power initially existing. Rather, such treaties tend to perpetuate the results obtainable from possession of an initial command of power." He proceeded to suggest that flexibility rather than rigidity "creates lasting stability." Nowhere had the architects of the "permanent peace" provided for the means to make appropriate modifications. Instead, they tried to maintain the status quo. That misconstrued the nature of power and, therefore, the conditions needed to preserve peace. Careful inspection of the record shows that Dulles had little faith in any single instrument of power; despite the impression he helped to create, he minimized the efficacy of military solutions. All tools were mere elements of power; all had to be used selectively. "Power," he wrote in *War or Peace* in 1950, ". . . includes not merely military power, but economic power and the intangibles, such as moral judgment and world opinion, which determine what men do and the intensity with which they do it."

By the time that book appeared, the cold war had matured beyond its origins. Mao Tse-tung had routed Chiang Kai-shek, the Soviets had secured their sphere of interest in Eastern Europe, and the establishment of both NATO and the Communist Information Bureau (Cominform) helped move the superpowers toward im- placable hostility. Despite the rhetoric about the "international Communist threat" and the concomitant evils that he and fellow Americans condemned so freely, the essentials of Dulles's thinking did not change. Communism was, of course, evil. He had no doubts about the inherent advantages of democratic capitalism. Given a choice between the opposing systems, he was certain which would be supported by a Christian sense of values. Still, what becomes fascinating in retrospect, after one recalls the evangelistic tone associated with Dulles as secretary of state, is that he did not, at that stage, permit the current simplistic assumptions to seduce him.

While sharing the common tendency to cite the sequence of events that led to World War II as a justification for existing policy, he did not assume that Stalin was a new Hitler bent on military conquest of the world; Russian expansionism did not follow that course. The Soviets had succeeded with military means in Eastern Europe as a result of successful pursuit of the Germans and lack of competing military forces in the area. More relevant to an understanding of the phenomenon was that communism thrived on internal discontent and decay. Americans had not, in the past, perceived that "misery and despair in Germany was breeding Nazism." To talk, therefore, of the inevitability of a new major war simply failed to account for the changes that had taken place as a result of the recent great war. The defeat of Nazi Germany, the horrors related to that experience, the establishment of the United Nations, the "balance of terror," and abhorrence toward even the thought of a major new conflict made such repetition most unlikely. Frustrating Soviet Communist methods of "fraud, terror- ism, and violence" by making "positive and well directed efforts" in fellowship with other free peoples would probably suffice to preserve peace. The Communist threat that did exist was less a result of ideology than their possession of enormous military power. Those expansionist impulses causing such concern were mainly related to traditional Russian aspirations. Overt aggression,

Dulles believed, would probably result from the Kremlin's inability to control the Red Army.

Essential to the Dulles analysis was the conviction that a major war, if it should come, would be "the result of miscalculating." Both world wars that brought American involvement had, he pointed out, come from failure of foreign leaders to understand how we would respond. That the North Korean southward drive across the thirty-eighth parallel had followed the Truman administration's implication that the area lay beyond the American military periphery was the most recent vindication of his belief. Further, the Russians, as he had found at the opening session of the United Nations Conference at San Francisco, respected an uncompromisingly firm position.

He spoke at Princeton in early 1952 and repeated his view of the nature of the cold war. "It is primarily through social ideas that Soviet Communism achieves its victories," he said. "Almost no part of its expansion has been due to the old-fashioned method of open military aggression. The successful weapon has been political warfare, with the main reliance placed on revolutionary slogans which arouse the masses to Soviet-dictated violence." He proceeded to point out that the determination of right and wrong stemmed from "a moral or natural law not made by man . . . and conformity with this law is in the long run indispensable to human welfare." Dulles agreed with Arnold Toynbee in attributing the "crisis of our civilization" to the contradictions of our practices from their Christian context, so that "while Soviet Communism fails to invoke moral principle, we ourselves are not doing much better."

Three years earlier, in a letter to his son Avery, Dulles responded to an inquiry about the inherent qualities of Soviet communism revealing interesting aspects of his thought. "I know you have a contempt for 'expediency,'" the Old Testament prophet wrote to his Jesuit son, "but that is what in fact determines most people's conduct, and when you ask whether as a practical matter communism can be expected to give up violent methods without first becoming converted to a Christian view of the nature of man, my answer is that all history proves that such a development is quite possible." [2]

2. Dulles to Brother Avery Dulles, 3 March 1949, Dulles additional papers, Princeton.

◇◇◇

If politics may be defined as the art of the possible, to Dulles expediency was the art of politics. Serving under Eisenhower brought him together with a fellow practitioner. Their obvious personal differences did not prevent a remarkably smooth relationship, one so harmonious, in fact, that the virtual absence of conflict was often interpreted as evidence of Eisenhower's supine subservience to Dulles, the man who really determined American foreign policy. In reality, their teamwork was made possible by a common view of the task. For all Eisenhower's platitudes and public displays of innocence and for all Dulles's blend of righteousness and bellicosity, they were in basic agreement about the political requirements of their mission.

More than has been generally realized, Dulles weighed domestic political factors and responded accordingly. At the outset, he was second to no one in appreciating the need for the Republican party to decimate the traditional Democratic vote as a means of winning the 1952 election. The old New Deal coalition was clearly in jeopardy, buffeted by the domestic conservative reaction of the late 1930s and, more recently, by the consequences of the wartime alliance. Many Americans, particularly Roman Catholics, felt repugnance toward friendship with the Soviet Union. Polish-Americans were alarmed about Russian success in controlling Eastern Europe after their westward pursuit of the fleeing Nazis. Even as early as 1944, months before the Yalta Conference, protests were being voiced about President Roosevelt giving Stalin too much freedom of action in that area. Jan Ciechanowski, the Polish wartime ambassador to the United States, advised Dulles that a Republican return to power would be hindered severely through failure to appeal to the ethnic Slavic vote. Dulles never forgot the point. At a luncheon meeting in Colorado after the 1952 convention, he expounded on how the forthcoming campaign should emphasize the party's platform pledge to secure the liberation of the "captive peoples" behind the iron curtain.

His display of political consciousness that day impressed his audience. Eisenhower's subsequent campaign against Adlai Stevenson virtually rivaled Joe McCarthy's contemporary appeal to the frustration and anger of millions of Americans, especially Roman Catholic Democrats. Protests about the immorality of the ideological alliance with McCarthy failed to dissuade Dulles of its political necessity.

With the new administration installed in Washington, Dulles moved decisively to avoid Acheson's pitfalls. Whereas Acheson's "personal relations with Congress were, in the opinion of most observers, abysmal," Dulles worked hard to establish a relationship with the Senate characterized by "complete frankness and honesty." Although Acheson had come before the Foreign Relations Committee only when summoned, the committee's records show forty-eight appearances by Dulles during his six years at the head of the State Department. He always took particular care to journey to Capitol Hill to consult with the senators both before and after important international conferences. He also worked to improve upon Acheson's relations with the press. Most journalists felt that Truman's secretary of state had dealt with them in a high-handed and contemptuous manner. Dulles, understanding the importance of their role, proved far more open and congenial.

Ever conscious of popular support, the secretary tailored every public address to ensure the proper reception. Sophisticated audiences tended to criticize his pious moralizing, but they comprised an insignificant segment of the population; further, they constituted the administration's natural critics. More appropriately, Dulles spoke to the mass audience. He was careful to avoid complex language and even cleansed his speech drafts of foreign words and phrases, particularly those in Latin. He felt they tended to reduce the impact of his message and would make vast segments of his audience doubt his sincerity. So while the nation's intellectuals sneered, Dulles found compensation in the glowing responses from the hinterlands.

More important, perhaps, and puzzling to those who thought they knew Dulles, was his reaction to the whole issue of internal security and Senator McCarthy. One of the ironies of the tumultuous state of American politics during that bitterly partisan stage of the cold war was that he became so closely associated with the dangerously ambitious senator, at least in the eyes of his critics. Having convinced a frightened public that Communist success came from laxity and even treachery in high American circles and having placed the diplomatic corps under suspicion, the anti-Communist crusaders managed to intimidate even those who viewed them with contempt and loathing.

This submission by Dulles to the McCarthy tyranny provided

persuasive evidence of the senator's power. Everything about
McCarthy's public and personal life was abhorrent to the secretary; a greater contrast between two men could hardly be
possible. Moreover, even conservatives close to the man from
Wisconsin have testified that his notions about communism were
hazy; and, certainly in contrast to Dulles, his emphasis upon
ideology as an internal menace was a gross distortion. For the
secretary, the hunt for domestic subversives held no significance
whatsoever. Further, the McCarthy style and tone reminded Dulles
of Nazi Germany, a point the secretary made to Senator Ralph
Flanders of Vermont as they both heard the senator deliver one of
his harangues. Yet, so thorough was McCarthy's ability to intimidate, so secure was his hold on the public and the Congress,
particularly Republicans, that, to Dulles, any freedom to conduct
the affairs of the State Department meant concessions. Conscious
of his own support for Alger Hiss, the secretary knew that further
suspicions could hinder his conduct of American foreign policy.
Anything that reduced his latitude or detracted from his main
purpose was a nuisance to be eliminated.

As his first concession to what he perceived as the political
realities of 1953, Dulles provided evidence that the new administration had brought changes; after all, the recent election had
been a massive protest against Truman's policies. Therefore, in the
climate of fear that had saturated Washington and the nation, all
suspicions had to be allayed. Even before his own confirmation by
the Senate, Dulles took the discreet step of requesting that his
own loyalty be scrutinized by a full FBI field investigation, a
procedure that became standard for all appointees. Then, shortly
after assuming his office, he addressed an outdoor gathering of
State Department personnel. He called for their "positive loyalty"
to the new administration. Undoubtedly he feared hostility from
Democratic holdovers, but the connotations of the word "loyalty"
during that period were sufficient to send reverberations throughout the staff, including the Foreign Service. Thereafter, as one of
Dulles's close aides has since observed, it was no longer enough to
demonstrate mere "loyalty"; one had to offer "consistent proof of
such fealty."

To dramatize further its reaction against past policies, the new
administration had to purge those who in the public and congressional minds had been made scapegoats for the "permissive"
Truman policies toward international communism. Thus, officials

who had been attacked by what became known as the China Lobby (a pro–Chiang Kai-shek pressure group financed by textile importer Alfred Kohlberg and a coterie of other businessmen and their congressional spokesmen) would have to be sacrificed for the greater cause. Dulles arranged for the departure of the "old China hands," Foreign Service officers John Carter Vincent, John Stewart Service, and John Paton Davies, Jr., whose crimes consisted of having offered perceptive analyses of the situation in China before Chiang's downfall. To further prove that the Eisenhower administration had reversed discredited policies, Dulles also facilitated the retirement of Kremlinologist George F. Kennan, who was far too intimately associated with the policies that the Republicans had promised to reverse by extending hopes of "liberation" for the "captive peoples." What better evidence that the immoral assumptions of "containment" had ended than the purging of the man who had become identified as the main theoretician of that policy!

Also needing correction were suspicions about the lack of security within the department. Dulles, without any illusions about the rationale for such a policy, turned over the problem to Scott McLeod. A former FBI agent and newspaperman, McLeod's mentality and methods invariably brought suspicions that he was one of Joe McCarthy's men. Actually, he had been brought in by Undersecretary of State Donald Lourie on the recommendation of Senator Styles Bridges of New Hampshire. Given a virtually free hand, McLeod went to work with the zeal of a Boy Scout uncovering "enemy agents." Heading a crew of nearly two dozen ex-FBI men, he focused on all the soft spots that had been publicized by McCarthy, particularly on the supposed relationship between homosexuality and security leaks. After three weeks on the job, McLeod publicized his success in removing twenty-one "deviants." His men also patrolled the State Department's corridors, even making after-hours forays into office files that had not been locked. By November, McLeod's mission was justified with the announcement that 306 citizen employees and 178 aliens had been separated from the department for security reasons.

After two youthful agents of Senator McCarthy returned from an inspection tour of overseas libraries operated by the International Information Administration, the agency was accused of harboring on its shelves over thirty thousand volumes by "Communist" authors, including the works of Dulles's cousin, Foster

Rhea Dulles, as well as Arthur Schlesinger, Jr. The State Department promptly announced remedial action. Not only would all such literature be banned in the future, it promised, but also "any publication which continuously publishes Communist propaganda." McCarthy approved, calling it a "good, sensible order." Far from restraining the anti-Communist hysteria of the period, the administration, with Dulles carrying out his part of the mission, succumbed to those political pressures that inevitably fostered fear and insecurity within the government.

Fulfilling certain other promises, however, was not that simple, particularly when they threatened to jeopardize rather than aid the interests of diplomacy. The Republican platform promise to "repudiate all commitments contained in secret understandings such as those of Yalta which aid Communist enslavements" had, of course, been entirely consistent with Dulles's desires to win the votes of Slavic Americans. To make a pitch for votes was one thing, however; to carry out a campaign promise was quite another. The Yalta Conference had confirmed the arrangements made in London in 1944 that gave the West a legal status in Berlin. If this, as well as occupation rights in Vienna, had been given under repudiated treaties, how could such rights be continued? Thoughts about the problems such action would create for the ability of Americans to negotiate in the future rendered an anti-Yalta policy untenable.

Dulles and Eisenhower, therefore, catered to both international and domestic political realities. When the secretary met with the party's congressional leaders on 16 February to present the administration plan, the impossibility of satisfying both needs became obvious. The resolution he unveiled for congressional approval simply condemned diplomacy at the expense of "captive peoples." Rather than denying past obligations, it blamed the Russians for "totalitarian imperialism" that had led to the "subjugation of free peoples." Rather than repudiating the Roosevelt-Truman diplomacy, it blamed Russian deceit. To the Republican party's congressional leaders, that sounded remarkably similar to Democratic explanations for the failures of the wartime conferences. Facing a GOP rebellion over the issue, Dulles appeared before the foreign relations committees of both houses and urged Republicans to forget about the past and to concentrate on the future. He also warned about the international implications of repudiation. Even his critics called Dulles's performance before the House committee the "greatest advocacy of his career," but they were not satisfied. Supported by Senator Taft, the Senate Foreign Relations Committee added an amendment declaring that "the adoption of this resolution does not constitute any determination by Congress as to the validity or invalidity of any provisions of the said agreements or understandings." With Democrats incensed about its implications and siding with the administration on the issue, Eisenhower and Dulles considered dropping efforts to get any resolution through Congress. The simultaneous death of Joseph Stalin salvaged the situation by suddenly rendering the resolution "inopportune." Diplomatically, the timing would be regarded as callous. The change in Soviet leadership demanded cautious assessment.

Still, political exigencies required substantial evidence of departure from past policies. Although neither Dulles nor Eisenhower had international views that differed in substance from Truman-Acheson policies, and although the world appeared remarkably similar to them as it had to the Democrats, rhetoric had to obscure the inevitable continuity.

The partisan rancor of the past, the blame and bitterness, the charges of incompetence and even treachery, the suspicions of a lack of a "will to win," and the frustrations of an interminable war in Korea left leaders in the Dulles era little choice but to confirm prevailing popular assumptions. However involved the origins of the cold war, however sophisticated Dulles's own view, the options open to American leaders were severely limited. In the process, as close as was the Eisenhower-Dulles association, the secretary was the expendable man, the one exposed to the voters as the cold warrior in contrast to the peace-loving president, and, significantly, the man whose now strident anticommunism was politic in its attractions for the party's conservatives, who were suspicious about Eisenhower's intentions. Just as the president delegated the more sordid political tasks to Vice-President Richard Nixon, so it was in the area of diplomacy. Dulles's role was to placate the right wingers, to convince them that changes had indeed occurred. Therefore, instead of altering previous policies, Dulles's six years were full of strident posturing. With the need to take a hard line in crisis after crisis, to stem the Communist tide that had plagued the Democrats, it became more important to avoid a nuclear showdown than to take bold new initiatives. His own ideas about flexibility vis-à-vis power were severely compromised. In retrospect, considering the political mission and the climate of the nation, there was little room for innovation in foreign affairs.

His tenure, therefore, came and went with essentially the same problems, largely unresolved and often verging on the catastrophic. By definition, his accomplishments were negative. No ground was lost to the enemy and major military conflicts were avoided. More active in his travels than any previous secretary of state, almost constantly flying from capital to capital, Dulles gingerly used his political support to consolidate incipient policies and thereby helped to make his years a sort of plateau of the cold war era. He did succeed in holding the line with a minimum of force. At his death, European recovery and rearmament fulfilled the hopes of its architects, but the division of Germany and the status of Berlin remained as menacing as ever; the Russian hold over the "captive peoples" had been diluted in Poland but reaffirmed with steel and bullets in Hungary, and, in either case, it remained untouched by American policy; a brief war had exacerbated the Middle Eastern muddle over oil, Zionism, Arab nationalism, and Russian intervention satisfying no one and compounding the job of finding a solution; the Korean War had ended and the thirty-eighth parallel was relatively quiet, but American forces were covertly engaged in South Vietnam, sustaining a regime that carried the blessings of Washington more than the support of its own people; recognition of the People's Republic of China was an act that would have meant political suicide and few doubted American readiness to go to war to defend Chiang Kai-shek's right to maintain his garrisons on Formosa, or even the dubious bastions on Quemoy and Matsu; a summit conference had taken place in Geneva and platitudes were expended in behalf of toning down the ever accelerating arms race without a scintilla of substantive progress; the "third world" nations that had just begun to "emerge" at the start of the fifties were providing evidence of nationalistic independence and seemed stubbornly immune to romancing by either Moscow or Washington.

At the outset of his tenure, Dulles delivered a speech that many interpreted as an attempt to regain for the State Department the support Acheson had lost. He chastised those Europeans who "want to go in their separate ways" despite the "deadly serious" threat of encirclement by the Communist bloc. Addressing a national audience via television, he enumerated all the world's trouble spots and detailed the dangers of Communist expansion. "So far as your Government is concerned," he said, "you may be sure that it will not be intimidated, subverted or conquered. Our nation must stand as a solid rock in a storm-tossed world. To all those suffering under Communist slavery, to the timid and intimidated peoples of the world, let us say this: you can count upon us." Only six days later, when the president delivered his State of the Union message, he made headlines by reading from a section written by Dulles. The Seventh Fleet, Eisenhower announced, will "no longer be employed to shield Communist China." Although the act was soon described as the "unleashing of Chiang Kai-shek," it did not in substance alter what had been happening all along in the Formosa Strait.

The presence of the Seventh Fleet no longer deterred the Nationalist forces from striking at the mainland. According to the official Nationalist China news service, raiders had "temporarily occupied" twenty-one cities, three hundred fifty villages, and nine islands during the preceding year. President Truman had actually reversed the policy of guarding against military activities in the area but without the propaganda threat of a wider war. Still, Dulles made his point. Pro-MacArthur and pro-Taft segments of the public and the press rejoiced that the new administration had rejected the "Marshall-Acheson doctrine" by responding vigorously to Russia's challenge. When Dulles reached London shortly afterward, he faced evidence of European dismay at the appearance of growing American belligerence. He assured them that his words presaged no real change.

The Dulles journey marked the start of the administration's efforts to bolster the strength of the Western alliance. Winning ratification of the European Defense Community was the immediate goal. Acheson had given the plan high priority; it would enable the development of a West German army that could be safely—and therefore acceptably—integrated within the European Coal and Steel Community. The Dulles efforts provided a clear example of the continuity of American policy. Since the end of World War II, the United States had spent about thirty billion dollars on Western Europe; it now regarded formation of EDC as vital for the non-Communist world's ability to resist aggression.

Although the plan had been conceived by French political economist Jean Monnet, it had become clear that its main obstacle was the political situation in Paris. A French National Assembly divided almost equally among six different parties and the dependence of Premier René Mayer's government on the anti-EDC nationalist supporters of General Charles de Gaulle dimmed the outlook. Further damaging EDC's prospects was the Soviet "peace offensive" that followed Stalin's death. Prime Minister Georgi Malenkov projected soothing tones from Moscow. His words offered a hopeful world the possibility that Russia's new leadership was looking for a détente with the West. Malenkov stated that there was no dispute that could not "be decided by peaceful means, on the basis of mutual understanding by interested countries." Was the Russian overture genuine, or was it a ploy to sabotage EDC?

Simultaneous developments seemed to indicate a real change. Moscow radio began to glorify the Russian and Anglo-American wartime partnership. Foreign Minister Vyacheslav M. Molotov agreed to cooperate to obtain the release of British citizens being held by the North Koreans. From the Korean War zone came the first significant Communist concession toward relieving the truce deadlock. There was agreement for an immediate discussion to facilitate the exchange of sick and wounded prisoners of war. In Berlin, too, the Russians displayed a more cooperative attitude and relaxed restrictions that had been plaguing the Western sector of the city. Even in the United Nations there was change. The Russians joined the West in support of Dag Hammarskjöld as secretary-general. For Dulles and the American president, all this created a dilemma. Fears of adverse propaganda made it difficult for them to appear insensitive to the "peace offensive." At the same time, its acceptance as heralding a genuine rapprochement threatened to dilute the urgent need to strengthen the Western alliance and complicated the administration's efforts in behalf of continued foreign aid and military spending.

Eisenhower's address to the American Society of Newspaper Editors in April of 1953, an event widely publicized by the United States Information Agency, served as the counter-stroke. The president contrasted the postwar behavior of the Communist countries and the democracies and called for more than words to substantiate Soviet sincerity. In the broader sphere of diplomacy, Eisenhower was executing his function as an advocate of peace,

while Dulles continued to pursue *Realpolitik*. The contrast between the public images of the two men was, of necessity, highly
exaggerated. After all, the state of American public opinion toward
both Russia and the concept of communism and the considerable
influence of the Republican party's right wing made any substantive concessions by the Eisenhower-Dulles team a most hazardous
undertaking.

In reality, the administration's established policy and rhetoric
had combined to make the American position virtually inflexible.
They could not abandon the public advocacy of a unified
Germany governed by free elections, nor could they even appear
to accept the permanence of the captive condition of Eastern
Europe. Abandonment of support for Syngman Rhee and his
Republic of Korea government was equally unthinkable, as was
the reduction of American arms without firm and politically
acceptable agreements with the East. Moreover, at that stage of
the cold war, an administration elected largely through public
belief that it could deal more firmly with communism than had its
predecessors could not suddenly admit that it was possible to deal
with the godless Communists who had, as millions believed,
"violated every treaty." Dulles's mission was the continued mobilization of the "free world" against the immoral enemy.

His determination and abrasive style became evident during
Dulles's subsequent efforts in behalf of EDC. At a session of the
NATO Council in Paris, in a desperate yet calculated effort to force
the issue, he expressed grave apprehensions about "whether
continental Europe can remain a place of safety" despite the
continuing schism between France and the German Federal
Republic. Speaking carefully, he warned that French failure to
ratify EDC "would compel an agonizing reappraisal of basic
United States policy." In other words, there could be an end to
American military support of Western Europe. Whether or not the
subsequent anti-EDC vote in the National Assembly resulted at
least in part from adverse reaction to the secretary's words, the
European community was dead.

The essentials of Dulles's policy survived, however. Creation
of the Western European Union salvaged the early restoration of
West Germany's full sovereignty and won the admission of the
Bonn government as an equal partner. At the suggestion of British
Foreign Secretary Anthony Eden, the Brussels Treaty of 1948, which
had provided for the mutual defense of five nations against a

remilitarized Germany, was revised and expanded. The new organization included Great Britain, which would not have been possible if EDC had been accepted. The administration had achieved its goal after all. Eisenhower's memoirs recall his agreement with Dulles "that the accomplishment of the transformation was a 'near miracle—a shining chapter in history.' "

Quickly, the distinctive characteristics of Dulles's diplomacy had become a stiff military posture and an apparent readiness to go to war if necessary. His "Policy of Boldness" article had pointed to the need to "retaliate instantly . . . by means of our choosing." Additional prominence was given in January 1954 to his statement before the Council on Foreign Relations of the importance to the United States of "a great capacity to retaliate, instantly, by means and at places of our choosing." Subsequent talk about more reliance on "deterrent power, and less dependence on local defensive power," more trust in air power and the efficacy of atomic weapons ("More bang for the buck!") brought the pejorative phrase "massive retaliation" into the speeches of Dulles's critics. While the secretary insisted that deterrence was his objective, those fearful of its implications considered it a dangerous concept. They feared an irresponsible use of atomic weapons and diplomacy that would leave little choice between all-out war or inaction because of the weakness of conventional forces.

In sharp contrast to the continuing depiction of the president as a man of peace, a *Life* article by James Shepley in early 1956 lent more substance to charges that Dulles was a warmonger. Shepley's authorized contribution described the secretary of state as advocating the need to be willing to go "to the brink" if necessary to avoid war. Thus, the author of "massive retaliation" was also a practitioner of "brinkmanship." The rhetoric virtually buried the substance of Dulles's concern with deterrence through the avoidance of miscalculation and ignored the fact that the concept he had expressed was hardly unique. At the same time, "actual manifestations" of the Dulles diplomacy displayed considerable prudence.

Liberating the "captive peoples" was one thing as a political slogan but quite another matter to carry out. Therefore, when the shortage of food and other grievances led to serious uprisings in East Berlin in 1953, there was no overt American response. Even more dramatically, the Hungarian "freedom fighters" of 1956, temporarily in possession of Budapest, found that their frantic

"Don't Be Afraid—I Can Always Pull You Back"

From Herblock's Special for Today *(Simon & Schuster, 1958)*

appeals for American assistance went unanswered. Nor was there aid for the Polish insurgents a few days earlier. Responding to such crises would, of course, have meant sending Western forces behind the iron curtain and a rather brazen provocation of a major conflict. It was pointed out that military force was never planned as the way to effect liberation.

Willingness to go to the brink did not imply lack of restraint. It did emphasize the need to maintain a position of power and guard against any temptation to weaken Western unification. Therefore, Dulles worked to help frustrate any legitimate progress toward disarmament, even when a Russian proposal presented in London in 1955 apparently complied with previous American demands. Dulles fully expected the Russians to continue to maneuver to throw the West off guard and constantly expected attempts by Moscow to promote a sense of euphoria.

Consistent with his thinking, he expressed strong reservations about the wisdom of having the president meet with the Russians in a summit conference in Geneva in 1955. British political pressures following the replacement of Sir Winston Churchill as prime minister by Anthony Eden ultimately led to the meeting. With general elections scheduled in Great Britain that May, it was politically wise for the incumbents to gain popular favor by arranging for a meeting with the Russians. Contrary to public impressions, Eisenhower was skeptical. The president pointed out to Foreign Minister Harold Macmillan, who was exerting pressure on Washington, that he understood why such a conference would be helpful to British conservatives but the more vehemently anti-Communist American public also had to be considered. In the end, Dulles may even have been somewhat less reluctant than the president, who was not ready to provoke the indignation of his party's right wing.

Once the gathering became inevitable, following the signing of the Austrian peace treaty and a meeting of the foreign ministers, Dulles drew up an advisory memorandum for the president. He warned against permitting the Russians to exploit the conference by establishing moral and social equality with the West. "These gains can be minimized," he wrote, "by the President avoiding social meetings where he will be photographed with Bulganin and Khrushchev, etc., while maintaining an austere countenance on occasions where photographing together is inevitable." Further, publicizing that the United States was using the occasion to "push for satellite liberation and liquidation of international communism"[3] could minimize whatever gains the Kremlin hoped to derive from the conference. Indeed, the subsequent conference with its "spirit of Geneva" afterglow did provide both sides with propaganda opportunities, with the American president unveiling his "open skies" inspection proposal, but it made no real progress toward mitigating cold war conflicts.

If Geneva's value was illusory, it at least marked the high point of Anglo-American cooperation, an issue that underwent considerable stress during the Dulles years. To begin with, his appointment as secretary of state contradicted advice given to the president by Anthony Eden. British sensitivities had been upset by claims that Dulles had reneged on an agreement to permit the Japanese government the choice of dealing with either of the two Chinas. Instead, Premier Shigeru Yoshida was informed that the United States expected them to side with Chiang Kai-shek. When Dulles arrived in London on his first official trip after the unleashing of Chiang, he found the British press denouncing him as a "double-dealer." Personality differences and continued mutual suspicion further strained the relationship between the two outstanding figures of American and British diplomacy. They exacerbated inherent distinctions between the policies of the two governments and complicated the handling of such matters as the Indochinese crisis of 1954, the dilemma over the Formosa Strait, the problem of the offshore islands of Quemoy and Matsu, and, most dramatically, the Suez Canal affair in 1956.

This was more than just Dulles's policy, for the position of the Eisenhower administration necessarily differed from considerations that underlined both British and French needs. In Indochina, the French had been in the throes of a colonial war since 1946; by the spring of 1954, there could be little doubt of the precariousness of their situation. French Union troops, supported largely by American matériel and financial aid, had been backed into a

3. John Foster Dulles, "Secret Paper #4: Estimate of Proscript of Soviet Union Achieving Its Goals," Dulles additional papers, Princeton.

corner—or, more precisely, into the valley that held their garrison at Dien Bien Phu. That Ho Chi Minh's forces were Communist was largely incidental to the French, who were struggling to salvage whatever bargaining hand they could retain at the Geneva Conference that was scheduled to open on 26 April. If they had to relinquish their colonial holdings, which had become a virtual certainty, they nevertheless wanted to retain economic concessions in the area. The British, with a colony to protect at Hong Kong and with continuing diplomatic and economic relations with the People's Republic of China, were in no position to provoke the Peking government. Opposition from the Labourites in Parliament further complicated matters, particularly since Churchill was expected to retire shortly as prime minister.

The Americans could ill afford to tolerate such considerations. Less than one year earlier, the administration had extricated the country from the Korean War. A combination of threatening the possible use of atomic weapons, a warning delivered by Dulles personally to the Indian prime minister obviously for transmission to Chinese ears, and the changed leadership of the Soviet Union after Stalin's death had facilitated an armistice. Acceptance of the Korean division by the American public, drawn along a line that deviated only slightly from the original thirty-eighth parallel boundary, was widely attributed to Eisenhower's personal prestige and its Republican sponsorship. Even then, the party's right wing, particularly William Knowland, then on the verge of becoming the new Senate majority leader upon Taft's death, was clearly unhappy. Further jeopardizing the administration's ability to fulfill its campaign promise of tough anticommunism was the coincidental timing of the Indochina crisis and the opening of Senate hearings that placed the government squarely against Senator McCarthy.

Moreover, neither Eisenhower nor Dulles operated on assumptions that differed from those inherited from Truman and Acheson. A policy statement drawn up by the National Security Council in early 1952 had linked the nation's security needs in that area to American holdings in the Pacific and such resources as natural rubber and tin as well as petroleum and "other strategically important commodities." To Washington, that made the French effort "essential to the security of the free world, not only in the Far East but in the Middle East and in Europe as well." Eisenhower himself cited such interests; at a governors' conference in Seattle in 1953, he warned that if "we lose Indochina" we would also sacrifice the "tin and tungsten that we so greatly value from that area." He also told a news session that the nations in Southeast Asia were like a "row of dominoes" that would collapse in the face of Communist take-overs of adjacent lands.

Nevertheless, Dulles and Eisenhower were in agreement about the inadvisibility of overt, unilateral American military intervention. All along, Dulles had feared the consequences to Indochina of a Korean settlement, which would free the Chinese to send more help to Ho Chi Minh. An administration that had won popular support in large part through faith in its ability to end the war in Korea could hardly commit American troops to another conflict in that part of the world so soon afterward. As Dulles pointed out privately later that spring, the American public had not been "educated" to undertake a war in Indochina. That was substantially confirmed by a Gallup poll that showed 76 percent of Republicans and 70 percent of Democrats opposed to sending troops. Such a move would also undermine the administration's efforts in behalf of its New Look defense policy that minimized the need for the same conventional forces that would have to be used in any such involvement. Helped by an elaborate analysis contributed by General Matthew Ridgway, Eisenhower also under-stood the persuasive arguments against fighting a land war in that part of the world.

There was little evidence of Senate support for the use of force. When congressional leaders of both parties were given a confidential briefing that informed them about Admiral Arthur Radford's Operation Vulture scheme calling for American air and naval power to aid Dien Bien Phu, there was general agreement that no such action should be undertaken without England and France. There was also substantial understanding that military power was inappropriate for what was basically a conflict over colonialism. Senator John F. Kennedy drew praise from both sides of the aisle when he stated that conviction in a major speech in the Senate.

Eisenhower and Dulles were determined to salvage the situation by strengthening the Western position before the Ge-neva Conference and by guarding against French temptation to make a hasty and unfavorable settlement. At the same time, Paris had to be handled carefully because ratification of EDC was still being sought. If nothing could be saved, disassociating Washing-ton from the wreckage could minimize at least political losses.

While still in command of NATO forces, Eisenhower had advised the French to "make this a matter between freedom and communism." [4] At a cabinet meeting during the crisis, Dulles acknowledged that many other countries did not regard communism as the most vital issue. "People have to understand," he added, "that there is something better in the world than just giving up to the Commies. It's a long hard road." Vice-President Nixon had already been dispatched on a tour of the Far East to make a series of speeches emphasizing that the conflict was to uphold the cause of "freedom and independence" and the "liberties of the Indo-Chinese peoples." In April of 1954, the vice-president dramatized the administration's stance by expressing the possibility that American land troops might have to be sent to the area. In other words, there should be no miscalculation of American intentions.

Dulles flew to London to meet with Eden. He found the foreign secretary still opposed to any pre-Geneva statement supporting a joint military strike; but two days of talk did end with a joint communiqué that, to Dulles, represented real progress. Both nations agreed to join with the other countries in "an examination of the possibility of establishing" such a coalition "to assure the peace, security and freedom of Southeast Asia and the Western Pacific." He returned home with the assumption that he had obtained the authority to convene a nine-power conference to form such a coalition, but the British ambassador soon informed him that Eden had forbidden participation by a representative of the United Kingdom in a meeting for that purpose. Dulles was angry, convinced that Eden had reneged. Those who knew Dulles well and understood his powers of persuasion guessed he had left London thoroughly convinced that Eden had bought his arguments. Actually, the communiqué had been ambiguous; it had made no definite statement about a coalition, only one that called for an "examination" of such united action as a "possibility." The French, too, opposed "united action." They wanted to end the war, not broaden it. For them, survival on the battlefield long enough for a decent settlement that preserved their economic interests was different from enlarging a war that was already unpopular at home.

Dulles went to Geneva in 1954 prepared to disassociate the

4. Dwight D. Eisenhower, Dulles Oral History Project, Princeton.

United States from any agreement that recognized the right of communism to exist in a part of Vietnam. Not only did he arrange to leave the sessions early by sending a substitute in his place, but the final draft did not carry an American signature. At the same time, the United States helped to install and support the regime of Ngo Dinh Diem with the aid of covert operations directed by CIA operative Colonel Edward Lansdale. As the Pentagon Papers released in 1971 confirmed, belief that the United States–backed regime in Saigon could not win the elections, scheduled for 1956 in accordance with the agreements made at Geneva, led Washington to support President Diem's successful move to cancel the voting. For Eisenhower and Dulles, it was the only possible solution.

Then, to salvage his attempts at containing communism, Dulles arranged a conference in Manila later in 1954 that resulted in the formation of the Southeast Asia Treaty Organization (SEATO). Providing for collective defenses of the area, it fell short of the NATO-type provision for an integrated military command for instant responses to aggression; but its existence, plus Eisenhower's offer to assist the Diem government "in developing and maintaining a strong, viable state, capable of resisting attempted subversion or aggression through military means," provided the justification for the overt intervention undertaken by subsequent administrations.

Anglo-American relations fared no better over Formosa and Suez. Both contributed substantially to weakening the rapport among the Western allies. In the face of Chinese Communist threats against Quemoy and Matsu, Prime Minister Churchill, fearing a new conflict in the Far East, and one that would be fought over insignificant rocks close to the mainland, thought Chiang Kai-shek's garrisons should evacuate the islands. During repeated threats in that area, however, Dulles intentionally avoided telegraphing the American intent to the People's Republic. His Formosa Resolution that was approved by the president and in the Senate by the lopsided vote of eighty-three to three authorized the president "to employ the forces of the United States as he deems necessary for the specific purpose of securing and protecting Formosa and the Pescadores against armed attack, this authority to include the securing and protecting of such related positions and territories of that area now in friendly hands and the taking of such other measures as he judges to be required or appropriate in assuring the defense of Formosa and the Pescadores." Intentionally left ambiguous were the criteria for deciding what kind of attack would constitute a "threat" to Formosa.

To the British, who had recognized the Peking government in 1950, the American attitude toward mainland China was unduly provocative. When Eisenhower met with Prime Minister Harold Macmillan at Bermuda in 1957, in the presence of Dulles, the president mentioned the strong American opposition to giving the People's Republic of China a seat in the United Nations. So great was that pressure, he added, that the successful seating of Peking might force an American walkout. During that conversation it was Dulles who pointed out that, contrary to the president's words, recent public opinion polls indicated that opinion was becoming more flexible on the issue. Macmillan, impatient with Eisenhower's position, retorted that the Americans seemed willing to throw out the UN when it stopped serving their interests.[5]

Even before that Bermuda meeting, the distinctive considerations behind American policy, as interpreted by Eisenhower and implemented by Dulles, had subjected the Atlantic alliance to its most severe blow. As had been the case during the war scare brought on by the 1954 Indochina crisis, Dulles again became the villain in the piece: he was blamed for undermining the British response in the Middle East and creating the crisis there, and it was his arrogance toward President Nasser's ambassador to Washington that prompted Egyptian nationalization of the Suez Canal. The subsequent part played by the United States in ending the rash Anglo-French and Israeli invasion of Egypt to retrieve the canal seemingly vindicated the hostile perceptions of Dulles's influence.

That interpretation simply gave too much credit to the secretary of state. At the same time, it minimized the president's active involvement in the affair. In the Middle East, as in Western Europe and the Far East, the administration's continuation of the containment policy meant drawing a sharp line against Communist expansion. Complicating such a maneuver, of course, was the real problem of nationalism and what was referred to as the "neutralist" attitude of the nonaligned nations. An additional

5. Memorandum of Conversation, 24 March 1957, Dulles papers, Princeton.

element of risk came from Arab-Israeli tensions. Washington therefore had to navigate a delicate course between Russia's desires for influence in that area, Arab oil holdings that involved the interests of American corporations, and Nasser's ambitions; moreover, the administration had to contend with an electorate that reflected significant support for Israel. To prop up the region's anti-Russian proclivities, Dulles inspired what ultimately became known as the Baghdad Pact. That mutual defense agreement included Great Britain, Pakistan, and Iran in addition to the original members, Iraq and Turkey. Unfortunately, it only created new problems. Egypt feared the pact would make Iraq dominant and the Soviet Union was thereby challenged to find new ways of penetrating the Middle East. As the Nasser regime drew closer to the Russians, the Egyptian position became more ominous and led to the American agreement to join with the British in helping Cairo to finance the construction of a dam at Aswan on the Nile River. Its purpose was to create hydroelectric power and new arable land for a rapidly increasing population.

Nasser, however, resented Anglo-American provisions that limited Egyptian expenditures for other major enterprises; the British, anxious to placate Iraq in order to preserve the security of two air bases in that country, bore the brunt of the resentment felt by Egypt's chief Moslem rival toward the deal being prepared for Nasser. Further, Nasser's actions became increasingly offensive to Washington. Not only did the Cairo government recognize the Chinese Communist regime, but Egyptian agents worked throughout the Middle East against rulers in Libya, Lebanon, Jordan, Iraq, and Saudi Arabia. Congressional anger grew when Nasser purchased additional weapons from the Soviet bloc and considered accepting a large interest-free loan from Russia. Fears that newly irrigated lands along the Nile would eventually produce long-staple cotton in competition with domestic growers fueled the growing antipathy toward United States financing of the dam.

It was not, then, merely that Egypt's policies had so offended the Dulles concept of morality that led the secretary to greet Nasser's ambassador with the information, just when Cairo had agreed to accept the money, that the loan was no longer available. More accurately, the positions of both the British and the Americans had changed. As Eden reports in his memoirs, he and Foreign Secretary Selwyn Lloyd had already decided that they "could not go on with a project likely to become increasingly onerous in finance and unsatisfactory in practice."

Eisenhower, not his secretary of state, considered a change in policy essential and led the way to its realization. At a meeting of the National Security Council at Camp David, he expressed doubts about the loan. Dulles also agreed that negotiations over the dam should be terminated. The members of the NSC approved the president's subsequent decision to cancel the offer.[6] This occurred before Dulles met with Nasser's emissary. Therefore, despite notions that became popular, the secretary did not precipitously fling the offer back to the ambassador just because the Egyptian had announced that the Russians were also willing to help. The subsequent nationalization of the Suez Canal, moreover, was a move that Nasser himself later admitted had been under discussion for two years. Considering that monitored telephone calls showed that the Egyptians also knew about the decision on the loan beforehand, there is ample reason to believe that Nasser used or even provoked the incident for his own purpose.

Aware of British and French fears that Nasser had the ability to close the canal at will and thus cut off the flow of oil to Western Europe, Eisenhower and Dulles labored feverishly to prevent or at least to delay any military action. The Israelis were also ready to exploit the situation, because Egyptian *fedayeen* raiders were harassing the tiny nation from Gaza Strip bases. Of particular embarrassment would be the start of a war in the Middle East just before the presidential elections in the United States. Eisenhower, mindful of his cooperation with Eden's domestic political needs when he had agreed to go to Geneva in 1955, informed the prime minister of the folly of impetuous action and said that American public opinion "would be outraged" if there were no efforts to solve the crisis by peaceful means. Dulles then fulfilled his mission by pressing London to delay hasty action. To keep the British and French hopeful, he dangled before them the prospect of American cooperation in the use of force if all other solutions failed. When the diplomatic effort collapsed and a concerted British-French-Israeli invasion began just before the 1956 elections, and without any prior notification to Washington, Eisenhower would have nothing to do with it. Instead, publicly and privately, he worked to

6. Dillon Anderson, Dulles Oral History, Princeton.

stop the invasion. General Andrew Goodpaster, then the president's staff secretary, has confirmed that Dulles merely worked within the parameters established by Eisenhower. By the time the president got the three nations to terminate their thrust just short of their goal (with the help of a threatened Soviet intervention), Dulles was already confined to Walter Reed Hospital for the removal of a cancerous growth.

Ten days after Eisenhower's landslide reelection, Selwyn Lloyd and Sir Harold Caccia, the new British ambassador to Washington, visited Dulles at his bedside.

"Once you started, why didn't you go through with it and get Nasser down?" Dulles asked.

"Foster," replied Lloyd, "why didn't you give us a wink?"

"Oh!" answered Dulles. "I couldn't do anything like *that!*" [7]

Dulles's diplomacy substantiates the conclusion that his own accomplishments were more noteworthy for holding the line than for new departures. His rhetoric masked the continuation of Truman's policies. Contradicting his own convictions about flexibility and the hope for change within the Communist world, Dulles's policies succumbed to domestic considerations and ignored the deterioration of so-called monolithic international communism. That approach certainly did nothing to relieve tensions. Some of his positions, particularly regarding disarmament, intentionally opposed the kind of rapprochement that was the objective of those American businessmen who wanted economic relations with the Communist world. From those quarters, there was annoyance that he had so little appreciation of the value of trade with the East. Without access to Soviet sources, it is virtually impossible to conclude that greater congeniality would have mitigated the cold war at that stage. Blaming Dulles for its perpetuation simplifies the problems; but one thing seems certain: he mobilized support for the Eisenhower presidency even from among the Republican party's most zealous cold warriors. The importance of that accomplishment should not be underestimated.

7. Herman Finer, *Dulles over Suez* (Chicago, 1964), p. 446; Hugh Thomas, *Suez* (New York, 1966), p. 147.

BIBLIOGRAPHIC NOTE

Much has already been written about the Eisenhower-Dulles era, but future studies of Dulles will follow the availability of his papers now stored at the Dwight D. Eisenhower Library in Abilene, Kansas. Of particular value, especially to those interested in unraveling the intricacies of the Dulles-Eisenhower relationship, will be the extensive files of cables from the secretary to the president. At present, researchers may use papers at the Princeton University Library that offer insights into both Dulles's thought and personal makeup; until more diplomatic material is released, much will continue to depend on the large number of contributions in the Dulles Oral History Project at Princeton. Additionally, both Columbia University and the Dwight D. Eisenhower Library have transcripts of the interviews from the Eisenhower Oral History Project.

For an understanding of Dulles, the student should begin by reading Louis L. Gerson's *John Foster Dulles* (New York, 1968). The book, which is part of the American Secretaries of State series, is without interpretive distinction but written with clarity and offers a useful chronicle. *The Time of Power: A Reappraisal of John Foster Dulles*, by Richard Goold-Adams (London, 1962), remains a worthwhile critique despite the absence of citations. Norman Graebner, *The New Isolationism* (New York, 1956), offers a critical analysis of the administration's earlier diplomacy. Intent on minimizing Dulles as a moralist and upgrading his diplomatic abilities is Michael Guhin's *John Foster Dulles: A Statesman and His Times* (New York, 1972). Two books by contemporary journalists, John R. Beal, *John Foster Dulles*, rev. ed. (New York, 1959), and Roscoe Drummond and Gaston Coblentz, *Duel at the Brink* (Garden City, N.Y., 1960), are limited but cannot be dismissed. A small but annotated sample of Dulles's own views on a variety of issues is available in a book by one of his press secretaries, Andrew H. Berding, *Dulles on Diplomacy* (Princeton, 1965). Eleanor Lansing Dulles has offered a humanizing and poignant account of his final struggle in *John Foster Dulles: The Last Year* (New York, 1963).

Dulles's most accessible writings are two books and several articles: *War, Peace and Change* (New York, 1939) and *War or Peace* (New York, 1950); "A Policy of Boldness," *Life* (19 May 1952) 146–60; "Policy for Security and Peace," *Foreign Affairs* (April 1954), 353–64; and "Challenges and Response in United States Policy," *Foreign Affairs* (October 1957), 25–43.

Many works examine the domestic setting against which Dulles worked. A book that is both a comprehensive view of the administration and a scholarly treatment of the political factors is Herbert S. Parmet, *Eisenhower and the American Crusades* (New York, 1972), from which has been drawn the bulk of the material for this essay. Arthur Larson's *Eisenhower: The President Nobody Knew* (New York, 1968) is a contribution by a White House staff member that does much to alter views of the Eisenhower-Dulles partnership that the president's detractors favored. A highly jaundiced view of Dulles by an insider is Emmet J. Hughes, *The Ordeal of Power* (New York, 1963). Indispensable although tedious and burdened by committee authorship are the two volumes that comprise Dwight D. Eisenhower's *The White House Years* (Garden City, N.Y., 1963, 1965). Fairly sensational at the time of its publication for its use of material provided by the administration was Robert J. Donovan's *Eisenhower: The Inside Story* (New York, 1956). Richard Rovere's *Affairs of State: The Eisenhower Years* (New York, 1956) is a collection of contemporary observations by a liberal journalist. I. F. Stone, *The Haunted Fifties* (New York, 1963), offers more critical and incisive views. Marquis Childs's *Eisenhower: Captive Hero* (New York, 1958) was the first significant evaluation not marred by sentimentality for the general in the White House. Garry Wills, *Nixon Agonistes* (Boston, 1970), is a pungent treatment that says much about Eisenhower and his vice-president. Most useful among the contributions by insiders, despite limited candor, are Sherman Adams, *First-Hand Report* (New York, 1961), and Richard M. Nixon, *Six Crises* (Garden City, N. Y., 1962). Two magazine articles that deserve particular attention are William V. Shannon, "Eisenhower as President," *Commentary* (November 1958), 390–98; and Murray Kempton, "The Underestimation of Dwight D. Eisenhower," *Esquire* (September 1967), 108.

A rapidly growing volume of analyses of the cold war provide useful insights into the Dulles era. Most worthwhile are Walter LaFeber, *America, Russia, and the Cold War, 1945–1966* (New York, 1967), Louis J. Halle, *The Cold War as History* (New York, 1967), Stephen Ambrose, *Rise to Globalism* (Baltimore, 1971), and Seyom Brown, *The Faces of Power* (New York, 1967). Traditional arguments supporting the American role may be found in Walt W. Rostow's *The United States in the World Arena* (New York, 1960) and in his *The Diffusion of Power, 1957–1972* (New York, 1972). More critical views are in Richard J. Barnet, *Intervention and Revolution* (New York, 1968), and Ronald Steel, *Pax Americana* (New York, 1967).

Personal memoirs by foreign and American diplomats help to round out the picture. See, in particular, Sir Anthony Eden, *Full Circle* (London, 1960), Harold Macmillan's *Tides of Fortune* and *Riding the Storm* (New York, 1969, 1971), George F. Kennan, *Memoirs, 1950–1963* (Boston, 1972), and Robert Murphy, *Diplomat among Warriors* (Garden City, N.Y., 1964). Milton S. Eisenhower's *The Wine Is Bitter* (Garden City, N.Y., 1963) is both compassionate and perceptive in viewing conditions relating to Latin America.

THE EDUCATION OF
JOHN F. KENNEDY

John F. Kennedy Library

Robert A. Divine

It was no accident that the cold war reached its height in the administration of John F. Kennedy, the youngest American ever to hold the office of president. Despite his sophistication and graceful style, Kennedy sincerely believed in the cold war shibboleths that men like Dean Acheson and John Foster Dulles had been voicing for a decade and a half. He was convinced that Russia directly threatened the security of the United States (Khrushchev really meant to bury us) and that only a tough, determined American response, grounded in military superiority, could ensure the nation's survival. In the course of his tragically short term in office, Kennedy's attempts to substantiate these beliefs brought the world to the brink of nuclear war and engulfed the United States in the Vietnam quagmire. Yet during his last year in the White House, JFK showed signs that he had learned that arms and will alone were not enough to master world affairs, that the qualities of human understanding and concern for mankind

317

might be equally important. In that sense, the education of John F. Kennedy not only broadened the horizon of one man; it also opened the way for his successors to move beyond the cold war.

Like all of us, Kennedy was a prisoner of his own past. In spring 1939, while a junior at Harvard, he had undertaken a grand tour of Europe. Through the good offices of his father, Joseph P. Kennedy, then ambassador to England, he had had a chance to observe diplomatic developments in Paris, Berlin, Warsaw, and Leningrad firsthand on the eve of World War II. He returned to the United States after the outbreak of fighting in September and then drew upon his experiences to write an honors thesis in political science entitled "Appeasement at Munich." Though he avoided his father's isolationist belief that Europe was doomed, he condemned England for permitting Hitler to rearm and then to outmaneuver the democracies at Munich. National weakness led to the inevitable surrender of Czechoslovakia to Germany, Kennedy argued, implying that security for any country rested on superior military force and a willingness to use it. With the help of his father and a family friend, Arthur Krock, Kennedy published a revised version of the thesis in the summer of 1940 under the timely title *Why England Slept*. Americans bought forty thousand copies of the slim volume, which offered both a facile explanation of Hitler's astonishing success and this advice to the United States: "We should profit by the lesson of England and make our democracy work. We must make it work right now."

The onset of the cold war served only to sharpen and intensify Kennedy's commitment to a philosophy of force. Winning election to Congress in 1946 on the basis of his attractive personality, fine war record, and family name, he soon criticized the Truman administration for failing to wage the struggle against communism with sufficient vigor. In January 1949, he rose on the floor of the House to condemn the State Department for "losing" China to the Communists repeating the familiar right-wing attack on FDR's Yalta Agreements by charging, "What our young men had saved, our diplomats and our President have frittered away." Kennedy cast votes for the Truman Doctrine and the Marshall Plan, but he had reservations about Point Four and economic aid for development, and when Truman sought to cut back on defense spending in 1949, Kennedy countered by demanding a seventy-group air force and a stepped-up civil defense program. At the same time, he opposed the export of strategic goods to Communist China, calling it "trade in blood." Despite his concern with Asia, he remained European oriented, defending the administration's plan to station troops on the Continent against Republican demands for withdrawal and warning after the outbreak of the Korean War against neglect of NATO, for that could lead to "a major disaster in Western Europe." The lesson of Munich continued to dominate Kennedy's thinking; he joined millions of Americans in transferring the tragic experience with Hitler's Germany to the confrontation with Stalin's Russia.

As cold war attitudes hardened in the 1950s, Kennedy showed few signs of dissatisfaction with the prevailing consensus. He did try to modify Eisenhower's Formosa Strait Resolution in 1954, hoping to avoid a commitment to defend the offshore islands of Quemoy and Matsu, and in 1957 he delivered a stinging indictment of the French refusal to grant independence to the Algerians. Kennedy's record on Vietnam was mixed. He criticized the French conduct of the war against Ho Chi Minh's guerrillas after two trips to Indochina in the early 1950s, but he joined Eisenhower and Dulles in supporting the Diem regime. In a speech in Washington on 1 June 1956, Kennedy, now a senator, declared that Vietnam represented "the cornerstone of the Free World in Southeast Asia, the keystone to the arch, the finger in the dike," and prophesied that if "the Red tide of Communism" flowed into Vietnam, "Burma, Thailand, India, Japan, the Philippines and obviously Laos and Cambodia" would be endangered. His deepest concern, once again, lay with the state of America's defenses. Alarmed by the Soviet *Sputnik* and Russian progress in developing an intercontinental ballistic missile, JFK warned in 1958 that by the early 1960s "the deterrent ratio might well shift to the Soviets so heavily . . . as to open to them a new shortcut to world domination." Kennedy urged Eisenhower to take heroic measures to close the missile gap, reminding him that "our experiences with the illogical decisions of Adolf Hitler" should have taught us the need to be on guard against totalitarian leaders. When Stuart Symington asked if Kennedy were comparing America in the 1950s to Britain in the 1930s, JFK replied, "The Senator is completely correct."

Kennedy was convinced that Eisenhower had let the United States drift dangerously in world affairs and in his campaign for

the presidency he adopted the slogan "Let's get moving again."
Dramatic events in 1960 seemed to confirm Kennedy's diagnosis.
In May, the Russians shot down a U-2 spy plane on the eve of the
Paris Summit Conference and when Eisenhower took full responsibility for the overflight but refused to announce cancellation of
future missions, Khrushchev called off the summit meeting with
an angry tirade that signaled an ominous deepening of the cold
war.

In the next few months, a sense of despair developed in
America as rioting students forced Ike to cancel a planned trip to
Japan, violence and near chaos overtook the newly independent
Congo, and Fidel Castro moved Cuba into the Communist orbit.
Nikita Khrushchev dominated American headlines; he declared
the Monroe Doctrine "dead," accused the United States of
"piracy" when the Russians shot down a second American
reconnaissance plane, and shocked the entire world with his
antics at the United Nations meeting in New York, particularly
when he took off his shoe and thumped it on his desk to express
his contempt for the West. Ignoring the advice of political experts,
Kennedy harped on foreign policy issues to drive home his belief
that the Republicans had failed to preserve America's leadership in
the world. "The harsh facts of the matter are that our security and
leadership are both slipping away from us," Kennedy charged at
the outset of the campaign, claiming that "the balance of world
power is slowly shifting to the Soviet-Red-Chinese bloc."

During the fall campaign against Vice-President Richard
Nixon, Kennedy made two serious foreign policy slips. The first
came during an interview with Chet Huntley, when Kennedy said
that the United States ought to urge Chiang Kai-shek to withdraw
from Quemoy and Matsu, describing the islands as indefensible.
In the second of four televised debates, Nixon jumped on this
remark to accuse Kennedy of advocating a policy of retreat and
withdrawal. Furious at being backed into a corner, Kennedy tried
to clarify his position, but finally he simply let the issue drop when
he realized that he had surrendered the initiative to Nixon, an
even more ardent cold warrior than Kennedy in 1960. Kennedy's
second mistake came on 20 October, when his aides released a
statement on Cuba advocating support of "fighters for freedom"
who were struggling to overthrow Castro's regime. When Nixon,
adroitly shifting to a soft line, accused Kennedy of proposing to
violate American treaty commitments and engage in naked aggres-

sion, JFK again backed away with the limp excuse that his position had been misunderstood.

At best, foreign policy contributed only marginally to Kennedy's narrow victory in November. Dissatisfaction with declining American prestige in the world, deepened by the release of secret USIA public opinion polls taken abroad, undoubtedly won Kennedy many votes, but his inept handling of the offshore island and Cuban issues probably cost him just as many. More importantly, Kennedy's actions suggested the dangers of electing so young and inexperienced a man to the presidency at a time of grave world crisis. His brash promise of support for the Cuban exiles and his tactless challenge to Ike's wise policy of ambiguity on Quemoy and Matsu raised serious questions about his leadership in world affairs. His rhetoric provoked even greater doubts. His constant reference to a world divided between freedom and slavery signaled a determination to escalate the cold war, as did the repeated call to increase America's military strength. The man who warned the American people that "the only thing that will deter Mr. Khrushchev from loosing his hounds of hell on us will be a strong America" was now president, with the power not only to get America moving again but also to blow up the entire globe.

Once in the White House, Kennedy set out to revitalize American foreign policy. He combed the ranks of the "Eastern Establishment" to find bright, dynamic men in the universities, foundations, and Wall Street law firms to replace the businessmen that Eisenhower had relied upon to lead the nation. Aided by Robert Lovett, Truman's secretary of defense (and the personification of the eastern internationalist elite) who declined a cabinet position on the grounds of ill health, Kennedy assembled an apparently brilliant team: Robert McNamara, the whiz kid who had risen to the presidency of the Ford Motor Company by applying techniques of systems analysis, as secretary of defense; McGeorge Bundy, the intelligent and supremely self-confident dean of the Harvard faculty, as national security adviser; Walt Rostow, MIT economic historian who had suggested the phrase "Let's get moving again" and who displayed a tough-minded approach to the cold war, as Bundy's deputy; and Maxwell Taylor, the intellectuals' favorite general who had fought a losing war against the Eisenhower-Dulles massive retaliation policy, as military adviser to the president and later chairman of the Joint Chiefs of Staff. The only lesser light was Secretary of State Dean Rusk, a deliberate, thoughtful man with proven bureaucratic skill, an inclination to defer to the military, and a streak of innate caution that led contemporaries to characterize him as an ideal subordinate without the stuff of command. Kennedy's choice of Rusk seemed a clear sign that he intended to formulate and conduct foreign policy himself.

The "New Frontiersmen" shared one vital quality: they all believed that the world was pliable and that, in the words of David Halberstam, they "could manage and control events, in an intelligent, rational way." They all assumed a tough, pragmatic style, thinking of themselves as "can-do" operators who had the courage, brains, and determination to meet the Soviet challenge and overcome it. Kennedy epitomized this new approach to world problems. He was cool and detached, rising above the moral concerns that inhibited Adlai Stevenson and contemptuous of the softness of so many American liberals. His warm smile and youthful vitality gave him an appealing public image, but reporters who observed him closely noted his aloofness, his refusal to become emotionally involved with either issues or personalities, and quickly dubbed him "Jack the Knife." His sense of irony served him especially well; he could stand back and examine himself critically, aware of his own shortcomings and the very real limits on his power. His wry sense of humor distinguished him from humorless men like Bundy and McNamara and gave him a humility that saved him from their arrogance.

Kennedy's first presidential speeches indicated that he fully intended to live up to his campaign rhetoric. In the inaugural address he and Theodore Sorensen prepared, Kennedy repeated his belief that Russia threatened the very existence of the United States ("Only a few generations have been granted the role of defending freedom in its hour of maximum danger") and reiterated his intention of relying on superior military force ("Only when our arms are sufficient beyond doubt can we be certain beyond doubt that they will never be used"). Ten days later, in his State of the Union address, he painted an even more chilling picture of the world. In each critical area he had examined "the tide of events has been running out. . . . time has not been our friend," he warned. He identified the Soviet Union and Communist China as the twin dangers facing the Republic, asserting that neither Communist nation "had yielded its ambitions for world domination." In words that revealed he was still haunted by Munich, he declared, "Our task is to convince them that aggression and subversion will not be profitable routes to pursue these ends."

The problems facing the new president were enough to stagger the wisest and most experienced statesman; Kennedy's belief that he could manage them was yet another sign of immaturity. In Africa, prompt action by the United Nations, under the skilled leadership of Secretary-General Dag Hammarskjöld, had helped restore a measure of order to the explosive Congo, where the death of Patrice Lumumba had eased fear of a Communist take-over. The chief threat now came from Moise Tshombe, leader of the mineral-rich province of Katanga, who attempted to assert his independence with the backing of European mining interests. Closer to home, Fidel Castro had forced President Eisenhower to break off diplomatic relations in early January by insisting that the American embassy staff be reduced drastically. Kennedy and his advisers feared that Castro and "Che" Guevara intended to spread their revolution to other Latin American states; at the very least, Cuba seemed to be a model for other nations unhappy with the traditional United States hegemony in the Western Hemisphere. In Southeast Asia, the Viet Cong were waging an increasingly successful guerrilla war against the Diem regime, whose large American-trained army had been created to meet an overt invasion from the north, not to fight a brush-fire war. The situation appeared to be much more critical in Laos, the tiny country where the Eisenhower administration had sponsored a right-wing overthrow of neutralist leader Souvanna Phouma in 1958 only to provoke a Communist counterattack that threatened to engulf the entire country. In Berlin, tension had been building since Nikita Khrushchev first announced plans to sign a separate peace treaty with East Germany in 1958 and thus undermine Western access rights to the city. The Soviets had delayed further action after the abortive Paris summit until the

American elections were over; now Kennedy would have to decide how to deal with the Russian insistence that, after sixteen years, the victors of World War II resolve the German problem.

Historians have tended to treat Kennedy's policies toward these crucial issues separately, taking them up one by one and thereby ignoring how they impinged on each other. Yet the only way to understand these crises is to see them as Kennedy did, as interrelated phenomena that came to him intertwined, never permitting time for calm, deliberate judgment. In the first eight months, JFK dealt simultaneously with Cuba, Berlin, and Southeast Asia, and his policies culminated in a major nuclear war scare in the summer of 1961 that served as a precursor to the more famous Cuban missile crisis of the following year.

The hallmark of Kennedy's early behavior in office was a lack of prudence. As a young, bright, but inexperienced president, he tried to deal quickly and pragmatically with these desperately complicated and dangerous issues, hoping to register immediate gains and thus establish his credentials with Nikita Khrushchev. He ignored the advice of moralists, men like Undersecretary of State Chester Bowles, Senate Foreign Relations Committee Chairman J. William Fulbright, and UN Ambassador Adlai Stevenson, who tried to point out the long-run consequences of Kennedy's contemplated actions. Bowles left the State Department in November; Stevenson quicky found himself without any effective influence on administration policy and began to suspect, quite rightly, that he was being used to divert world attention from Kennedy's hard-line actions; Fulbright continued to be consulted, but his advice was disregarded with monotonous regularity. Instead the realists, led by Bundy, Rostow, and McNamara, dominated the administration's inner councils and reinforced Kennedy's own hawkish inclinations. The president and his advisers simply did not have any patience with the long-winded, moralistic objections of the idealists; the world was on fire, and they had to rush to put out the flames.

The acquisition of power gave Kennedy access to information that did not always confirm his prior beliefs. In the first few weeks in office, he and McNamara discovered that the missile gap was an illusion; far from trailing the Soviets in strategic striking power, the United States was opening up an impressive lead. At the time of the inauguration, America had more than one hundred ICBMs, compared with less than fifty for Russia; nearly seventeen hundred long-range bombers to the Soviet Union's one hundred fifty; and eighty Polaris missiles on board five nuclear submarines, while the Russians had none. After studying the figures, the forthright McNamara told reporters on 6 February that there was no missile gap, only to have the White House issue an immediate denial. Two days later, John F. Kennedy informed the press that it was "premature to reach a judgment" on the issue, thus deliberately keeping from the American people the fact that a gap existed in reverse. In the course of the next few months, Kennedy sent three messages to Congress requesting a total increase of six billion dollars in defense spending, a major portion designated for strategic weapons. As a result, by the time of Kennedy's death, the United States had opened up an enormous lead over the Soviet Union in ICBMs and Polaris missiles, creating a dangerous imbalance in the arms race that insured a massive Soviet effort to catch up. The huge nuclear arms buildup of the sixties, which culminated in the ABM, the MIRV, and the SS-9, thus became Kennedy's grimmest legacy.

Kennedy made an equally significant decision in regard to Cuba in his first few weeks in office. Shortly after the election, CIA Director Allen Dulles informed Kennedy of the plan Eisenhower had approved earlier in 1960 to train a group of Cuban exiles in Central America and help them invade Cuba to overthrow the Castro regime. In late January 1961, Kennedy told Dulles to go ahead with the CIA plan, which at that time called for a landing near the Escambray Mountains in south-central Cuba. The plan underwent numerous revisions in the next two months, until finally the landing site was changed to the Bay of Pigs, some eighty miles from the mountains, which were to serve as a sanctuary for the exiles if the invasion failed. Chester Bowles and William Fulbright opposed the scheme; the latter told Kennedy that he had permitted his hatred of Fidel to cloud his judgment. "The Castro regime is a thorn in the flesh," Fulbright said, "but it is not a dagger in the heart." Even Dean Acheson, a superhawk, was appalled, calling it "a wild idea." Kennedy could not forget his campaign promises to help free Cuba and listened instead to the CIA and the Joint Chiefs, who approved the plan without giving it the rigorous analysis it deserved.

Some fourteen hundred brave but misguided exiles splashed ashore on the morning of 17 April. Castro responded decisively; he used his air power to gain control of the skies and sank several support ships. The next day his militiamen quickly overcame the lingering resistance of the survivors and took over one thousand prisoners. Arthur Schlesinger, Jr., sat glumly in the nearly deserted naval air base at Opa-Locka, on the outskirts of Miami, explaining to the leaders of Free Cuba why the United States could not intervene to save their comrades at the Bay of Pigs. Meanwhile, Dean Rusk told the press that the United States was not "intervening in Cuba" and Lem Jones, a New York public relations man, issued press releases in the name of the "Cuban Revolutionary Council" declaring that the "action today was largely of a supply and support effort" and calling upon the Cuban people to rise up in "a coordinated wave of sabotage and rebellion." John Kennedy ruefully admitted that "we will be kicked in the can for the next couple of weeks," but he took the long view, adding, "but that won't affect the main business."

The main business was the cold war with the Soviet Union, and on 19 April Kennedy dispatched a reply to Khrushchev's angry note pledging "all necessary assistance to Castro." The United States, Kennedy informed the Russian leader, had no intention of invading Cuba, but if any foreign power sent troops into the hemisphere, "we will immediately honor our obligations under the inter-American system to protect this hemisphere against external aggression." The events in Cuba, the president explained, simply indicated the growing restiveness of the Cuban people under Castro's dictatorial rule and then concluded, "The great revolution in the history of man, past, present, and future, is the revolution of those determined to be free." Kennedy was equally belligerent in a speech to the American Society of Newspaper Editors on 20 April. He took full responsibility for the fiasco, but at the same time he did not retreat an inch. He repeated his determination to prevent further "communist penetration" in the Western Hemisphere and then stated his personal conclusion from the Bay of Pigs tragedy: "Only the strong, only the industrious, only the determined, only the courageous, only the visionary who determine the real nature of our struggle can possibly survive." The lesson of the Cuban disaster, according to Kennedy, was that harder work, greater sacrifice, and heavier reliance on military force were necessary to win the cold war. In other words, the only thing wrong at the Bay of Pigs was that the United States did not do enough to defeat the Communists.

Kennedy moved quickly to apply this analysis to Indochina.

Laos remained the most crucial spot in the early months of the Kennedy administration as the neutralist forces of Kong-le joined with the Communist Pathet Lao against the American-supported government of Phoumi Nosavan, gaining control of the strategic Plain of Jars in February and beating back a government counterattack in April. Determined to stand firm after the Bay of Pigs, Kennedy ordered CIA advisers in Laos to don American uniforms and called an emergency session of the National Security Council. The Joint Chiefs of Staff opposed a civilian suggestion for a quick airborne strike against the Plain of Jars; remembering Korea, they insisted that if the United States intervened in Laos, it should do so with at least two hundred fifty thousand men and the willingness to use nuclear weapons if China or the Soviet Union entered the conflict. Sobered by this advice, Kennedy began to consider the alternative of diplomatic negotiation to achieve a neutral Laos. At a White House luncheon in May, General Douglas MacArthur reinforced Kennedy's growing doubts by stating bluntly that the U.S. should not "put one American soldier on the continent of Asia—we couldn't win a fight in Asia." (At the same luncheon, the general told the president with evident relish, "All the chickens are coming home to roost and you are living in the coop.") By mid-May, Kennedy had decided against using force and instead sent Averell Harriman to Geneva to work out a diplomatic solution. Harriman helped arrange for a new coalition government under Souvanna Phouma in October, and in July 1962 the United States signed an international agreement at Geneva to guarantee the neutrality of Laos. In succeeding years, both sides violated the terms as the Pathet Lao and the CIA-controlled Laotian army continued to skirmish, but at least Kennedy had avoided full-scale American military involvement in a remote area.

The president's relative softness on Laos undoubtedly contributed to the firmer position he took on South Vietnam. When he assumed office, he had renewed the Eisenhower administration's commitment to the Diem regime, despite growing signs that the people of South Vietnam were more responsive to the National Liberation Front and its Viet Cong guerrillas. A staunch believer in the domino thesis, Kennedy saw Vietnam as far more than just a struggle for one country or even one region. He viewed the violence there as a crucial test of the concept of wars of national liberation which Khrushchev had announced as the new Communist tactic for world control in a January speech. The entire third world, which held the balance of power between the East and the West, was at stake, thereby justifying a major American effort in Vietnam.

The president made his first significant move on 29 April 1961, when he approved recommendations by Walt Rostow to send Vice-President Lyndon Johnson to Saigon and to authorize one hundred additional American military advisers in South Vietnam, thus violating the limits set by the Geneva Agreement of 1954. On 11 May the president adopted revised recommendations of a special task force on Vietnam which included the dispatch of four hundred Special Forces troops (the Green Berets) and the beginning of covert operations against North Vietnam: infiltration, sabotage, commando raids, and even occasional air attacks. The official goal, stated in the highly secret National Security Council memorandum 52, was "to prevent Communist domination of South Vietnam" and "to create in that country a viable and increasingly democratic society." Thus, Kennedy committed the United States to participation in a bloody civil war in the mistaken belief that American vital interests were directly involved.

The president made the decision despite the advice of more experienced world leaders. Not only did General MacArthur warn him against committing American forces on the mainland of Asia, but Charles de Gaulle offered a prophetic view of what that participation would mean. "For you," he told Kennedy on 31 May, "intervention in this region will be an entanglement without end." He went on to cite the French experience in Indochina and said the Americans could not escape the same fate. "I predict to you," de Gaulle declared, "that you will, step by step, be sucked into a bottomless military and political quagmire despite the losses and expenditures that you may squander." Kennedy listened to the old man politely, but the words had no effect. His exposure to world affairs, from Munich on, told him that the only thing that aggressive dictators understood was superior force and the courage to use it. He had failed to stand firm on Cuba and Laos; he felt he must draw the line at Vietnam.

In mid-May, just as Kennedy was making his initial commitment to defend South Vietnam, Khrushchev suggested that the two men hold a summit conference in Vienna in early June. The president, eager to dispel any notions of his softness after the Bay of Pigs, quickly accepted and agreed to an agenda limited to Laos, the issue of nuclear testing, and Berlin. When the two met on 3

June, Khrushchev immediately took the offensive, asserting the Marxist thesis that communism was bound to triumph in the third world and insisting that wars of national liberation were the result of revolutionary nationalism, not Soviet diplomacy. Taken off guard by the ferocity of Khrushchev's attack, Kennedy replied by stating that the responsibility of both superpowers lay in maintaining the existing world balance and avoiding direct confrontations that might lead to nuclear war. Turning from ideological issues, the two leaders discussed Laos and nuclear testing without reaching any agreement and then took up the far more urgent question of Berlin.

Kennedy came well prepared on Germany. In March he had asked Dean Acheson to canvass the European situation and give him recommendations on Berlin. Predictably, Acheson rejected the idea of a negotiated settlement, arguing that the status quo of a divided Germany suited American interests. If the Russians tried to change the situation, the United States should respond with a series of measures, beginning with a new airlift and ranging from the use of conventional forces to a willingness to participate in a nuclear exchange. Acheson did not think such a showdown likely; he saw Berlin as a test of will in which a firm American stance would force the Russians to back down, as they had in 1949. At Vienna, Khrushchev renewed his request for negotiations, and when Kennedy refused to enter into talks once again imposed a six-month deadline, saying he intended to sign a peace treaty with East Germany at that time and turn over Berlin access rights to the Democratic Republic of Germany. Kennedy declared that the United States would insist on asserting its wartime rights in Berlin regardless of such a treaty; Khrushchev replied, "I want peace, but if you want war, that is your problem."

"It is you, and not I, who wants to force a change," Kennedy answered.

On that somber note the talks ended.

Instead of easing the cold war, the Vienna meeting escalated it. Berlin had become a test of will for both sides. Adamantly refusing the negotiations Khrushchev wanted, Kennedy tried to escape from the awful choice of surrender or nuclear war that had always confronted American leaders dealing with an isolated Berlin. He sought a way out by strengthening American conventional forces in Europe, and in a dramatic broadcast to the American people on 25 July he spelled out his program. Denying

Daily Mirror Newspapers Ltd., London

Franklin in The London Daily Mirror

that the city was indefensible ("And so was Bastogne. And so, in fact, was Stalingrad. Any dangerous spot is tenable if men—brave men—will make it so"), Kennedy asked Congress for an additional 3.5 billion dollars in defense funds, authority to increase the armed services by nearly three hundred fifty thousand men, and permission to call up one hundred fifty thousand reservists to active duty. Then he announced plans for a sweeping civil defense program to protect the nation against a nuclear attack. "In the coming months," Kennedy informed the American people, "I hope to let every citizen know what steps he can take without delay to protect his family in case of attack." He thereby touched off a mania for home fallout shelters that brought out the worst rather than the best in the American character (a rush for profits by overnight promoters, the purchase of guns to keep less fortunate neighbors out of a patriot's backyard shelter).

The message to Khrushchev was clear: the United States would fight a nuclear war before giving way on Berlin. The Soviet leader, who had asked only for negotiations to end the abnormal German situation sixteen years after the war's end, took two steps that caught the Kennedy administration completely by surprise. Worried by the steady flow of East German citizens, especially the young and the talented, who fled via Berlin to West Germany on the order of thirty thousand a month, Khrushchev sealed off East Germany by building the Berlin Wall and thus provided a unilateral solution to an urgent problem. The danger of war seemed great, but to his credit, Kennedy acted with restraint, sending Lyndon Johnson to reassure the people of West Berlin and reinforcing the meager garrison with a fifteen-hundred man battle group, yet refusing to challenge the Soviet action as right-wing Americans urged. Khrushchev then dropped the other shoe; on 30 August, he announced that Russia would resume nuclear testing in the atmosphere, breaking the voluntary suspension that had been in effect since 1958. Over the next few weeks, the Soviets exploded over forty nuclear weapons, including one massive hydrogen bomb of nearly sixty megatons, prompting Kennedy's response, "Fucked again."

The Berlin crisis gradually ebbed in the fall of 1961. Kennedy relented on negotiations and allowed Dean Rusk to begin talks with Soviet Foreign Minister Gromyko at the United Nations in mid-September. In October Khrushchev called off his six-month deadline; but the cost was high. Kennedy had raised tensions to a dangerous level by threatening nuclear war over Berlin and had provoked Khrushchev into taking steps that destroyed any chance for a détente in the near future. The world watched in horror as refugees from East Germany died in brave attempts to scale the wall, while everywhere radiation levels increased as the fallout from the Russian tests rained down from the skies.

Kennedy's first eight months in office had been filled with bitter lessons. Setting out to prove that he was tougher than the Communist leaders, he had only demonstrated the futility of such an aggressive approach by the Bay of Pigs, the weapons buildup, his commitment to South Vietnam, and, above all, the dangerous Berlin policy. He mistook action for courage, tough talk for diplomatic strength, realism for wisdom. Yet he had learned that the problems were not so simple nor the solutions so easy. Above all, he now knew the limits of rationality in world affairs. Hugh Sidey commented on one evening during the height of the Berlin crisis when the president and his brother sat up late discussing the ominous situation. "All his days had been spent planning the steps up to and into nuclear war, should it be required of this country," Sidey wrote. "On that night as they talked, there was the eerie realization that war could be the product of a whim, a misunderstanding, a human mistake."

Vietnam reflected the new urgency Kennedy brought to world problems after the Berlin crisis. His initial commitment of additional advisers and four hundred Green Berets had failed to halt the Viet Cong insurgency. President Diem, who earlier had resisted suggestions that he ask for American combat troops, submitted a formal request for such assistance in late September 1961. Despite CIA reports that 80 to 90 percent of the Viet Cong guerrillas were southerners engaged in a civil war against a repressive regime, Kennedy's advisers, notably Walt Rostow, argued that Hanoi directed the insurgency and that only heroic measures directed against North Vietnam could win the war in the south. Groping for a clearer assessment, Kennedy sent Rostow, acting as White House representative, and Maxwell Taylor, spokesman for the Pentagon viewpoint, on a crucial mission to South Vietnam in early October; significantly, no one of similar stature represented the State Department. After a hurried tour of the country, the two advisers reported to Kennedy that the situation was bad but not hopeless. They recommended increased support for Diem, never questioning his leadership, and the introduction of eight thousand American combat troops disguised as flood relief workers to repair recent ravages of the Mekong River. Taylor, who wrote the report, recognized the dangers involved, but he assured the president that "the risks of backing into a major Asian war by way of SVN are present but are not impressive. . . . NVN is extremely vulnerable to conventional bombing, a weakness which should be exploited diplomatically in convincing Hanoi to lay off SVN."

Kennedy received this naïve report skeptically. "It will be just like Berlin," he told Arthur Schlesinger, Jr. "The troops will march in; the bands will play; the crowds will cheer; and in four days everyone will have forgotten. Then we will be told we have to send in more troops. It's like taking a drink. The effect wears off, and you have to take another." Secretaries Rusk and McNamara, however, endorsed the Taylor-Rostow recommendations, reminding the president of the stakes involved. "The loss of South Viet-Nam would make pointless any further discussion about the importance of Southeast Asia to the free world. . . . The loss of South Viet-Nam to Communism would not only destroy SEATO but would undermine the credibility of American commitments elsewhere." This classic restatement of the domino thesis may have impressed Kennedy, but even more influential was the sober reminder that the loss of Vietnam to the Reds "would stimulate bitter domestic controversies in the United States and would be seized upon by extreme elements to divide the country and harass the Administration. . . ." Kennedy remembered all too well how the fall of China had discredited the Truman administration (after all, he had even participated in a small way in the process) and paved the way for the Republican return to power under Eisenhower in 1952. Vietnam must not become another China; political realities at home made military commitment abroad imperative.

On 13 November 1961, Kennedy approved stepped-up economic assistance for Diem, increased military aid, especially in the form of helicopters to give the South Vietnamese forces mobility in fighting the Viet Cong, and additional American military advisers, but not the combat troops Diem wanted and Rostow, Taylor, and McNamara advocated. Nevertheless, the increased American participation fundamentally changed the character of

the Vietnamese conflict. American prestige was now fully engaged; the distinction between advisers and combat troops
gradually broke down as U.S. officers and soldiers began to take an
active role in the fighting.

Kennedy faced an equally difficult decision in fall 1961 on the
question of nuclear testing. The United States had suspended all
tests in October 1958 and had entered into negotiations for a test
ban treaty with the Soviets in Geneva. The talks quickly reached a
deadlock on the vital issue of underground tests. It was easy to
detect nuclear explosions in the atmosphere, but scientists had
great difficulty distinguishing small underground tests from earth-
quakes. The United States insisted on frequent on-site inspections
inside the Soviet Union to investigate seismic disturbances reported by "black boxes," clusters of instruments scattered strategically across the world. The Russians finally agreed to a maximum
of three inspections a year, but they also demanded the right to
veto the findings of the international supervisory body, a condition the United States felt it could not accept.

Khrushchev's resumption of atmospheric nuclear testing in
September 1961 put Kennedy on the spot. The president was
already under intense pressure from the Pentagon to resume
testing, despite an impressive American lead in nuclear technology. Kennedy resisted demands for explosions in the atmosphere,
but he announced plans for underground tests on 5 September
saying, "In view of the acts of the Soviet Government, we must
now take those steps which prudent men find essential." The
dramatic news of the Soviet detonations led to increasing public
uneasiness, though the president's science adviser Jerome Wies-
ner assured him that while American tests in the atmosphere
would "certainly contribute to our military strength, they are not
critical or even very important to our over-all military posture." By
the end of the year, however, the president had decided to resume
tests in the atmosphere, and after overcoming the strenuous
objections of British Prime Minister Harold Macmillan (Britain's
Christmas Island was to be the site of the tests), Kennedy
announced his intentions in a nationwide radio and television
appearance on 2 March. He expressed regret for the dangers to
health from fallout, but he felt he could not risk a "relative decline

in our nuclear strength." On 25 April, the first in a series of explosions began in the Pacific.

Kennedy acted for psychological and political reasons. The United States had opened an enormous lead over the Russians in the arms race by 1962; Congress had authorized funds for the building of 1,000 Minuteman solid-fuel ICBMs and 656 Polaris missiles on board 41 nuclear submarines. The Russian resumption of testing was a desperate effort to close the widening American nuclear lead, a lead made doubly dangerous by Kennedy's apparent willingness during the Berlin crisis to risk all-out war. The Soviets were acting out of weakness, not strength; yet the president, trapped by his own excessive reliance on a philosophy of force and fearful of appearing soft when confronted with Khrushchev's belligerence, felt he had to meet the Soviet challenge. Inevitably, American resumption provoked a second series of Russian tests and led Khrushchev to reject a renewed American proposal for a comprehensive test ban treaty.

The ultimate Russian response to America's growing nuclear superiority came in Cuba. Sometime in the first half of 1962, Khrushchev decided to take the dangerous gamble of installing forty-two medium-range ballistic missiles in Cuba. Afterwards, the Russian leader claimed that his sole motive was to defend the Castro regime against an expected American invasion. Others speculated that he wanted to catch the United States off guard in order to impose a favorable settlement in Berlin, while still others thought he strove to reestablish Soviet primacy over China within the Socialist camp. The simplest explanation is that Khrushchev, realizing how far behind the U.S. his nation was falling in nuclear striking power, hoped to redress the strategic balance by placing offensive missiles in Cuba. Even with these weapons in place, the Russians could not overcome the American lead in ICBMs and bombers, but Khrushchev would gain a psychological initiative that he presumably intended to convert into a diplomatic victory.

Whatever his motives, Khrushchev badly miscalculated the impact of his gamble on John F. Kennedy. In early September, Washington had knowledge of an impressive Soviet arms buildup in Cuba, though as yet there was no inkling of the missiles. Republican leaders, hoping to win control of Congress in the November elections, made the Russian action in Cuba a major campaign issue. Richard Nixon, running for governor of California, called for a "quarantine" of Cuba; Senator Barry Goldwater demanded a blockade; Senator Kenneth Keating of New York, relying on often unreliable exile reports, warned that the Russians were bringing in missiles. Kennedy discounted the GOP oratory, but he publicly informed the Russians in September that he would not tolerate introduction of offensive weapons.

On 14 October, an American U-2 flew over the area of Cuba where work on the missile sites had been under way for several weeks; the next day photo-analysts spotted the evidence and on 16 October McGeorge Bundy informed the president. Kennedy immediately made a fateful decision. Instead of confronting the Russians with the evidence of their hostile acts privately, and trying to force them to retreat without fanfare, he decided to say nothing while exploring alternative courses of action with a select group of advisers. For the next six days, the Executive Committee of the National Security Council discussed a wide range of options, including a surprise attack on the missile sites, invasion of Cuba, a blockade of the island, and even a sit-and-wait policy to see what the Russians would do. Surprisingly, no one advocated a diplomatic approach to the Soviets until the president finally consulted Adlai Stevenson, his ambassador to the United Nations. Stevenson proposed a trade: the United States would withdraw its intermediate-range missiles from Italy and Turkey (Kennedy had already ordered their removal the previous summer), as well as evacuate the naval base at Guantánamo Bay, in return for a Soviet pullout from Cuba. The president rejected this suggestion, apparently without any careful reflection. He also rejected, at least temporarily, the hawkish proposals for a bombing strike and invasion, preferring to begin instead with a quarantine of Cuba to prevent the introduction of any more missiles and a virtual ultimatum to force Khrushchev to withdraw those already in Cuba. In effect, Kennedy opted for a nuclear confrontation to force the Soviet leader to back down.

The American people first learned of the missiles in a dramatic presidential television address on Monday, 22 October, only an hour after Secretary of State Rusk had informed the Russian ambassador of American intentions. Kennedy condemned the Soviets for "this sudden, clandestine decision" to effect "a deliberately provocative and unjustified change in the status quo," and he declared that the United States could not accept it "if our courage and commitments are ever to be trusted again by either friend or foe." Then he outlined his plan of action. The navy would enforce a strict quarantine of Cuba, turning back any ship carrying offensive weapons. The United States would bring the Soviet threat to world peace before both the Organization of American States and the United Nations, but the president relied on an implicit nuclear threat to force Khrushchev to remove the missiles already in Cuba. He warned that any nuclear attack on any nation in the Western Hemisphere launched from Cuba would be regarded "as an attack by the Soviet Union on the United States, requiring a full retaliatory response upon the Soviet Union." Kennedy directed his most chilling words to Khrushchev personally, calling on him "to move the world back from the abyss of destruction—by returning to his government's own words that it had no need to station missiles outside its own territory. . . ."

Khrushchev accepted the nuclear challenge, sending Kennedy a message on 23 October in which he refused to honor the quarantine and accused the president of leading mankind "to the abyss of a world missile-nuclear war." For the next few days, the world watched in fascinated horror as the Russian ships approached the U.S. Navy's patrols in the Atlantic while construction continued around the clock on the Cuban missile sites and an American invasion force assembled in Florida. The first break came on 25 October when more than twenty Soviet ships altered course, signifying Russian acquiescence to the blockade. Work on the missile bases intensified, however, and officials in Washington realized that the real showdown had not yet come. On Friday, 26 October, a long, rambling letter from Khrushchev arrived which revealed the Soviet leader's fear of war and contained a possible solution: withdrawal of the missiles in return for an American promise never to invade Cuba. The Russians confirmed this offer through unofficial channels and the president was ready to accept it when a second message from Khrushchev arrived on Saturday morning. Much more formal and unyielding in tone, this note offered a very different way out: the swap of American missile bases in Turkey for those in Cuba. Kennedy, unwilling to back down in public under pressure, refused to consider this bargain, and his military advisers, almost gleefully telling him he had been naïve in relying on limited measures, recommended an air strike on the missile sites within two days, to be followed by a full-scale invasion of Cuba. At this crucial point, the president's brother, Attorney General Robert F. Kennedy, suggested a peaceful alternative. Why not, he asked, ignore the second note and respond

instead to Khrushchev's first letter, pledging not to invade Cuba in return for a Soviet withdrawal of the missiles. The president agreed, and late on Saturday sent such a message to Khrushchev. Leaving nothing to chance, the president asked his brother to meet that evening with the Soviet ambassador and make clear, as Bobby Kennedy wrote later, that "we had to have a commitment by tomorrow that those bases would be removed. . . . He should understand that if they did not remove those bases, we would remove them." He then outlined the contents of the note that his brother had just sent to Khrushchev and added that while there was no mention of American missiles in Italy and Turkey, "President Kennedy had been anxious to remove those missiles . . . and it was our judgment that, within a short time after this crisis was over, those missiles would be gone."

The next morning, Khrushchev accepted Kennedy's offer, and the crisis ended. The president promised not to invade Cuba and the Russians dismantled the bases and removed the missiles under American aerial inspection. A few months later, the United States took its missiles out of Italy and Turkey, as President Kennedy quietly lived up to the secret aspect of the missile settlement.

At the time, Kennedy won virtually unanimous praise for his cool and courageous handling of a dangerous situation. The Democrats retained their control of Congress and Kennedy's ratings soared in the Gallup poll. In retrospect, the president's conduct appears to have been unnecessarily provocative. Although he did resist the pressure for a military solution, he failed to explore the possibility of a diplomatic negotiation. Kennedy dismissed Stevenson's suggestion for a *quid pro quo,* yet in the final analysis he made such a swap privately. The tragedy is that his own fear of appearing weak prevented him from approaching the Russians privately and negotiating a solution before threatening the world with a nuclear confrontation. Kennedy handled the crisis with great technical skill, but the doubt remains that he need not have gone to the brink of disaster to achieve his goals.

The Cuban missile crisis marked a decisive shift in John Kennedy's approach to world problems. During the last year of his life, he displayed a new and far more mature concern for the ultimate question of war or peace in the nuclear age, a concern that culminated in the nuclear test ban treaty and a belated effort to reassess the American role in Vietnam.

The first sign of Kennedy's determination to profit from the missile crisis came the very day that Khrushchev capitulated. In a statement to the press welcoming the news of the Russian withdrawal, the president expressed his "earnest hope" that "the governments of the world can . . . turn their urgent attention to the compelling necessity for ending the arms race and reducing world tensions." Two months later, on 19 December 1962, Khrushchev responded by writing Kennedy his conviction that the "time has come now to put an end once and for all to nuclear tests, to draw a line through such tests." To prove his sincerity in working for "the noble and humane goal of ceasing nuclear weapons tests" the Russian leader agreed to accept three on-site inspections a year to ensure against secret underground explosions. Kennedy cut the American demand for twenty such inspections to seven, but then a deadlock developed as Khrushchev, though Kennedy had unofficially signaled to him a willingness to accept three, returned to the original Soviet refusal to allow any inspections. In a last-ditch effort to break the stalemate, Kennedy joined with British Prime Minister Macmillan in an offer to send senior representatives to Moscow to negotiate directly with Khrushchev. In May, the Soviet leader accepted his proposal (with a noticeable lack of enthusiasm) and the talks were scheduled for late June or early July.

The president decided to inform the American people of his efforts for a test ban treaty in a major speech at American University on 10 June 1963. In eloquent and moving language, Kennedy addressed himself to "the most important topic on earth: world peace." He carefully avoided cold war rhetoric, denying any desire to achieve "a Pax Americana enforced on the world by American weapons of war," and called upon his countrymen "to re-examine our attitude toward the Soviet Union." He spoke admiringly of the Russian people and the huge losses in life and property they had suffered at the hands of Germany in World War II. The United States and Russia, he declared, now had a common interest in halting the arms race and preventing the far greater devastation of a nuclear holocaust. Differences between the two nations were bound to persist, he continued, but "at least we can help make the world safe for diversity. For, in the final analysis, our most basic common link is that we all inhabit this small planet. We all breathe the same air. We all cherish our children's future. And we are all mortal."

It was hard to believe that this was the same man who only two years before had called for an all-out offensive against communism to win the battle of freedom over slavery. Two years of adversity had taught President Kennedy that negotiation and compromise were more vital than military strength and determination in resolving world problems. With a new insight born of the Cuban missile crisis, he told the American people that they must reexamine their attitudes toward the cold war and stop trying to pile up "debating points." "We must deal with the world as it is," he concluded, "and not as it might have been had the history of the last eighteen years been different." Then he announced that the United States and England had agreed on high-level talks in Moscow to seek a test ban treaty and that meanwhile the United States "would not conduct atmospheric tests as long as other states did not do so."

Nikita Khrushchev later told Averell Harriman, the veteran diplomat Kennedy sent to Moscow to conduct the test ban negotiations, that the American University address was "the greatest speech by any American President since Roosevelt." The Russian leader's formal response was more restrained; on 2 July, he offered to negotiate a test ban treaty limited to environments where detection did not require on-site inspection: the atmosphere, outer space, and underwater. Kennedy accepted this proposal for a limited test ban treaty, and in mid-July Harriman arrived in Moscow, along with British diplomat Lord Hailsham. After only ten days, they initialed an agreement that bypassed the earlier deadlock by outlawing all but underground nuclear tests.

In announcing this achievement to the American people, President Kennedy declared that "for the first time in many years, the path of peace may be open." He added that the agreement was only a first step, saying, "No one can be certain what the future will bring." He was wise to admit the limited nature of the treaty. The military leaders accepted the agreement with great reluctance and were persuaded to go along only after Kennedy promised the Joint Chiefs an extensive program of underground nuclear tests and gave them a written commitment to resume tests in the atmosphere "should they be deemed essential to our national security." In testifying to the Senate Foreign Relations Committee, Secretary of Defense McNamara portrayed the treaty as a victory for the United States, asserting that the U.S. had greater experience and profficiency in underground testing to argue that "we can at least retard Soviet progress and thereby prolong the duration of our technological superiority." Undoubtedly this belief that a limited test ban conferred important strategic advantages on the United States was as influential as the idea of a first step in halting the arms race in leading the Senate to ratify the treaty by a sweeping margin of eighty to nineteen. Nevertheless, Kennedy had achieved a goal that Adlai Stevenson had first advocated against overwhelming opposition in 1956. Despite its limitations, the test ban treaty marked the first break in the cold war; it was Kennedy's finest legacy.

In the summer of 1963, Kennedy also seemed to be in the process of changing his mind about Vietnam. The war there had improved following the limited American involvement the president had sanctioned in late 1961. The use of helicopters, the presence of the Green Berets, the adoption of a strategic hamlet policy in the rural areas, above all, the sheer lift in South Vietnamese morale resulting from the infusion of American aid, had set back the Viet Cong. Improvement proved temporary; by early 1963, the guerrillas had regained the initiative in the war and were widening their hold on the countryside. More significantly, Diem created a grave political crisis when he tried to repress the Buddhists in the spring of 1963. On 11 June, a day after the American University speech, an aged monk doused himself with gasoline in Saigon, lit a match, and burned to death before a chanting crowd of Buddhist supporters and the camera of Associated Press reporter Malcolm Browne. The widely published photograph of the self-immolation horrified the American people and forced President Kennedy to question the wisdom of continuing to back the Diem regime.

In the last few months of his life, Kennedy agonized over Vietnam. He sympathized with Averell Harriman and others within the administration who saw the war primarily as a political struggle and who wanted to force Diem into instituting democratic reforms as the only way to win the confidence of the people. He even permitted the State Department to send a famous cable in late August which permitted the new American ambassador, Henry Cabot Lodge, to give South Vietnamese generals the green light in their plans to overthrow the government in Saigon. In a CBS interview with Walter Cronkite on 2 September, Kennedy revealed his belief that only a greater effort by the South Vietnamese could turn the tide. "In the final analysis," he commented, "it is their war. They are the ones who have to win it or lose it. We can help them, we can give them equipment, we can send our men out there as advisers, but they have to win it, the people of Viet Nam, against the Communists."

Yet at the same time, the president allowed the military to continue backing the Diem regime. In an interview with Chet Huntley and David Brinkley on 9 September, he expressed his belief that the loss of South Vietnam would open up all Southeast Asia to the Chinese Communists, revealing that he was still under the grip of the domino thesis. "I think we should stay," he concluded. "We should use our influence in as effective a way as we can, but should not withdraw." Privately, he told aide Kenneth O'Donnell that he planned to negotiate an American withdrawal in the future, but that he could not act until after the 1964 elections, which suggests that the memory of Truman and the fall of China still haunted him. The overthrow and murder of Diem on 1 November probably forced him to reconsider this long-term strategy. The United States, having used its influence to remove Diem, now bore the responsibility of backing his successors; there was no longer any graceful way for Kennedy to withdraw.

Despite the worsening situation in Vietnam, the theme of peace cropped up more and more in Kennedy's speeches in the fall of 1963. On a speaking tour of the West suggested by Majority Leader Mike Mansfield, he drew his warmest response when he spoke about his efforts to end the cold war. In Billings, Montana, the audience came to life when he talked about the confrontations with the Soviet Union over Berlin and Cuba and expressed his heartfelt desire "to lessen the chance of a military collision between these two great nuclear powers which together have the power to kill 300 million people in the short space of a day. . . . That is why I support the test ban treaty, . . . because we have a chance to avoid being burned." He was even more eloquent the next evening in Salt Lake City. Warning against both a return to isolationism and a simplistic, "black and white" approach, he pleaded for "a world of diversity" and expressed the hope that "the world of the future will have room for a diversity of economic systems, political creeds, religious faiths, united by the respect for others, and loyalty to a world order."

The president who spoke these words had undergone a fundamental change in outlook during the thousand days he had been in office. He had taken up his duties believing essentially in a two-dimensional world, one in which overwhelming American power and the willingness to use it would cure all problems. He learned that international affairs were neither so simple nor so malleable. The real world—in which guerrillas in the jungles of Indochina successfully defied the power and technology of the greatest nation on the earth, in which a rival leader would risk nuclear war by placing missiles on the doorsteps of the United States—intruded on Kennedy's rational approach to foreign policy and taught him that there was a third dimension to international affairs whose existence he had not even suspected.

The ultimate tragedy was that John F. Kennedy never had the opportunity to put his hard-won education to work. No one can say what he would have done in Vietnam had he lived; yet it is possible that he could have avoided his successor's escalation of that conflict. Instead, it fell to his bitter rival of 1960, Richard Nixon, to inherit the possibilities for peace that Kennedy had glimpsed and to pursue them to end the long years of hostility toward Communist China, enter into a meaningful arms control agreement with the Soviet Union, and bring about a cease-fire in Vietnam. Perhaps only John Kennedy, with his fondness for the ironies of history, could have fully appreciated this final twist of fate.

BIBLIOGRAPHIC NOTE

The literature on John F. Kennedy's foreign policy divides into early, favorable accounts and more recent critical ones. This essay relies heavily on James MacGregor Burns, *John Kennedy: A Political Profile,* 2nd ed. (New York, 1961), Arthur M. Schlesinger, Jr., *A Thousand Days: John F. Kennedy in the White House* (Boston, 1965), and Theodore C. Sorensen, *Kennedy* (New York, 1965) for information in this study, while rejecting their sympathetic view of the president. This analysis reflects the more skeptical viewpoints expressed by Richard J. Walton in *Cold War and Counterrevolution: The Foreign Policy of John F. Kennedy* (New York, 1972) and Louise Fitzsimons, *The Kennedy Doctrine* (New York, 1972). Other books used include Robert F. Kennedy, *Thirteen Days: A Memoir of the Cuban Missile Crisis* (New York, 1969), Roger Hilsman, *To Move A Nation* (Garden City, N.Y., 1967), David Halberstam, *The Best and the*

Brightest (New York, 1972), the *New York Times* edition of *The Pentagon Papers* (New York, 1971), edited by Neil Sheehan and others, for Kennedy's Vietnam policies, and Hugh Sidey, *John F. Kennedy, President* (New York, 1963), which provides an admirably detached view of Kennedy's years in the White House.

Courtesy, Senator Fulbright

THE CONGRESS AS CLASSROOM:

J. WILLIAM FULBRIGHT

and the Crisis of American Power

David F. Trask

Congress historically has acted negatively with regard to American foreign relations. The elder Senator Henry Cabot Lodge symbolizes this more notoriously than any other congressional leader. Only a few legislators have ever sought to exercise intellectual influence on foreign affairs; one is the junior senator from Arkansas, J. William Fulbright, Democrat, chairman of the Senate Committee on Foreign Relations. Once, musing on his activities, he said rather wistfully: "I don't exercise direct power, I don't cut people's heads off, politically speaking or symbolically speaking. I don't make people do things." What seemed to Fulbright possibly useful was the educational effect of his commentaries on public issues. "I

Biographical information on this essay is drawn largely from Haynes Johnson and Bernard M. Gwertzman, *Fulbright: The Dissenter* (Garden City, N.Y., 1968), and Tristram Coffin, *Senator Fulbright: Portrait of a Public Philosopher* (New York, 1966).

think these discussions are like any form of education. It's hard to prove, but I think it's there. . . . It seems to me that ideas you advance begin to develop." Perhaps recalling his stormy relations with more than one president, most importantly Lyndon Baines Johnson, he wondered whether his activity had made any great difference. "There are so many prejudices and bitter hatreds and feeling that people have." Despite his self-doubt, it is clear that Fulbright has contributed to the American people's education in the intricacies of international politics, delivering lectures from the Senate during the cold war years, seeking to introduce novel opinions into the public debate of great international questions.

   Fulbright's early experiences prepared him well for the vocation of educator. Born in 1905 to an affluent family who eventually settled near Fayetteville, Arkansas, the seat of the state university, he enjoyed an active, comfortable youth. As an undergraduate at the University of Arkansas he became prominent in intercollegiate sports, particularly football, and student government. These endeavors and a good academic record led to his selection as a Rhodes Scholar in 1925. While at Oxford Fulbright read European history and politics and traveled extensively on the Continent, where international affairs attracted his attention. Returning to Fayetteville in 1929, he planned to help manage his family's multifarious businesses, but on a chance visit to a friend in Washington he met his future wife and decided to attend the George Washington University Law School, from which he graduated second in a class of 135. After a brief apprenticeship in the Antitrust Division of the Department of Justice (he helped argue the famous NRA case, *Schechter* v. *New York*), he returned to George Washington as an instructor in law, his first pedagogical experience. These eventful years ended in 1936 when, at thirty-one, he returned to Arkansas to teach at the university's law school. To others at this time he must have appeared a well-bred and well-educated southern patrician, possibly destined for some public service in the future but hardly for a role as dissenter.

   In September 1939, Fulbright became president of the University of Arkansas, an assignment that gave him his first opportunity to comment publicly on international questions. He engendered controversy, particularly when he took the interventionist side in the great debate that preceded American entry into World War II. On one occasion, he planned to say at the University of Missouri that the "weaseling, timid, and fearful policy of the isolationist senators is one of the greatest dangers to our true interests," but his invitation to speak was withdrawn in deference to the anti-interventionist views of Senator Champ Clark. In that same year, 1940, a new governor of Arkansas, Homer M. Adkins, took umbrage at some derogatory remarks about him made by Fulbright's mother, Roberta, who wrote a column in a newspaper owned by the family. "It seems," she had noted, "that the people of Arkansas want a hand-shaking governor instead of one who accomplishes something." In June 1941 the board of trustees of the university, dominated by Adkins's appointees, summarily discharged Fulbright.

This catastrophe marked an important turning point in the life of the young educator. The following year he ran for the House of Representatives as a Democrat from the Third Congressional District. An energetic campaign produced a comfortable victory, and he took his seat in the Seventy-eighth Congress in January 1943. He obtained a place on the House Foreign Affairs Committee, where his activities soon began to attract considerable notice.

A convinced internationalist, Fulbright immediately interested himself in the question of postwar security. During his campaign he had sounded the principal theme he pursued in Congress, that there could be no return to the "so-called good old days of extreme nationalism." The Democratic party "must again catch the spirit of 1918 and 1932 and attack the problems of the world with the same daring and originality that we attacked that peace and that depression."[1] When another freshman member of Congress, Clare Boothe Luce, attacked internationalist views as "globaloney," Fulbright answered that the "narrow, imperialistic policy of grab . . . carries within itself the seeds of its own destruction." He then organized support for a brief statement, known as the Fulbright Resolution, that endorsed a postwar security organization. The House "hereby expresses itself as favoring the creation of appropriate international machinery with power adequate to

1. This quotation and most others cited for the years to 1963 are drawn from Karl Meyer, ed., *Fulbright of Arkansas: The Public Positions of a Private Thinker* (Washington, D. C., 1963).

prevent future aggression and to maintain lasting peace, and as favoring participation by the United States therein." With President Roosevelt's support Fulbright was able to push his resolution through the House on 21 September 1943 by a vote of 360 to 29. Together with a similar resolution sponsored by Senator Tom Connally of Texas, which passed in the Senate, Fulbright's act laid the foundation for congressional acceptance of the United Nations Charter. His successes encouraged him to run for the Senate in 1944 against the incumbent Mrs. Hattie Caraway, knowing that his old adversary, Governor Adkins, would also enter the contest. Despite allegations that Fulbright was both a draft-dodger and a visionary he won a runoff election against Adkins by thirty-four thousand votes. His mother could not resist a parting shot. "Homer Adkins," she wrote, "has came and went."

Fulbright's first labor in the Senate was to champion the United Nations. As he would do throughout his career he adduced historical arguments for this campaign. Looking back to 1919 he maintained that rapid change had confused the people, leading to a public reaction against the League of Nations that adversely affected policy throughout the interwar period. "We made pious declarations against war . . . and yet did nothing concrete when Manchuria and Ethiopia were invaded." Americans had misconceived their role in world politics and had "failed to examine and agree upon certain basic convictions which are essential to any policy." The resulting bewilderment led to emotional responses and to improvisation from day to day; of foreign policy Fulbright urged that policy stem from clearly articulated principles. Although exhilarated when the Senate accepted the United Nations Charter, he immediately grasped the sinister portent of the atomic bomb. The threat of nuclear destruction, Fulbright believed, strengthened the internationalist case against conventional power politics. A strain of pessimism—that deepened in later years—began to appear in his speeches. The discovery of extermination camps in Germany had provided "an ugly but powerful demonstration of what lies beneath that thin crust of civilization so laboriously acquired by man." Such thoughts underlay Fulbright's belief in an international rule of law, enshrined in the charter. The only alternative was "constantly recurring warfare of rapidly increasing destructiveness." Binding legal constraints were required because goodwill alone rarely had ensured peace and order.

In one most important respect Fulbright went beyond the spirit of the charter. He spoke eloquently against the principle of absolute national sovereignty, claiming that it was totally inconsistent with the development of international laws having sufficient force behind them to gain general confidence. His hopes for the UN waned as he realized that conditions necessary to sustain collective security—political and social solidarity among the great powers and the will to enforce charter obligations—had not materialized. The world had attempted, unwisely, "to outrun history, to move in a single leap from world anarchy to world community." Security would come only if people abandoned nationalism, only if people broadened their loyalties, "never forgetting . . . that it is the human individual, and not the state or any other community, in whom ultimate sovereignty is vested." Sponsorship of the Fulbright Scholarships and of other projects for international education derived from the view, expressed regularly, that such programs cultivated "perceptions and perspectives that transcend national boundaries." In 1972 he still maintained that supranationalism, as an alternative to the balance of power, was "not only the course of realism but the only available course of sanity." [2].

Fulbright launched a commentary on Soviet affairs even before the end of the war, recognizing that the future of the UN depended on cooperation among the great powers. To counteract the anti-Bolshevik sentiment that had grown between the wars, he went so far as to claim that "the Russian experiment in socialism is scarcely more radical, under modern conditions, than the Declaration of Independence was in the days of George III." Capitalism, in which he believed, was neither divine nor inviolable, and challenges to it were neither sacrilegious nor treasonable. By May 1946, however, Fulbright had become alarmed by Russian initiatives. His mind went back to the Munich pact of 1938, when Germany had assumed that the United States favored peace at any price. Now the Arkansas senator feared that America's resolve to participate in world politics might decline in the aftermath of war. Complaining about precipitous troop withdrawals from Europe, he

2. Fulbright's opposition to nationalism may be traced in later books, such as *Prospects for the West* (Cambridge, Mass., 1963), *Old Myths and New Realities, and Other Commentaries* (New York, 1964), *The Crippled Giant: American Foreign Policy and Its Domestic Consequences* (New York, 1972), p. 177.

wondered aloud, "Are we, or are we not, going to use our influence and play a leading role in foreign affairs?" The United States must show the world that, "while we do not seek war, yet we are willing and able to fight whenever we believe any power threatens the right and opportunity for men to live as free individuals under a government of their own choice." In this statement Senator Fulbright anticipated the Truman Doctrine by nearly a year.

Nothing seemed more important than the reconstruction of Western Europe. Fulbright supported the principal measures of containment developed during the period 1947–49, though he later criticized the broad scope of the Truman Doctrine, maintaining that the country, frightened by Stalin's policies in Eastern Europe, had converted "from Wilson to Machiavelli in the same zealous spirit in which a repentant Communist may become a devout believer in a religion or a repentant hawk may offer himself as a martyr for peace." He even claimed that the UN had failed not simply because of Russia but because Dean Acheson and others had not wanted it to work. At the time, however, he supported the objectives of the Truman administration.

Any reservations he had related to means rather than ends. Fulbright again anticipated evolving administration ideas by proposing a startling change in the political organization of Europe as the best method of curbing Russian ambitions. Standing alone, European nations could not hope to resist Russian pressure. In April 1947, recalling the Continent's ancient unity under the Romans and the Carolingians, he envisioned revival of a parallel system, which he deemed possible because of roughly similar institutions throughout non-Communist Europe. If Germany became a loose grouping of small states and merged into a larger government representing some three hundred million people, German militarism could be controlled and Germans could not dominate the federation. All manner of economic benefits would result, not to mention the political gains. Moscow would oppose this change, but, should France provide leadership, supported by the United States and Britain, a United States of Europe could be built and a new renaissance might occur. Fulbright's Oxford tutors must have been thoroughly proud of this analysis by their old student!

Meanwhile, Fulbright had begun to manifest those maverick qualities that later came to be his most characteristic attributes. In

November 1946, when the Republican party gained control of Congress, he suggested offhandedly that Truman appoint a leading Republican as secretary of state and then resign, awarding the presidency to the majority party since there was no vice-president. This proposal, derived from Fulbright's admiration for the British pattern of government, would have substituted parliamentary practice for the presidential system. For this act of lese majesty he earned the formidable enmity of Truman, who on more than one occasion referred to him as "that overeducated Arkansasan, you know, Senator Halfbright." He did not improve his standing in 1949 when he presided over an extensive investigation of the Reconstruction Finance Corporation and uncovered extensive corruption in Washington, an issue used to advantage by the Republicans during the elections of 1950 and 1952.

These setbacks aside, Fulbright finally gained his heart's desire in 1949: membership on the Senate Foreign Relations Committee; from this vantage point he observed the era of Senator Joseph R. McCarthy and President Dwight D. Eisenhower. He stepped forward as one of the most outspoken critics of the senator from Wisconsin, a service that won him the respect of civil libertarians and of many liberals, despite their dislike of his stand on racial issues. During these years he built an impressive reputation and acquired seniority, and although he was not as frequently in the public eye as before, he greatly increased his knowledge of American foreign policy and his prestige as an authority in the field.

By 1956 Fulbright discerned a dangerous shift in the balance of power, to which the United States had not responded. America's nuclear superiority and ability to distribute foreign aid had held Russia in check; but now the Soviet Union had become competitive. What increasingly alarmed Fulbright was the administration's commitment to deterrence, the belief that the maintenance of sufficient power to damage aggressors seriously would lead such powers to refuse to accept the costs of an attack. Such a policy would fail because it required a degree of expertise that could not be expected indefinitely of mankind. Moreover, this strategy assumed that the Soviet Union was the only likely instigator of international conflict. A great struggle might start in the Middle East or even in Southeast Asia, where neither superpower would necessarily exercise restraint.

The tendency of the country to make an unreasoning defense

of the status quo, just when the world was caught in "a ferment of cataclysmic change," impressed Fulbright at this time; he attributed the policy to the malign influence of John Foster Dulles. He did not yet discern any change in Soviet objectives, but he emphasized the flexibility of Russian policy under Khrushchev. The United States must demonstrate comparable flexibility if it wished to maintain peace and spread freedom in the world. As the nation headed into the 1960s, nothing seemed more wrongheaded than a global crusade in behalf of the established order. Americans, he argued, were "neither omniscient nor omnipotent. . . . We cannot aspire to make the world over in our own image." He favored action, but he opposed "indiscriminate military intervention in response to every provocation and every disorder, regardless of its character and cause." At this time, he was almost alone in raising these questions, considered heretical in the golden age of brinkmanship and containment.

The senator gradually formulated a comprehensive view, historical in nature, of the course of events from 1945 to 1960, and this served as a basis for new proposals. The American response to the revolution in world politics that began after 1945 had come in the form of containment, and this was well and good during the immediate postwar years; but such policies no longer sufficed. The nuclear stalemate, Europe's recovery of economic vigor, development of flexibility in Russia, and stirrings of nationalism in the third world dictated a new approach. In the future, the United States would have to deal not with crude forms of aggression but with "the insidious challenges of psychological penetration, of political subversion, of economic conquest, of the use of foreign aid and trade as political weapons."

Of great concern to Fulbright was the rise of military influence in American policy, convinced as he was that warfare no longer offered a solution to international tensions. He argued that in present circumstances wars, even those ending in total victory, "generate more problems than they solve." Only qualities such as perseverance and sacrifice could further security. In the long run the *character* of Americans rather than magical formulas and prescriptions would decide whether the nation dealt successfully with what he still called the "Communist challenge."

He had long argued that a sound foreign policy rested on moral strength at home; he now sought explanations for the decline not simply in morals but in tastes and values that was shaking the nation. Perhaps, he speculated, this deterioration was unavoidable, given the American past. Preoccupied with growth, the nation had failed to develop a philosophy and culture to support expansion. America now required "qualities that are associated with maturity rather than youth; qualities of wisdom, as well as resourcefulness; persevering determination, as well as righteous indignation; and perhaps most of all, moral courage in the place of adolescent bravado." He admired a sense of mission, but only in proper measure. He did not advocate default on America's international tasks to further essential domestic reforms, but he inveighed against the "globalism" of the Eisenhower years, a pattern that continued in modified form into John F. Kennedy's tenure. As a sound example to follow, he cited Great Britain during the nineteenth century. As director of the European concert, London "led but did not dominate," participating in a system of shared responsibility.

From the beginning of his congressional career, Fulbright was interested in the perennial question of the relations between the executive and the federal legislature. As early as 1943 he had adopted a moderate position, holding that the president should administer policy, but according to broad guidelines that should emanate from the Senate. Shaping this view was his old complaint about the lack of clear policy and the resulting American tendency to improvise foreign relations. The legislator's responsibility to curb potential executive oppression remained in force, however. A responsible Congress encouraged "a climate in which the genius of individual beings can flourish." He criticized violations of appropriate functions by legislators, most notably in his comments on Senator McCarthy. He had voted for censure of McCarthy in 1954, he claimed, not because of his colleague's character or views, but because of his "official degradation of the power of the Senate, by which he has gravely injured the United States and the Senate." Although the Senate's investigatory role must be safeguarded because this power stood at the heart of the legislative process, Fulbright also argued that a legislator "ought to consider himself a teacher, offering by precept and example a style and method of deliberation that can be imitated by the community at large, as it seeks on its own to know and then to do the

Vadillo in La Prensa, Mexico City

"Mr. Fulbright and the blind giant."

good." The legislator, however, like the teacher, "must be prepared to accept banishment or destruction at the hands of the people because he has aroused their anger in the very act of serving them well."

Fulbright became more and more concerned about executive irresponsibility during the Eisenhower years, but he kept these earlier views. The Senate could not "initiate or force large events, or substitute its judgment for that of the president, without seriously jeopardizing the ability of the nation to act consistently, and also without confusing the image and purpose of this country in the eyes of others." The Senate should confine itself to another, even more important responsibility: to "explain and rationalize the burden which the people bear, to help them to that degree of understanding which will compel their agreement." If this were properly done, a consensus would emerge upon which the president could base his initiatives.

Senator Fulbright spoke with greater confidence and authority as the 1960s began. He possessed the great prestige and not inconsiderable power conferred by his chairmanship of the Senate Committee on Foreign Relations, a post gained in 1959 with the assistance of his old and good friend, Lyndon B. Johnson, then majority leader. Further, he stood apart from the rest of the Senate in his understanding of foreign affairs. With Kennedy, a Democrat, in the White House (and one with whom Fulbright seemed to have in common intellectual if not personal ties), and with a Democratic majority in both the House and Senate, a bold new era of executive-legislative collaboration in foreign affairs seemed about to dawn. It was a safe bet that Fulbright would play a pivotal part in the new diplomatic initiatives of the Kennedy administration. That was not to be, largely because the intellectual differences between the senator from Arkansas and the Bostonian who moved into the White House proved as great as their personal differences. One may assert that a major cause of this falling out was that Fulbright continued to grow intellectually, while Kennedy and his circle of advisers never moved beyond the prevailing wisdom about foreign affairs.

In 1963, Harvard University invited Fulbright to deliver the prestigious Clayton lectures, and in preparation for this pedagogical opportunity he drew together his thoughts about U.S. foreign policy, offering certain broad prescriptions for American diplomacy in accord with his views on the proper role of Congress in foreign affairs. Fulbright began these lectures, which were later published under the title *Prospects for the West,* by recourse to history, as was his wont. During the twentieth century the West had declined in its power relative to other parts of the world. Outside challenges no longer permitted the West to consider its ideas and values as having universal applicability. In addition, the West could not redress its position by resorting to war. Unfortunately, an inveterate tendency toward "baleful nationalism" had prejudiced the West's position. Fulbright's solution to the crisis of the Western world represented a refurbishing of his old dream of a

United States of Europe, which he now expanded into an Atlantic
partnership including the United States. However much he desired a world community, it was unattainable. "We must therefore," he continued, "focus our efforts on the more modest goal of
building new bonds among those people of the free world who
have some feeling of shared values and interests, some feeling of
the ability to communicate freely, some feeling of trust and
confidence in each other's purposes." He did not approve General
de Gaulle's plan for a strictly European organization, based as it
was on outworn nationalism and exclusion of the English-speaking
nations. Through an Atlantic partnership the West could become a
model and a magnet for Asia, Africa, Eastern Europe, and even for
the Russians.

Fulbright's analysis reflected a changing appraisal of the
Soviet Union. Stalinism had represented a renewal of nationalism
and imperialism in the crudest form. Under Khrushchev the Soviet
Union still hoped to destroy Western unity, but it now was using
sophisticated means. To counteract the Russian challenge the
West had to maintain its defenses, but it must make clear that its
policy was to counteract Russian imperialism, not ideology. "The
Soviet Union, insofar as it renounces expansionist and subversive
ambitions, can enjoy a safe and honorable life without threat or
danger from the West." As a further measure, the West must
strengthen its internal fabric, making itself safe against alien
ideologies and an example of social and material well-being. Such
a course might encourage moderation in Russia, even a withering
away of the idea of a Russianized world.

Fulbright never had manifested more than a qualified optimism about human nature, and the stress of the cold war
reinforced his proclivity for an endorsement of human reason that
was, at best, ambiguous. Events had shown that "free societies,
including our own, have acted foolishly or disastrously as a result
of their own shortsightedness and irrationality." This reality might
force changes in traditional actions, but Fulbright remained
committed to "belief in the moral sanctity of the free mind and
the free individual." These views reflected his preoccupation with
conservative thinkers such as Alexis de Tocqueville and Walter
Lippmann, whom he quoted more frequently than any others in
support of his opinions.

Fulbright expanded his views on domestic conditions. Melioration at home determined a nation's success with other nations.

The West would survive if it proved more successful than its enemies in creating "an economic system that provides material abundance, a political system based on justice and freedom and human dignity, and an educational system that cultivates individual excellence and spiritual fulfillment." The United States must further important reforms at home. Postwar prosperity had "benumbed" the American social conscience, diverting attention from pressing domestic problems such as unemployment, deteriorating schools, and urban blight. Progress would not result either from expanding a vulgar consumer culture or pursuing overseas adventures. "If America is to achieve excellence in life and greatness in history," he concluded, "these can only come from the decision of our people to find purpose and direction in their lives, to give shape and coherence to their civilization."

The Clayton lectures represented for Fulbright both an end and a beginning. In them he drew together his earlier experience, when he had struggled with the problems posed by the Russo-American confrontation that followed World War II. If he differed from Acheson and Dulles, he shared the pervasive Europocentrism of those two exponents of containment. Like others at the time he dissented not from the broad views of the cold war entertained in the executive branch but from the tactics of those in power. His more advanced theories (such as his attitude toward national sovereignty) do not seem to have had much if any influence. Fulbright did not ignore the problems of the third world, but he looked at the area in terms of Western interests without undertaking a truly detailed analysis of developments outside the Atlantic region. In 1963 Fulbright had gained the respect of many in the country because of his articulate statements, but he was not considered to be outside the establishment. Very soon, however, he turned to issues that related more to future policy in Latin America and Asia than to the defense of the West, and events during the presidency of Lyndon Johnson forced him to adopt marked changes in his diagnosis of world problems as well as new prescriptions for their cure.

Fulbright had long been a close associate of Johnson. He had supported the majority leader's presidential candidacy in 1960 and campaigned for him in 1964, praising the programs of domestic reform that became known as the "Great Society." In their days in the Senate, Johnson would proclaim, "Bill's *my* Secretary of State." This mutual admiration society did not endure long beyond the election of 1964. When Fulbright began to adopt a critical stance toward the administration's foreign policies, Johnson attempted to cajole the senator, exposing him to "the treatment," a term journalists used to describe the president's forceful methods of persuading others to support his policies. This method did not sway his old friend from Arkansas. Fulbright's alienation from Johnson during the period 1964–66 paralleled his retreat from the conventional wisdom about American foreign relations at the same time the United States committed itself to war in Southeast Asia. The senator's two important books of this period, *Old Myths and New Realities* (1964) and *The Arrogance of Power* (1966), reveal striking departures from earlier views.

Ironically, he seems to have thought for a time that Johnson would sponsor constructive change. He intended *Old Myths and New Realities* to point the way in foreign relations. The old myth of greatest importance was the view that the Communist world constituted a monolithic conspiracy seeking to overthrow free-dom. Adherence to this idea blinded its exponents to great changes in the pattern of world politics as well as to appropriate adjustments. The new reality turned on a sharp change in Russo-American relations, which Fulbright associated with the outcome of the Cuban missile crisis in 1962 and the signing of the limited test ban treaty of 1963. In these situations Moscow had shown restraint, and both sides had implicitly repudiated the idea of achieving total victory. Russia had accepted America's strategic superiority because of indications that it would be exercised responsibly. Some Communist powers posed danger, but others did not. In any event, the real threat remained that of imperialism not ideology. The United States "must deal with the Soviet Union as a great power, quite apart from differences of ideology." Normal relations might not become possible for many years, but thoughtful policies could lessen Russo-American tensions.

It was not clear that the country would take full advantage of these new options. The United States was entrapped by an "excessive moralism, by a tendency to equate means with ends and therefore to attach a mythological sanctity to policies and practices which in themselves have no moral content or value except insofar as they contribute to the achievement of some valid national objective." Fulbright thus confirmed his tendency to identify his own country rather than the Soviet Union as a deterrent to constructive change in international relations. He realized that no dramatic solution could resolve the cold war; it could neither be won nor ended immediately. These notions he labeled the favorite myths of the American Right and the American Left. He drew attention more clearly than in earlier works to the limits rather than the vistas of power. Americans, he urged, should recognize "the realities of a world in which neither good nor evil is absolute and in which those who move events and make history are those who have understood not how much but how little it is within our power to change."

The critical concern was not to end the cold war but to preclude a holocaust. Those nations with nuclear weapons, he noted, were most likely to serve as nuclear targets. Neither of the superpowers needed nuclear arms; they could exist without them. Proliferation of nuclear capability would constitute a "great equalizer" among nations large and small. These realities created Russian and American interest in arms control. The senator was devastatingly critical of calls for general and complete disarmament, labeling such proposals "an exercise in cold war fantasy." They stimulated false hopes and caused disappointments, heightening rather than resolving tensions. More modest initiatives, sustained over time, could lead to constructive change. Cold war encounters might turn to more tolerable rivalries that did not distract mankind from "the creative pursuits of civilized societies."

Fulbright gave increasing attention to places other than Europe, particularly to Latin America where the rise of Fidel Castro in Cuba had created new problems. He believed that Kennedy had overreacted. "We have flattered a noisy but minor demagogue by treating him as if he were a Napoleonic menace." Fulbright opposed unilateral action toward Cuba, arguing that the inter-American system should deal with acts of aggression mounted by Cuba. The Alliance for Progress, an attempt to facilitate peaceful social revolution in Latin America, hopefully would achieve its goals, but he warned that violence was always possible "in countries where feudal oligarchies resist all meaningful change by peaceful means."

Asian problems also came within his purview, especially instability in Southeast Asia. In 1961 he had criticized U.S. policy in Laos, which he thought was unrelated to actual circumstances

there, but had spoken differently of South Vietnam where "qualified success" had rewarded American efforts. Future developments would depend on the Diem regime's capacity for reform.
He placed little faith in paramilitary operations. "The proper
course," he insisted, was "to continue sustaining and supporting
efforts of the Vietnamese army to cope effectively with the foe in
being—tough bands of hit-and-run Communist guerrillas—while
devoting at least as much effort to assisting and guiding the
Vietnamese people in their struggle for dignity and economic
independence." By 1964 second thoughts had come. He opposed
complete American withdrawal and favored supporting the Geneva agreements of 1954 and 1962 which envisioned independent
states free of outside domination, but he argued that this goal did
not require either hostilities between the Indochinese states or an
imposing American presence. Fulbright entertained modest hopes
for the improvement of relations with mainland China. He
dismissed the concept of the "two Chinas," agreeing with those
who proposed that the U.S. consider the option of improving
associations with Peking. He thought that Taipeh and Peking
might someday end the civil war and open up "the possibility
of entirely new patterns of international relations in the Far East."

Fulbright also expanded his early critique of military influences in the making of foreign policy. National security depended
on many elements besides armaments. He lamented the tendency
of civilians to surrender decision making to "highly specialized
technical experts whose experience and knowledge have only very
limited relevance to the complexities of international politics." He
objected to congressional haste in voting huge appropriations for
the Department of Defense, an approach that contrasted with
careful surveillance of expenditures on social programs at home.
The most dangerous consequence of the cold war was its
tendency to force diversion of resources from peaceful to warlike
pursuits. His scathing criticism of the space program reflected
these views. If Russia got to the moon first, but the United States
achieved the objectives of the Great Society, "whose prestige
would be higher, who would then be ahead in the world-wide
struggle for the minds of men?" [3]

3. For a detailed work on the military threat see J. William Fulbright, *The Pentagon
Propaganda Machine* (New York, 1970).

Throughout this analysis, Senator Fulbright continued to rely heavily on historical judgments based on his knowledge of modern history. To him the utility of history lay not in the use of analogy but "in its broad distinctions of the kinds of human effort that are likely to fail; in its empirical distinctions between the desirable and the possible; in its suggestions as to the limits as well as the possibilities of human capacity." He argued that if history contained a lesson it was that "we must be cautious in our prescriptions and modest in our aspirations." Grand designs had led to evil consequences for the Communists, and at times the West had also acted without regard to its limitations. By 1972 he spoke even more pointedly against the use of unsound historical analogies, having in mind reference to the Munich Conference of 1938 and other examples of appeasement to justify unyielding resistance to communism in all situations. Decisions could only be determined by considering existing facts in historical context and not excluding "an active awareness that, whatever our fears of repeating past mistakes, and whatever we think we owe to generations yet unborn, we have a prior obligation to those already born and now alive."

A new theme that would continue in later writings appeared in *Old Myths and New Realities*. Fulbright increasingly felt a need to attain deeper insight into the wellsprings of human behavior, particularly as he grasped the extraordinary solidarity of established attitudes toward policy. This concern drew him to the insights of psychology and even psychoanalysis as possible means for developing capacity to change. "In our quest for world peace," he reasoned, "the *alteration of attitudes* is no less important, perhaps more important, than the resolution of issues." Wars were spawned in the minds of men. To act on the mind was "to act upon the source of conflict and the potential source of redemption and reconciliation." What interested him most was the possibility of "generating a *logical process* in which peoples and statesmen come increasingly to think of war as undesirable and unfeasible." If this process took place, then the world might become capable of the political creativity required to cope with the awful problem of nuclear warfare. These ideas, still inchoate, would play an important role in Fulbright's thought as he headed into the most trying years of his senatorial career, the era of the Vietnamese War.

In 1964–65 several episodes forced Fulbright to extend his revisionist views into full-blown dissent. In August 1964, he shepherded the Tonkin Gulf Resolution through the Senate, a statement Johnson used as a blank check to pursue the war in Vietnam. Fulbright later regretted his action deeply, claiming that he had been misled as to the facts in the matter. He also considered Johnson's intervention in the Dominican Republic during 1965 an egregious overreaction. Most important was intensification of the Vietnamese War early in 1965, leading to the bombing of North Vietnam and commitment of hundreds of thousands of troops in pursuit of total victory. This activity marked out for the Republic what appeared a quixotic, dangerous course. His reactions to these events appeared in *The Arrogance of Power* (1966), still another book based on speeches delivered in the Senate and elsewhere.[4]

His newfound interest in psychology provided the theme for this volume. Considering the causation of wars, he came to the conclusion that the usual reasons given by historians—to obtain territory, markets, and resources or to defend principles—did not point to roots. Such answers were "explanations or excuses for certain unfathomable drives of human nature," drives he summarized in the term "arrogance of power." Under the compulsion of this drive, nations assumed that "force is the ultimate proof of superiority." The causation of war might "have more to do with pathology than with politics, more to do with irrational pressures of pride and pain than with rational calculations of advantage and profit." Armed with this concept, he proposed to reexamine foreign policy as a "humanist," as one who "weighs human behavior against human *needs,* notes the discrepancy, notes as well the irrational elements in human nature and the limitations these impose, and then tries to find ways, within those limitations, of narrowing the gap between behavior and needs."

Fulbright now viewed the cold war as an outgrowth of total victory in 1945, which had created a vacuum of power in Europe

4. J. William Fulbright, *The Arrogance of Power* (New York, 1966).

and east Asia, filled "quickly and eagerly by Russia and belatedly and reluctantly by America." After twenty years of contention, the condition of the protagonists could be stated clearly. Russia had become a conservative power with a major stake in the status quo, which helped more to explain its course than did its philosophy of world revolution. The United States showed "some signs of that fatal presumption, that overextension of power and mission, which has brought ruin to great nations in the past." Warfare in Vietnam could only accelerate this tendency, which meant that America might become the leader of an international counterrevolution.

According to Fulbright, two strains struggled to dominate American thought: democratic humanism and intolerant puritanism. In troubled times intolerance seemed to control affairs. Given this fact and the danger of nuclear war, radically new attitudes were essential. The world needed no more crusades by high-minded men seeking regeneration. Such endeavors always foundered because of human perversity, because "men are loutish and ungrateful when it comes to improving their souls and more often than not have to be forced into their own salvation." He concluded that the nation required a truly conservative foreign policy, one that would conserve peoples, one that accepted the world "as it is, with all its existing nations and ideologies, with all its existing qualities and shortcomings." The great conservatives, had they been reborn into the twentieth century—men like Burke, Metternich, and Castlereagh—would not have become cold warriors. They would try to deal with the world as it was rather than as they wanted it to be because "they believed in the preservation of indissoluble links between the past and the future, because they profoundly distrusted abstract ideas, and because they did not think themselves or any other man qualified to play God."

Fulbright's idea was reconciliation. The Communist world was no longer monolithic; it was being nationalized and humanized. Remembering that reconciliation posed psychological demands since it required "cultivation of cooperative attitudes and a sense of having practical common objectives," he proposed that the U.S. and Russia eschew great enterprises and instead undertake lesser initiatives, "a great many projects of practical cooperation." The total effect of such measures might alter attitudes. As appropriate activities he mentioned the test ban treaty already accomplished, possible reductions in production of fissionable materials, improved cultural exchanges, arrangements for cooperative space exploration, opening of new consulates, and creation of additional airline connections.

Fulbright remained convinced that strength at home was essential to an effective policy overseas, but he extended analysis of this question to fit his changing views. Nothing troubled him more than the tendency to postpone domestic reform in favor of commitments elsewhere, a frequent cause of national disaster. Sensitive to the charge that he was reverting to the old isolationism, he argued forcefully that he sought not to turn back the clock but to redress the balance between domestic reform and international activism. "Our commitments abroad," he concluded, "are about as permanent as anything can be in human life and . . . the postponement of domestic action until foreign needs subside probably will mean its postponement forever."

For some time Fulbright had been a sharp critic of foreign assistance, commenting frequently on the dangerous consequences of military as opposed to technical or economic aid and maintaining that long-range goals rather than "short-sighted, trivial, and superficial objectives" should guide its distribution. By 1966 he brought this line of thought to maturity. Bilateral aid, he claimed, was operated "as a kind of charity, demeaning to both recipient and donor. In addition, it is becoming a vehicle for deep American involvement in areas and issues which lie beyond our vital interests and our competence." He did not favor eliminating appropriate forms of assistance. He wanted to administer aid as a "community enterprise" on a multilateral basis through institutions such as the UN and the World Bank. In this form economic assistance could foster some redistribution of wealth from the richer to the poorer nations. The aid program in Vietnam had become dangerous because it had fostered "a *state of mind* among American policy-makers under which it was felt that the United States had a proprietary investment in Vietnam—an investment of prestige and money which those responsible were naturally unwilling to see go down the drain."

Fulbright continued his interest in Latin America in *The Arrogance of Power*. He thought American policy contradictory, since Washington supported the Alliance for Progress but also pursued indiscriminate anticommunism. In concrete situations the United States encouraged reactionary governments, a course that played into the hands of the Communists. Having in mind the intervention in the Dominican Republic, he argued that the country should compete with Communists for influence in reform movements rather than abandon such movements to them. Support for economic development and social justice would counteract communism more effectively than military aid and CIA manipulation. Since Latin America would undoubtedly experience more social revolution, the only question was whether it would adopt Communist or democratic methods. In the short run, perhaps, the best course was to loosen existing bonds with Latin America, remembering that voluntary ties ultimately constituted the closest associations. Let the Latin Americans decide for themselves what relations they wished to maintain and what they wished to discard, and even let them develop arrangements among themselves and with nations outside the hemisphere in which the United States did not participate, a direction that would strengthen pride and mitigate past feelings of indignity and inferiority in relation to the United States.

Almost all of these recommendations were at variance with those of President Johnson—who implicitly represented a prime example of the arrogance of power—but the senator's tendency to root-and-branch dissent came to the surface most clearly in his comments on the Vietnamese War. That struggle was a terrible mistake, if only because the United States could not achieve the end in view with the means at hand. How could Western nations "go into a small undeveloped Asian nation and create stability where there is chaos, the will to fight where there is no tradition of it, and honest government where corruption is almost a way of life?" American policy, motivated by fear of communism, now amounted to what he called the "Asian Doctrine," a commitment comparable to the Monroe Doctrine for Latin America. Johnson's policy envisioned for America a primary role as policeman of the Orient. Unlike earlier commitments of this nature, which were either qualified or exercised cooperatively with other nations, the Asian Doctrine was "unilateral and virtually unlimited in its objectives." The United States was fighting in Vietnam for vague purposes, involving itself on one side of a domestic insurrection. The application of the Asian Doctrine in Vietnam meant not only a commitment to military victory but to long-term engagement: protection of a stable government in Saigon, maintenance of massive power indefinitely in Southeast Asia, and supply of unlimited foreign assistance to create a Vietnamese "great society." All these entanglements clearly went beyond America's true national interest. Fulbright detected both domestic and foreign dangers stemming from the Vietnamese adventure. It stood in the way of promising East-West negotiations and prejudiced relations with old friends in Europe. At home it aborted the program of domestic reform launched by Johnson.

He did offer a plan for relieving the crisis in Southeast Asia: neutralization of the region. Any settlement that did not take into account the growing conflict there between the United States and Communist China would be futile. Since neither power could accept defeat, neutralization seemed logical. "In such circumstances," wrote Fulbright, "it is the fact of neutralization rather than the political or ideological complexion of the small countries concerned that has made for stability and peace."

Behind this proposal lay broader views on the revolutionary future of the third world. He did not envision any quick transition to democratic government in Asia, Africa, and Latin America; for most countries a time of troubles would ensue. Americans found it difficult to understand social revolution because their own society was so unrevolutionary. They lacked any "genuine feeling of empathy," even if they thought of their own tradition as revolutionary and as a proper model for others to emulate. Fulbright believed that to relate properly to revolutionary radicalism, the United States must support local nationalism rather than merely oppose communism. Vietnam provided a grisly example of what happened when an anti-Communist policy led the United States to oppose the forces of nationalism.

To express such views was certain not only to result in exclusion from the inner circles of the Johnson administration but also to engender more public attention than had ever come Fulbright's way. As a leading antiwar spokesman he became a minor folk hero among liberals (and even radicals) despite his proclivity for moderate and at times quite conservative outlooks. He was at the center of the turbulence that overwhelmed the country during the latter years of the 1960s, and his activities then are the services for which he will perhaps be best remembered. As chairman of the Senate Foreign Relations Committee he periodically conducted inquiries associated with the war—to the accompaniment of praise from dissenters and often bitter criticism from those who supported the administration's policies. Fulbright's "unthinkable thoughts" continued to mature as the United States finally backed away from its attempt to achieve victory in Vietnam but failed to negotiate an early peace.

The *Crippled Giant*, which appeared in 1972, for the most part extended analyses first presented in 1964–66. Fulbright began with an assumption he had not made before, that nuclear holocaust seemed unlikely because a reasonable balance of power seemed to have developed. In the Nixon-Kissinger foreign policy he saw a shift from ideological crusading to classical power politics. If Henry Kissinger's geopolitics improved on earlier approaches and frequently dictated departures often advocated by Fulbright in the past, the senator nevertheless found fault. A geopolitical approach was both amoral and without substantive purpose. It was also unstable: "Managed with agility, it can hold war off for a time, but war in the end is what it comes to." Once exercised, power could not be allowed to rest. "If you *can* be a bully, then you must be—on pain of being thought a 'pitiful, helpless giant.'" Kissinger's strategy might depict the facts of human experience, but it was unacceptable because of its "utter irrelevance to human needs."

In even more forceful terms than during the 1960s, Fulbright gave witness to his Wilsonian internationalism. The idea of collective security he deemed the one really new thought to develop in the field of international relations during the century. It constituted a critique not only of traditional *Realpolitik* as practiced by the Nixon-Kissinger team but of isolationist thought as well. Recognizing that Metternich and Bismarck had been internationalists of a sort, he insisted that those like himself, who were frequently labeled as neo-isolationists, in fact distinguished between the new and the older variety of internationalism. He and others, he wrote, "welcome the reversion to the old power politics as an improvement on the ideological crusade but regret it in all other respects [retaining] some faith in the validity and viability of the United Nations idea." Looking beyond the Vietnamese War he wondered whether the American people would take advantage of this relative stability to pursue basic changes in the international system. If so, Americans might then shake free of the material and spiritual costs associated with World War II and after. Because the nation had attempted to play a role for which it was unfit—that of international power broker—it had depleted its resources, becoming a crippled giant.

Updating his commentary on Russia, the senator saw further signs of recovery in the balance of power. Giving full credit to Nixon for his successful negotiations in Moscow during May 1972, he saw in this event "the final, belated acceptance by the United States of the postwar balance of power in Europe and in Soviet-American relations." He doubted that the future held much promise unless the country adopted a course that in essentials reverted to Woodrow Wilson's concept of world order. He argued that a corrupted version of this outlook had dominated recent American history, defining Wilson's central premise as the view that "the nation's vital interests are essentially domestic in character, that it is our own democracy that is to be defended, that our proper concern is not with what we can make of the world but what must be done in the world to create conditions under which we will be free to make what we want of ourselves."

As a fundamental guide for the future, Fulbright advocated a much limited foreign policy, not forever and not to the extent of wholesale abandonment of commitments, but long enough "to replenish our depleted resources, renew our neglected society, and restore our endangered democracy." Gone was his earlier preoccupation with grandiose schemes such as a concert of free nations. Changing conditions had reduced the concept of an Atlantic partnership to "little more than a lingering sentimentality." Europe could take care of itself. To those who called him a neo-isolationist for advocating a modest course, Fulbright had harsh words. This charge was "an invention of people who confuse internationalism with an intrusive American interventionism, with a quasi-imperialism."

His views on the latter stages of the Vietnamese War echoed this moderate approach. The policy of Vietnamization, which he considered a disguised extension of the Johnsonian goal of victory, was doomed. Because President Nixon's visit to China pointed toward improved relations with that country, Fulbright felt this development, of and by itself, repudiated the idea that war in Vietnam had to be waged to discredit wars of national liberation. He marveled at the importance attached to the conflict by its defenders. "From the standpoint of American security and interests, the central fact about Indochina is that it does not matter very much who rules in these small and undeveloped lands." He did not favor Communist domination, but such an outcome seemed at least tolerable. He agreed with those experts who believed that a Communist regime in Southeast Asia would erect a more effective barrier to Chinese expansion than a weak non-Communist state, especially since China represented more a political and cultural than a military menace to the region. Given the damage at home wrought by years of struggle abroad, he counseled Americans "to acknowledge and liquidate our mistake and, by that very act, initiate the process of social—and moral—reconstruction of which our country is in so great need."

True to his earlier beliefs, Fulbright remained convinced that an unduly optimistic appraisal of human capacity would lead only to greater difficulties in the future. Man, despite technological accomplishments, remained a "moral primitive." Thought about attaining true human community must begin with "the candid recognition that man's capacity for brotherly love is limited, and so is his capacity for voluntary restraint of his competitive and destructive impulses." Mankind must find means of restraining international lawlessness as it had managed to curb domestic anarchy in order to sustain hopes for the survival of the race. "If that is not the most promising of foundations on which to build," he concluded, "it has at least the solidity of truth."

Fulbright's thought over the past thirty years contains many elements of continuity. While he has been innovative and flexible in his search for ways of conducting American diplomacy, he has always acted in terms of a moderately pessimistic evaluation of human nature. This fundamental philosophical conviction aligns him against the views of both conservative and liberal thinkers. His recommendations over time have increasingly emphasized caution and restraint. He is a moderate and a realist in the great tradition of the intellectual guides with whom he feels most at home, de Tocqueville and Lippmann. Another sustained commitment has been his rejection of absolute national sovereignty as a principle for organizing international relations. To his mind the system of nation-states is obsolete, and he has always searched for ways of moving the world to supranational modes of organization.

Within this pattern of continuity Fulbright has gone through considerable changes of view, a natural consequence of experiences during an era of profound historical discontinuity. The more important modifications in the realm of policy are related to his growing pessimism. If in his early years there was a strong sense of American power and responsibility, his later commentary stresses partnership with other nations. At the outset he embraced the views of those who advocated containment of Russian expansion, although he advanced as an institutional vehicle the concept of Atlantic partnership. Most recently he has emphasized the need for a sound social and political system at home. In this respect, his views parallel those of the great Progressives of the early twentieth century, including Wilson, who recognized that international involvement might threaten liberal reform. No neo-isolationist, Fulbright believes that the United States must forego the active role it followed during the cold war because of the necessity for overhauling the great tradition of American democracy. Again, overshadowing all else is his strong conviction that foreign policy begins at home, that external success rests on a strong internal polity.

Fulbright has not been a particularly original thinker; his most important function has been to mediate between the intelligentsia and the public. He has synthesized for popular consideration the drift of informed opinion and frequently has served as public advocate for fresh ideas well before the country has been prepared to accept them easily. The validity of his most recent pronouncements will depend primarily on whether he is right in discerning the emergence of a rough new balance of power and whether he is right about the preeminent importance of domestic reform as a basis for continuing successes in foreign affairs.

Fulbright has been a most constructive legislator in the sense of that function that he himself considers so important: as an educator helping to build sound public attitudes toward great questions of policy. He has suffered much in the service of this ideal. No student of his public life can fail to admire his humanity, his sympathy for the lot of ordinary folk despite his patrician proclivities. Fortune cast him in the role of dissenter, not a part that he desired for himself or that came easily. Always a historian, seeking guidance in the study of the changing past, he proved able to explore new learning, especially psychology, when he discerned a need for deeper understanding of human motives at a late point in his career. This capacity marks him as a man of intellectual courage, an appropriate and admirable quality for one who has pursued the vocation of teacher.

BIBLIOGRAPHIC NOTE

The best sources of information for the views of Senator Fulbright are his numerous books and other writings. These include *Prospects for the West* (Cambridge, Mass., 1963), his contribution to *The Elite and the Electorate: Is Government by the People Possible?* (Palo Alto, 1963), *Old Myths and New Realities, and Other Commentaries* (New York, 1964), *The Arrogance of Power* (Cambridge, Mass., 1966), *The Two Americas* (Storrs, Conn., 1966), and *The Crippled Giant: American Foreign Policy and It's Domestic Consequences* (New York, 1972). See also Fulbright's muckraking book, *The Pentagon Propaganda Machine* (New York, 1970). The compilation of Fulbright's public statements by Karl Meyer, *Fulbright of Arkansas: The Public Positions of a Private Thinker* (Washington, D. C., 1963), is informative.

Useful biographical accounts are Tristram Coffin, *Senator Fulbright: Portrait of a Public Philosopher* (New York, 1966), and Haynes Johnson and Bernard M. Gwertzman, *Fulbright: The Dissenter* (Garden City, N.Y., 1968). The characterization of Fulbright in David Halberstam, *The Best and the Brightest* (New York, 1972), is brilliantly done.

The White House

AN AMERICAN METTERNICH:

HENRY A. KISSINGER

and the Global Balance of Power

Michael Roskin

In the late 1960s and early 1970s America suffered a Pearl Harbor in reverse: Vietnam. The former catastrophe had pushed the United States into tremendous overseas involvement; the latter threatened to turn the nation inward. The economy, public opinion, and Congress all pressed for reduction of U.S. commitments abroad. The word "neo-isolationism" was in the air. Coming to the presidency in 1969, Richard M. Nixon recognized the trend toward disengagement, feared it, and contrived to circumvent it. He fervently wished to keep the United States in the international game in a leadership role. The massive U.S. interventionism of the 1940s through the 1960s, however, was no longer possible, so Nixon turned to a body of assumptions that had received little

This essay is based in part on Professor Roskin's doctoral thesis, "Turning Inward: The Effects of Vietnam on U.S. Foreign Policy."

373

prior attention in American foreign policy: balance of power diplomacy. In practice, balance of power thinking amounted to a radical revision of U.S. foreign policy. The Nixon administration dropped the ideological rhetoric of the cold war and sat down to do business with Moscow and Peking.

This major shift required new concepts, careful planning, and meticulous, even personal, implementation. The traditional executive departments were too large and sprawling to carry out such a program, even if they had been intellectually capable of it. Nixon rather needed a single person who would understand precisely what he was trying to achieve and in whom he could place the highest confidence. It was further important that this agent or alter ego be thoroughly grounded in the principles of international equilibration. A forty-six-year-old Harvard government professor named Henry Alfred Kissinger suited the role admirably.

While Nixon and Kissinger achieved a rare rapport with each other, from the beginning Kissinger served merely as Nixon's personal adviser with no freedom to act on his own. Indeed, Kissinger often described himself as little more than a good and faithful servant to the president, laying out options for his choice and giving advice only when asked. This skirted the question of how often Nixon asked, which was probably quite often. "Frankly, I can't imagine what the government would be like without you," Nixon told Kissinger at the time he decided to stay on and not return to Harvard after two years in the White House. The two men needed each other; their relationship seemed symbiotic. Nixon established the general direction of policy and supplied the power, and Kissinger elaborated the tactics of diplomacy and carried them out, often in highly personal style.[1]

So involved did Kissinger become in the execution of policy, making dozens of flights overseas for delicate negotiations that stunned the world when revealed, that he frequently eclipsed President Nixon in the public's attention. As a celebrity of the 1970s Kissinger had few equals. He stood out both in relation to the colorless, nonintellectual administration in which he served and in relation to his diplomatic predecessors. Of the two dozen

1. The first item on an agenda for future research should be the determination of how much of U.S. foreign policy in the early 1970s was Kissinger's and how much was Nixon's. It may, of course, be impossible to untangle the two.

or so figures in this work, Kissinger is the only Jew, the only one
born in Europe, the only divorcé, the only career scholar of
international relations, and, most importantly, the only man to
have served a president directly with no official position in the
State Department, Congress, or the military services. His unique
status changed only in 1973, when he was named secretary of
state.

That Kissinger was Jewish, German born, and divorced may
have little relevance to his foreign policy thinking. Psychoanalyti-
cally oriented writers suggest that Kissinger's birth and boyhood in
Fürth (near Nuremberg) scarred his psyche with fear of revolutionary upheavals, causing his conservative, power-oriented viewpoint. Why being a Jewish boy in Nazi Germany should make one
a conservative rather than a leftist or Zionist (Kissinger took little
interest in Jewish affairs) remains unclear. Further, Kissinger
shrugged off his boyhood experiences as "not a key to anything. I
was not consciously unhappy. I was not so acutely aware of what
was going on." When he was fifteen, in 1938, the family moved to
America and settled in upper Manhattan. The only evident
remnant of Kissinger's life before 1938 is his German accent, which
he has never lost.

Kissinger seems to have harbored no special grudge against
Germany; he waited to be drafted in 1943 rather than volunteering
earlier. He graduated from George Washington High School in
1941 with a straight A average. Then, intending to become an
accountant, he took evening courses at New York City College and
worked days in a shaving brush factory. His pursuits were totally
conventional.

Army service sharply changed Kissinger's orientation from
bourgeois to intellectual. A key figure in this process seems to
have been Fritz Kraemer, another German-born immigrant, sixteen
years older than Kissinger and a holder of two doctorate degrees.
The two men met as privates in the Eighty-fourth Infantry Division,
and Kraemer apparently awakened the intellect of his younger
friend. "He told me I had a good political mind," Kissinger
reflected years later. "It was a thought that had never occurred to
me." Kraemer's connections seem also to have produced some
choice assignments for Kissinger, including interpreting for a

general, administering a German district in the occupation government, and, after Kissinger left the army as a staff sergeant in 1946,
teaching as a well-paid civilian at an army intelligence school in
Oberammergau.

By this time, however, Kissinger yearned for an intellectual
career and in the fall of 1946 entered Harvard on a New York State
scholarship. Picking up a Phi Beta Kappa key on the way, he
breezed through to a B.A. in government in 1950, an M.A. in 1952,
and a Ph.D. in 1954. His mentor during this period was Professor
William Yandell ("Wild Bill") Elliott, a strongly anti-Communist
scholar of world affairs and an influential Washington adviser in
the Roosevelt and Truman administrations.

In 1949, while still an undergraduate, Kissinger married Ann
Fleischer, also of German-Jewish background. The marriage ended
two children and fifteen years later. Since his 1964 divorce, and
even a little before, Kissinger has enjoyed the company of
numerous attractive women. In the early 1970s he and his dates
were so photographed that he earned the reputation of "swinger."
How much actual swinging he did is uncertain—he often worked
eighteen hours a day—but the pose served him well as a cover to
distract the press from his more serious activities. Once in 1971,
for example, he was spotted in a Paris restaurant with a female
American television producer and got a sly wink from newsmen
who, luckily for Kissinger, failed to unearth the real purpose of his
visit to Paris: ultrasecret negotiations with the North Vietnamese.

Coincidentally, Kissinger's presumed model in international
diplomacy, Austrian Prince Metternich, was an inveterate woman-
izer. Kissinger's relationships with women, however, remained
opaque because he adroitly deflected curiosity by means of his
self-deprecating humor. Explaining his dates with writer Gloria
Steinem, Kissinger announced that she was "not now and has
never been my girl friend. But I am not discouraged. After all, she
did not say that, if nominated she would not accept or, if elected,
she would not serve." Kissinger termed such ploys "humanizing
devices," but left unclear whether they actually served to human-
ize him or merely to convince others that he was human. At any
rate, his female companions turned the portly former academic
into a superstar, which in turn may well have enhanced public
acceptance of his diplomacy.

Kissinger's intellectual foundation was set by the time he
wrote his doctoral dissertation (published in 1957), a highly

regarded analysis of Metternich's and Castlereagh's power-balancing maneuvers after the Napoleonic wars. In current political science language, the dissertation was thoroughly "traditional" in that it used no "variables" or statistics to validate hypotheses. Instead, Kissinger dug into Metternich's and Castlereagh's papers, many in French and German, to paint with grand strokes a picture of balance of power diplomacy in its heyday. Today a political science department might reject such a "wisdom" approach and direct the student to the history department (which might disparage the effort as metahistorical). The work contained at least as much history as political science.

Although it would not satisfy a behavioralist's thirst for empirical verification, Kissinger's approach did distill considerable wisdom that might be of some policy use, which is precisely what Kissinger intended. While his doctoral dissertation dealt with the post-Napoleonic era, the work seems clearly designed as a springboard to twentieth-century problems. The wisdom Kissinger extracted from Metternich's time he applied intact in his best-selling *Nuclear Weapons and Foreign Policy* (1957). He even began both works with the same allusion to Greek mythology: that Nemesis sometimes punishes man by fulfilling his wishes too completely.

Kissinger wrote only one carefully researched and richly documented book, *A World Restored*, a revised and expanded version of his dissertation. His four subsequent books and more than forty articles, aimed at policy thinkers rather than scholars, contained little original research or documentation.[2] These works simply presented Kissinger's views on current strategic and diplomatic problems, supported by little evidence but beautifully (if somewhat turgidly) argued and written.

Kissinger always seemed to find the lessons of his Metternich study closely applicable to the current scene. He argued in his dissertation, for example, that a revolutionary state (in this case France) in a world of status quo powers would feel insecure and would try to alleviate this insecurity by crushing other states. Such a situation of chronic mistrust Kissinger dubbed a "revolutionary"

---

2. An exception to this might be his 1968 article on Bismarck, which shows a flash of the old depth: "The White Revolutionary: Reflections on Bismarck," *Daedalus* 97 (Summer 1968), 888–924. This study also uses the line, "But the gods sometimes punish pride by fulfilling man's wishes too completely," p. 890.

Absolute Security Promotes Insecurity

world system, the chief cause of which was the revolutionary state's quest for absolute security. "Only absolute security—the neutralization of the opponent," wrote Kissinger in his *World Restored*, "—is considered as sufficient guarantee, and thus the desire of one power for absolute security means absolute insecurity for all the others." Opposed to this is what Kissinger called a "legitimate" world order in which status quo states have no deep fears of their neighbors' intentions and thus neither need nor strive for absolute security. It was a profound and well-expressed insight, and Kissinger repeated it in books and articles from 1955 to 1966. "Absolute security for one power means absolute insecurity for all the others."

Kissinger's writings were repetitive. Many of his arguments published in the 1960s could be found in his dissertation, sometimes word for word. Such behavior is hardly unique to Kissinger; indeed, it is probably typical of most academics. Kissinger, however, could have been a large cut above this; he might have grown intellectually if he had pursued a straight scholarly career; but he was too busy. His repetitive writings were not cheap or dishonest; they appear to be simply the mark of a man in a hurry. Kissinger hoped to influence policy and he seems to have used his many books and articles to build a reputation in policy-making rather than academic circles. Thus, there was an inevitable tendency to rely on his original insight rather than to set aside months for fresh research and reflection.[3]

Kissinger had little time for such an introspective existence. Even as a Harvard graduate student he was immersed in other activities, from running the Harvard International Seminar (which he headed until 1969) to consulting for the army's Operations Research Office and Psychological Strategy Board. Appointed an instructor in government at Harvard in 1954, the thirty-one-year-

---

3. One widely anthologized article can be strongly recommended, both because it is well written and because it contains in a few pages all the main points of Kissinger's four earlier books. "Domestic Structures and Foreign Policy," which first appeared in *Daedalus* (Spring 1966), consists of little more than pasted-together portions of *World Restored* (chapter 1), *Nuclear Weapons* (chapter 3), *Necessity for Choice* (chapter 6), and the 1965 *Troubled Partnership* (chapter 7). It has been reprinted in James N. Rosenau, ed., *International Politics and Foreign Policy* (New York, 1969), Frederick H. Hartmann, ed., *World in Crisis* (New York, 1973), Robert L. Pfaltzgraff, ed., *Politics and the International System* (Philadelphia, 1972), and Henry A. Kissinger, *American Foreign Policy* (New York, 1969).

old Kissinger boldly applied for the vacant managing editorship of *Foreign Affairs*. Although he was turned down, he attracted the attention of Hamilton Fish Armstrong, the quarterly's august editor, who recommended him for an eighteen-month appointment as director of a research program to study methods of dealing with the Soviet Union short of all-out war. From this project came Kissinger's *Nuclear Weapons and Foreign Policy* (1957), which soon became required reading in Washington and in university courses on defense policy.

The basic thesis of the book was not startling; it was, rather, the conventional wisdom of the day, one of many refutations of John Foster Dulles's policy of "massive retaliation" to counter Soviet expansion. Criticism of Dulles's strategy had actually begun in 1954, the year in which he first articulated the policy. By the late 1950s scores of books and articles argued that reliance on nuclear retaliation alone boxed America into the untenable position of having either to ignore minor Communist incursions or make them the potential cause of global war. Massive retaliation left the United States with either/or choices when a spectrum of responses was needed. The argument became more urgent as the decade progressed and the Soviets appeared to have developed warheads and rockets equal or superior to America's. *Nuclear Weapons and Foreign Policy* simply said what many other strategic thinkers were arguing at the time, but said it better than most. Kissinger did not stand apart from the mainstream nor did he lead it. His criticisms had nothing to do with the fundamental assumptions of American foreign policy; he rather criticized methods. He left unexamined the prevailing dogmas that communism was monolithic, expansionist, Kremlin controlled, and responsible for uprisings in the third world. The conventional wisdom of the 1950s, lasting until the late 1960s, saw strategic import in all conflicts; few or none were merely local squabbles. Kissinger accepted this view. With the United States locked into a strategy of "all-out war," he wrote in *Nuclear Weapons*, "the Soviet bloc may then decide, as its nuclear arsenal grows, to absorb the peripheral areas of Eurasia." He lumped the Middle East together with Korea and Indochina as areas where "Soviet and Chinese aggressive moves have occurred." The possibility that Indochina and the Middle East might be scenes of intense, local, nationalistic conflicts rather than Sino-Soviet pincer movements did not occur to Kissinger, just as it did not occur to most Americans.

To block Communist expansion on the Eurasian periphery, Kissinger and others recommended that the United States immediately develop capabilities for fighting limited wars. At this point, however, Kissinger differed somewhat from other critics by urging development of limited nuclear capability as well as conventional capability. Most Dulles critics feared that any use of nuclear weapons would soon escalate into all-out war. They wanted to develop conventional forces to preclude use of nuclear ones. Three years after publication of *Nuclear Weapons* Kissinger dropped his tactical nuclear suggestion and fell into line with the other critics. He shifted in part because the growing Soviet nuclear capability had offset America's former superiority.

Senator John F. Kennedy picked up the debate over strategy, embellished it with urgent rhetoric, and used it effectively in his presidential campaign. He launched the "missile gap" controversy in a 1958 Senate speech, predicting that the "critical years" of Soviet superiority would be 1960 to 1964. Kissinger accepted this view in his *Necessity for Choice* (1960), a book fully as alarmist as a Kennedy speech. Kissinger saw imminent doom for the United States if it did not turn to a flexible response strategy of the sort that Kennedy was advocating. There never had been any missile gap, however, as the Democrats admitted after Kennedy's inauguration; like many others, Kissinger had fallen for Democratic campaign rhetoric. Indeed, American missile strength in the early 1960s so overshadowed Soviet capabilities, some scholars believe, that it prompted Moscow to put missiles in Cuba in 1962 to redress the strategic imbalance. After all, absolute security for one power, in this case the United States, meant absolute insecurity for all the others.

In *Necessity for Choice* Kissinger criticized the Eisenhower administration for reducing the army to a mere fourteen divisions, leaving the United States "in no position to fight a limited war." President Nixon reduced the army from nineteen and two-thirds to thirteen divisions, but by the early 1970s Kissinger and most other defense intellectuals did not protest; the advocates of limited war had had their fingers burned in Vietnam. During the Kennedy presidency their views had been implemented. They got a bigger defense budget, a larger army, a counter-insurgency committee, Green Berets, and Vietnam. They wanted limited war, and they got it. One might almost say, recalling Kissinger's overworked aphorism, that the figure of Nemesis haunted the 1960s, punishing man by fulfilling his wishes too completely.

Kissinger changed a number of his perceptions during the agony of Vietnam, as did America as a whole. He ceased using the words "Soviet" and "Communist" interchangeably. He discarded the monolithic image of communism and stopped referring to the "Sino-Soviet bloc." Kissinger in 1970 was less bellicose and alarmist than he had been in 1960. It is tempting to say that Kissinger the practitioner had turned his back on Kissinger the theorist; that would be an exaggeration, for he preserved the basic framework he had constructed early in his scholarly career, and he took it with him to the White House.

Perhaps the key element of this framework was Kissinger's rather firm belief in a general balance of power approach. Although he conceded that the classic balance of power game was inapplicable to the twentieth century, Kissinger persistently returned to the concepts and phrases of balancing as the only reasonable way to construct a world order. In a 1973 interview, for example, he explained that balance of power was obsolete but that we "must have a certain equilibrium of strength." Kissinger, to be sure, had no fixed formula but rather a general approach that depended as much on the subtleties and sensitivity of the practitioner as on anything else. Power balances do not fall from heaven; the artist-statesman, who must use nuance, ambiguity, and intuition to patiently construct a durable edifice, creates them. One of the greatest errors—to which Americans are particularly prone, according to Kissinger—is to aim directly for peace. A statesman who wishes nothing but peace is at the mercy of any expansionist, revolutionary power willing to risk war. Statesmen who pursue reasonable national interests rather than peace itself may be able to balance and limit their demands. The resulting equilibrium, which Kissinger called a "legitimate" international order, then brings peace as a by-product.

The "revolutionary" world system of the mid-twentieth century was surely due to the destabilizing influence of the Soviet bloc, Kissinger believed. The Kremlin was the revolutionary maverick that felt it must remake the world in its own image to protect itself from hostile outside forces. Kissinger remained untouched by the wave of revisionism that grew in the wake of Vietnam, which posited United States behavior as an important contributor to international tensions. This did not mean that Kissinger presumed permanent Soviet-American hostility. He believed that a firm stance in the face of expansionism can gradually induce revolutionary powers to become legitimate without threatening their existence. The Kremlin could eventually be brought around to play by the rules of a legitimate world order; that is, they would not threaten because they would not feel threatened. The beginning of this process is extraordinarily difficult, Kissinger admitted, because initially a status quo power and a revolutionary power have nothing in common. "Diplomats can still meet but they cannot persuade for they have ceased to speak the same language," he repeated.[4]

To carry out this delicate process, Kissinger firmly believed, bureaucracies are worthless, incapable of policy innovation. He regarded the conventional institutions of United States foreign policy with little more than contempt. He saw a clear incompatibility between "inspiration" and "organization": inspiration brings fresh ideas, but the organization functions only by routinizing old ones. Both may be necessary, but they will not be found in the same place. The State Department might satisfactorily handle daily paper flow, but the American penchant for staffing the higher positions there with businessmen and lawyers produced "pragmatic" compromises between bureaus rather than bold new approaches. For inspiration, Kissinger modestly suggested, outside intellectuals should be recruited, particularly those who understand the historic processes of world politics.

Kissinger's general orientation can be compared to that which George F. Kennan claimed he had in mind in his containment doctrine. Kennan later denied that his 1947 "X" article aimed at a military and ideological standoff between the Soviet Union and the West; it was, rather, to be a flexible tool to teach the Russians international good behavior. Kissinger saw this better than did his postwar predecessors who had turned containment into an ideology. Both Kennan and Kissinger, it should be noted, shared the same "realist" approach to world politics.

In part because of his many books and articles, Kissinger's

---

4. The phrase may not have originated with Kissinger. Raymond Aron said in a 1953 French article, "It takes two to negotiate a settlement; both sides must speak the same language and follow the same principles."

academic and political careers prospered during the 1960s. He became a full professor at Harvard in 1962, and his course on foreign policy was one of the most popular in Cambridge. Kissinger had to miss many classes, though, because of his extensive outside consulting assignments: for the National Security Council in 1961–62, for the Arms Control and Disarmament Agency from 1961 to 1967, and for the State Department from 1965 to 1969. Kissinger attained no position of prominence in the Washington of Kennedy and Johnson, however. In the first place, Kennedy made little use of the National Security Council, preferring instead to conduct policy with the help of former Harvard dean McGeorge Bundy. Bundy monopolized access to President Kennedy and did not much utilize the part-time consulting of Kissinger, who in any case did not like playing second fiddle. On a more philosophical level, Kennedy and Johnson were global crusaders rather than subtle balancers of power. Kissinger's approach was far removed from the "can do" enthusiasm of the Kennedy people and the "shoot from the hip" style of Johnson.

Kissinger had greater success on the Republican side, particularly with Nelson A. Rockefeller, governor of New York and serious contender for the Republican presidential nomination in the 1960s. The two first met as a result of Kissinger's 1954 appointment to the Council on Foreign Relations study project. In 1956, Rockefeller named Kissinger to a Rockefeller Fund study project that resulted in *Necessity for Choice*. At the same time Kissinger started advising Rockefeller on foreign policy matters and then writing speeches for him. Kissinger even had a Telex machine installed in his Harvard office to transmit texts to Albany. The political ties lasted until 1968.

Kissinger's concern with temporal power seemingly marks him as an opportunist, but with two reservations. In the first place, probably all political scientists long for power in the real world; Kissinger was just more obvious and more successful. Everything Kissinger wrote, even his dissertation, related to current policy. This is not necessarily a criticism; indeed, many believe the university should be "relevant" to practical action. Secondly, there is nothing wrong with a scholar wanting to become a practitioner, especially when he is more able in the latter role.

With his consulting in Washington, it was inevitable that Kissinger become involved in the Vietnam question. In 1965 he visited South Vietnam as a State Department consultant for a firsthand report—a pessimistic one—on how things were going during the year of the major U.S. buildup. In 1967 he helped open contacts between Washington and Hanoi through French acquaintances, journeying to Paris several times to convey messages. The operation, code named "Pennsylvania," stayed secret until 1972 when it surfaced as part of the Pentagon Papers. Until 1969, Kissinger published nothing on the Vietnam War, nor did he even take a conspicuous public stand.

By 1968, however, he was ready to admit that Vietnam had been "a very critical failure of the American philosophy of international relations." He neglected to name himself as a contributor to this philosophy or to find any connection between Vietnam and his earlier enthusiasm for limited war capabilities. By the time Kissinger appeared with an article of his own on Vietnam it was 1969 and his perceptions were banalities: "We fought a military war; our opponents fought a political one." Bernard Fall and Sir Robert G. K. Thompson had touted such conventional wisdom for years; by then it was a shopworn observation in Washington. Kissinger's ideas on the difficulties of getting out, however, were remarkably prescient: Saigon would balk; there would be a scramble for territory before a cease-fire; and a Saigon–Viet Cong coalition could not possibly work.

While admitting that the war had been based on false premises, Kissinger argued that the huge American involvement itself made Vietnam a matter over which the United States must not lose credibility. "Other nations can gear their actions to ours only if they can count on our steadiness," he wrote. Kissinger flatly ruled out a unilateral U.S. withdrawal from Vietnam. On the surface this would appear to be a hawkish position, but Kissinger advocated neither a drive for "victory" nor a policy of indefinite continuation. What he may have had in mind, but did not state publicly, appeared only in private conversations at Harvard in 1968, according to Daniel Ellsberg of Pentagon Papers fame. There, said Ellsberg, Kissinger repeatedly urged a policy of "decent interval," that is, a delay of two to three years between American withdrawal and Communist take-over. This implied that the best the United States could hope for from the Vietnam imbroglio was merely avoiding the appearance of direct defeat.

Kissinger's elaborate concern for appearances, a concern that made him considerably less a thoroughgoing realist than someone like Hans Morgenthau, seems to have matched the views of President-elect Nixon. Nixon, too, wanted United States forces withdrawn, but not in a way that would trigger "neo-isolationism" at home or loss of credibility abroad. A sudden, unilateral American withdrawal and quick Communist take-over could do just that, they feared. An America that believed it had been defeated in war would be divided, rancorous, and unable to play a leading role in world politics. Nixon used these themes repeatedly during his first term.

The newly elected Nixon, who claimed a special interest and expertise in foreign affairs, had followed Kissinger's writings for some years but had met him only once, in 1967, at a social function given by Clare Boothe Luce. In late November 1968 Nixon summoned Kissinger to New York and elicited his views on foreign policy at length. Kissinger had not thought much of Nixon previously, but he emerged from the meetings impressed. Nixon named Kissinger his assistant for national security affairs, and the following January Kissinger moved into a White House office and a $42,000-a-year job.

It soon became apparent that Nixon was using Kissinger as far more than a consultant. Kissinger also became executive secretary of the National Security Council, a body whose fortunes had fluctuated since its establishment in 1947. Eisenhower relied on it heavily, but Kennedy and Johnson preferred to work informally with a few individuals. Nixon upgraded the NSC and used it as the control center for all important foreign policy matters. The reorganizer and master of the NSC's staff was Kissinger. As a result, the Harvard professor soon became far more important than either the secretaries of state or defense.

Kissinger brought together a staff of 46 professional assistants and 105 administrative personnel (more than double the previous administration's) with an annual budget of $2.3 million. The NSC staff commanded compliance from State, the Pentagon, and the Central Intelligence Agency, ordering studies, reports, and options, and then structuring them as Kissinger saw fit. During Nixon's first three years in office, for example, the NSC staff supervised more than one hundred forty National Security Study Memoranda from the traditional departments, sometimes returning them if they were not sufficiently thorough. In 1969 the NSC staff rated studies produced by the State Department only "50 to 70 per cent acceptable."

The State Department's subservient status did little for its employees' morale, which had long been in decline as major foreign policy decisions were increasingly taken over by presidential assistants and the Pentagon. Kissinger and his staff, however, brought this trend to a new high point. An especially stinging remark came in 1971 from Senator Stuart Symington, Democrat of Missouri, who charged that Kissinger rather than William P. Rogers was "the actual architect of our foreign policy" and that Rogers was "laughed at" in Washington. President Nixon called the charge a "cheap shot" at his "oldest and closest" cabinet appointee; nonetheless, the charge was absolutely right, and all official Washington knew it. Even foreign ambassadors often preferred an appointment with Kissinger than with Rogers; they knew where the power lay.

From a functional viewpoint, the swollen (36,600 employees) bureaucracy at State was ill equipped to take foreign policy firmly in hand, considering especially the don't-rock-the-boat caution of career Foreign Service officers and the tendency to staff the top positions with lawyers (such as Rogers), a practice about which Kissinger had written earlier. State retained a certain residual importance in the daily workings of foreign affairs, but not in the actual formulation of policy. The gigantic U.S. overseas involvements after World War II led to specialization: Defense took strategic questions and the disposition of American forces abroad; the CIA did faster and sharper political reporting than State; the Commerce Department played a major role in economic policy; public diplomacy went to the U.S. Information Agency; State tried to play its old role of gentlemen generalist, but the ball slipped from its fingers. Increasingly, presidents turned to small coordinating staffs right in the White House. Kennedy was so exasperated with the State Department's slowness that he formulated most of his own policy in consultation with McGeorge Bundy. Johnson similarly used Walt Rostow, even down to planning bombing targets in North Vietnam. With Kissinger, however, the process probably became irreversible and institutionalized. This by itself was one of Henry Kissinger's major contributions to United States foreign policy.

There was little doubt that Kissinger's NSC staff formulated policies—or, in the special terminology used by President Nixon, "policy options" from which he chose—better than traditional departments. Even if a later president tried to restore decision-making initiative to State, he would still feel compelled to have a coordinator and staff close at hand. Relatively placid times might allow the traditional departments to take over more decisions, precisely because they would then be only routine. Until placid times return—an unlikely event—every future president will want his own Kissinger.

Even more embarrassing for State was the fact that Kissinger was not merely Nixon's idea man but his agent in diplomatic negotiations as well. Important matters were not handled by ambassadors or by the State Department in Washington, but rather by Kissinger personally. He so bypassed the American embassy in Moscow that one diplomat complained, "I have to go to my Soviet counterpart at the ministry to find out what has been going on in these talks." U.S. missions around the world sometimes felt that they served as little more than Kissinger's hotels. This situation was actually a long-term trend. With the development of jet aircraft many of the world's capitals were but a few hours from Washington. It was easier for a president to send his alter ego to discuss exactly what he wanted than to brief a series of State Department people who might not convey precise nuances. Further, Nixon had a penchant for *coups de théâtre,* dramatic international moves that surprised everybody. One man could carry out the groundwork for such moves in reasonable secrecy; a bureaucracy could not. Kissinger became resident philosopher, master planner, and personal executor of the Nixon policy.

To do this Kissinger worked himself and his staff hard. "There can't be another crisis this week," he once quipped. "My schedule is already full." Many of the NSC staff resigned, either under pressure of his demands or over continuation of the Vietnam War, especially at the time of the 1970 United States invasion of Cambodia. By mid-1971 only about a fourth of his twenty-eight original professional-level staffers were still there. Kissinger's treatment of his assistants amused Washington. One story related that he became so angry over a State Department cable that he backed its bearer against a wall and berated him for ten minutes. "I'm not going to clear that cable unless changes are made in it," said Kissinger, "and you can march back down to the state department and tell the secretary. . . ." His victim protested, "But Dr. Kissinger, I work for *you.*"

'. . . . AND, HENRY, I WANT YOU TO MAKE IT PERFECTLY CLEAR TO THEM THAT OUR BOMBING ALONG THEIR BORDERS IS NOTHING REALLY SERIOUS!'

Editorial cartoon by Pat Oliphant. Copyright the Denver Post. Reprinted with permission of Los Angeles Times Syndicate

Brutal or not, in short order a markedly different United States foreign policy began to emerge from this machine. Twelve days after his inauguration, Nixon instructed Kissinger to put out feelers to Peking through Eastern European contacts. Later in 1969 Kissinger began meeting secretly with North Vietnamese representatives in Paris to try to reach a plausible compromise to cap American disengagement in Vietnam. On the theoretical level, Kissinger and his staff turned out a new and more limited orientation for U.S. policy as a whole. This first surfaced in Nixon's Guam Doctrine of 25 July 1969, and the president elaborated on it in subsequent "state of the world" messages each February.

Major changes were surely due. By 1969 the United States showed signs of war weariness. Even then the Vietnam War, which was to drag on another four years, was the longest in U.S. history (dating it from 1961, as the military does). The public mood was frustrated and snappish. Much of the remaining support for the war had evaporated in the wake of the 1968 *Tet* offensive, which demolished the Johnson administration's claims of progress.

If Johnson had been able to fool the public and Congress about the burdens of the war, he could not fool the economy. Starting with the major U.S. escalation in 1965, the overheated American economy went into an inflationary spiral that developed a life of its own and refused to end with Nixon's wage and price controls. The inflation fueled severe balance of payments deficits and runs on the dollar abroad. By August 1971 Nixon had to do the hitherto unthinkable: devalue the dollar. The move accomplished little, and he had to do it again in February 1973. In total, the dollar lost about one-fifth of its value, even more in relation to German and Japanese currencies. The United States experienced trade deficits for the first time since the 1890s. Large sectors of U.S. industry and labor demanded protectionist trade legislation. America discovered that it no longer had the means to finance major overseas military commitments.

Partly to save money and partly to deflate the biggest single source of discontent, Nixon ended the draft in 1973 and trimmed the armed forces from 3.5 million in 1968 to 2.3 million in 1973. The cuts fell especially hard on ground forces, the army and marines, without which there could be no overseas interventions.

Nixon's biggest problems, however, came as he faced an inflamed, Democrat-controlled Congress that seemed to be looking for excuses to hamstring the executive in foreign policy. Too cowardly to move against the war at the height of the fighting, congressmen tried to make up for lost time by massacring foreign aid, undermining American troop commitment to Europe, limiting presidential war powers, and blocking the bombing of Cambodia. Kissinger emerged as a major irritant to Congress. Shielded by "executive privilege" from direct congressional probing, he appeared as a sort of unreachable secretary of state, neither confirmed by nor answering to the Senate. He claimed he met with members of the Senate Foreign Relations Committee frequently though unofficially, but these meetings appeared to calm the Senate little or not at all.

Given the factors of public opinion, economic difficulties, shrunken armed forces, and a newly reassertive Capitol Hill, any president in the early 1970s would have had to limit United States engagements abroad. Nixon and Kissinger thus appear as the right men at the right time. Their Democratic predecessors had expanded the postwar interventionism until it met with disaster; Nixon and Kissinger picked up a shipwrecked foreign policy and put it back together, this time with a sense of limits, of the "do-able," that Kennedy and Johnson lacked.

This is not to say that Nixon and Kissinger led an American retreat from world involvement. Indeed, Nixon labeled such a retreat "new isolationism" and sought to avoid it. Instead, he articulated a theme of carefully controlled pullback from Kennedy-style globalism. Speaking to newsmen informally on Guam in 1969, Nixon explained that the United States would provide a nuclear umbrella for its Asian allies in case of direct invasion, but the Asians would have to defend themselves against internal, guerrilla-type attack. The 1970 state of the world report to Congress, written by Kissinger and his staff with no help from the State Department, said that "America cannot—and will not—conceive *all* the plans, design *all* the programs, execute *all* the decisions and undertake *all* the defense of the free nations of the world. We will help where it makes a real difference and is considered in our interest." To sense the change that had occurred in American thinking over the decade, one need only compare this passage with President Kennedy's inaugural promise to "pay any price, bear any burden, meet any hardship, support any friend, oppose any foe to assure the survival and success of liberty."

The mind of America and the external world had both changed over the 1960s; more important than which had changed more, however, is the fact that changes in American orientation enabled its leaders to *perceive* that the external world had altered. The Sino-Soviet dispute had for some time fragmented the Communist world, but it took the anguish of Vietnam to elevate this perception to national policy. In the 1970 state of the world message, Nixon-Kissinger noted that "international communist unity has been shattered." Kissinger helped lay to rest one of his earlier stock themes, the presumed monolithic quality of the Communist bloc.

Indeed, American orientations had changed so much during the Vietnam era that a two-minute televised announcement by President Nixon on 15 July 1971 was greeted with amazement and approval: Nixon would visit Communist China and Kissinger had already been there secretly to work out the details. On 21 February 1972, TV satellite brought back from Peking images of the old Red baiter beaming at his Communist hosts, and the American people loved it.

It may be argued that a new United States–China relationship had been in the making for some time. The Kennedy administration dropped discreet hints in 1963 that things might change between the two countries. Peking reportedly extended initial feelers to the Johnson administration in 1964. By late 1968, China experts tended to agree, the Soviet invasion of Czechoslovakia so disturbed Peking that it reconsidered its hostility to America. Lyndon Johnson, however, busy waging a war against supposed Red Chinese surrogates and encumbered by a frozen-minded secretary of state who insisted that Peking be called by the old Nationalist name of Peiping, was in no position to strike off in new directions had he wished to.

Nixon was free to act with regard to China because he had striven for room to maneuver, with Kissinger's help. He backed up his Guam call for Asian self-reliance by cutting back American forces in Korea, Japan, Okinawa, Thailand, and the Philippines, to say nothing of withdrawing more than half a million U.S. troops from South Vietnam. Additionally, he relaxed trade and travel restrictions to China. Peking slowly reciprocated, and in April 1971 signaled its interest in a new relationship by inviting an American table tennis team to tour China; the breakthrough was dubbed "ping-pong diplomacy."

The evolution of the new China policy clarifies Kissinger's role in the Nixon administration. The basic idea seems not to have originated with him. Nixon came to the White House with such a détente in mind and ordered his assistant to get to work on it, but the execution of the idea was firmly in Kissinger's hands. Kissinger made two trips to Peking to set up the president's visit and another trip in February 1973 to conclude an agreement for each nation to open a "liaison office" (an embassy in all but name) in the other's capital. During that visit, a photograph of Kissinger emerging from a two-hour chat with Mao Tse-tung appeared on the front page of China's, and later the world's, newspapers.

At the same time, Soviet-American relations improved dramatically. This was possibly related to the Sino-American détente; perhaps the balance of power technique had worked with such precision that the specter of a tacit Peking-Washington entente pushed Moscow into new flexibility. Indeed, much happened in Soviet-American relations in 1972. The first part of the strategic arms limitation talks (SALT I) concluded in May with an agreement to limit defensive nuclear weapons. SALT II started with much broader aims in the fall of the same year. A three-day Kissinger visit to Moscow broke deadlocked talks on expanding bilateral trade. In November preliminary talks on a European security conference opened in Helsinki, and the conference itself began in July 1973. At the same time discussions on the mutual reduction of military forces in Eastern and Western Europe began in Vienna. Nixon and Brezhnev exchanged effusive visits in 1972 and 1973.

The cold war logjam was giving way; before attributing this solely to balance of power (or equilibrium of strength, as Kissinger might have it), one must be aware that the *sine qua non* of Soviet-American détente came with Willy Brandt's settlement of the German question in the Moscow Treaty of 12 August 1970. Bonn in effect admitted that German territories lost to Poland and Russia during World War II were gone for good and would never be claimed by Germany. The treaty between the two Germanies of 21 December 1972 further confirmed Bonn's acceptance of the results of the war by recognizing the division of Germany as all but permanent. The rapidity with which Moscow-Washington relations improved at this time suggests that, as far as the Russians were concerned, the cold war had been mostly a geopolitical question of German and Soviet boundaries rather than ideology. The détente in Europe, however, arose as much from Brandt's *Ostpolitik* as from the Soviet need to shift army divisions to the China frontier. The Soviets had considerable incentive for securing their European flank during a period of tension with China. Brandt's *Ostpolitik* gave them this opportunity. The importance of the China factor in Soviet policy toward Western Europe was not clear. The higher one appraises it, the more one turns to balance of power concepts; the lower one appraises it, the more one turns toward ideological, historical, economic, and other factors unrelated to balance of power. Perhaps the best one can say is that Brandt's election as chancellor and the Ussuri River clashes, both events occurring in 1969, were conducive to détente in Europe.

A little-noticed practical consequence of the Nixon-Kissinger policy was the American acceptance of the Soviet and Chinese positions in Europe and Asia, respectively. By supporting Brandt's treaties, Washington accepted division of Germany and implicitly the division of Europe. In coming to terms with Peking, Washington left the Nationalists on Taiwan to "negotiate" their future with the mainland. The only objections to these accommodations came from right wingers who were dismayed at America's "surrender" to communism. There was a grain of truth in such views; America had surrendered—not to communism, but to reality.

If the rapprochements with the Soviet Union and China were successful, some other Nixon-Kissinger policies were not. Kissinger's most spectacular triumph seemed to be the cease-fire agreement reached with the North Vietnamese and Viet Cong in Paris on 27 January 1973. Kissinger worked on this for four years, making a total of twenty-four trips to Paris, at first secretly but later with crowds of newsmen outside the suburban meeting places.[5] President Nixon called the truce "peace with honor," but critics charged that it brought neither and could have been reached four years earlier. In truth, the Paris agreement had but two operative

---

5. The "official" Paris peace talks that proceeded simultaneously achieved nothing in 174 meetings, except perhaps agreement on the shape of the table.

clauses: the United States pulled out its last few thousand troops from South Vietnam, and the Communists released almost six hundred American prisoners of war. The rest of the document, a vague and complex variation of the 1954 Geneva accords, was inherently unworkable. The agreement left several North Vietnamese divisions in the south, did not delineate which side controlled which areas, and the fighting did not stop. Kissinger returned to Paris in June 1973 to reaffirm with the North Vietnamese the truce's provisions. The firing still did not cease, but the Americans were out, even if Saigon's long-term future was highly uncertain.

Kissinger, who as a professor had harped repeatedly on the impossibility of true negotiations between status quo and revolutionary powers, probably did not really think he had achieved a workable peace in Vietnam. His minimum goal was extrication without humiliation; for this he needed a "decent interval" between U.S. withdrawal and Communist take-over. The 1973 truce provided this interval, but not much else. It delayed both domestic and international reactions to the spectacle of America losing—or at any rate not winning—a war. The eventual fall of Saigon could bring those reactions out into the open with a vengeance. The "new isolationism" that Nixon strenuously sought to avoid was merely held in abeyance, not definitively squelched.

Vietnam had been an albatross around Kissinger's neck, and he clearly wanted to be rid of the miasma so he could move on to the overriding diplomatic questions of the epoch. As he expressed in 1971, "What we are doing now with China is so great, so historic, the word 'Vietnam' will be only a footnote when it is written in history." Kissinger was cognizant, however, of the other possibility. "Vietnam," he told newsmen early in his White House career, "may be one of those tragic issues that destroys everyone who touches it."

While American relations with the Soviet Union and China improved dramatically under Nixon, ties to Western Europe and Japan deteriorated noticeably. Chronic balance of payments deficits and related runs on the dollar gave Europeans and Japanese the impression that America did not have its economic house in order and shirked responsibility by accusing its trading partners of trade discrimination. Washington created further mistrust by dealing with Moscow and Peking over the heads of European and Japanese allies, respectively. Both Western Europe and Tokyo began to go their own ways, a backhanded testament to the efficacy of Nixon's balance of power maneuvers. If enemies did not need to be permanently hostile, allies did not need to be permanently friendly; partners could become rivals.

One clear-cut failure of the Nixon-Kissinger policy came in south Asia. While proclaiming neutrality in the 1971 India-Pakistan war over Bangladesh, word soon leaked out that Nixon had ordered Kissinger to "tilt" the United States in favor of Pakistan, which was in a morally indefensible position for slaughtering Bengalis. Informed observers held that Nixon wished to repay Pakistan for its help in arranging the China visits and to demonstrate to pro-Pakistan Peking that the United States and China had common interests against pro-India Moscow. If so, the move was a gratuitous one that gained America nothing but India's enmity.

The Kissinger period marked a major change in the thrust of post–World War II United States foreign policy. Kissinger helped end the cold war and make Washington's relations with its erstwhile archenemies, Moscow and Peking, almost normal. In doing so, he may have triggered unpredictable forces in Western Europe and Japan. He tried to reduce Vietnam to a footnote, but it loomed as a large, sad chapter. Probably his longest-lasting contribution, however, lay in helping introduce nonideological balance of power thinking into U.S. foreign policy.

The Kissinger legacy contained a distinct danger, namely, that after Kissinger moved on lesser figures might misuse a balance of power approach. For Kissinger, balance of power was a general attitude, not a fixed formula. Overeager policy makers might someday seize upon it and reduce it to an oversimplified doctrine. One is sobered to recall that a generation of policy makers thought they understood the "realist" lessons of Hans Morgenthau and George Kennan while they had merely picked up the surface toughness of the two thinkers, not their underlying rationality. One of Kissinger's pupils seems to have done just that. "I think it will be a safer world and a better world if we have a strong, healthy United States, Europe, Soviet Union, China, Japan, each balancing the other, not playing one against the other, an even balance," said Richard Nixon in 1971.

Kissinger sensed the problem in his 1968 essay on Bismarck: "Bismarck's less imaginative successors failed even when they strove for 'calculability' or 'reliability.' These qualities seemed more easily attainable by rigid commitments than by the delicate, constantly shifting balancing of Bismarck's policy." Thus the problem of how to institutionalize inspiration faced Kissinger as he became secretary of state in September 1973. The reinvigoration of the moribund State Department bureaucracy was perhaps his greatest challenge. If he failed to impart his individual wisdom to that unreceptive institution, then his comment on Bismarck eventually might serve as Kissinger's own epitaph: "Statesmen who build lastingly transform the personal act of creation into institutions that can be maintained by an average standard of performance. This Bismarck proved incapable of doing."

BIBLIOGRAPHIC NOTE

Kissingerology is a new field, and little has been published on Kissinger himself. One book-length treatment by David Landau, *Kissinger: The Uses of Power* (Boston, 1972), is extremely useful on Kissinger's background, but concentrates excessively on Vietnam as if it were Kissinger's policy rather than Nixon's, and came out before the Paris agreement. Landau adopted the view, current among many critics at the time, that the various Nixon escalations (Cambodia, Laos, mining of North Vietnamese ports, etc.) indicated an obdurate refusal to end American participation. This view is time bound, and the Landau book was dated within a few months of its publication. British journalist Henry Brandon explores the relationship between Nixon and Kissinger in *The Retreat of American Power* (Garden City, N.Y., 1972), which also ends before the Paris accord. A detailed analysis of Kissinger's published works appears in Stephen R. Graubard, *Kissinger: Portrait of a Mind* (New York, 1973).

To understand Kissinger's times, the quarterly *Foreign Policy* (not the stodgy *Foreign Affairs*) is indispensable. It first appeared at the end of 1970 with a generally reformist-critical orientation. Particularly important is number 5 (Winter 1971–72), which contains two helpful articles: "Kissinger's Apparat," by John P. Leacacos, and I. M. Destler, "Can One Man Do?" The radical commentator I. F. Stone cast jaundiced looks at Kissinger in *The New York Review of Books*, 19 October and 2 November 1972.

Although the China breakthrough came as a surprise in 1971, an article in 1969 was oddly prescient and may have paralleled thinking that was going on in the White House. See John Paton Davies, "The U.S. Invented the 'Imbalance of Power,'" *New York Times Magazine*, 7 December 1969. Davies, a former State Department China hand, was purged by Dulles. The article can be read as an exhortation to pursue the course Nixon and Kissinger ultimately did follow.

NOTES ON THE CONTRIBUTORS

Russell D. Buhite, associate professor of history at the University of Oklahoma, studied with Paul Varg at Michigan State University, where he received his Ph.D. in 1965. He has written biographies of two important figures in American-Chinese diplomacy: *Nelson T. Johnson and American Policy toward China, 1925–1941* (East Lansing, Mich., 1968), and *Patrick J. Hurley and American Foreign Policy* (Ithaca, 1973). In addition, Professor Buhite has edited the volume on the Far East in *The Dynamics of World Power: A Documentary History of U.S. Foreign Policy, 1945–1973* (New York, 1973), and is currently writing a book on Soviet-American relations.

Charles DeBenedetti, associate professor of history at the University of Toledo, studied with Norman Graebner and J. Leonard Bates at the University of Illinois, where he received his Ph.D. in 1968. He has published a number of articles on American diplomacy and is currently completing a book on the peace movement and American foreign policy during the period 1919–29.

Robert A. Divine, professor of history at the University of Texas, Austin, studied with Ralph Gabriel at Yale University, where he received his Ph.D. in 1954. Among other works, he has published *American Immigration Policy, 1924–1952* (New Haven, 1957), *The Illusion of Neutrality* (Chicago, 1962), *Second Chance: The Triumph of Internationalism in America during World War II* (New York, 1967), and *Roosevelt and World War II* (Baltimore, 1969). He is general editor of the Wiley series on American diplomatic history, and his most recent work is *Foreign Policy and U.S. Presidential Elections, 1940–1960* (New York, 1974).

Robert H. Ferrell, professor of history at Indiana University, studied with Samuel Flagg Bemis at Yale, where he received his Ph.D. in 1951. He has published voluminously on the subject of diplomatic history and has served as editor of the updated American Secretaries of State series (for which he wrote the volumes on Kellogg-Stimson and Marshall). His major works include *Peace in Their Time: The Origins of the Kellogg-Briand Pact* (New Haven, 1952) and *American Diplomacy in the Great Depression* (New Haven, 1957), and he is now working on a volume in the New American Nation series covering the years from 1917 to 1921. Professor Ferrell is a past president of the Society for Historians of American Foreign Relations.

John Lewis Gaddis, associate professor of history at Ohio University, studied with Robert Divine at the University of Texas, where he received his Ph.D. in 1968. He is the author of *The United States and the Origins of the Cold War* (New York, 1972), which received the Bancroft Prize for history. He is currently writing an analysis of Russian-American relations from 1781 to 1973 and is preparing a sequel to his book on the origins of the cold war.

Ross Gregory, professor of history at Western Michigan University, studied with Robert H. Ferrell at Indiana University, where he received his Ph.D. in 1964. His *Walter Hines Page: Ambassador to the Court of St. James's* (Lexington, Ky., 1970) won the Frederick Jackson Turner Prize; in addition, he has published *The Origins of American Intervention in the First World War* (New York, 1971). Professor Gregory's current project is a study of American life during World War II.

Helen Dodson Kahn resides in Columbus, Ohio; she studied with Walter LaFeber at Cornell, where she received her Ph.D. in 1968. She is now working on a full-length biography of Willard Straight.

William Kamman, professor of history at North Texas State University, studied with Robert H. Ferrell at Indiana University, where he received his Ph.D. in 1962. He has published *A Search for Stability: United States Diplomacy toward Nicaragua, 1925–1933* (South Bend, 1968), and he is writing a multiarchival study of American–Central American relations in the 1930s.

Richard D. McKinzie, associate professor of history at the University of Missouri, Kansas City, studied with John Wiltz at Indiana University, where he received his Ph.D. in 1969. A research associate at the Harry S. Truman Library Institute since 1969, Professor McKinzie has written a number of articles on the diplomacy of the Roosevelt-Truman period; he is the author of *The New Deal for Artists* (Princeton, 1973) and (with T. A. Wilson) is working on a study of foreign aid in the Truman administration. In addition, he is a coauthor of a forthcoming textbook of twentieth-century United States history.

David McLellan, professor of political science at Miami University (Ohio), received his Ph.D. from Yale University in 1954. He has written *The Cold War in Transition* (New York, 1966) and coauthored *The Theory and Practice of International Relations* (Englewood Cliffs, N.J., 1970). Professor McLellan is currently preparing a biography of Dean Acheson.

Frank J. Merli, associate professor of history at Queens College of The City University of New York, studied with Robert H. Ferrell at Indiana University, where he received his Ph.D. in 1964. He has written *Great Britain and the Confederate Navy, 1861–1865* (Bloomington, 1970), and is currently preparing a book on nineteenth-century neutrality from 1819 to 1919.

Herbert S. Parmet, associate professor of history at Queensborough Community College of The City University of New York, has written widely about American political history and biography. His published works include *Aaron Burr: Portrait of an Ambitious Man* (New York, 1967) (with Marie B. Hecht), *Never Again: A President Runs for a Third Term* (New York, 1968), and *Eisenhower and the American Crusades* (New York, 1972). Professor Parmet is currently writing a history of the Democratic party since 1945.

Thomas G. Paterson, professor of history at the University of Connecticut, received his Ph.D. in 1968 from the University of California, Berkeley. He is the author of *Soviet-American Confrontation: Postwar Reconstruction and the Origins of the Cold War* (Baltimore, 1973). In addition, he has written a number of articles and edited several important books on recent diplomacy, including *Cold War Critics: Alternatives to American Foreign Policy in the Truman Years* (Chicago, 1971); *The Origins of the Cold War* (Lexington, Mass., 1970), *American Imperialism and Anti-Imperialism* (New York, 1973), and *Containment and the Cold War* (Reading, Mass., 1973). Professor Paterson is currently writing a book on the Truman Doctrine and containment, 1945–75.

Michael Roskin, assistant professor of political science at Lycoming College and former Foreign Service officer and newspaperman, studied with Marian Irish at American University, where he received his Ph.D. in 1972. He has published articles on American diplomacy in *Foreign Policy* and *Le Monde Diplomatique.*

Eugene P. Trani, associate professor of history at Southern Illinois University, studied with Robert H. Ferrell at Indiana University, where he received his Ph.D. in 1966. In addition to a large number of articles, he has published *The Treaty of Portsmouth: An Adventure in American Diplomacy* (Lexington, Ky., 1969), and he is working on a study of Woodrow Wilson and Russia, 1913–21, which has been supported by a NEH Younger

Humanist Award. During 1972–73, Professor Trani was a fellow at the Woodrow Wilson International Center for Scholars.

David F. Trask, professor of history and chairman of the department at the State University of New York, Stony Brook, studied with Ernest May at Harvard University, where he received his doctorate in 1958. He has written *The United States in the Supreme War Council: American War Aims and Inter-Allied Strategy, 1917–1918* (Middletown, Conn., 1961), *General Tasker Howard Bliss and the "Sessions of the World," 1919* (Philadelphia, 1966), *Victory without Peace: American Foreign Relations in the Twentieth Century* (New York, 1968), and, most recently, *Captains and Cabinets: Anglo-American Naval Relations, 1917–1918* (Columbia, Mo., 1972). He was a coeditor of *A Bibliography of United States-Latin American Relations since 1810* (Lincoln, Nebr., 1968) and has edited *World War I at Home: Readings on American Life, 1914–1920* (New York, 1970). His current project is a military and naval history of the Spanish-American War.

Theodore A. Wilson, professor of history at the University of Kansas, studied with Robert H. Ferrell at Indiana University, where he received his Ph.D. in 1966. He has published *The First Summit: Roosevelt and Churchill at Placentia Bay, 1941* (Boston, 1969), which was awarded the Francis Parkman Prize. Professor Wilson has served as senior research associate at the Harry S. Truman Library Institute and has received fellowships from the National Endowment for the Humanities and the Guggenheim Foundation. He is currently completing a study of the origins of foreign aid, 1943–53 (with Richard McKinzie), and preparing a biography of Henry A. Wallace.

INDEX